SHAW: THE ANNUAL OF BERNARD SHAW STUDIES

VOLUME 33

Edited by

Michel W. Pharand

THE PENNSYLVANIA STATE UNIVERSITY PRESS
UNIVERSITY PARK, PENNSYLVANIA

Quotations and excerpts from published Bernard Shaw writings are used in this volume with the permission of the Estate of Bernard Shaw.

Cover illustration: Unpublished 9″ x 12″ drawing by Richard A. Roff entitled "G.B.S." Collection of Michel Pharand.

Library of Congress Cataloging-in-Publication Data

ISSN: 0741-5842
E-ISSN: 1529-1480
ISBN: 978-0-271-06372-0

The Pennsylvania State University Press is a member of the Association of American University Presses.

It is the policy of The Pennsylvania State University Press to use acid-free paper. Publications on uncoated stock satisfy the minimum requirements of American National Standard for Information Sciences—Permanence of Paper for Printed Library Material, ANSI Z39.48–1992.

Publication of SHAW: The Annual of Bernard Shaw Studies is made possible in part through the sponsorship of the International Shaw Society. An application for membership in the Society is available at www.shawsociety.org.

Note to contributors and subscribers: SHAW's perspective is Bernard Shaw and his milieu. As "his life, work, and friends"—the subtitle to a biography of GBS—indicates, it is impossible to study the life, thought, and work of a major literary figure in a vacuum. Issues and people, economics, politics, religion, theater, and literature and journalism—the entirety of the two half centuries the life of GBS spanned—was his assumed province. SHAW, published annually, welcomes articles that either explicitly or implicitly add to or alter our understanding of Shaw and his milieu. Manuscripts may be sent as email attachments (in Word) to Michel W. Pharand at michelpharand@yahoo.com; or to Julie A. Sparks at Julie.sparks@hotmail.com. All subscriptions, claims, and changes of address should be directed to Johns Hopkins University Press, PO Box 19966, Baltimore, MD 21211, phone 410-516-6987, jrnlcirc@press.jhu.edu. In matters of style, please refer to recent volumes of SHAW.

CONTENTS

REVIEWS

PASSINGS

A CONTINUING CHECKLIST OF SHAVIANA   231

CONTRIBUTORS   270

NOTICES   274

INTERNATIONAL SHAW SOCIETY   278

Introduction

MICHEL W. PHARAND

This volume of the sHAW opens with the transcript of a public lecture given by Shaw, near the end of a six-week holiday in Ireland, during his second return to Dublin (after emigrating in 1876). "Poor Law and Destitution in Ireland," delivered on 3 October 1910 in Dublin's Antient Concert Rooms, is printed here for the first time since its publication in *The Freeman's Journal* (4 October 1910). We are grateful to Nelson O'Ceallaigh Ritschel for bringing Shaw's lecture to our attention and for so thoroughly annotating it.

The range of topics covered by the eleven essays in this volume is evidence that Shaw, to use his own derogatory expression, was no "pure specialist." The first essay, by the late Sidney Albert, is "The Time of *Major Barbara*," an inquiry into the "compelling" reasons for Shaw selecting 1906, when the play takes place, rather than the year before, when it was written. A convincing case indeed. Charles Carpenter then provides "the inside story" on how Shaw, Bertrand Russell, and Gilbert Murray reacted to Britain's 3 August 1914 declaration of war on Germany: Murray approved of the decision, Shaw regretted it, Russell was outraged. Three months later came Shaw's "Common Sense About the War," with Murray countering in mid-1915 with *The Foreign Policy of Sir Edward Grey, 1906–1915*, an attempt to exonerate the Foreign Office, and Russell attacking in December with *The Policy of the Entente, 1904–1914: A Reply to Professor Gilbert Murray*.

Next, Lagretta Tallent Lenker examines how A. S. Byatt incorporates "a heavy dose of GBS, intentionally or unintentionally," in her 2009 novel, *The Children's Book*, where allusions to Shaw's life and work illustrate how

Fabianism pervades her book. In "Authorship and *Shakes Versus Shav*," Christopher Wixson "seeks to reframe the grappling portrayed in *Shakes Versus Shav* within the larger idea of the uniquely vexed creative authority for playwrights," arguing that "Shaw presciently muses over the ramifications for the Shavian text upon the death of the author."

The next three essays are international in scope. Peter Conolly-Smith finds that with *Jitta's Atonement*, Shaw's 1922 adaptation of his German-language translator Siegfried Trebitsch's *Frau Gittas Sühne* (1920), Shaw "cheats" on Trebitsch's original text by changing its ending, a "belated revenge" on Trebitsch's translation of *Pygmalion*, which "had similarly changed the thrust of that play's ending." Barry Keane then surveys the stage productions of *Mrs Warren's Profession* from 1907 to 1952 in partitioned Poland, where the play's translation, production, and reception "generated impassioned debate . . . while also reaffirming for each era that Poland occupied the moral high ground in terms of its treatment of women and the working classes." And Kay Li analyzes John Woo's 2009 film adaptation of *Pygmalion*, *My Fair Gentleman* (*Yao Tiao Shen Shi*), and its portrayal of how the entrepreneurial peasant Charles Zeng Tian-gao, the Eliza Doolittle figure, moves to metropolitan Shanghai and amasses his fortune. His transformation by Candice Wu Jia-qian, the Henry Higgins figure, from country bumpkin to gentleman, is an analogy for how China quickly emerged from the devastating poverty caused by the Cultural Revolution to the affluence resulting from modernization.

Sallust, writes Stanley Weintraub, "is a mysterious and subtle signifier" in Shaw's writings, appearing in only Shaw's last completed novel, *An Unsocial Socialist*—"and there only as the hideaway address of the hero." Weintraub explores what Shaw may have known about the Roman political philosopher and finds numerous echoes of Sallust in Shaw's works.

Derek McGovern examines Shavian elements in the 1964 *My Fair Lady* film (based on the 1956 Broadway musical) to determine, first, to what extent it is "a faithful adaptation of its stage musical counterpart"; second, in what specific ways "the film's aesthetics convey the likelihood of a Higgins-Eliza romance"; and third, in what respects the film is "more faithful to the stage version(s) of Shaw's play than the 1938 film version of *Pygmalion*."

Gustavo A. Rodríguez Martín probes "Shaw's acquaintance with the cultural centrality of numbers" by looking at "the stylistic and symbolic function of number words . . . in specific plays, in the speech of particular characters, and over his entire dramatic canon." He also makes the link to

Shaw's "socioeconomic critique" and "to numbers whose literary function relies on some sort of religious significance."

Finally, the late Isidor Saslav shares what he discovered in some of the seventy-six scrapbooks compiled by Shaw biographer Archibald Henderson. Saslav dubs what he calls a "treasure trove of Shaviana," held at the University of North Carolina at Chapel Hill, "Carolina gold"—and rightly so, as many of these heretofore unknown and unrecorded letters, articles, reviews, and reports by and about Shaw are sure to open for Shavians new avenues of research.

On Irish Destitution

BERNARD SHAW

[The occasion of Bernard Shaw's second return to Dublin, after emigrating in 1876, was a public lecture on 3 October 1910 on the Poor Law and Irish destitution.[1] The lecture occurred near the end of a six-week holiday in Ireland for Shaw and his wife, Charlotte, and it was delivered at Dublin's Antient Concert Rooms for the charitable middle-class Irish Committee to Promote the Break-up of the Poor Law.[2] Shaw's Dublin lecture was part of Beatrice Webb's effort in London to revitalize the Fabian Society by unleashing a "crusade" against the Poor Law.[3]

The Poor Law went into effect in 1838 throughout the British Isles, and by 1910—and much earlier—there was little evidence that the system humanely alleviated the severest poverty. Webb's crusade extended from her 1909 Minority Report, based on her time on the Royal Commission on the Poor Law and her opposition to the Commission's "Majority" recommendations—which she felt did not go far enough in combating poverty.[4] Webb hoped that the crusade would draw on the energy of the younger Fabians, and she turned to her husband Sidney Webb and others from the old Fabian guard to launch the initial steps. Sixteen days before Shaw addressed Dublin, Sidney began the crusade with an address against the Poor Law in London. The next move was Shaw's in Dublin, followed weeks later by both Shaw and Sidney lecturing in Edinburgh.

Shaw's lecture in Dublin proved to be an important historical moment for Shaw and the socialism in Dublin that was precariously emerging by 1910.[5] Weeks before Shaw reentered Dublin, the socialist agitator James Connolly returned to Dublin from seven years in America, where he had worked as a union organizer and socialist editor. Almost immediately Connolly provocatively sought to energize the fragile Irish socialist movement as it reeled in the wake of the Catholic Church's efforts to nullify and eradicate socialist ideology during the spring of 1910. To mark his return to Dublin, and to seize an initiative, the working-class Connolly published a pamphlet, *Labour, Nationality, and Religion,* that countered the Church's charges against socialism that had been authored by a Jesuit priest, Father Robert Kane, and printed nationally in the *Irish Catholic* newspaper.[6] Connolly's pamphlet generated intense controversy within some Dublin circles, and that controversy provided the Irish context of Shaw's Dublin lecture. In fact, Dublin's *The Freeman's Journal* noted that while Shaw's lecture attracted many, the audience "included an exceptionally large number of representatives of the Church."[7] Arguably, the Church's many representatives were present due to the Church's campaign against socialism, and no doubt the public exchange with Connolly had increased the Church's concern with what Shaw, perceived in 1910 Dublin as Ireland's most famous socialist, might say to Dubliners.

Shaw's "Poor Law and Destitution in Ireland" lecture has only been published in third-person transcripts in two contemporary Dublin newspapers on 4 October 1910, *The Irish Times* and *The Freeman's Journal.* This marks the first publication of the lecture since 1910. The transcripts in the two newspapers are remarkably similar; outside of a few very minor differences, the two transcripts are identical.[8] Even the respective openings of the lecture-transcripts of the speech—starting with Shaw's rising as a "signal for a sustained burst of applause"—are identical.[9] This may well suggest that a text of the lecture was provided to the two newspapers—but in the third person with indications of audience applause and laughter.[10] However, one witness to the lecture recorded that Shaw chastised his audience for having denounced John Millington Synge's *The Playboy of the Western World* when it premiered in 1907, and both newspaper transcripts omit the mentioning of Synge's play.[11] At the very least, the two papers left out one angle of Shaw's lecture—or perhaps the Synge comment was not scripted, if Shaw had indeed provided a text to the newspapers.[12]

The covering of Shaw's lecture in the Home Rule *Freeman's Journal* and the conservative pro-British *Irish Times,* but not in the nationalist and class conservative *Irish Independent,* bespoke of Dublin's growing industrial tensions. *The Irish Independent,* part of the pro-employer newspaper holdings of capitalist extraordinaire William Martin Murphy, was either not sent a transcript of the lecture—if one existed—or chose not to provide any coverage. It was Martin's newspaper *The Irish Catholic* that had printed Father Kane's attacks on socialism and trade unionism that the then mostly unknown James Connolly had answered in his *Labour, Nationality, and Religion* pamphlet. And despite Shaw's near celebrity status, Murphy's papers were not to record or comment on Shaw's lecture within the backdrop of the urban Irish class divide that only a year later would erupt into trade union wars with Irish employers—with William Martin Murphy eventually leading and unifying Dublin employers against the syndicalist union movement. In an extraordinary way, the lack of coverage in Murphy's papers of Shaw's lecture strangely anticipated the radical coming together of Shaw and Connolly on 1 November 1913, during the Dublin Lockout, on the speakers' platform at a rally in London's Royal Albert Hall on behalf of locked-out Dublin laborers and their movement. Shaw's 1910 Dublin lecture represented a crucial step in the development of Irish socialism that would march toward revolution.

The following transcript of Shaw's "Poor Law and Destitution in Ireland," from *The Freeman's Journal*, provides the existing text for Shaw's first address in Beatrice Webb's crusade against the Poor Law, and provides critical insight into one of Shaw's more direct actions on behalf of the Irish proletariat within an increasingly revolutionary and radical Dublin. Four days after Shaw's 1910 Dublin lecture, Connolly's friend and socialist colleague in Dublin, Frederick Ryan, wrote to Connolly of the now-charged Dublin political atmosphere: "I somehow feel—one senses these things in the air—there is the best opening now in Ireland that I remember for making a real forward move and ripping into the whole fabric of moral and intellectual tyranny in the country. There is no doubt one can get an audience to listen now to things that 5 years ago or even 3 or 4 years ago would have frightened them."[13] Shaw's lecture delivered an indisputable impact on the Irish socialist movement, and six years later James Connolly led the socialistic Irish Citizen Army into Irish revolution, known as the 1916 Easter Rising.[14]

NELSON O'CEALLAIGH RITSCHEL]

"Poor Law and Destitution in Ireland"[15]

Mr. Shaw, whose rising was the signal for a sustained burst of applause, commenced by saying that the very kind reception which had been accorded him was rather an embarrassing one, because he was not going to be as complimentary to the audience as they had been to him. The Chairman had suggested that what he was aiming at was taking all the Poor Law officials and Guardians of this country, pouring paraffin oil on them and setting them on fire. That was not what he had in view. He really wanted to take the audience and submit them to the paraffin oil treatment (laughter) or any other treatment that would really rouse them to a sense of their Civic duty. He had no doubt that in their private capacity they were extremely amiable people, but

HE COULD NOT ACQUIT THEM OF THE MOST MONSTROUS CIVIC CRIMES[16] when he thought what destitution, and what the Poor Law system was in Ireland at present. He would very much rather they gave up the practice of private virtue, and took up the practice of civic virtue—if they felt they had to make the choice between them. As a private person the amount of harm they could do was very small—a few murders, perhaps, or an embezzlement, which would cause a slight amount of inconvenience to people around them (laughter). He had spent part of that afternoon in the South Dublin Workhouse. It was possible he might spend longer time later on in a workhouse (laughter), but he hoped it would not be an Irish workhouse (laughter). There were some very conspicuous things about the Irish workhouse. In the first place they had got too many of them (hear, hear). There was another thing. No child should ever be in a workhouse, under any circumstances (hear, hear). In the workhouses of Ireland to-day they had 8,000 children. That was

A PRETTY LARGE ITEM OF CIVIC CRIME TO BEGIN WITH (hear, hear). They had no business to have any one of those children in the workhouse. It was the fact of the child being there that helped to make the workhouses as horrible as they were. He did not want to appeal to their instincts to humanity, which might probably lead them wrong. He did not want to appeal to their sentimentality. He wanted to appeal to their economic sense; their sense of justice. Poverty was a crime—a crime, not of the poor, but of the people who allowed them to be poor. Poverty was a crime of society—a preventable crime. Nineteen hundred years ago a great Leader of the human race said, by way of reproach: "The poor ye have always with you." There were a great many Christians at the present time,[17] instead of understanding that this was a reproach, interpreted it as a warning of something inevitable—"The poor ye have always with you"—as if such blasphemy could come out of the mouth of Christ. There was another interpretation—"The poor ye have always with you; I congratulate you; keep them with you." That, of course, was utterly wrong. If they looked at the Press[18] they would see a long string of figures presented with regard to the expenditures of the Corporation. With three thousands of pounds they could put an end to pauperism; but they were manufacturing the paupers, and when they had manufactured them they turned round and said: "That is the pauper's own fault." They could not say that about the children, at all events. He

WONDERED IF THEY BELIEVED IN THE DAY OF JUDGEMENT: if he were to judge by their civic conscience he would say they did not (laughter). Well, on the day of Judgment, when it came, these eight thousand children that were in their workhouses to-day would stand up and say: "What crime have I committed?" (applause). He should not advise them to get up and ask what crimes they (the audience) had committed, because the eight thousand children would be able to give an answer, and it would require all the mercy in Heaven to prevent them from going to a place which would not be as bad as the ordinary workhouse (laughter), or so disorderly, or wasteful, or murderous and unpatriotic, but it might be quite as uncomfortable— therefore let them be careful (laughter and applause). What was it they did in the workhouses in Ireland? They took a number of people of all kinds, threw them into a building higgledy-piggledy. They took the most hardened scoundrels and placed them side by side with comparatively innocent young men. They took a young woman, whose only crime was to be poor, in close association with other women whose company was extremely bad. He found, however, that in Dublin attempts were made at separation and classification.

THEY WERE VERY CAREFUL ABOUT SKIN DISEASES BUT CARED NOT IN THE SLIGHTEST FOR SOUL DISEASES—the only conclusion he could come to was that they believed people had skins, but did not believe that people had souls. The very worst skin disease was not so dangerous or contagious as a soul disease. The Poor Law system had been in existence for about one hundred years, and English and Irish Commissions had dealt with the subject, which had also been considered by every serious person who had given any serious attention to the question. Pauperism was increasing, and there were more people in their unions than there used to be, and there would be more still, as long as things went on as at present. The remedy was comparatively simple,

ALMOST ALL THE THINGS THEY WERE DOING IN A CRUEL AND WASTEFUL WAY THEY WERE DOING TWICE OVER. The duplication of charitable services in this country was something extraordinary. In London, he could assure them a man who made a really scientific study of charity as it existed at present could get on extremely well. Side by side with public charities they had private charities to which people largely subscribed. There was a time when a certain scandal was created in Europe by the too liberal sale of indulgences, but when he grew up and began to look about him he found that the sale of indulgences was going on like anything and that even Protestants were buying them (laughter). When a Protestant wanted to buy an indulgence he sent a cheque to the secretary of a charitable institution (laughter). "You may generally depend," added Mr. Shaw, "that if he sends a cheque for £ 100 he has £500 that he is not entirely satisfied about (laughter).

IN ORDER TO TRY AND MAKE THEIR CONSCIENCES FEEL EASY they were throwing thousands of pounds into the coffers of charitable societies, who set up large offices with a number of gentlemen with liberal salaries. Accordingly they found there were in London—he did not suppose there were such persons in Dublin—people who know the run of charities so well that they would first go and get outdoor relief from the Guardians and would then go to five or six different charitable societies and get relief from every one—the result being that they had about £ 5 10s a week (laughter). Now that money was wasted, except from the point of view of the persons whose consciences were made easy.

Proceeding, Mr. Shaw said that in England there was a separate authority which had nothing to do with the poor law and which could easily deal with all the cases that arose. They had the same thing in Ireland with one exception—the Education Authority. In England all the local authorities— through Councils, County Councils, and so on—appointed an Education Committee, who could co-opt very many ladies and gentlemen who were interested in and willing to do some public work. In that way they were able to get up a pretty strong committee, who took charge of the schools in the place. His contention was that

THERE SHOULD BE FORMED EDUCATION COMMITTEES IN IRELAND by whom they[19] would be properly treated instead of being put into the workhouses under the public charities with the pauper taint on them for all their lives. For if they started a child as a pauper that[20] child would afterwards come back to the workhouse (hear, hear). Again they should have School Clinics. He had driven around a great deal of Ireland and being a writer of plays he was naturally of a romantic disposition and took notice of the young women whom he saw (laughter). And he observed the fact that, as a rule, they had remarkably few teeth (laughter). Yes, that was so, and it was a disgrace to a country that everybody had not a good set of teeth—either real or artificial (a laugh). These girls were sent to school and taught to read and write—a very useful thing; they were taught history—mostly untrue, geography, mostly unnecessary, and that could be obtained from a steady reading of Bradshaw (laughter). Many were taught

AN EXTRAORDINARY LANGUAGE SUPPOSED TO HAVE BEEN SPOKEN IN ANCIENT IRELAND (laughter), but which never was, and never would be spoken anywhere on the face of the earth (laughter and hisses). Yet, it is so, but they were not taught to take care of their teeth (laughter). And let him tell them this. It might be a very amusing thing. If he had been brought up in that language instead of in that which he spoke and wrote, he would have lost his grip of the world. Let them teach and learn it as an accomplishment or as a kind of mental gymnastics, like Greek or Latin, but let them not set up fresh barriers between one nation and another at this time (applause). They need not despise his language because it is English—which was a language spoken by a large number of the human race, and if they hissed him any more, as had just done, he would—well

HE WOULD BEGIN TO TALK TO THEM IN GAELIC AND THEN THEY WOULD SEE WHERE THEY WERE (laughter). But he would make a compromise and say if he admitted frankly that it was delightful that these Irish girls should be taught Gaelic, would they admit that there should be some Clinic to look after their teeth (laughter); granting, if they liked—and he did it for the sake of a quiet life—that they should speak Gaelic, did they not think that they desired the girls to have some teeth to speak it with (applause and laughter). And, furthermore, it was not only bad teeth but bad hearts and blood that they had to teach and deal with. They allowed the seeds of tuberculosis to be sown, which they took so much trouble to cure, but which they might prevent. No, they waited until it became incurable, and then began to tinker with it (hear, hear). He first proposed[21] was that they should take their 8,000 children now within the walls of the workhouses—they should take them out of the hands of the Guardians altogether, and place them in the hands of an education authority who would be made responsible for their bringing up in good health worthy of being called the children of Ireland (applause). They had

AN EXCEPTIONALLY GOOD MEDICAL SERVICE IN IRELAND. Why should the epileptic and consumptive be sent into the workhouses? They were not the proper places for such people—who should be in hospitals where proper nurses and not pauper nurses were employed to tend to them (applause). If they were Irishmen and Irishwomen they would take that view. But it was absurd for them to be bragging of being Irishmen and Irishwomen—they were hardly Rathmines or Clontarf men (laughter), and the tendency was to develop a curious social being—a slanted kind of little Robinson Crusoe (laughter), without even the excuse of Robinson (laughter), for after all, he had no one to be social with. The sooner they became conscious of this the better. They should remember that the man who said merely "I don't want a room I live in to be a dirty room" was not saying much. The real man with a real sense of cleanliness said,

I DON'T WANT THE CITY I LIVE IN TO BE A DIRTY CITY (applause). The other man said in a sort of narrow way, "I don't want my children to associate with poor and dirty children": but as long as they lived in a city with poor and dirty children they had to associate with them, and they caught their diseases, and their death rate spread to them. Their children growing up heard their language in the street as they shouted and swore, and got steeped in this atmosphere. And yet, they imagined that they could keep aloof.

IF THEY WANTED TO HAVE DECENT LIVES FOR THEMSELVES they must get rid of the dirt and filth in the country together. Instead of bringing up people to be paupers they could bring them up to be decent people. The problem they had to deal with was not altogether the people that were inside the South and North Dublin Unions. Altogether the South Dublin Union was not a place he would like to live in, it was a place compared with the places in which thousands of people in this city had to live who were not paupers at all, and some day or other the intelligent Irish people would discover what they did not all know at present, namely, that if they went and announced themselves as destitute persons the Guardians must take them in, and the result would be that they would have a much cleaner bed than that to which they were accustomed and they would have no rent to pay. Soon they would begin to realize this more generally.

Mr. Shaw went on to say that, instead of taking their sick people and putting them in hospital, they should throw them on the Public Health Service, and tell that Public Health Service that they had not only to cure disease, but to prevent disease. They had to employ a large number of medical offciers—new sorts of doctors who,

INSTEAD OF KEEPING YOU SICK AS LONG AS POSSIBLE, INSISTED ON KEEPING YOU WELL AS LONG AS POSSIBLE (laughter). He did not speak as a literary man. He had sat on a Public Health Authority, and he had passed through a severe epidemic, and he had seen medical officers of health—very able men—growing very anxious during that epidemic, and he had seen their faces blossom like flowers in water because of that epidemic and all the money it was brining to them. The sensible state of things was to have their medical men paid and honoured altogether according to their vital statistics. When the death rate went down they should let that be a score to the medical profession. At the present time—and the chairman would confirm him—

THE ABOLITION OF DISEASE IN IRELAND WOULD SIMPLY MEAN THE RUIN OF THE MEDICAL PROFESSION AS IT WAS ORGANIZED AT PRESENT. To keep a city healthy required very hard work on the part of everyone. Among other things, they had to make people understand the laws of health. There was a horrible infant mortality in Glasgow, a frightful infant mortality in Liverpool, a terrible one in London, and a higher one in Dublin. How could they look a London man or a Liverpool man in the face, and how could they talk about the superiority of the Irish intellect and Irish character when they know all the time that they were killing children faster than they were. If they only took half the trouble to eradicate ill health that they did to eradicate ordinary crime, they would very soon have no trouble with crime or disease. How were they going to deal with their old people? Well, they had already made a beginning. It was entirely right that old age pensions should be given people who had worked hard all their lives from the time they were children. They were just as entitled to their pensions as any Cabinet Minister that ever qualified for a pension. The old age pensions had created a new department of officials, and the proper way to deal with the old people was to hand them over to that authority, which should have no stigma of any pauperism about it. Dealing with

THE VERY DIFFICULT QUESTION OF THE ABLE-BODIED PAUPER, he said that man came on their hands because in most cases he was an unemployed man. Sometimes he was a man who had got something of him (Mr. Shaw) in him (laughter), he having tried to do honest work for some years, but did not like it (a laugh), and accordingly he took to the vaga-bond pursuits by which he had become famous (laughter). In going over to the workhouse that day the thing that struck him was that almost the majority of the men he saw were respectable men—men who would take a job if they could get it. Here they were right up against the problems of unemployment, to which he would devote the remainder of his time. They should get out of their heads the idea that unemployment was a thing that could ever be put a stop to. The nature of work in this world was such that, organize it as they would, a great number of people must at a particular moment be unemployed. But under the present system they allowed industrious men to be thrown out of employment and did not help them in any way. They pretended he was a bad character; and the retribution was that he became a bad character, and they made him a bad character (applause). He depreciated the idea of working men being thrown out into the streets—it was not even good business. He urged the advisibility of

ELABORATING THEIR SYSTEM OF LABOUR EXCHANGES. He was quite recently in Tralee, and saw a notice set up stating that the nearest Labour exchange was at Limerick, some sixty miles away (laughter).

OF COURSE ALL THE UNEMPLOYED HAD COMMAND OF MOTOR CARS, and so it would not matter (laughter). They should be able to send the unemployed person to, say, the next street, and in that way they could effectively reduce the number of the unemployed, so as to include only those who were unavoidably unemployed, and keep them out of workhouse. He held that the guardians of the poor were not the proper persons to undertake such a duty. The proper persons to deal with those who could work and had the opportunity of working, and who would not work—the proper persons were the prison authorities (hear, hear). Once they were quite certain that a man was loafing, and that it was his own fault, he should be regarded as a social criminal (hear, hear), and he should be detained and put where he would have to work, whether he liked it or not (hear, hear). They could not do that now, for they could not tell the deserving from the undeserving. In conclusion, he would only say it should be their pride to pay back what their rearing and nurturing and education cost, to

SUPPORT THEMSELVES IN A DIGNIFIED AND DECENT POSITION; To provide for their old age and retirement in some way. Anyone who did less than that inflicted injury on his country by being born in it. They should keep that ideal before them, and leave their country in their debt, and would have done more than by all the talk they could indulge in as to Robert Emmet or any other patriot. They would make their country great, and when they spoke of "going to their account" they should remember that they must do that humbly and lead lives that would leave their country better than they found it (loud applause).

NOTES

1. Shaw's first known return to Dublin since 1876 was in October 1908, during which he was observed at the Abbey Theatre attending performances of *The Suburban Groove*, by W. F. Casey, and *The Piper*, by Shaw's friend Conal O'Riordan (who wrote under the pseudonym Norrys O'Connell). The constant Dublin playgoer of the period, Joseph Holloway, recorded on 2 October 1908: "In the evening the [Abbey] theatre was well attended; many distinguished people were present including George Bernard Shaw whom W. B. Yeats captured and held in conversation" (Joseph Holloway, *Joseph Holloway's Abbey Theatre: A Selection from His Unpublished Journal "Impressions of a Dublin Playgoer,"* ed. Robert Hogan and Michael J. O'Neill [Carbondale: Southern Illinois University Press, 1967] 116). *The Piper* is a satirical look at Irish nationalism and is set in 1798. The "many distinguished people" who were at the Abbey on 2 October 1908 did not include one of the theater's three directors, J. M. Synge, who had sparred with Shaw in their master plays, *John Bull's Other Island* and *The Playboy of the Western World* (see my *Shaw, Synge, Connolly, and Socialist Provocation*, University Press of Florida, 2011). On the very day, Synge, still recovering from recent surgery, wrote to his fiancée, actor Molly Allgood (who acted as Maire O'Neill), "I am not going to the Abbey today as I have been in town every day since Sunday [2 October 1908 was a Friday]" (J. M. Synge, *The Collected Letters of John Millington Synge, Volume II, 1907–1909*, ed. Ann Saddlemyer [Oxford: Clarendon Press, 1984] 204). As Synge makes no mention in his letter of Shaw attending the Abbey, it is most probable that Shaw's attendance on 2 October was unannounced and unknown, even to W. B. Yeats, prior to the evening. If Yeats had advance knowledge, he most likely would have notified Synge—and Synge's explanation for his absence would have mentioned Shaw. Synge had unwittingly, perhaps, missed his last chance to meet Shaw. After Synge's death in March 1909, O'Riordan was named a director of the Abbey Theatre, but resigned shortly afterward. Shaw's Poor Law lecture in 1910 was certainly his first publicized return to Dublin. Even when the Abbey Theatre premiered Shaw's *The Shewing-up of Blanco Posnet* in August 1909, Shaw remained outside Dublin. It is interesting that his first publicized appearance in Dublin was as the public socialistic intellectual. (Peter Gahan has forthcoming research that details Shaw's 1908 Dublin visit as an informal venture over a few days before returning to London.)

2. Many cultural events took place in the Antient Concert Rooms during the 1890s–1920 period, with connections to many of Ireland's major writers of early (and later) modernism: Shaw, Synge, Yeats, Lady Gregory, James Joyce, to name a few, and many artists. And decades earlier, Shaw's mother had sung at the Antient Concert Rooms with the Amateur Musical Society.

3. Norman and Jeanne MacKenzie, *The Fabians* (New York: Simon and Schuster, 1977), 366.

4. MacKenzie, *The Fabians*, 358.

5. A socialist movement in Ireland, namely, Dublin, had begun to appear during the late 1880s and early 1890s, which culminated in the formation of the

Irish Socialist Republican Party (ISRP) in 1896. However, Irish socialism faded, if temporarily, in 1903, when the ISRP collapsed.

6. The *Irish Catholic* paper was part of the newspaper empire of Dublin business leader William Martin Murphy. Murphy would emerge as the leading figure in the trade union wars in Dublin during 1911–14. Murphy organized major Irish employers into the Dublin Employers Federation, which sought to crush the syndicalist movement of the Irish Transport and General Workers' Union during the 1913 Dublin Lockout.

7. "Mr. Bernard Shaw in Dublin," *The Freeman's Journal*, 4 October 1910, 7.

8. Notes are provided in the following text of Shaw's lecture that indicate the minor differences between the two contemporary transcripts.

9. "Mr. Bernard Shaw in Dublin. 'Poor Law and Destitution in Ireland,'" *The Freeman's Journal*, 4 October 1910, 7.

10. In its coverage of Shaw's lecture, *The Freeman's Journal* made no value judgments on Shaw's lecture, but *The Irish Times* did as one of its leader writers (unnamed) labeled Shaw a "jester," and reported that the lecture was spoiled "by the same dogmatising and the same extravagance of simile and illustration that mark his plays." "Poor Law System," *The Irish Times*, 4 October 1910, 6. Shaw most likely did provide both papers with a transcript. In a 1911 letter to Margaret Halstan, in response for advice on delivering a public speech, Shaw suggested she "get a few copies" of her speech and "give them to the press" if she wanted press coverage (George Bernard Shaw, *Bernard Shaw: Collected Letters* 1911–1925, vol. 3, Dan H. Laurence, ed. New York: Viking, 1985. 62).

11. Holloway, *Joseph Holloway's Abbey Theatre*, 142.

12. Both *The Irish Times* and *The Freeman's Journal* were among the Dublin newspapers that attacked Synge's *Playboy* in 1907. In 1910, the year after Synge's early death, Synge's collective works were published in Dublin with favorable critical response.

13. Frederick Ryan, *Between Comrades: James Connolly, Letters and Correspondence, 1889–1916*, ed. Donal Nevin (Dublin: Gill and Macmillan, 2007), 443. *The Freeman's Journal*, which named a handful of publicly known attendees to Shaw's 1910 lecture, did not name Frederick Ryan, but did name the leftist journalist Francis Sheehy-Skeffington. Ryan certainly was not a well-known figure to most of *The Freeman's Journal*'s readers, despite having been the Irish National Theatre Society's first secretary, 1902–4, and its treasurer, 1904–6. But as a Dublin socialist, it was Ryan who introduced Connolly to Sheehy-Skeffington on the very night Connolly returned to Dublin, 26 July 1910 (Thomas J. Morrissey, S. J. *William O'Brien, 1881–1968: Socialist, Republican, Dail Deputy, Editor, and Trade Union Leader.* [Dublin: Four Courts Press], 2007, 44). Not only did Ryan and Sheehy-Skeffington greatly admire Shaw, Ryan introduced Shaw's reputation and ideologies (as perceived by Ryan) to the fledging Irish socialist movement in 1899 when he lectured the minuscule Irish Socialist Republican Party on Shaw's Fabian lectures, essays, and early plays. The ISRP's founder and secretary was James Connolly. Ryan, whose Dublin socialist play *The Laying of the Foundations* (1902) is heavily based on Shaw's

Widowers' Houses, undoubtedly attended Shaw's lecture on 3 October 1910 and helped forged a bridge between the lecture and Connolly. The poverty-stricken Connolly was unable to attend the lecture as he was in Scotland speaking to small socialist gatherings trying to scrape together enough funds to send for his family still in New York.

14. For a fuller discussion of the Irish context and Irish impact of Shaw's 1910 "Poor Law and Destitution in Ireland" lecture, see my *Shaw, Synge, Connolly, and Socialist Provocation*.

15. "Mr. Bernard Shaw in Dublin. Poor Law and Destitution in Ireland," *The Freeman's Journal*, 4 October 1910, 7–8. The transcript of Shaw's lecture is reprinted in the third person with no alterations from the original form as it appears in *The Freeman's Journal*.

16. The various phrasing printed in all caps are unique to *The Freeman's Journal*'s transcript of Shaw's speech. *The Irish Times* did not use all caps for any phrase, but the phrases are identical in both transcripts. *The Freeman's Journal* may have used the caps in an effort to assist in the reading of the speech, with perceived areas of emphasis. Perhaps Shaw even emphasized such phrases when he delivered his lecture—or used caps in the transcript he provided, if he provided a transcript.

17. *The Irish Times* inserted "who" after "present time." "The Poor-Law System: Mr. George Bernard Shaw on Destitution in Ireland Lecture," *The Irish Times*, 4 October 1910, 6.

18. *The Irish Times* printed "Irish Times" instead of "Press." "The Poor Law System," 6.

19. "They" refers here to the poor children in Ireland who were then in workhouses.

20. *The Irish Times* printed "the" instead of "that." "The Poor-Law System," 6.

21. *The Irish Times* used the phrase "His first proposal" rather than "He first proposed." "The Poor-Law System," 6.

The Time of *Major Barbara*

SIDNEY P. ALBERT

In "The Time of *Major Barbara*" (Notes and Documents, *Theatre Survey* 23, no. 1 [May 1982]: 110–11), Bernard F. Dukore wondered why Bernard Shaw chose to have his play take place in January 1906 rather than in 1905, the year in which it was written and first performed. He advanced some conjectures for this decision and welcomed "a quotation from the playwright that would settle the matter" (111). The question Dukore raised hardly strikes me as a matter of great moment, and I seriously doubt whether Shaw ever made such a desiderated explanation. Nevertheless, what he had to say prompts a number of observations that I trust are germane.

To the question, "Why 1906 rather than 1905?" one might well respond, why not? The reasons for selecting 1906 are clearly more compelling than those for the year before. The time of composition may have some bearing on the dating of a contemporary play, but it need not be decisive. The time of stage production may be more significant, but in this instance, as Dukore reported, it spanned the two years, so other considerations were bound to be pivotal.

Shaw began writing *Major Barbara* late in March 1905, finished it in Derry, Ireland, on 8 September, returned to London at the end of that month, and after reading it to Gilbert Murray and Granville Barker on 1 October, undertook a revision that was not completed until 15 October.[1] Evidently he was writing it for a planned production in November because late in September—after the original version was written—he expressed uncertainty as to whether he would have a prompt copy by November in view of the need for cutting that lay before him. As it turned out, he did prepare a prompt copy in time, and the drama opened on schedule on 28 November. Still, some measure of doubt about the possible production date may have been in the playwright's mind in the immediately preceding months.

As Dukore points out, in the manuscript and original prompt copy of 1905, as well as in the first published edition of the play in 1907, only the month of January is given as the time, with no mention of year.[2] It is in the theater programs of the initial production that the time is specified as January 1906. Once Shaw selected January as the month for his play, 1906 became inevitable as the year to insert in the program. January 1905 would have made no sense.

Why the author preferred the month of January for his setting is another question. Here my surmise differs from that of Dukore: January is *mid*-winter, the middle of the three winter months, a time when cold weather has already been experienced and more is in store. It also marks the beginning of a new year. From the production standpoint, a January date for the play would keep it contemporary throughout 1906; setting it any time in 1905 would not, relegating it to the past virtually from its opening. That would hardly do for a drama that is prospective in outlook, not retrospective.

Pertinent to our consideration too are several points about the consecutive series of engagements at the Court Theatre. The first six matinee performances, presented on successive Tuesdays and Fridays, were stretched out over three weeks. The first, on 28 November, was the only one in that month; the final one took place in mid-December on the 15th. Thus five-sixths of the matinee run occurred in December, barely squeezed into the end-of-year schedule at the Court. Interestingly enough, the play was not licensed by the Lord Chamberlain until 9 December. It is also noteworthy that the "January 1906" entry in the program during the November-December performances elicited not a single comment from the numerous reviewers of the new Shavian drama: 1905 was rapidly waning, and the new year was imminent.

With but a two-week hiatus for the Christmas season, this *Major Barbara* production resumed on 1 January for six weeks, "promoted" to the evening bill in accordance with Court Theatre repertory custom (as one of the reviews tells us).[3] That this was essentially a continuation of the November-December run, with but a single cast replacement, has been somewhat obscured by an error in the record preserved by Desmond MacCarthy in his *The Court Theatre, 1904–1907*. Soon after the 10 February end of these six weeks, *Major Barbara* returned to the Court stage, substituted for an unsuccessful matinee presentation (of two plays), on 13, 16, 20, and 23 February. Unfortunately, in the appendix of his book, MacCarthy has conflated the programs for the two 1906 runs, which differ only in cast changes. On 1 January, only the Lady Britomart was replaced; on 13 February, there was a new Cusins and Lomax as well. MacCarthy puts all three replacements on the 1 January program, suggesting more cast alteration than actually took place.[4] In any event, of the fifty-two performances of *Major Barbara* at the Court, forty-six were in 1906, so that for the greater part of its run, as Dukore indicates, the 1906 dating was quite timely.

Dukore's speculation about the inappropriateness of designating the time of the play as "the present" during the pre-Christmas matinees—because then "the Salvation Army has less difficulty collecting donations than at any other time of the year," and because it would entail further extraneous and time-consuming dialogue "to explain its non-Christmastime problem"—invites further comment. First of all, in *Major Barbara* Shaw seeks to show the futility of charity as a way of dealing with "the crime of poverty." The economic problem he addressed was pervasive: it encompassed Christmastime as well as the rest of the year.

It so happened that November and December 1905 marked a period of exceptional economic distress in London, and indeed in all of England—a time well suited to highlight Shaw's wide-ranging politico-economic message in *Major Barbara*. Conditions were so bad that in November 1905 London witnessed a procession of several thousand unemployed, who also sent an impressive deputation of wives and mothers to call upon Prime Minister A. J. Balfour. But they were appealing to a government leader who believed that the problem stemmed from "fundamental economic laws which are not laws of society but laws of nature, and which no legislation will enable us to overcome."[5] On 13 November, Queen Alexandra made a public appeal for funds "to assist me in alleviating the suffering of the poor starving unemployed during the winter."[6] She initiated the fund with her own contribution of £2,000. Before the end of the month, £100,000 had been raised, and the amount eventually rose to more than £250,000. In a letter to the editor of the *London Times* dated 13 November 1905, Shaw hailed the queen's fund as a response to government ineffectuality and a challenge to statesmanship to find alternatives to charity (the text of his letter is printed below).[7] His suggestion was that the unemployed be put to work destroying their squalid homes and replacing them with better ones.

At the same time, the West Ham Distress Committee reported more than two thousand unemployed in that borough—the locale of Act II of *Major Barbara*—totaling more than eighty thousand persons when dependent women and children were taken into account. Hundreds of people were ineligible to receive assistance under the newly enacted but very limited Unemployed Workmen's Act. At the London School of Economics, a committee was formed to investigate the extent and causes of, as well as remedies for, the widespread poverty to be found among the nearly three hundred thousand inhabitants of West Ham. Poverty there was described as a permanent problem demanding national attention and concern, and contributions to the committee's Outer London Inquiry Fund were solicited.[8]

Balfour, who attended the first performance of *Major Barbara,* resigned as prime minister six days later on 4 December. His Conservative government was succeeded by a Liberal cabinet under Sir Henry Campbell-Bannerman and the general election took place in January 1906. Before resigning, Balfour had appointed a Royal Commission on the Poor Laws, with Shaw's Fabian colleague Beatrice Webb as one of its members.

Patently there was no want of economic and political turmoil when *Major Barbara* came upon the scene. But well before all these events occurred, Shaw had of course fixed the time of the play as January. Even so, it is unlikely that he would have wanted to move the time back to late 1905, all its turbulence notwithstanding. The problems and anxieties of the time were persistent and unyielding. One month would do as well as another in that respect: there was no prospect of immediate improvement.

It does appear odd that Shaw would specify the year 1906 in the theater programs but not in the early text of the play. Perhaps it was an oversight— not the only one in this play, as Dukore knows well. However, he may have wanted the year pinned down for the actual production, and left indeterminate for subsequent readers of the play. That would also leave revivals free to decide whether to designate a year and, if so, which one.

This possibility gains some credibility from inspection of the programs of most of the revivals of *Major Barbara* during Shaw's lifetime—especially those upon which he very likely exerted influence. The first documented revival of the play took place in Berlin (in Siegfried Trebitsch's German translation) in December 1909. Its program lists the *Zeit* as "*Gegenwart*" ("the present"). Trebitsch's published German text, in contrast, follows Shaw's 1907 one in giving the time only as "*Januarabend*" (a January evening"). The program of the 1915 Grace George–Louis Calvert American revival has Act I taking place "After dinner on a January night," but, in addition, indicates "Time—The Present." (Unfortunately, inaccessible to me at present are the programs for the 1921 and 1923 revivals by Norman MacDermott at the

Everyman Theatre, Hampstead, but in his book *Everymania*, MacDermott reports that Shaw "had not come to rehearsals but came to performances."[9] Lacking to me also is the relevant part of the program of the Theatre Guild revival in New York in 1928.)

In 1929, Leon M. Lion, Charles Macdona, and Lewis Casson revived the play at London's Wyndham Theatre, with Casson as Cusins and his wife, Sybil Thorndike, as Barbara. Sir Lewis told me years ago that Shaw was an active participant in that revival, which was modeled after the original production. The Wyndham program sets the first act as follows: "After dinner on a wintry night early in the century . . ." If by this Shaw thought that the play no longer belonged in the present, but needed to be returned to the era of its composition—however vaguely indicated—he may well have thought differently a few years later, for the program of the Old Vic revival of 1935, in the preparation of which Shaw was deeply involved, omits all mention of time.[10] So does the program of the Westminster Theatre revival in 1939.[11]

With respect to Shaw's addition of the year 1906 in his revision of the published text of *Major Barbara,* it is necessary to make a minor correction in Dukore's account. The author did not make this change for the first time in the 1931 Constable Standard Edition, but rather did so one year earlier in the 1930 Constable limited edition of the *Collected Works of Bernard Shaw.* (The 1929 Globe edition retained the wording of the original Constable edition.) After the Standard Edition, Shaw published another edition of the play: the Penguin screen version in 1945. In that edition the only time reference in the new prologue with which the drama begins is seasonal: "Bitter winter weather."[12] Following the prologue, the scene shifts to Wilton Crescent "some weeks later." But in the second-act stage directions, the references to January remain intact as in all the other editions of the play.

To the limited extent that any pattern of intent on Shaw's part is discernible in these variations over the years, it would appear that he may well have taken a separate approach to text and stage production. The published play focuses initially on the month of January, kept indeterminate as to year until the 1930 revision, which situates it in 1906; then for the screen version, all specificity of year is abandoned. For the first stagings, January is particularized in 1906—the year at hand—then released to a shifting "present" time in early revivals. Subsequent revivals, in which the playwright appears to have had a hand, suggest a movement toward indefiniteness not only in year but even in month. This leaves revivers with a relatively free hand. What does remain constant and invariable is the Shavian emphasis on bitterly cold wintry weather in the second act alone.

THE QUEEN'S COUP D'ÉTAT.
TO THE EDITOR OF THE TIMES

Sir

Like everybody else in London with a spark of social compunction
I am boundlessly delighted with the very womanly dash made by
the Queen [Alexandra] to do something for the unemployed. She
has waited for parliament to deal with the question, and parliament
has done nothing—has, indeed, with great difficulty been prevented
from doing less. She has waited for the Prime Minister to advise,
and the Prime Minister avows his utter helplessness. The resources
of the Constitution being thus exhausted, she has boldly thrown
the Constitution to the winds and taken the matter in hand herself.
She has said, in effect, to our wise men: "Well, if you cannot get my
people work, I will give them bread. Who will come and help me?"

In doing this the Queen has precipitated a crisis that was bound to
come sooner or later. The situation is not new. In cities like ancient
Rome or modern London competitive commerce always finally creates
a proletariat too numerous to be effectually coerced and too clever to
be duped by spurious political economy and pious platitudes about
the sacredness of law and order. In 1886, when the windows of the
clubs in Pall-mall were broken, the classes represented by those clubs
immediately paid £49,000 ransom to the Mansion-house fund, most
of which went into the hands of the anything-but-hardworking. Trade
revived and staved off the emergency for a time; but it is upon us again,
and now the question is, Are we to accept *Panem et Circenses* [bread and
circuses] as a regular part of our metropolitan organization? We must,
if the alternative is to leave the unemployed to choose between starva-
tion and plunder. The Queen will not allow us to starve her people. She
has forced our hand, and is going to organize Panem (the circuses will
come later) with her own hands, unless we find work and wages for the
unemployed, who, by the way, will very soon acquire a taste, like their
social superiors, for incomes without work.

It is a critical situation, and one that may become dangerous
if those who understand it are too courtly or too cowardly to
speak out. The Queen's charity is the last resource of a bankrupt
civilization. If we can do nothing better we must adopt it, and she is
right to force the alternative on us. But can we do nothing better?

For my part I see no difficulty in finding work for the unemployed. Take the places they live in, for instance. There is the urgently necessary work of knocking those places down, burning their putrid *débris*, and replacing them with decent dwellings in airy and handsome streets. The spots to begin with are already marked by Mr Charles Booth on the map of London in black. If instead of directing the attention of the unemployed as in 1886 to the possibility of extorting a demoralizing ransom by destroying the houses of other people, we could set them to the eminently desirable and honourable work of destroying their own and building better ones to replace them, the Queen would not need to empty her private purse with the heartbreaking knowledge that her money would save her people's lives at the expense of their characters.

It is true that there is no commercial demand for a new and decent city; but pray for what great social work is there any commercial demand? How long more will it take us to see that great nations work for national profits, and keep the little souls who can understand nothing but commercial profits out of the national councils? I wish I could persuade the Queen that there is no lack of money, no lack of work, no lack of charity. It is character and statesmanship that we want, and these, alas! cannot be created by cheques and subscription lists.

Yours truly,

G. BERNARD SHAW.

10, Adelphi-terrace, W.C., Nov. 13.

NOTES

1. The details are traced in my article, "'In More Ways Than One': *Major Barbara*'s Debt to Gilbert Murray," *Educational Theatre Journal* 20, no. 2 (May 1968): 123–40, especially 124–25.

2. The Act II stage directions in the original Derry manuscript read: "for it is an abominably cold, raw, January day." The 1907 printed edition adds an opening sentence, "*The yard of the West Ham shelter of the Salvation Army is a cold place on a January morning,*" then reads, "*for it is a grindingly cold raw January day.*"

3. *The Bystander,* 10 January 1906, 72.

4. London: A. H. Bullen, 1907, 146; reprinted in Desmond MacCarthy's *The Court Theatre,* 1904–1907, ed. Stanley Weintraub (Coral Gables: University of Miami Press, 1966), 130, which Dukore cites, and in which the error inadvertently persists.

5. William Scovell Adams, *Edwardian Heritage: A Study in British History, 1901–1906* (London: Frederick Muller, 1949), 216.

6. Ibid., 218.

7. Shaw's letter appeared in *The Times* on 14 November 1905. The transcription printed here, taken from the *Times* digital archive online, differs only slightly from the version published in Ronald Ford, ed., *The Letters of Bernard Shaw to "The Times,"* *1898–1950* (Dublin: Irish Academic Press, 2007), 50–51.

8. *Morning Post*, 1 December 1905.

9. Norman MacDermott, *Everymania: The History of the Everyman Theatre, Hampstead, 1920–1926* (London: The Society for Theatre Research, 1975), 57.

10. On Shaw's involvement in the production, see Harcourt Williams's *Old Vic Saga* (London: Winchester Publications, 1949), 136.

11. There were two more London revivals prior to Shaw's death, one at the Arts Theatre in 1948 and the other at the Bedford Theatre, Camden Town, in 1949. I have not seen the program of the former; the latter gives the time for Act I as "After dinner on a January night," reverting to the language of the first published edition. But Shaw, by then in his nineties, could scarcely have had much to do with these productions.

12. *Major Barbara: A Screen Version* (Harmondsworth: Penguin, 1945), 37.

Shaw and Bertrand Russell versus Gilbert Murray on Britain's Entry into World War I

The Inside Story

CHARLES A. CARPENTER

What follows is a brief history of bitter strife among lifelong friends. It expands into a revelation of what lies beneath and remains concealed in those people when their friendships are severely challenged. Because all three of them happened to be unquestioned geniuses, dedicated activists, and highly prolific writers, their interaction during a time of extreme stress becomes all the more revealing. The key individual who touched off this cultivated but disquieting conflict was Sir Edward Grey, British Foreign Secretary from 1906 to 1915; the key event was his decision to commit his country to war against Germany on 3 August 1914.

By that time, approaching the age of sixty, Bernard Shaw had completed his triumphant "reign" at the Court Theatre and had resigned from the Executive Board of the Fabian Society. He was one of England's most conspicuous figures, constantly arguing his opinions from whatever pulpits would risk his voice and whatever publications cared to exploit his popularity. He was relentless in pursuing and exposing scandals which derived from the government and its bedfellow, the aristocracy, and which threatened to affect the lower echelons of society in disastrous ways. The decision to go to war became a prime target.

One of his very best friends and a favorite correspondent, although a decade younger, was an Australian / English classics professor named Gilbert Murray, whose vocation would normally have been enough to draw little but scorn from Shaw. Murray's scholarly brilliance was confirmed when, in 1908, he was appointed to the highest academic honor in England at the time, Regius Professor of Greek at Oxford University. Shaw's greatest achievement to date was his successful campaign, bolstered mainly by his own plays, to influence susceptible English playgoers to prefer intellectually stimulating drama to the "popular" fare. The friendship of the two was mutually respectful: they sent each other the drafts of nearly all of their writings and assumed that they would take the time to read them carefully and comment upon them at length. This despite the fact that both were also otherwise occupied as earnest campaigners for worthy causes and cultivators of a host of valued relationships.

Bertrand Russell, one of the most respected British philosophers in the early twentieth century, was a cousin of Murray's wife and member of an aristocratic family. But like Shaw he had a strong iconoclastic bent directed especially toward conventional ideals that were typically evoked by his fellow aristocrats. A socialist at heart while eschewing an active commitment, his chief expertise was in logic, which he used as an instrument of persuasion on social and political issues as well as in philosophy and mathematics. His collaboration with Alfred North Whitehead on the landmark work *Principia Mathematica* was his most notable achievement during the prewar period. Russell corresponded extensively with Murray in those years.

Shaw was won over to Murray in the late 1890s partly because of his famously engaging manner and wide-ranging erudition, but more immediately by the fact that he yearned to become a playwright.[1] Influenced by Euripides and Ibsen and nudged by Shaw, after a few false starts he shifted his focus to composing a kind of play that was unparalleled at the time: modernized translations of Greek dramas aimed at converting theater audiences from "Sardoodledom" (Shaw's term for the French well-made play *à la* Victorien Sardou) to "the New Drama" chiefly exemplified by Shaw but also by Harley Granville Barker, St. John Hankin, John Galsworthy, and (in Murray's and Shaw's minds) Euripides. Shaw appropriated Gilbert's looks, mannerisms, and translations for the character of Cusins in *Major Barbara*—a problematic episode for Murray, but not severe enough in itself to cause a breach.[2]

The three were destined to clash head-on when, on 3 August 1914, Sir Edward Grey surprised half the nation and many members of Parliament by announcing that Britain was joining its fellow members of the "Triple Entente," France and Russia, in declaring war on Germany and its allies. The clinching event was the German army's invasion of Belgium on its way to attack France. Murray wholly approved of Grey's decision; Shaw regretted it but mainly deplored the way it had been reached; Russell was outraged by his country's commitment to such a self-destructive action taken with little or no consent from Parliament, much less the people who would be on the front lines.[3] Three months later Shaw published an eighty-page supplement to *The New Statesman* entitled "Common Sense About the War," later issued as a pamphlet, which attacked Grey's progress toward war in the mode of a well-documented exposé; in mid-1915 Murray countered with *The Foreign Policy of Sir Edward Grey, 1906–1915*, a book-length attempt to exonerate the Foreign Office and refute its detractors; then Russell attacked that attempt head-on in December 1915 with his longer book, *The Policy of the Entente, 1904–1914: A Reply to Professor Gilbert Murray*. Interspersed were lesser steps in the ongoing conflict that refined and intensified the continuing argument.

Historical Background

During the spring and summer of 1914, war had seemed to most Europeans both unlikely and ill-advised. An authoritative study of World War I explains that the International Tribunal at the Hague, set up in 1900 to settle disputes between sovereign countries,

> was a symbol of the determination of the civilised world not to allow itself to become embroiled in mutually destructive conflicts. Socialists throughout Europe denounced the very concept of war and urged the working class everywhere to refuse to be a part of capitalist enthusiasm for war. Bankers and financiers, like the landed aristocracy with whom they were in competition, felt themselves part of a wider international grouping, which, whether by trade in the one case or intermarriage in the other, had nothing to gain by war, and much to lose.[4]

In his widely read book, *The Great Illusion*, Norman Angell put the situation in a nutshell when he wrote that "even a victorious warring power would suffer extraordinary economic and financial loss as a result of war"—which of course turned out to be true.[5]

Early in the century Murray had classified himself as a Radical Liberal, with capitalist and aristocratic leanings but some sympathy with socialist aspirations. His criticism of his country's treatment of the Boers during the South African War of 1899–1902, one of his granddaughters recalled, got him "pelted with rotten eggs for his unpopular anti-war views."[6] Bertrand Russell, in his relatively unformed twenties, reacted to the war by undergoing a conversion from "an imperialist more or less" to a humanist with "a horror of force," and thus a pro-Boer (Clark, 86).

Much more pragmatically, Shaw correctly assumed the British would win and annex the Transvaal region with its hoards of gold, and focused his energy on fitting the postwar situation there into the Fabian vision of gradually changing the entire world into a socialist one, with the more advanced countries guiding the underdeveloped ones.

By this time, to paraphrase Duncan Wilson, Murray had become one of the Liberals' most coveted intellectuals, and he profited from his relations with the political establishment. But he remained a dedicated Radical: he had been associated with the Webbs and other Fabians in their efforts to reform the Poor Law, and with Christian Socialists on social issues. He sympathized with the Independent Labour Party and other groups on the left who argued that it was working-class families who would suffer most from war because their breadwinners would necessarily be the chief source of manpower, which in this case could truly be described as cannon fodder (Wilson, 217). Most of his associates were strong advocates of peace.

Sir Edward Grey had risen to his position of Foreign Secretary through his aristocratic family and the partisanship of fellow "country gentlemen." Preferring sports, fishing, and other pleasures to the rigors of education, he was sent down from Oxford in 1884 for incorrigible idleness.[7] At nineteen he inherited the title "Sir" along with a two thousand-acre estate and ample income to continue doing what he wished. At twenty-three, he somehow won an election for the House of Commons as a Radical Liberal; at twenty-four, he was favored with a typical stepping-stone position with the Foreign Office, parliamentary Under-Secretary. There, he earned the approval of the Secretary, Lord Rosebery, as a man with well-defined qualifications: his addresses impressed the House, Rosebery stated, "not by brilliance of speech or sharpness of retort but by soundness of grasp and sincerity of tone" (Robbins, 44). He weaved his way upward into greater and greater appreciation, if not influence, until Rosebery told the new Foreign Secretary that Grey was "one of the most important members of the Govt . . . Moreover he is persona gratissima to the H. of C., popular, admired, and respected . . . If he sticks to political life, he is certain to make his mark" (Robbins, 51–52).

In line with this prophecy, Grey became the Foreign Secretary in 1906. This was a precarious choice for a peace-seeking administration, since he had already developed a strong dislike for Germany. As early as 1903 he had described the country as "our worst enemy and our greatest danger."[8] One of the first problems he had to deal with as Foreign Secretary was "the Denshawai affair," an incident that occurred on 13 June 1906 in a small Egyptian town when five British officers visited it to go pigeon shooting and started firing. The farmers, for whom the pigeons were the main source of revenue, were enraged, tried to stop them, failed, and sought redress. British tribunals sentenced the delinquent villagers to awful punishments, including four hangings and many floggings, but the British officers involved were all cleared. Before the trials were concluded, Lord Cromer, Consul-General of Egypt, sought Grey's approval for the sentences. Grey exposed his weakness as the man in charge who had to make tough decisions: he "had a hurried conversation with the Prime Minister and Asquith, but decided to take no action, although he found the verdicts startlingly severe . . . The more the Foreign Secretary studied the affair, the more uncertain he became. Nevertheless, he considered that he had been right not to interfere, since the authority of the man on the spot had to be upheld" (Robbins, 166). Murray was surely aware of this event because he would have read Shaw's lengthy discussion of it in the last section of his 1912 preface to *John Bull's Other Island*, "The Denshawai Horror."[9] In *Common Sense About the War* Shaw cites this incident as proving that the kind of man who could behave with such squeamish deference to people responsible to him had the wrong kind of character for the position he was in. For Shaw it became an analogy to Grey's allowing Britain to send tens of thousands of middle- and lower-class men to die in the war because, well before, he could not play the bully and tell Germany outright that if it attacked Belgium and France it would have to defeat not only their forces (and that of their ally, Russia) but also Britain's well-trained volunteer armed forces and dominant armada.

Grey Acts and Murray Reacts

When Britain, France, Germany, Austria, Russia, Serbia, Italy, Turkey, Morocco, Japan, and other countries were jockeying to maneuver advantageous alliances in the European and Asian balance of power competitions, Murray was hesitant to favor war as a means to that end. Besides hating war, this would ally him with militant anti-German sentiment expressed by Lloyd George, Winston Churchill, and other leading Conservative and Liberal voices. As an academic, he admired much German literature and the cultivated milieu out of which it emerged. One of his most valued friends was the distinguished German classicist Ulrich von Wilamowitz-Moellendorff, who assisted him with an edition of Euripides' plays in 1901 and stayed in contact for many years (Wilson, 54–56). Just before the war began, Murray had signed a letter prepared by the British Neutrality Committee urging that Britain remain neutral if war broke out between other great powers. Ironically, and perhaps symptomatically, the letter was delayed and did not get published until the war had already started, with England as its anti-German centerpiece.

Several times Murray had voiced the widespread pre-1914 belief that European nations had become so civilized that there could never be war again. He later admitted that he had been shortsighted in this tenuous assumption, prompted by his own Hellenic faith in the power of reason to influence man. Shortly before the war broke out, he was walking through St. James's Park and encountered Sir Edward Grey. When he commented that surely war was unthinkable, he was shocked to hear Grey respond that it was certain to come, and come in the near future.[10] Grey was of the same stock that the great majority of British cabinet members and parliamentarians boasted: aristocrats who assumed that they had the proper qualifications to run the country and its colonies as leaders of its political and military establishments, and whose highest ambitions were to do just that. Murray himself was not quite in this class, lacking their wealth and lofty ambitions. However, he felt a personal kinship with it, and had managed to marry into the aristocracy by wooing and finally winning the daughter of the Countess of Carlisle at her home, Castle Howard. (The Countess was the "formidable" woman whom Shaw approximated as the model for Lady Britomart in *Major Barbara*.)

On the eve of by far the most momentous and destructive war the world had ever experienced, 3 August 1914, Murray was swayed toward favoring Britain's entry into it by a single speech of Grey, his long and hastily prepared address to Parliament. After hearing that Germany had just invaded neutral Belgium in order to attack France advantageously, which to Grey made war Britain's only alternative, Murray came away convinced that his country "had no choice" but to oppose Germany's chosen path.[11] Close friends, among them Shaw, Russell, J. L. Hammond, and John Morley, strongly disagreed with this, but he was not swayed from his view that the British government's determination had been correct. He wrote to his wife, Lady Mary, on 7 September:

> I have hours in which I feel as you do, utterly abased and crushed by the misery of the war, feeling that the death and maiming and starving of Germans and Austrians is just as horrible a thing as the same suffering in Englishmen. But mostly I feel strung up and exalted by a feeling of the tremendous issue and the absolute duty that lies upon us to save Europe and humanity. We did not know until the war revealed it what this German system meant. Once it is revealed I do feel that we must strike it down or die. (Quoted in Wilson, 218)

Shaw and Russell React

The first indication to Murray that Shaw might have conflicting views came in mid-September when he naively asked him to join the "greatest possible number of eminent writers" in signing an official manifesto in support of the war (Wilson, 219). This was the initial gesture of a newly formed unit of the Foreign Office, the Bureau of Information, which had solicited and received Murray's assistance. Clearly irked, Shaw rewrote parts of the document to turn its message on its head, signed it, and invited Murray to send this new version out. Then, in a serious post-script, he urged him not to support the original Manifesto. "What it says is not true and not new," he said, "and it gives Grey a testimonial just when the war gives us a chance of discrediting all this Cromer-Milner-Grey diplomacy & reviving what is valuable in the Liberal tradition."[12] Shaw had already published an article that Murray must not have seen: "The Peril of Potsdam: Our Business Now." It begins, "Now that we are at war, it is as well that we should know what that war is about." He denounces the acclamations of patriotism and manly aggression, declaring: "Our national trick of virtuous indignation is tiresome enough in peaceful party strife at home. At war it is ungallant and unpardonable. Let us take our pugnacity to the field and leave our hypocrisy and bad blood at home." Then he asserts: "This war is a Balance of Power war and nothing else." His finale takes satiric aim at Grey: "History will not excuse us because, after making war inevitable, we run round at the last moment begging everyone not to make a disturbance, but to come to London and be talked to kindly but firmly by Sir Edward Grey."[13]

Four days later Bertrand Russell's more strident voice was heard in a brief article, "The Rights of the War," published in *The Nation* (15 August). Dejected by learning that several of his friends favored the war—among them Whitehead, George Trevelyan, H. W. Massingham, and his brother—he registered both shock and indignation:

> Those who saw the London crowds, during the nights leading up
> to the Declaration of War, saw a whole population, hitherto pea-
> cable and humane, precipitated in a few days down the steep slope
> to primitive barbarism, letting loose, in a moment, the instincts of
> hatred and blood-lust against which the whole fabric of society has
> been raised. "Patriots" in all countries acclaim this brutal orgy as a
> noble determination to vindicate the right; reason and mercy are
> swept away in one great flood of hatred . . .

And all this madness, all this rage, all this flaming death of our
civilization and our hopes, has been brought about because a set
of official gentlemen, living luxurious lives, mostly stupid, and all
without imagination or heart, have chosen that it should occur
rather than that anyone of them should suffer some infinitesimal
rebuff to his country's pride.

He then directed his attack on the Foreign Office, singling out Grey for a
special rebuke:

Our diplomacy . . . has not been guiltless. Secret arrangements,
concealed from Parliament and even (at first) from all the Cabinet, in
spite of reiterated denials, an obligation suddenly revealed when the
war fever had reached the point which rendered public opinion tol-
erant of the discovery that the lives of many, and the livelihood of all,
had been pledged by one man's irresponsible decisions. Yet, though
France knew our obligations, Sir E. Grey refused, down to the last
moment, to inform Germany of the conditions of our neutrality or
of our intervention.[14]

Shaw's letter to Murray quoted above concludes: "I am struggling labo-
riously through a Manifesto of my own on the subject." That document,
Common Sense About the War, begins, "The time has now come to pluck up
courage and begin to talk and write soberly about the war." Flaunting his
"Irish capacity for criticizing England with something of the detachment of
a foreigner," he rails against the widespread jingoistic reaction to the war's
alleged progress, and traces the path of British anti-German propaganda
from the 1870s to the present (16, 20–22).[15] He mentions Murray only once,
en passant (61–62).[16]

The framework for his argument about how the war started is to describe
what governmental spokesmen and accommodating journalists identified
as Germany's war-mongering *Junkers* and equate them with those high-level
British officials who, in his mind, fit the definition themselves:

I see the people of England united in a fierce detestation and
defiance of the views and acts of Prussian Junkerism. And I see
the German people stirred to the depths by a similar antipathy
to English Junkerism, and angered by the apparent treachery and
duplicity of the attack made on them by us in their extremest peril
from France and Russia. I see both nations duped, but alas! not quite

unwillingly duped, by their Junkers and Militarists into wreaking
on one another the wrath they should have spent in destroying
Junkerism and Militarism in their own country. (17)

Shaw cites a German dictionary which says that the term *Junker* actually
denotes wealthy young noblemen or country gentlemen whose natural
course is to rise to positions of power and influence in the government.
His prime example is not a German but Sir Edward Grey, whom he calls
"a Junker from his topmost hair to the tips of his toes." He grants that the
Kaiser is also a Junker, but "much less autocratic than . . . Grey, who . . .
sends us to war by a word to an ambassador and pledges all our wealth to his
foreign allies by a stroke of his pen." In fact, to him Grey's Foreign Office is
a virtual "Junker Club" (18–19). While documenting the Byzantine political
maneuvers of diplomats in several countries, Shaw focuses especially upon
Grey, whom, he says, an autocratic foreign policy permitted to make war
"without consulting the nation, or confiding in it," resulting "inevitably" in
"a disastrous combination of war and unpreparedness for war" (43).

He then offers a distinctly different view of the role played by the German intrusion into Belgium. Undeniably this event was the provocation
on which England declared war, but in Shaw's eyes the rationale offered
by Grey had little to do with the underlying reasons, which traced back
to secret balance-of-power diplomacy. Britain had been prepared for this
contingency since 1906, having secretly told France and Belgium that it
would not permit any military power to invade the continental shores of
the North Sea. When Germany did, Prime Minister Asquith had what Shaw
later called "a perfectly presentable and correct pretext for entering on a war
to which he was already secretly pledged, Belgium or no Belgium."[17]

Only about a third of *Common Sense About the War* is concerned with
how England became involved in it, but Shaw's arguments so far drew little but venom from those who read them and heard about them. Murray's
reactions seem to be unrecorded. In retrospect, Shaw summed up the general effect by saying that his inflammatory statements were "so revolting
to Englishmen in the delirium of the war fever, and so contradictory to
the current legends of melodramatic patriotism, that [the essay], launched
in November 1914, when the war fever was at its height, produced furious demands for my immediate execution as a pro-German, a Pacifist,
a traitor, . . . and what not."[18] The polemic was excoriated by several of
his close friends (chief among them Henry Arthur Jones, William Archer,
and H. G. Wells), and he was expelled from the Dramatists' Club, one of
whose members was Murray. He took small consolation in cheers from

rigid pacifists (like Bertrand Russell at the time) or extreme socialists (like
Keir Hardie). The howls of execration, especially in the press, were almost
as hysterical as those which greeted Bertrand Russell from a Cambridge
University group assembled by a divinity professor after he issued the
pamphlet *War, The Offspring of Fear* on 7 November 1914.[19] He was told:
"[A]fter a very careful discussion it was gravely burned with the consent of
the whole company; and one of their number expressed the opinion that
it ought to have been burned by the common hangman" (38).

This cogent, forceful thirteen-page essay, published by the left-
leaning Union of Democratic Control, is a call for understanding what
causes underlay the outbreak of the war as viewed by the various nations
involved. Its basic premises are axiomatic: "[T]here are higher goals than
victory and nobler ideals than the destruction of hostile armies" (39), and
"the horror of this war should produce the will for peace" (46). Russell
implicitly measures Britain's jingoistic response to entering the war
against a criticism of the decision by two distinguished German intellectuals, who had characterized it as "an indelible shame to England"
and stressed a crucial angle on the conflict which its enemies had down-
played: the factor of Russia's "barbarism" threatening their homeland
with their hosts of armed divisions. It was that nation's partial mobiliza-
tion that prompted Germany to declare war against the third member
of the Triple Entente before moving on Belgium and France. "England
fights to please a half-Asiatic Power against Germanism," the writers
state, and then generalize:

> It is the fault of England that the present War is extended to a
> world-war, and that all culture is thereby endangered. And why all this?
> Because she was envious of Germany's greatness, because she wanted
> at all costs to hinder a further extension of this greatness. She was only
> waiting for a favourable opportunity to break out to the detriment of
> Germany, and therefore she seized most promptly on the necessary
> German advance through Belgium as a pretext in order to cloak her
> brutal national selfishness with a mantle of respectability. (39–40)

Murray Defends Grey

At about the same time that Russell's pamphlet appeared, another from a
fellow member of the UDC was published which attempted to refute the
prewar policies of the Foreign Office: H. N. Brailsford's *Origins of the Great*

War. Brailsford argues that "the war hinged entirely on conflicts in the East ... rather than on German designs on France or desire for naval supremacy." If there was moral responsibility for the war, "it must be shared between Germany and Russia."[20] Murray's first response to these two diatribes was a pamphlet published in October by his university's press, *How Can War Ever Be Right?* The style he adopted reflects the fair, balanced, but finally accusing mode of Grey:

> From the point of view of one who really believes that great nations ought to behave to one another as scrupulously and honourably as ordinary, law-abiding men, no Power in Europe, or out of it, is quite blameless. They all have ambitions; they all, to some extent, use spies; they all, within limits, try to outwit each other; in their diplomatic dealings they rely not only on the claims of good sense and justice, but ultimately, no doubt, on the threat of possible force. But as a matter of degree, Germany does all these things more than other Powers. In her diplomacy, force comes at once to the front; international justice is hardly mentioned.[21]

Murray then proceeded to write a 140-page book, published in early 1915 by what had become the Bureau's chosen outlet, Oxford University Press: *The Foreign Policy of Sir Edward Grey, 1906–1915.* It is a careful, well-documented attempt to describe Grey's rationale in persuasive terms. He sent a copy to Grey, describing it as an "act of homage from one of your rather critical supporters," and drew a mildly favorable response: "[T]he terms in which you write are a very real pleasure and encouragement" (Wilson, 223). However, when Grey wrote his two-volume memoir in 1925, *Twenty-Five Years, 1892–1916,* he did not make a single reference to his staunch defender.[22]

Murray touches off his defense by lumping Russell and Brailsford in with a hardly defensible category he calls "pro-Germans,"

> who are in a very small minority and have to fight hard. And many of them become naturally so wrapped up in their own immediate controversy that, as far as their combative feelings are concerned, the central enemy of the human race is Sir Edward Grey; next to him come the British Cabinet and the most popular generals. The Kaiser is to them a prisoner in the dock, a romantic unfortunate, to be defended against overwhelming odds. (7)

Murray does not single out Shaw for criticism, preferring to incriminate him indirectly:

> These writers are in their way high-minded, disinterested,
> courageous, and often very clever, but they are not at present in a
> state of mind which enables them to see or even to seek the truth.
> They are impassioned advocates, not fair-minded inquirers. They
> might one and all utter the famous plea of their ally, Mr. Shaw: "Who
> am I that I should be just?"[23]

Later he will echo this in two memorial statements about his friend.

Replying to the UDC's claims of secret diplomacy and evasion of parliamentary control, Murray argues that Grey (as Wilson cogently summarizes it) "knew of German aggressive designs, and had to build up a system of alliances to counter them, without openly denouncing Germany and thereby closing the door to peaceful accommodation with her" (223). If one is not yet aware of important elements of Grey's diplomacy that breed suspicion, Murray's rebuttals ring soundly enough. His analysis of the historical background, and especially of the twelve crucial days that led up to the war, would strike most readers as extremely careful and thorough. His *grande finale* is impressive, even if susceptible to criticism from determined opponents:

> . . . No one can read the debates of the last few years on Foreign
> Politics in the House of Commons without feeling that the House was
> under some heavy shadow and members' tongues not moving freely.
>
> This shadow, this overhanging peril, must never be forgotten in
> any judgement which we pass on Sir Edward Grey's conduct of our
> foreign affairs. . . . If here and there on some point of detail he has
> not driven as clever a bargain as he might; if he has not stood up to
> our friends Russia and France as defiantly as some of his less responsible
> critics would have done; even if, here and there, he has not
> pressed fearlessly forward in support of some weak nation to which
> British liberal sympathies went naturally forth; if under his guidance,
> with all our enormous naval expenditure and prestige, Great Britain
> has sometimes seemed to have little spare strength for the running of
> avoidable risks or the championing of disinterested causes; let those
> criticize him who can still say that he over-rated our danger. The
> rest of us will only be grateful for ever to one who through all these
> years of crisis acted justly and sought no aggrandizement, who kept

faith with his friends and worked for a good understanding with his enemies, who never spoke a rash word to bring the peril nearer, and never neglected a precaution to meet it when it should come. (137)

Murray's instinctive as well as reasoned favoritism for Grey often manifested itself in unguarded statements crying out for a raised-eyebrow response from many who had followed Grey's prewar career. A glaring example: "Sir Edward Grey's policy was exactly right. I am thankful to have a Foreign Minister who does not aim at bluff or cunning, but who has established his great reputation in Europe because he is known to be disinterested and faithful to his word" (34). It would be more accurate to say that his reputation depended to a great extent upon the alliance of the observer with the standard norm of British statesmanship, well defined by Shaw as that of imperialist Junkers.

Shaw and Russell Attack

Shaw read Murray's book and wrote a review to be published in *The New Statesman*. Intending to prepare his friend for the shock of reading it, he sent him one of his most enigmatic and puzzling letters, the relevant part of which follows:

14 July 1915

My dear Murray . . .
I have done you in (the Grey book) for this week's New Statesman. I thought it better to slaughter you myself than leave you to some young butcher with no respect for his elders. And you have done Grey in. What ironic fiend possessed you? The horrid cruelty with which you put all his footle in italics would revolt Euripides. Even that damning passage in which he says that he is not quite sure whether the neutrality of Belgium is a fighting matter is there. Poor Edward, with the vials of wrath slowly turning upside down over his head in the hands of the avenging angel of Denshawai, fluttering about and saying to the Germans, "If you can only suggest something—I assure you I'm quite reasonable."

Dont you KNOW that youve destroyed him? Your dramatic faculty has enabled you to get into his skin in the most wonderful way: you defend him exactly as he would have defended the King of the Belgians if he had accepted the German offer (as Grey would have accepted it); but there come bits where the laughter of the subconscious Murray breaks through and gives the show away. Those Persians sawn in two with the dear delightful Russians marching between them—the Caudine forks up to date—and Grey taking it like a mixed biscuit at afternoon tea, though shocked to his soul by Shuster's bad form in not paying his calls: did you really see that with Grey's eyes as you wrote?

The knock-out is perfection. He was always guided by circumstances. Not like Napoleon, who said "I make circumstances." Youve really handled the man barbarously in your dramatic delirium.

It is funny; but I feel a certain remorse about it. Ever since that Egyptian horror I have raged against the folly of leaving Grey at the Foreign Office after such a sensational revelation of his utter want of character. But that is not quite the truth. It is not that he has no character, but that he has the wrong character for the job. . . . Will he ever realize that he could have stopped the war, probably, by a shake of his fist, and that he was too nice and cautious to do it. Do the ghosts of the million slain never come to his bed and point to their mangled entrails and Edipusted eyes and say "Thus didest thou"? I hope not. The only consolation one has in thinking of him is that he will never know. He will say, to the end, "I asked them to come and confer. They *wouldnt*. Simply wouldnt. And I'd have given them such nice tea. And we could have talked about Servia. What more could I do? I may as well think about something nice and go to sleep."[24]

It would take pages of sophistry to unravel what Shaw really means by his most startling statements here, which characterize a highly intelligent man congenitally incapable of detecting hidden motives in himself as being possessed by an "ironic fiend" who compelled him to apply his "dramatic faculty" not of the Euripidean but of the Keatsian sort, "negative capability," to "get into [the] skin" of one of the most prominent and respected leaders of his country's government and "destroy" him—all without realizing it.

Shaw's review incorporates most of these galling comments, but also contains criticisms with objective substance.[25] The most important is that Grey could have prevented the war simply by intimidating Germany as David Lloyd George had done during the "Agadir crisis" (the second crisis involving Morocco) in 1911. Responding to audacious German demands, backed by a gunboat, for "compensation" in return for negotiating a French protectorate in Morocco, Lloyd George delivered his legendary Mansion House speech in which he declared that national honor was more precious than peace. Its key statement: "If Britain is treated badly where her interests are vitally affected, . . . then I say emphatically that peace at that price would be a humiliation intolerable for a great country like ours to endure" (*Wikipedia*; verified). The speech was interpreted by Germany as a warning that she could not impose an unreasonable settlement on France, which was, of course, its intention. This is what Shaw is referring to when he says,

> Here was England, with Continents for colonies, with her mighty fleet, her stirring tradition, her unbeaten record, her millions of men spoiling for a fight, . . . towering, in spite of all Germany's laurels, as the most formidable single-handed Power on this earth. Her sword was in Sir Edward Grey's hands, her purse in his pocket, her men at his back. There was no need to shout: England's whisper was the thunder of Europe. In 1911, Mr. Lloyd George had shaken his mailed fist just once at the threat of war, and the sky cleared obsequiously in a moment. (349)

Shaw also quotes Murray on the frequency of Grey's refusal to propose anything definite during the crucial ten days preceding the war, and his earnest requests for Germany and other countries involved to "suggest something." Grey also hedged his bets to withhold how Britain really would act or react in crucial situations: for example, "Great Britain cannot promise to intervene, but will not necessarily stand aside." Shaw: "And during all these ifs and ans, and appeals to Germany and everyone else to suggest something, the allies were positively shouting to Sir Edward to say straight out whether he was going to fight or not: in other words, what England would stand and what she would not. And he could not even bring himself to say positively that he would fight if Belgian neutrality were violated!" (350). This culminates in Shaw's one piece of mockery directed at Murray: he couldn't believe his fellow literary genius had written the sentence, "Whether Grey's policy was right or wrong, it was from the beginning *quite definite* [Shaw's italics]." He sums up ironically:

> Sir Edward Grey . . . is spoken well of by all men. But he too is the victim of a mysterious fate. He is, as Professor Murray repeatedly testifies, the most truthful of men. Yet he never opens his mouth without deceiving us. He is the most loyal of simple manly souls; yet he is accused of betraying every country and every diplomatist who trusted him. He is the kindest of men; and yet he has [implicated us in the tortures of Denshawi and] brought upon us the slaughters of Armageddon. (351)

Another significant set of responses went unmentioned by both Shaw and Russell, although they surely reflected their opinions: those of House of Commons members who voiced their dissent after Grey's crucial speech.[26] The Leader of the House, Ramsay MacDonald, stated bluntly: "I think he is wrong. I think the Government which he represents and for which he speaks is wrong. I think the verdict of history will be that they are wrong" (1829–30). Then he chided Grey for doing what so many politicians had in the past: as Keir Hardie crisply put it later, "Our honour is said to be involved in entering into the war. That is always the excuse" (1841). Philip Morell rejected Grey's chief justifications for declaring war and countered: "I believe we are going to war now because of the fear and jealousy entertained in this country unfortunately, and fostered by large sections of the Press—the fear and jealousy of German ambition." Echoing others, he added that one concealed motive was "to preserve the despotism of Russia" (1835). The socialist T. Edmund Harvey deplored the coming "terrible wreckage of human life" and sermonized that this "is no people's war. It is a war that has been made . . . by men in high places, by diplomatists working in secret, by bureaucrats who are out of touch with the people of the world, who are the remnant of an older evil civilisation which is disappearing by gradual and peaceful methods" (1839). To top it off, the peace activist Arthur Ponsonby made an urgent plea:

> In the future, which is so black, I trust that my fellow countrymen will not embark on this light-heartedly and in a spirit of aggression. I trust that, even though it may be late, the Foreign Secretary will use every endeavour to the very last moment, disregarding the tone of messages, and the manner of Ambassadors, but looking to the great central interests of humanity and civilisation, to keep this country in a state of peace. (1842)

The most recent judgment I have found on Murray's reaction to Sir Edward's speech, "the defining moment of his political career," occurs in Martin Ceadel's 2007 essay, "Gilbert Murray and International Politics" (Stray, 217–37). In explaining the Liberal government's position, Ceadel states:

> Grey's ill-prepared performance proved unexpectedly persuasive, for a reason which the historian Cameron Hazelhurst neatly put his finger on: "The one massive virtue of Grey's speech was the stumbling manner, mistaken this time, as so often before, for honesty. Here was a man, it seemed, who had struggled for peace." . . . Murray was one

of those taken in: he evidently felt sympathy for a fastidious Oxonian statesman from an old Whig family struggling to do the right thing. What thus separated Murray from those radicals who maintained their neutralism and suspicion of secret diplomacy . . . was as much a difference of temperament as an alternative reading of international politics. Murray was temperamentally disposed to trust certain members of the Liberal establishment, whereas others were decidedly not." (223–24)

No recorded response from Murray to Shaw seems to exist, and indeed, as far as I was able to discover, no letters between the two are extant between November 1915 and February 1918.[27] Murray did reply after a fashion, reasserting his main judgments in an October 1916 letter to the editor of *The Times* in which he acclaimed another speech by Grey defending the war. Even though many more voices criticizing the Foreign Secretary had been raised in the past two years, Murray simply reiterated that Grey went "patiently and with absolute truthfulness over the whole ground, showing again exactly why we were compelled in honour to declare war and are now compelled to continue it; how we entered the lists as the champions of all national safety and freedom, and can appeal to the brotherhood of civilized mankind to support us simply because we are fighting for the right and not for conquest" (printed in Stray, 333).

Close acquaintance with writings by and about Gilbert Murray, as well as his activities throughout his life, will preclude almost anyone from attributing his repetition of these ultrapatriotic sentiments to anything but his honest convictions, with no trace of an intention to curry favor with the elite or console the suffering masses. He shared this attitude with many intellectuals, including his occasional collaborator and close friend of both himself and Shaw, William Archer, who, in a pamphlet entitled *The Thirteen Days* (1914), first condemned the German government of behaving with "criminal recklessness," then applauded "the skill, the tact, the temper, the foresight, the unwearied diligence and the unfailing greatness of spirit" of Grey.[28] Both men tended to be awed by their aristocratic superiors to the point that they could rationalize or suppress their possible flaws. Murray had in the meantime been transformed into a thoroughgoing patriot, actually joining a local branch of the armed forces in late 1914 at the age of forty-eight, the Oxford Volunteer Training Corps. He was diligent enough to be promoted to corporal in June 1916, and did not resign until 18 May 1917. In a 1915 letter to a longtime compatriot, J. A. K. Thomson, he declared: "It is right to offer oneself. I shall be delighted to die of a chill on the liver in Flanders if Lord Kitchener wishes it, and will kill as many Germans as I can in the process." "But," he added cutely, "if I were K I don't think I should send me" (Wilson, 234–35). In mid-1915, Murray's prewar translation of Euripides' *The Trojan Women* was touring the United States under the sponsorship of the radical Woman's Peace Party headed by Jane Addams. It was billed as "The World's Greatest Peace Play." He drafted a preface (never published) that clearly articulates his views on the war and the eventual peace:

> While I am heart and soul with the Woman's Peace Party in their
> abomination of War and Militarism and their pursuit of Peace,
> and while I feel the continuance of the present war a daily and
> nightly horror, taking the ease and joy out of life, I do not wish my
> co-operation in this National Tour to be interpreted as meaning
> that I am in favour of making peace with Germany on whatever
> terms the German Government may propose. To "crush Germany"
> is fortunately a sheer impossibility, deliberately to "hate Germany"
> is a sin against civilization. But I believe that in order to secure the
> rule of Peace and Public Rights in Europe certain safeguards must
> be obtained and certain reparations must be made. And there-
> fore, as I believe it was the duty of my country to declare war on
> 4 August 1914, so I believe that it will be her duty, both to herself
> and to humanity, to scrutinize earnestly, though I hope gener-
> ously, the proposed terms of Peace.[29]

Jumping to conclusions about a matter as serious as going to war obviously has its questionable aspects. It can put one on the defensive, and in Murray's case the people calling him wrong were as bright and high-minded as he. Their assaults on his convictions were extremely difficult to parry. Both Shaw and Russell had done their research into the past actions of Grey and the Foreign Office, Shaw at least since 1904 and Russell mainly just before and after the war started. In the same way that Murray searched— and found—evidence to support his convictions and reasons for fending off critics, so Shaw and Russell pounced on weak spots in Murray's exposition and found documentary evidence to buttress their own arguments.

An authoritative account of the onset of the war, written by two historians who are quite critical of Sir Edward Grey, will provide balance to the conflicting opinions of our three principals:

> The crisis of 1914 was the fifth in a series since 1905. Each produced
> tensions, bitterness, and resentment, which mounted with

the progress of the series. A war might have come earlier if the combination of elements in the crisis had been somewhat different, or it might have been postponed until the next crisis if certain aspects of the situation had been different in 1914. At that time the mixture of elements was just right for the explosion. Although we cannot say that war was inevitable in July 1914, we can say that, given the conditions that existed—the ambitions and goals of the great powers, their shifting strength, the institutional and domestic factors, the temper of the times, and especially the deeper forces favorable to a political upheaval—the conclusion can hardly be avoided that a great conflict was bound to break out sooner or later.[30]

Shaw and Russell on Murray the Individual

Both before and after finding reason to criticize his friend so disconcertingly for the faults of *The Foreign Policy of Sir Edward Grey*, Shaw deeply admired Murray and valued his opinions of his own work. Again and again, to anyone and everyone, he hailed his translations of Greek plays and other classical literary works as great and enduring contributions to world literature. On 29 October 1909, he wrote to Margot Asquith, the prime minister's wife, about the possibility of a knighthood for Murray: "If a high-literary knight or baronet, or even baron is wanted, Gilbert Murray, now Regius Professor of Greek at Oxford . . . , is the very man. His translations of Euripides are magnificent." Murray was eventually offered a knighthood, but declined.[31] A month later Shaw strongly recommended Murray for membership in the Dramatists' Club even though by its standards he was not a playwright of "established reputation": he is "one of those very rare men who combine the genuine artistic anarchic character and sympathies with academic distinction and political and social attachments to the big outside world."[32] Shaw also showed great respect for Murray's analyses of his own plays and prefaces, even urging him to help him with the last act of *Major Barbara* and incorporating several of his suggestions. In this context, his letter about "the Grey book" is a graphic record of tortuous psychological speculations about what had prompted Murray to "destroy" Grey inadvertently.[33] It has no resemblance to the finely honed assault that Bertrand Russell unleashed on the professor.

Russell had nothing like Shaw's admiration for Murray. He had once succumbed to the beauties of his *Hippolytus* to the extent of saying that it enhanced his emotional life forever, and the two families had a warm friendship at least until 1914.[34] However, in 1913 he had described Murray to his mistress, Lady Ottoline Morell, as "soft and squashy, and untruthful in his soul" (letter of 3 March); and when *The Foreign Policy of Sir Edward Grey* appeared he told her that he could "make a terrible piece of invective" on it, since he could not "discover any infamy in the whole wide world which the Foreign Office had not done its best to support—it is beyond belief. I think every word the Germans say against us is justified" (*Prophecy and Dissent*, 202). He also wrote an American acquaintance, Lucy Donnelly: "Gilbert Murray is a snivelling sentimental ass," and his "book on the war shows absolutely no attempt to tell the truth" (*Prophecy and Dissent*, 557). Such hysterical vilifications reflect what the philosopher George Santayana detected in Russell: "the fault common to the political radicals of being disproportionately annoyed at things only slightly wrong or weak in others." Clark notes that this was "a widely held professional view" (201). His behavior may also have been accompanied by a severe, understandable bout of depression similar to those his father had often experienced. Shortly after the war had begun, he confided to Ottoline: "I seem to feel the weight of Europe's passion, as if I were the focus of a burning glass—all the shouting, angry crowds. Emperors at balconies appealing to God, solemn words of duty & sacrifice to cover red murder & rage. It seems as if one must go mad or join the madmen" (Clark, 246).

Russell on Shaw the Individual

It is instructive to note that Russell viewed Shaw in much the same way that more conventional aristocrats than himself did. Like Murray before the war, he described himself as a Radical Liberal with progressive leanings. He first encountered Shaw, sixteen years his senior, at early meetings of the Fabian Society, but did not get caught up in their gradualistic program. In a 1904 letter to Goldsworthy Lowes Dickinson, he characterized the best-selling author of *Man and Superman* in his typical analytic and testy manner:

> I think Shaw, on the whole, is more bounder than genius, and
> though of course I admit him to be "forcible," I don't admit him to
> be "moral." I think envy plays a part in his philosophy in this sense,
> that if he allowed himself to admit the goodness of things which he
> lacks and others possess, he would feel such intolerable envy that he
> would find life unendurable. Also he hates self-control, and makes
> up theories with a view to proving that self-control is pernicious.
> I couldn't get on with *Man and Superman*: it disgusted me. I don't
> think he is a soul in Hell dancing on a red-hot iron. I think his Hell is
> merely diseased vanity and a morbid fear of being laughed at.[35]

In 1911 Russell shared an honorary dinner for Henri Bergson with Shaw and others. He was angered when Shaw joked that Bergson had adopted his own views on creative evolution, and offered a sample. "Bergson said it wasn't quite that way, but Shaw set him right, and said Bergson evidently didn't understand his own philosophy." Everybody but Bergson (and Russell) congratulated themselves and each other on their shared freethinking, but to Russell they seemed "like naughty children when they think (mistakenly) that the governess is away."[36] In a brief, largely laudatory, essay written shortly after Shaw's death, Russell quipped: "Shaw, like many witty men, considered wit an adequate substitute for wisdom." Summing up his career, he credits Shaw for publishing *Common Sense About the War*, and then digresses: "Although he did not write as a Pacifist, he infuriated most patriotic people by refusing to acquiesce in the hypocritical high moral tone of the Government and its followers. He was entirely praiseworthy in this sort of way, until he fell victim to adulation of the Soviet Government and suddenly lost the power of criticism and of seeing through humbug if it came from Moscow." In sum, "As an iconoclast he was admirable, but as an icon rather less so."[37]

Realities Underlying Murray's Defense of Grey

In his reply to Murray's book, Russell taunted the author that his defense of Grey had been written "under the tutelage of the Foreign Office."[38] Murray of course denied it, but it is far from a clear-cut case. In early 1915, Murray had volunteered with many other academics and writers to contribute treatises of this type for the Foreign Office's secret War Propaganda Bureau, a hive of one-sided publications, photographs, and films innocuously referred to by its location, Wellington House. Its declared aim was "to counteract German propaganda among the neutral countries," but this also involved keeping British civilians enthusiastic about the war so that they would be inclined to join the armed forces, and ultimately to win enough support from Americans to have them eager to join their allies.[39] Murray helped out repeatedly even while referring to it in private as the "Mendacity Bureau" (Wilson, 219). In April 1915, he had discussed the attacks on the Foreign Office by Russell and Brailsford with officials in the Bureau and apparently urged them to respond, whereupon they in turn encouraged him to undertake the task. Murray's biographer reports that Murray's own papers reveal that while they may not have "inspired" his work, their officials in charge of propaganda, delighted with Murray's involvement, helped him by providing key documents since he would surely promote the government's ends. Neither Russell nor Shaw mentions this or other things they may have learned about the benefits that Murray reaped from his modest volume: the Foreign Office had arranged to finance and distribute at least nine thousand copies to teachers, a thousand to the branch secretaries of various trade unions and other union members, and many to all the instructors on the Oxford University Extension Board. By doing that, chief executive officer Sir Claud Schuster wrote Murray on 8 July 1915, his work would reach many influential people "without giving the show away."[40]

Historians generally accept Murray's defense of Sir Edward Grey as commendable, given his perspective from outside the inner workings of the government. What seems like a sensible, though slyly critical, recent judgment is that of Peter Clarke in *Hope and Glory: Britain 1900–1990*: "It was to be a Liberal professor of Greek at Oxford, Gilbert Murray, who wrote the classic defence of Grey's foreign policy in 1915. It may have made an anti-war protestor like Bertrand Russell angry, and left the sceptical Shaw unmoved, but it tapped a rich vein of Liberal self-righteousness, which, stage by stage, helped to invest war-making and peace-making with high moral objectives" (72).[41]

Murray on Shaw the Individual

The norm of the long Murray-Shaw relationship was certainly harmonious cooperation. The two asked endless favors of the other, and fulfilled them in a way that may have elicited a few frowns but mostly feelings of gratitude and good fellowship. Nevertheless, in his honest deliberations over Shaw's plays, prefaces, articles, and controversial books, Murray returns again and again to Shavian modes and manners that troubled him. The chief ones were those that intelligent but tradition-bound critics such as Archer and A. B. Walkley were prone to repeat: in capsule form, write plays that are *plays*, and when you *are* serious *be* serious.

His first comments on a Shaw play, in a 1900 letter to Archer about *Caesar and Cleopatra*, are typical: "I think C & C rather a magnificent thing in its way, but of cours[e] desperately guyed and with its flashes of insight marred by somewhat pedantic details on the one hand and large historical misconceptions on the other" (Wilson, 93). In a review of *Three Plays for Puritans*, he lectures Shaw obliquely on the same play: "There is a delightful figure (which ought to be ruthlessly cut out!) in *Caesar and Cleopatra*, an ancient Briton, . . . who on certain occasions observes, 'Caesar, this is improper,' and 'O Caesar, great Caesar, if I could but persuade you to regard life seriously, as men do in my country!' I heartily echo his words."[42] He never seemed capable of understanding a distinctive pillar of Shaw's literary and philosophical strategy: "Every jest is an earnest in the womb of time."[43]

Murray's vacillating, digressive critique in a letter to Shaw of the virtues and vices of his greatest comedy, *Man and Superman*, extends to a psychological analysis of Shaw himself:

> It makes on me, in general, the same kind of impression as Caesar and Cleopatra, of an extraordinarily good thing gone somehow wrong. I wonder when you will write the real thing that is in you— the thing that will not go wrong!
>
> My main theory of what is wrong with you—for of course I keep several—is that you suffer from a lack of moral courage. This is borne out by the way you boast of your shamelessness; as a worldly man always boasts of his unworldliness. You express divers original or unpopular or odd opinions (always with a sense of your own courage, I think!) but do you ever stick to one and take the consequences? . . . Never. You lead your admirers on and on; and then, in a sudden panic, thinking that you may be laughed at, you laugh yourself and say it was a joke. Which it was not!
>
> This damnable vice is intimately connected with another, which you share with Ruskin, Carlyle and, I think, Tolstoy: a fundamental preference for rhetoric to truth . . . You sacrifice the accurate statement of fact to something that will make a proper effect on your audience—or, it may be, to something that gives you artistic pleasure. That leads to overstating things in order to get your effect. Then, at last, the ordinary Human Fool, whose instinct is after all a wonderfully fine organ, sees to his great comfort that you are saying more than you can possibly mean; therefore you do not mean what you say; therefore whatever he likes to believe is right, and the rest is "brilliant" paradox.[44]

That note of preferring rhetoric to truth will recur in several later contexts. One that amounted to an acid test arose from a collaboration of Shaw and Murray on a letter to the editor of the London Times in late April 1941, entitled "The Bombing of Cities: Military and Non-Military Objectives." Shaw had drafted it and sent copies to both Murray and H. G. Wells, hoping both would co-sign it. Wells turned down the invitation flatly, partly because he had already proposed the idea long ago, and Murray, realizing that it would never be published with some of Shaw's rhetorical flourishes included, replied that he would sign only if certain passages were cut. Shaw agreed readily, telling Wells, "Of course I will cut as he desires: in fact I should have cut these Shavian touches myself."[45] One half-facetious example, though logical enough to qualify as a jest in earnest, will suffice. The Swiftian touch in the last sentence of the following was excised:

> If raids could be maintained nightly and each raid killed 1000 persons, half of them women, it would take over a century to exterminate us and a century and a half to exterminate the Germans. Meanwhile, as both sides are depending for victory on famine by blockade, the reduction in the number of mouths to be fed would be a relief to us. *If the Germans, instead of dropping tens of thousands of bombs on us, had parachuted thousands of live babies, they would have embarrassed us and reduced our food supplies much more effectively.* (my italics)

The Times published the letter on 29 April after cutting more of these "Shavian touches."[46]

Two final demonstrations of Murray's belief that one of Shaw's major drawbacks was his addiction to style rather than substance occur in tributes written after his death. The first returns to their most noteworthy disagreement:

> [Shaw] never wrote as a judge, always as an accuser or an advocate. He attacked the things he considered wrong, showed them up as ridiculous, illogical, oppressive; he vividly over-stated his case against them. It was for others to pronounce judgment. I once came away with him from hearing a speech of Sir Edward Grey's. It had been just in Grey's manner; a moderate, unadorned, fair and absolutely convincing statement. Shaw thought it very poor indeed. It had none of the qualities that he valued; no wit, no eloquence, no happy phrase, no new point of view or illuminating paradox. [What he had heard] was, in fact, the just judge speaking, not the brilliant advocate.[47]

The second tribute is less focused, but amounts to much the same idea:

> With all his amazing brilliance he is one of the kindest and most generous of men. I would not say he was one of the wisest. His genius in practical affairs is analytic rather than constructive. He once wrote in defence of some article of his in the *Saturday Review*, the remarkable words: "Who am I that I should be just?" It was a true defence. It was not his business, or his gift, to weigh all the

elements of a dispute, to sum up carefully and recommend the safest course. Officials and administrators can do that. Shaw's business was to show something that was wrong and not known to be wrong; to throw a dazzling light upon it, even by exaggeration and unfairness, to compel people to see something which they were unable or unwilling to see.[48]

Mutually Gratifying Finale: Murray and Russell

Great Britain had been the only major nation to depend for its armed forces upon qualified volunteers. For a time a great many younger members of the aristocracy were willing to serve, partly because they assumed that they would join the officer ranks. Huge numbers of ordinary working men were driven to enlist by their habitual patriotism intensified by jingoist pressure or simply by the need for a decent-paying job. But as the war continued to decimate the empire's troops and discourage volunteering, the government felt compelled to take drastic measures. On 16 January 1916, the first Military Service Act was passed, imposing conscription on unmarried men between the ages of eighteen and forty-one. Men who refused to bear arms were treated as conscientious objectors, but at first this required a commitment to noncombatant duties, mostly supporting troops at the front. Anyone who refused these duties was sent to prison, often under humiliating conditions.

Bertrand Russell became the most prominent intellectual who fought stubbornly against this law, mainly by campaigning with a new organization called the "No Conscription Fellowship." Gilbert Murray also devoted much energy to the relief of men suffering under the established system, but he could not agree with the extreme position that Russell advocated. Coincidentally, and fortunately for their lapsed friendship, the case that turned out to command most of his attention was the persecution of Russell on a minor charge of seditious conduct; the government was clearly out to get him. In 1917, the United States had at last declared war against Germany, and early the next year Russell was prosecuted for "statements likely to prejudice His Majesty's relations" with its much-needed ally in a low-circulation periodical entitled *The Tribunal* (3 January 1918). He was first deprived of his lectureship at Cambridge University by a vote of his peers, then sentenced to six months' imprisonment. Russell knew he had risked such treatment, and he rationalized by welcoming the free time it would give him for study and writing. However, he soon learned that he was to be placed in a Second Division area, which had no amenities for intellectual pursuits. Upon hearing this Murray wrote to him, expressing contempt for the Lloyd George government and its unjustified treatment of him. Russell replied warmly and gratefully, and Murray employed his high-level connections to get his penitent friend's location changed to the First Division, where he could pursue his studies (Wilson, 237–42). The ultimate sequel to this event occurred on 11 September 1951, when Russell, in a message to the Philosophical Society (copied to Murray), summed up his reasons for admiring his "close friend for over half a century":

> He and I have not always agreed on public issues, but we have,
> I think, throughout whatever divergence on this or that question
> been conscious of a deep underlying agreement on fundamentals.
>   Gilbert Murray is a great and steadfast humanist, who adheres
> to liberal beliefs, now, alas, not so common as they were when he
> and I were young. As growing darkness descends upon the world,
> stars shine more brightly, and of these stars Gilbert Murray is among
> those of the first magnitude.
>   If the international world could listen to him, many of our
> troubles would quickly end, and the sombre fears that rob our age of
> hopefulness would be dissipated.[49]

Murray replied the day after: "I was greatly touched by that letter . . . about our fifty years of close friendship. It is, I think, quite true about the fundamental agreement; I always feel it—and am proud of it" (210). Taking this in from the skies far above, Shaw would have waved his wings at his two friends with the benevolence befitting his present status as omniscient judge.[50]

NOTES

1. Duncan Wilson, *Gilbert Murray, OM, 1866–1957* (Oxford: Clarendon Press, 1987), 79–81. Wilson died before he finished this authoritative biography; his wife, using his detailed notes, finished the last quarter of it. A convincing sample of Murray's intellectual charm: Bernard Berenson, the distinguished American art critic, told Russell: "The really great event of the last few weeks has been Gilbert Murray . . . Conversation spread before us like an infinite thing, or rather like something opening out higher and greater with every talk. I found him so gentle, so sweetly reasonable— almost the ideal companion." (Letter of 22 March 1903 printed in *The Autobiography of Bertrand Russell, 1872–1914* [Boston: Little, Brown, 1951], 291.) Quotations from Murray's letters have been kindly authorized by Alexander Murray, his grandson.

2. As a faithful teetotaler, Murray was irked by being likened to a character who is provoked to drink too much, and, as a person who had fashioned his own name out of George Gilbert Aimé Murray, by being forced to endure "Adolphus." (Letter of 11 August 1905 in *Granville Barker and His Correspondents: A Selection of Letters by Him and to Him*, ed. Eric Salmon [Detroit: Wayne State University Press, 1986], 223.)

3. Russell aired his attitude to Lucy Donnelly on 21 October 1914, saying that "Clearly the Germans are the worst—but Maeterlinck & Gilbert Murray & Robert Bridges are almost as bad." Oddly, shortly after the war started he had told her that Shaw "favours" the war. Both quotations are in Ronald W. Clark, *The Life of Bertrand Russell* (New York: Knopf, 1976), 247.

4. Martin Gilbert, *The First World War: A Complete History* (New York: Holt, 1994), 12.

5. Quoted in Gilbert, *The First World War*, 12.

6. Ann Paludan, "Remembering Our Grandfather I," in Christopher Stray, ed., *Gilbert Murray Reassessed: Hellenism, Theatre, and International Politics* (Oxford: Oxford University Press, 2007), 21 (hereafter cited as "Stray").

7. On this period of Grey's life, see Keith Robbins, *Sir Edward Grey: A Biography of Lord Grey of Fallodon* (London: Cassell, 1971), 14–17.

8. Quoted in Zara S. Steiner and Keith Neilson, *Britain and the Origins of the First World War*, 2nd ed. (Basingstoke: Palgrave Macmillan, 2003), 42.

9. *The Bodley Head Bernard Shaw: Collected Plays with Their Prefaces*, ed. Dan H. Laurence, 7 vols. (London: Reinhardt, 1970–74), II, 853–72. For a detailed, authoritative account of the event, see Kimberley Luke, "Order or Justice: The Denshawai Incident and British Imperialism," *History Compass* 5, no. 2 (2007): 278–87. She makes a convincing case for the ultimate impact of the incident: "As a result of Denshawai, British imperialism in Egypt was painted in stark relief and found wanting" (278).

10. Paludan, "Remembering Our Grandfather I."

11. He said this in a letter to his wife, Lady Mary, three days after the war had begun (Wilson, 219).

12. Letter of 12 September 1914 (letter 78) in Charles A. Carpenter, ed., *Bernard Shaw and Gilbert Murray: Selected Correspondence* (forthcoming).

13. *London Daily News and Leader*, 11 August. Quoted and described in Stanley Weintraub, *Journey to Heartbreak: The Crucible Years of Bernard Shaw, 1914–1918* (New York: Weybright and Talley, 1971), 29.

14. Russell, *Prophecy and Dissent 1914–16*, ed. Richard A. Rempel et al. (London: Unwin Hyman, 1988; *Collected Papers* 13), 7–8. On the days just before Grey's speech, Russell had expressed his opposition to the threatened war by organizing a petition that sixty Cambridge University dons signed. It expressed "their conviction of the supreme importance of preserving England's neutrality . . . considering that at the present juncture no vital interest of this country is endangered such as would justify our participation in a war." However, Grey's speech convinced many of these signatories to change their minds (481–82).

15. Quotations and paraphrases from *Common Sense About the War* refer to pages 16–84 in J. L. Wisenthal and Daniel O'Leary, eds., *What Shaw Really Wrote about the War* (Gainesville: University Press of Florida, 2006), hereafter cited as "Wisenthal."

16. *Common Sense About the War*, 61–62. As part of deploring the alliance with Russia, Shaw grants "Gilbert Murray's plea that the recent rate of democratic advance has been greater in Russia than anywhere else in Europe," then follows it by mocking the actual quantity of that rate.

17. "The Great War and the Aftermath: A Dialogue between Bernard Shaw and Archibald Henderson," *Fortnightly Review* 697 (1 January 1925); repr. in *Table-Talk of G.B.S.: Conversations on Things in General Between George Bernard Shaw and His Biographer*, ed. Archibald Henderson [London: Harper, 1925], 140–41).

18. Preface for an unpublished French edition of his "Peace Conference Hints," printed in Wisenthal, ed., 242.

19. *Prophecy and Dissent*, 39–47.

20. London: Union of Democratic Control, 1914 (19 pages). During Murray's first teaching position at Glasgow University, Brailsford had been an admiring student and they had remained friends. When the young man was about to leave to fight in the Greco-Turkish war, Murray apparently gave him a pistol— rather than a textbook, Cusins says in *Major Barbara*. F. M. Leventhal in *The Last Dissenter: H. N. Brailsford and His World* (Oxford: Clarendon Press, 1985), from which his pamphlet is quoted (130), notes that Murray's recollection of this may have been confused (32f.).

21. Quoted in William Bruneau, "Gilbert Murray, Bertrand Russell, and the Theory and Practice of Politics," in Stray, 209.

22. 2 vols. (New York: Stokes, 1925).

23. The statement actually occurs in a musical review of 30 March 1889 (reprinted in Shaw's *London Music in 1888–89 as Heard by Corno di Bassetto* [New York: Dodd, Mead, 1937], 91).

24. Shaw, *Collected Letters*, 4 vols., ed. Dan H. Laurence (London: Reinhardt, 1965–88), III, 300–301 (hereafter *CL*).

25. "Professor Gilbert Murray's Defence of Sir Edward Grey," *The New Statesman* 5 (17 July 1915): 349–51.

26. *The Parliamentary Debates (Official Report)*, 5th series, vol. LXV: Fourth Session of the Thirtieth Parliament of the United Kingdom of Great Britain & Ireland, House of Commons, 8th vol. of Session 1914, comprising period from Monday, 20th July, to Monday, 10th August, 1914 (London: His Majesty's Stationery Office, 1914).

27. However, by 4 June 1917 the two were at least communicating indirectly: Murray had told Charlotte Shaw that he would like to attend a scheduled reading of Shaw's latest play, *Heartbreak House*, and she replied by inviting him (unpublished letter quoted by permission of the Sidney P. Albert estate). Shaw also reached Murray indirectly: after the long hiatus, he wrote to Lady Murray on 8 February 1918, and his words were surely meant as much for her husband as for her: "The whole world is realizing that it went raving mad four years ago; but it locked the asylum doors in its frenzy and threw the keys out of the window; and now it must go on raving when it is in its right mind again" (*CL* III, 528).

28. Peter Whitebrook, *William Archer: A Biography* (London: Methuen, 1993), 313.

29. Recorded in Sybil Thorndike, "The Theatre and Gilbert Murray," in Murray, *An Unfinished Autobiography, with Contributions by His Friends* (London: George Allen and Unwin, 1960), 163. Bernard F. Dukore details the fortunes of the play in "Maurice Brown and the Chicago Little Theatre," *Theatre Survey* 3 (1962): 59–78: in fifteen weeks it was performed in thirty-one cities to about thirty-three thousand people. See also Marie Louise Degen, *The History of the Woman's Peace Party* (Baltimore: Johns Hopkins University Press, 1939).

30. Bernadotte E. Schmitt and Harold C. Vendler, *The World in the Crucible, 1914–1919* (New York: Harper and Row, 1984), 23.

31. Letter of 29 October 1908 to Margot Asquith, wife of Prime Minister Sir Herbert Asquith, in *Theatrics: Selected Correspondence of Bernard Shaw*, ed. Dan H. Laurence (Toronto: University of Toronto Press, 1995), 94. He declined the knighthood in early 1912 (Wilson, 193).

32. Shaw, *CL*, II, 882, 885.

33. None of its prophecies materialized; on the contrary, Grey profited in many respects from Murray's encomium.

34. *The Autobiography of Bertrand Russell, 1872–1914* (Boston: Little, Brown, 1951), 135–36. On 9 February 1901, he had heard Murray read excerpts from his translation of *Hippolytus*, and proclaimed it "a wonderful experience" (234).

35. Letter of 20 July 1904, *The Autobiography of Bertrand Russell*, 288–89.

36. Letter of 28 October 1911 to Lucy Donnelly, *Selected Letters*, 2 vols. (London: Routledge, 2001–2), 1:400. Bergson's *L'Evolution créatrice* (1907) postdated *Man and Superman* by four years.

37. *Portraits from Memory, and Other Essays* (New York: Simon and Schuster, 1956), 75–80.

38. When he wrote about this to Russell, he received a surprisingly gracious—though perhaps disingenuous—reply on 28 December, in which he says, "I am very sorry I gave a wrong impression about your connection with the F.O. I certainly thought you had more to do with them . . . I thought it necessary to answer you, just as you thought it necessary to write your pamphlet, but I did not mean that there should be anything offensive in my answer; if there was, I am sorry. I feel that our friendship still lives in the eternal world, whatever may happen to it here and now" (*Autobiography*, II, 54).

39. See M. L. Sanders and Philip M. L. Taylor, *British Propaganda During the First World War, 1914–18* (London: Macmillan, 1982), especially 38–43, and "Recruiting the Intelligentsia: Charles Masterman," in Gary S. Messenger, *British Propaganda and the State in the First World War* (Manchester: Manchester University Press, 1992), 24–52.

40. Editor's note in Russell, *Prophecy and Dissent*, 204–5. Citing a 1978 study by D. G. Wright, "The Great War, Government Propaganda and English 'Men of Letters'" (*Literature and History* 7 [Spring 1978]: 81), Messenger states flatly that Masterman "persuaded" Murray to write his defense of Grey, which was "dutifully" published by Oxford's Clarendon Press and "widely distributed by Wellington House in Britain and abroad" (63–64). On its own, Oxford University Press had previously encouraged faculty members to write what became 87 *Oxford Pamphlets*, three of them by Murray; how closely this series became tied in with the bureau

is unclear but may be inferred (James Duane Squires, *British Propaganda at Home and in the United States* (Cambridge: Harvard University Press, 1935, 17). Moreover, since Murray was known as a popular lecturer, the agency took advantage of this by arranging and financing some of his appearances. He often complied even though he had to agree not to reveal who had sponsored him (*Prophecy and Dissent*, 205). On his later regrets for having willingly contributed to the actual "mendacity" of government propaganda, see Peter Edgerly Firchow's cogent account in *The Death of the German Cousin: Variations on a Literary Stereotype, 1890–1920* (Lewisburg, Pa.: Bucknell University Press, 1986), 114–26: "Wellington House and the Strange Death of a Liberal Professor." Firchow quotes many self-incriminating remarks in Murray's publications late in the war, when the treatment of conscientious objectors had especially drawn his ire, and soon afterward, when he deplored the vengeful motives underlying the disastrous Versailles Treaty.

41. London: Allen Lane; the Penguin Press, 1996.

42. "Mr. Bernard Shaw's New Plays," *Speaker*, 9 February 1901.

43. The "mad" priest, Peter Keegan, says this in *John Bull's Other Island* (*The Bodley Head Bernard Shaw*, II, 1021). Shaw elaborates upon it in the revised *Quintessence of Ibsenism* (*Major Critical Essays* [London: Constable, 1932; first published in 1913], 126ff.). I describe the theory, with examples from several of Shaw's plays, in "The Strategy and the Bacteriology: Scrutinizing the Microbe in Shaw's *Too True to Be Good*," SHAW: *The Annual of Bernard Shaw Studies*, 27 (2007): 137–46.

44. Letter of 30 September 1903 (letter 19) in Carpenter, ed., *Bernard Shaw and Gilbert Murray: Selected Correspondence*.

45. *Bernard Shaw and H.G. Wells: Selected Correspondence of Bernard Shaw*, ed. J. Percy Smith (Toronto: University of Toronto Press, 1995), 196.

46. The draft is printed in *Bernard Shaw and H.G. Wells*, 196. *The Times* version is in *The Letters of Bernard Shaw to The Times*, ed. Ronald Ford (Dublin: Irish Academic Press, 2007), 230–31.

47. "A Few Memories," *Drama*, n.s. 20 (Spring 1951): 9.

48. "A Foreword," pp. 13–15 in Stephen Winsten, ed., *G.B.S. 90: Aspects of Bernard Shaw's Life and Work* (London: Hutchinson, 1946), 14.

49. Russell, "A Fifty-Six Year Friendship," in Murray, *An Unfinished Autobiography*, 211.

50. Bernard F. Dukore read an early draft of this article and suggested vital improvements. I am indebted to him for his help.

The Fabian Mystique

GBS and ASB

LAGRETTA TALLENT LENKER

What is the difference between a City Fabian and a Country Fabian? Based on A. S. Byatt's remarkable novel The Children's Book, *depicting the late Victorian and Edwardian eras, one of the principal differences is that the minor Fabians found in the country seem to be far more interesting as characters than are the City Fabians, the major celebrities such as Shaw, the Webbs, Wells, etc, who make cameo appearances in this novel and are often cited for their inspiration.*

—R. F. Dietrich[1]

I've always had trouble with Shaw.

—A. S. Byatt[2]

I see no reason to croak about the critics.

—G. B. Shaw[3]

A. S. Byatt and Bernard Shaw may seem an unlikely pair, not only because they lived in different eras and usually wrote in different genres, but especially because of Byatt's public statements about her problems with her predecessor. Byatt tells Ramona Koval in a 2009 interview that her mother had a

huge collection of the works of George Bernard Shaw, including socialist advice for young women, and I reacted against that in some sort of way. . . . It's a deeply unreadable book to be truthful. I've got it out of piety towards my mother. . . . I can't get on with it. It's like Shaw's novels. I can't read those either. I've been reading his little book on Ibsen which is sort of brilliant and that about Ibsen's feminism and somehow I can manage that."[4]

This difficulty with Shaw's essays and novels does not stop Byatt from incorporating a heavy dose of GBS, intentionally or unintentionally, throughout her novel, *The Children's Book* (TCB 2009).[5] In creating the Fabian milieu that permeated the late Victorian era, Byatt evokes the historical Shaw by name nine times. Even Shaw's Jaeger suit makes an appearance (TCB 45). Also, part of Shaw's biography as the neglected child of a blended, bohemian family resonates with the fictional account of the Wellwoods,[6] the primary family around whom the novel revolves. The allusions to Shaw, his life and work, prove apt, as Fabianism pervades both Byatt's novel and Shaw's oeuvre; consequently, the strong influence of Fabianism on both writers—and Byatt's engagement of Shaw to depict the zeitgeist of the era—forms the basis for this study.

Critics place A. S. Byatt's imposing compendium, *The Children's Book*, in the genre of Neo-Victorianism, which began to flourish in the 1990s and includes Byatt's most famous work, *Possession* (1994). Joseph Bristow suggests that "neo-Victorian narratives present alternative visions of a nineteenth-century world that is much queerer, more bohemian, and altogether more politically enlightened than established types of historical fiction insist we should behold" and evinces a fascination with a wealth of information that suggests its fictional universe is historically accurate down to the smallest detail.[7] Byatt herself speaks more broadly about the increased popularity of historical fiction, recounting the story of a journalist who interviewed "various novelists about ten years ago about why they were writing historical novels, expecting some answer about paradigms of contemporary reality, and got the same answer from all of them. They wanted to write in a more elaborate, complex way, in longer sentences, and with more figurative language," in short, in the style of the earlier periods that they were depicting.[8] Byatt shares this rhetorical desire and sees it as a revolt of sorts against the prevalent "exactness" of contemporary writing. This analysis of a "revolt" that signals a change in prevailing literary trends supports previous discussions of our fascination with *fin de siècle* culture and the radical changes in society that often occur around the turn of centuries.[9] Bristow also recognizes Byatt's novel as part of our twenty-first-century fascination with World War I and its upcoming

centenary as manifested in novels, films, and television productions[10]—
the immense popularity of the current Masterpiece series *Downton Abbey*
is just one example of this fascination. *The Children's Book* also depicts a
continued interest in the many societal, cultural, and philosophical groups
spawned during this time of experimentation and change, including the
Society of Psychical Research, the Social Democratic Federation, the
Fellowship of New Life, the Positivists, the Theosophists, and the Fabian
Society, to name a few.[11] The Fabian Society proved especially interesting
to Byatt, in large measure because of the public/private dichotomy associated with the group. In personal terms, the Fabian Society was influenced
by a kind of "Bohemianism" toward sexual morality, with consequences
for the women (and their children) involved. However, in public terms, the
Fabians created a legacy of lasting influence as founders of the London
School of Economics and what Bristow terms their "god child," the modern
British Labour Party.[12]

Although summarizing such a complex work proves difficult, through
its plots and subplots *The Children's Book* tells several stories of different
British families and their German friends living during the Edwardian *fin de
siècle*, roughly 1895 to 1915. The many characters of the novel participate in
a story of near-epic proportions, as Byatt's Victorian-sized novel teems with
their "artistic temperaments, forbidden passions, dark secrets, bohemian
parents, and the idylls and perils of childhood—all set against a turbulent
backdrop of political and social change."[13] Of special interest to this study
are the lives of prominent female characters, many of whom inhabit the
Wellwood family home, Todefright, and who "bear witness to the gathering
momentum around female education and employment of the period. . . .
The span of female characters range from Olive Wellwood and her daughter
Dorothy, representing an influential Fabian family surrounded by various
intellectuals and artists, to women struggling with poverty and precarious
social position. Griselda Wellwood stems from a successful banker's family whereas Elsie Warren and her mother illustrate the corollaries of the
Industrial Revolution."[14] These female characters explore their own freedom, intelligence, and independent capabilities, but all suffer at the hands
of various male characters—fathers, friends, and especially notorious philanderers, all gathered under the banner of social change, most notably in
the form of Fabianism.

The Fabian Society provides the principal nexus between Bernard Shaw
and A. S. Byatt—one lived during the era under discussion in the novel
and the other depicts it from a present-day perspective. Shaw, a founding
member of the Fabian Society in 1884, served on its Executive Board until

1911 but remained an interested and informed member all of his long life. Byatt, who spends 675 pages depicting Fabian characters and their social, cultural, and personal milieu, confirms the lasting interest in this group of groundbreakers, forward thinkers, feminists, philanderers, statesmen, bohemians, and creative artists. Diana Maltz posits that Byatt did not write a *roman a clef* of the Fabian Society; rather, she studies "the ways that socialist identity played out through home and family."[15] However, through her narrative style, sometimes labeled "fictism,"[16] Byatt not only creates the socialist atmosphere surrounding a fictional family and their forward-thinking set, but also, by incorporating actual historical dates and events in a minute detail that often includes the weather on a given date, she situates her story amid the "political storm cloud that slowly steals upon this unsuspecting family."[17]

Byatt and Shaw also share evolving feminist ideals, each conceived under the historical, social, and cultural influences of their respective times. Although Shaw should not be judged according to twenty-first-century standards, he consistently recognizes in his writings the plight of marginalized women and often transforms their "problems" into "opportunities" for a discussion of the "woman question," one of the predominant issues of his day. Shaw's extraordinary female characters, especially his daughters—Ellie Dunn and Major Barbara, to mention only two—often exemplify his message of social and gender equality and reinforce his status as a radical author.[18] By her own admission, Byatt's feminism is evolving. In a 1996 interview in which she describes herself as a political not a literary feminist, Byatt proclaimed, "It's because I'm a feminist that I can't stand women limiting other women's imaginations [referring to academic gender studies]."[19] Jane Campbell calls Byatt's feminism the impetus behind her growing canon, filled with "powerfully imagined female characters."[20] Her descriptions of women at various stages of their lives and the societal and gender-related challenges faced by each (see discussion below) reinforce this feminism. Thus both the late Victorian and the contemporary writer share a desire for social justice and pen their feminist values by emphasizing the real obstacles faced by their dominant women characters and the manner in which they cope with these challenges.

Although the writings of Byatt and Shaw coalesce on several points—including the blending of myth, fairy tales, fantasy, and cultural archetypes into their literary creations—my interest focuses on how Fabian socialism, as practiced during the time span of the novel, becomes the meeting point for these very different writers, living in vastly different times. The well-chronicled history of the Fabian Society begins with the aptly titled "The

History of the Fabian Society by Edward R. Pease Secretary for Twenty-five Years."[21] Pease recounts the origins of the Society and the influence on it of Thomas Davidson, whose "socialism was ethical and individual rather than economic and political" and whose teachings served as the "occasion rather than the cause of the Fabian Society."[22] Pease continues, "The Fabian Society was founded for the purpose of 'reconstructing society,' based on the competitive system 'in such a manner as to secure the general welfare and happiness.'"[23] Members of the Fabian Old Gang, also known as the "Essayists" for their writing of the Fabian essays and tracts, guided the fledgling group's early efforts. Members so designated include Hubert Bland, Sidney Webb, Bernard Shaw, Graham Wallas, and Sydney Olivier, who recorded the group's collective positions and galvanized the young organization. H. G. Wells, speaking in 1906, characterizes the Society's original value and continuing potential as a "common meeting ground, a field for frank discussion, and wherever practicable a means of reconciliation and concerted action for Socialists of every party and type, however diverse their ideas of the political methods necessary for the attainment of their common social and economic ideals'"[24] Ian Britain summarizes the historical perspective from 1984:

> Dogmatic certainty, then, was absent even in the attitudes of the most conservative members of the Old Gang, and this serves to confirm doubts about the existence of any such phenomenon as orthodox Fabianism. The Fabians' approaches to socialism, if they can be summed up at all, may be defined by their very lack of doctrinal rigidity and uniform principles. Sidney Webb's description of "the work of the Fabian Society" as consisting in "the work of individual Fabians" may be applied to the thought of the Society as well.[25]

Yet this group of individualists, primarily through the efforts of Shaw, produced extraordinary statements of purpose, including the Fabian Basis, which all members were required to sign, as well as a seventeen-point Manifesto and numerous tracts and essays that recorded their collective positions on such varied topics as land rights and happy homes for children.[26] These concerns, also taking the form of stimulating lectures and lively debates, reflected the attempts of this diverse band of intellectuals to change their world, or at least influence it for the better, providing great material for artists and other creative individuals wishing to participate in the "permeation" (never "revolution") of the group's positions into the society at large through their personal activities as well as their art.

According to Britain, the Fabian artistic interests included musical compositions, theatrical productions, translations of various literary works into English, concerts, and recitals, which contributed to the "club-like atmosphere" of the society. "The Fabian Society even encouraged the setting-up of various sub-groups . . . that catered specifically . . . for the artistic interests of members. The Fabian Arts Group was but one of these; there were others, such as the Stage Society and the Fabian Summer School . . . . They helped make it fun to be a Fabian."[27] Later, the creative, fun-loving founding Fabians passed this spirit to the younger generation, through the Fabian Nursery and Summer School, whose members continued the group's clublike socialist pursuits.

These artistic elements of Fabianism became a natural haven for the more "bohemian" intellectuals searching for like-minded, or at least open-minded, fellowship. Although certainly not a formal part of Fabian philosophy, the exploits of prominent members such as H. G. Wells, the young Shaw, Edward Aveling (not technically a Fabian but a prominent socialist featured in Fabian histories), and Hubert Bland are the stuff of legend—the famous Fabian "fun" with often disastrous consequences on those around them. Hubert Bland, one of the Fabian Old Gang, serving on the Executive Committee for twenty-five years, was serious about his socialism but apparently more relaxed in other settings.[28] Bland married Edith Nesbit when he was unemployed but brought a mistress and illegitimate child to the marriage and into Nesbit's household, although Edith and "Maggie" supposedly knew nothing of each other until three years into the marriage. According to Anne Fremantle, Bland, a "scamp clothed in a frock coat, striped trousers, and a monocle," repeated this fertile infidelity, this time with one of Edith's friends, who had moved into the Bland home. Edith soon recognized the situation as one of her husband's making. "When Edith proposed to turn the woman and baby out of the house, her husband said he would go with them, and Edith weakly kept the lot. Literally, too, for it was by her successful writing that she supported her husband, their own three children, the illegits, and the various lady friends."[29] This scenario of the woman as breadwinner for her own family and the offspring of her husband's affairs plays a featured role in *The Children's Book*.

When the stalwart Fabians Beatrice and Sidney Webb invited the already-prominent H. G. Wells to join the Society, it was "full of young people mostly engaged to each other. The married Wells proceeded to have affairs with young daughters of two notable Fabians, Mrs. Pember Reeves and Hubert Bland (in a curious twist of history repeating itself). Wells seduced the child of one of Bland's "strays, one of those children brought up as her own by Mrs. Bland."[30] And so the Fabian bohemianism came full circle, with Wells earning the lasting reputation of doing "more than any of the other Fabian heretics to spread and perpetuate the philistine image of orthodox Fabianism, as represented by the views of the Webbs.[31] A blend of Bland and Wells appears in Byatt's book as Herbert Methley, the philandering Free Lifer whose actions refute the rights-for-women message he preaches. Thus, the bohemian element associated with the Fabian Society often went beyond the celebrated open lifestyle to inflict real harm and pain on the families of those involved, especially the wives and children of the notorious libertines.

Yet the Society's reputation rests on more than the apparent revolt of a philandering few against the strict mores of the moribund Victorian society. Britain assesses the intangible contributions of the Fabian Society as recognizing the challenges of reconciling a "free and open society with ever-increasing technical competence and centralization. . . . The Fabians from early on were not unaware of this problem: the very origins of the Society may be seen as a response to it, and an engagement with various aspects of it can be traced in the subsequent pronouncements of the Society's more articulate and active members. . . . They never produced an actual solution. . . . but they did suggest many positive and illuminating lines of approach."[32]

On a more concrete level, the bequest of Fabian Henry Hutchinson enabled the founding of the London School of Economics under the direction of the Fabian Executive, especially Sidney and Beatrice Webb, who insisted that the school be dedicated to teaching and research on economic and social issues and not to serve as a propaganda arm for socialism.[33] Similarly, although never expressly involved in politics as an organization, the group and its individual members produced a "god-child," as Bristow describes the modern British Labour Party. However, despite these stellar achievements, the Fabian Society remains best known for its remarkble individual members, including the most famous of all, Bernard Shaw.

In addition to playing the part of "favorite son" in many early Fabian households,[34] Shaw performed a vital role in the Society between 1884 and 1911, when he resigned from the executive committee. In 1898, Shaw married the Fabian Charlotte Payne Townsend, whose fortune funded many of the Fabian projects. Shaw wrote and spoke for the society during these years: "[H]is major achievement was in establishing that the Fabian Society would be the only Socialist society with any intellectual authority (This is why he made sure that [Annie] Besant, Webb, Wallas, and Olivier joined it). He wrote continuously about all sorts of subjects of political relevance. He edited the famous *Fabian Essays in Socialism* in 1889, but wrote nothing else that attempted to make systematic sense of politics until he belatedly wrote *The Intelligent Woman's Guide to Socialism* in 1928 and *Everybody's Political What's What* in 1944."[35]

In his writings, Shaw amended the motto of the Social Democratic Federation, "Educate, Agitate, Organize," to drop the "agitate" and substitute "Permeate,"[36] which better reflected the Fabian Society's "slow but sure" attitude toward political and social change. As Shaw's artistic success increased, his involvement in the Fabian Society waned, but he remained a dedicated Fabian for the rest of his life. Especially during this later period, Shaw's Fabianism became more an attitude of mind than a political cause.[37]

Yet Fabianism fueled Shaw's artistic imagination from his early novels to his great dramas and forms the basis for many of his works. Numerous Shaw plays take aim at the unfortunate structure of society and were written to offer corrections or at least point out that failing.[38] Richard Dietrich elaborates,

> His first three plays—*Widowers' Houses* (1892), *The Philanderer* (1893), and *Mrs. Warren's Profession* (1893)—were designated as "unpleasant" when published in 1898 because they ostensibly dealt with social crimes that were considered by many to be unmentionable in polite society. The surface subjects of Shaw's three plays—slum landlordism, the degradations marriage laws force upon ""people, and prostitution—though fit for the blue books of governmental investigative committees, had not been thought proper for the stage.[39]

Dietrich recounts Shaw's adverse reactions to the popular plays of Pinero, Jones, and Wilde, and his attempts to write in the style of the "new drama," based on the writings of Henrik Ibsen: "Shaw's plays were tougher-minded right from the beginning. . . . Shaw's plays, though ending happily enough from the Shavian point of view, ended unpleasantly from the conventional point of view."[40] More specifically, Tracy C. Davis identifies land ownership as the issue that turned Shaw into a socialist writer. This perennial English problem evolved into a discussion about the existing theory of rent that produced tenement slums that enrich absentee landlords.[41] *Fabian Tract 3*, written by GBS, addresses this problem from a socialist and political perspective, while *Widowers' Houses* treats it from a dramatic vantage point. Although few actual socialists appear in Shaw's plays, "Fabian permeation emerges most conspicuously in two of Shaw's first three plays, *Widowers' Houses* and *Mrs Warren's Profession*, and two of his early discussion dramas, *John Bull's Other Island* and *Major Barbara*. These plays combine an ingredient found in most of his plays, education on economic issues, with subtly covert attacks on capitalist institutions, attitudes and assumptions."[42] As with all of his plays, in *Mrs Warren's Profession* the villain is not the individual, in this case a prostitute, but the society that forces a person into a conventionally unacceptable role in order to survive.

While Shaw contends that all of his plays were written with a purpose ("I am not an art for art's sake man"),[43] critics often single out several plays in addition to those mentioned above as having a particularly Fabian message. Almost thirty years after joining the Fabian Society, Shaw wrote *Misalliance*, which features a family consumed with generational struggles, "around the sixth of this Tract 2 proposals: 'that the state should compete with private individuals—especially with parents—in providing happy homes for children, so that every child may have a refuge from the tyranny of neglect of its natural custodians.'"[44] Also, *Fanny's First Play*, written as a "pot-boiler" in 1911,[45] features Fanny O'Dowda, a child of privilege, who was sent to Cambridge and reunites with her absentee old-fashioned father, having acquired modern tastes in drama as part of her education. Ellen Gainor surmises, "Fanny has adopted Fabianism as her guiding force at Cambridge, thereby substituting the doctrine shaped by Shaw (and the Webbs) for any familial precepts introduced in her sequestered childhood."[46] After viewing Fanny's first play, Count O'Dowda and the family friend, theater critic Mr. Trotter (based on the eminent London critic A. B. Walkley [IV: 442]) "deprecates Fanny's efforts, saying 'Any clever modern girl could turn out that kind of yarn', which addresses such issues as cross-class marriage and force-feeding of suffragettes, while his fellow critics speculate on whether Shaw might be the author. And after the truth of Fanny's authorship comes out, she demurs at their comparisons: 'Oh, of course it would be a little like Bernard Shaw. The Fabian touch, you know.'"[47]

Next, in 1912, Shaw produced his most popular and enduring play, *Pygmalion*, which appears an unlikely candidate for this study of Shaw's Fabian plays.[48] As Arthur Ganz explains however,

> *Pygmalion* does not . . . seem like a socialist, much less a Fabian play, but it is. Higgins . . . has noticed . . . "a woman that looks like a worn out drudge of 50 a year after she's married." Later Higgins explains . . . that changing Eliza into a different being by creating a new speech for her is "filling up the deepest gulf that separates class from class and soul from soul." . . . It is reasonable to suppose that the elimination of such nefarious social distinctions and the

gradual—that is Fabian—evolution of a classless society in which speech patterns are not a barrier is the ultimate aim of Higgins' "Universal Alphabet" [and Shaw's similar spelling reform].[49]

Thus, Shaw subtly weaves his firm belief in the need for a classless society through "permeation" even in his most enduring work, and the message still resonates, even with those who can hear Shaw's words amidst the song and dance of the stage and film adaptation of that work, *My Fair Lady*.

The next play considered, *Heartbreak House* (1917),[50] does not offer the Fabian hope for world improvement; in fact, just the opposite. Disillusioned by World War I and convinced that the younger generation—especially young Fabians—had taken his maxim "the golden rule is that there is no golden rule" too far with their self-absorption and disregard for building a better society, Shaw created a play that marked a turning point in his writing. Eric Bentley explains: "*Heartbreak House* might be called The Nightmare of a Fabian. . . . You *might* learn from it his teachings on love, religion, education, politics. But you are unlikely to do so . . . because the play is not an argument in their favor. It is a demonstration that they are all being disregarded or defeated. It is a picture of failure."[51] Bentley continues that the men of influence—Mangan, Utterword, and even Hushabye—stand for personal power and enrichment, even favoring a world war at the expense of society. Only the octogenarian Captain Shotover seeks societal improvement by uniting wisdom and power. Bentley states further: "The Fabians had tried by 'permeation' to make the men of power wiser. But these authority figures preferred a world war to the world's wisdom. Shotover has given up on them as hopeless. The young ingénue Ellie Dunn still looks for "life with a blessing," but her soul mate is now "old and crazy."[52] However, this air of pessimism is soon lifted for Shaw with the writing of the universally praised and accepted *Saint Joan*, but in the time frame under consideration in this study (1895–1919), *Heartbreak House* sounds a somber note about the relevance of the Fabian Society that Byatt instills in *The Children's Book*.

While Shaw boldly sought to change the world with his art, Byatt reveals a more subtle and more reflexive motivation. She reports being intrigued with the intersection of two things that appear unconnected: "In this case [*The Children's Book*] I observed that this was the period of both all the socialist initiatives in Europe and a generation that found children's fantasy the most exciting literary form."[53] She becomes more specific in another interview: "I was interested when I started reading about the life of E. Nesbit that she and her very strange husband were founding members of the Fabian Society." Byatt then recounts the story of Hubert Bland

and Edith Nesbit Bland and their blended family, discussed above.[54] And so the prominent Fabians Edith and Hubert become the models for Olive and Humphrey Wellwood, whose family and circle pervade *The Children's Book*. Many famous Fabians make cameo appearances in the novel: H. G. Wells, Beatrice and Sidney Webb, and Sydney Olivier, among others, are discussed by Byatt's characters or appear in the historical accounts that occur throughout the novel. And yet Shaw and his work influence Byatt's tome in ways that few other historical personages do.

On an artistic level, Byatt alludes, wittingly or not, to themes and story lines from several of Shaw's major works to present the lives of several prominent characters in *The Children's Book*. Byatt creates twenty-five prominent characters in the novel. Explaining the difficulties inherent in such a large cast, she notes: "I don't think I've ever had so many characters, and the technical thing you have to learn as a novelist is to give them very strong characteristics."[55] The characteristics and identities that Byatt creates often relate to the Fabian socialism of Shaw and The Old Gang, which serves as one of the predominant anchors for the diverse group that inhabits the novel. Byatt, fascinated by the way socialist identity played out through the home and subculture, also reveals "how those living in bohemian communities can be rankled by the standards of their own people."[56] This interest dovetails nicely with Shaw's perennial theme of family and how this basic societal unit represents the condition of society at large.[57] More specifically, from a family perspective, Byatt portrays "the blocking of women's energies by domesticity and social expectations" again and again in her fiction,[58] while Shaw's heroines fight the same battles, earning him the badge of an early feminist.

Shaw's notorious *Mrs Warren's Profession* appears in *The Children's Book* via a version of the white lead factory from which the Shavian sisters Kitty and Liz escape. Two of Byatt's characters not only carry the family name of "Warren" but also must abandon home and family to escape the industrial death trap of lead poisoning that claims their mother (TCB, 175). Byatt's Phillip and Elsie Warren, brother and sister from the London slums of Burslem, flee the fate of poison and neglectful extended family by different routes, but both eventually find their way to the home of the renowned potter, Benedict Fludd and his family, neighbors of the Fabian Wellwoods. Although both are orphaned and penniless, Phillip, an aspiring artist himself, finds work as an apprentice to Fludd. Nevertheless, the young man often earns no pay for the backbreaking labor in the pottery; however, he has opportunities through Fludd and his contacts that his sister does not share. She too dreams of creating art, but Elsie becomes in effect the housemaid to the hapless Fludds, a bohemian family *par excellence*. While Elsie does not enter into prostitution like her Shavian counterpart, Kitty Warren, she does fall victim to the lecherous Herbert Methley (the Bland-Wells character) and becomes pregnant, thus doomed by both "the domestic and societal expectations" that haunt both Byatt's and Shaw's creative works. A group of community women, including the common-law wife of Methley, rescue Elsie from having "to go away," enable her to raise her own child, and ultimately help her join the blended family of one of the rescuing women. Although they have vastly different circumstances, Elsie Warren's story stirs a memory in the Fabian Olive Wellwood of her own flight from indigence in the north, as Olive recalls a past that offers another echo of *Mrs Warren's Profession*, that of a woman forced into drastic measures to escape a dire fate as an unattached woman in a poverty-stricken community.

The struggles of Elsie Warren also call to mind the frame of another Shaw play, *Pygmalion*. In this famous play, based on the Pygmalion and Galatea myth, a Svengali figure transforms the guttersnipe Eliza Doolittle into a "lady" worthy of high society by teaching her proper speech and diction. In the process, Eliza loses the cockney accent that marks her as a lower-class girl of the streets who supports herself by selling flowers, thereby removing this stigma of her true origins and class distinction. Both Byatt and Shaw "de-romanticize" the myth of Pygmalion and the fairy tale of Cinderella by emphasizing the class and gender struggles involved in the saga of both young characters.[59] Elsie does not have the good fortune of falling into the hands of a Henry Higgins, the obtuse but ultimately well-meaning professor of languages who effects Eliza's transformation. Instead she falls prey to the lecherous Herbert Methley, who tells her (and many other girls and women) that sexual liberation is their right (*TCB*, 327–28). After helping her learn to dress properly and buying her a much-desired red belt, Methley seduces Elsie at the conclusion of a lecture series entitled "The Woman of the Future" (327). Elsie, of course, becomes pregnant and, convinced of society's scorn, labels herself a "fallen woman" (349). Elsie escapes this fate with the aid of the enlightened women who suspect the identity of the child's father, and Elsie, with their help, prepares to raise her child and train for a profession. Much like Eliza in *Pygmalion*, Elsie dreams of becoming a teacher and with the assistance of her "three good fairies" (351), she eventually begins the training to realize her goal. Also like Eliza, Elsie eventually marries above her own station, becoming by marriage a member of the influential "city" Wellwood family, whose patriarch is Basil, the highly respected and more conservative brother of the Fabian Humphrey Wellwood. Elsie's path to respectability and to overcoming class and gender barriers proves much darker than Eliza's, however both emerge as images of the much heralded "New Woman." Byatt contrasts the travails of Elsie with those of the upper-class and pregnant Florence Cain, whose loving father and family money assure that this single girl will evade the "fallen woman" stigma that haunts the working-class Elsie when both are impregnated by the same man, thus underscoring the issues of class that distinguish groups of characters throughout the novel.

Daughters also become radicalized in the works of both Shaw and Byatt. In *The Children's Book*, Hedda Wellwood, youngest daughter of Olive and Humphrey, becomes a more radical form of the New Woman than her mother and sister. Although an active and participating family member, Hedda has been a "rebel without a cause" (*TCB* 624), until she discovered the Women's Social and Political Union (530). Inspired by the ultimate sacrifice made by the historical suffragette Emily Davison, Hedda eventually realizes that an act is required, and she attacks a perceived symbol of an oppressive society, the precious Gloucester candlestick in the Victoria and Albert Museum. The candlestick had "fascinated Olive and Tom Wellwood, as well as Phillip Warren . . . [and] the object momentarily entrances Hedda, and the stone she launches is ineffectual. She is discovered by guards before she can do further damage." While others find comfort and beauty in the valuable object, Hedda views it as only a symbol against which to rebel.[60] Hedda lands in jail and is force-fed after refusing to eat out of solidarity with other Suffragettes; eventually officials release her into the arms of the WSPU and her sister Dorothy (625–30). Like Elsie, Hedda also resembles a character from the Shavian oeuvre. In *Fanny's First Play*, religion, not the women's movement, inspires Margaret Knox to rebel against authority. The daughter of parents obsessed with respectability and with keeping up appearances, Margaret, the winner of good-conduct medals in school, revolts against authority and respectability after her first taste of freedom. She attends a prayer meeting that "sets her free" and enables her to defend herself against brutal treatment by police.[61] According to Gainor, *Fanny's First Play* provides Shaw the opportunity to discuss such ideas as cross-class marriage and force-feeding of Suffragettes.[62] However, while Byatt's Hedda plans her rebellious act with great care, the protest of Shaw's Margaret is impulsive, catalyzed by witnessing the rough treatment of women by police in a theater (IV: 393). Nevertheless, the results of these two revolts are the same: previously sheltered young girls enter jail as a result of their rebellious acts and emerge as enlightened New Women, ready to contribute to efforts to reform society.

The bohemian atmosphere that pervades much of *The Children's Book* links the novel to Shaw's *Heartbreak House*, previously described as a Fabian nightmare. "Captain Shotover, representing the bohemian father figure, has raised his daughters in a moral vacuum . . . and they consequently blame him for their own unhappiness."[63] Ariadne Shotover Utterword returns from years away from her family and soon sheds light on the reasons for her absence. She indicts her bohemian parent whose philosophy embodies Shaw's own early maxim—"The golden rule is that there is no golden rule"[64]: "But let me warn you . . . that I am a rigidly conventional woman. You may think because I'm a Shotover that I'm a Bohemian, because we're all so Bohemian. But I'm not. I hate and loathe Bohemianism. No child brought up in a strict Puritan household ever suffered from Puritanism as I suffered from our Bohemianism" (*HH*, V: 96).

Ariadne's brother-in-law Hector Hushabye, one of the bohemian inhabitants of Heartbreak House whom Ariadne rails against, plays a number of roles in the drama—Hesione Shotover, Hushabye's husband and Shotover's son-in-law, as well as the fictitious "Marcus Darnley," adventurer and breaker of young hearts.[65] He claims to be a Socialist (V: 82), fights imaginary duels, and enjoys making a striking appearance, with his "mousquitaire moustaches, . . . dandified curly brimmed hat, . . . and elaborate walking stick" (V: 83), and spends the evening of the play wearing a "handsome Arab costume" (V: 130). When Hector first meets his sister-in-law, sparks fly as they recognize familiar traits in each other:

HECTOR: You are neither a Bohemian woman nor a Puritan woman. You are a dangerous woman.

LADY UTTERWORD: On the contrary, I am a safe woman. . . . [And] you are an exceedingly clever lady-killer, Hector. And terribly handsome. I am quite a good player myself, at that game. Is it quite understood that we are only playing? (V: 97)

And so Hector plays the dashing lady-killer much as Humphrey Wellwood does in *TCB*. Yet he also understands the effects of the aura of bohemianism that pervades the house: "Something in the air of the house has upset you. It often does have that effect," he tells the visitors who feel the strain of living in the Shotover household (V: 152). However, despite his seeming awareness of the family's bohemian circumstances, he and the other inhabitants of Heartbreak House, like many of their generation in England, fail to see the ominous signs of the cruel fate that is at least partially of their making as they revel in their bohemian lives and "fascinate" each other for sport. World War I literally crashes into their world when the German zeppelins approach, dropping bombs and lighting up the night sky. The dazzled but clueless group compares the sound of the bombs to Beethoven (V:178), and Hesione voices the naive unawareness of all assembled: "But what a glorious experience. I hope they'll come again tomorrow night," as the play ends. Of course, the zeppelins did come again, with disastrous results for England.

Perhaps more than any other Shaw play, the themes of *Heartbreak House* pervade *The Children's Book*. Although the action of *Heartbreak House* occurs in one day and that of *The Children's Book* covers twenty-four years, the two works represent the mood of the Neo-Victorian age in unmistakably similar ways. Byatt depicts the bohemian atmosphere of the era described above in much the same way as Shaw creates it in *Heartbreak House*, with the parents living unconventional lives that affect everyone around them. The children of Olive and Humphrey Wellwood indict their upbringing in much the same way as do the Shotover offspring, revealing how bohemianism can scar as well as liberate.[66] In one of the historical accounts of the time, Byatt describes the children as "solemn," watching their playful parents relive their carefree childhoods, pulling juvenile pranks and writing "wonderful tales" of a longed-for carefree past (*TCB* 434). Phyllis Wellwood is one of those "solemn" children: "Like many children of shifting, insecure Bohemian households, she had a romantic vision of an ordinary, comfortable household that kept strict hours and was warmly predictable" (443), echoing Hector's description of the Hushabye children in *Heartbreak House*, who long for respectability and conventionality and spend all of their holidays in the homes of their respectable friends (*HH*, V: 96). Dorothy Wellwood expresses the same concerns, "I can't bear mess and muddle," referring to the news that Humphrey is not her real father. As she considers her childhood and what she believed to be the happy reality of her home life, she realizes "only nothing was what it seemed," finding it hard to sleep in the confusion that becomes a new reality for the organized, purposeful young woman who knows what she wants in life. Demonstrating how different children cope with the stress of their haphazard family life, Dorothy aspires to the purposeful life of a doctor, while her sister releases her frustrations very differently. Hedda commits her act of rebellion described above out of "rage with her past life, which would now end . . . the dreamy, comfortable, unsatisfactory muddled order of Todefright" (*TCB*, 626–27). Thus, Byatt reifies the dissatisfaction of children from "muddled" families, only described by Hector in *Heartbreak House*. However, the adults who live the free lifestyle also admit uncertainty about their choices. In *Heartbreak House*, Hesione confides to Ellie "[W]hen

I am neither coaxing and kissing nor laughing, I am just wondering how much longer I can stand living in this cruel, damnable world" (*HH*, V: 123). Byatt similarly undercuts Olive Wellwood's bohemianism with the following revelation: "She tried to be broadminded—she would have liked to be bohemian—but felt in fact a squeamish distaste" for action of some of the more notorious bohemians of the day such as Oscar Wilde (*TCB*, 393).

Byatt continues the allusion to Shaw's work, connecting her own Lothario Humphrey with the flirtatious Hector Hushabye in several ways. They are both socialists, and Humphrey, like Hector, loves elaborate costumes, such as the ones he and Olive wear in their backyard theatrical production (*TCB* 43). Also like Hector, he admits his need to fascinate women even as he grows older: "He had hoped that his inconvenient need for new women would slacken with his muscles. Women his age were no longer desirable, why should he be? And yet, he was. He kept testing it—women lecturers at summer schools, youngish ladies in bookshops, Fabians, socialists, he excited them, and through them, himself" (*TCB*, 448). Thus the two bohemian male characters rely on escapades conducted outside their respective marriages to fulfill some need deeper than their domestic life can provide, in ways often mocked by their creators.

The final similarity between *Heartbreak House* and *The Children's Book* concerns the attitudes toward impending war. Much like the unwitting inhabitants of Shaw's play, the Wellwoods and their contemporaries fail to see World War 1 approaching, as Byatt admits in a series of interviews: "I started working on the 1890s without thinking it through that all of these children would die in the war. . . . I'm a naturally pessimistic animal and there's a sort of innocence about these people. They came after the high Victorians. . . . I feel they [the high Victorians] understood that the world might be tragic whereas the Shaw, and even the Woolf generation . . . [failed to grasp life's tragic implications before World War 1]."[67] Byatt reports in another interview, "I remember school history classes where we wrote down The Causes of the First World War, in lists, as though there was an inevitable scientific process which inexorably led to the war. The more I read, the more I thought there were no such hard causes—only muddle and the fact that the Kaiser was mad."[68] Byatt transfers this belief to the characters in her novel as she realizes that readers would expect to know what happened to her young characters, and she provides a factual account of the "run up" to the war in two pages (663–35), detailing her fictional account of the fate of the children who served and that of their parents in thirty-nine pages (636–75). In those passages, Robin and Harry Wellwood die in battle, while Florian Wellwood returns alive but badly wounded, all victims of a war that no one foresaw.

"Through the fictional Olive Wellwood, Byatt conjures the period of Peter Pan and H. G. Wells, Fabianism and *The Wind and the Willows*."[69] The Fabian portion of this equation is germane to this study. While Maltz contends that *The Children's Book* is not a factual account of the Fabian Society,[70] the novel's plot is loosely structured around tales of infamous Fabians, actual activities and issues attributed to the Fabian society, and the influence of the "Fabian Mystique" on many of Byatt's characters. She sprinkles descriptions of actual Fabian events and gatherings liberally throughout the novel. For example, she notes the founding of the Society in 1884 and makes it relevant to the novel by having Violet Grimwith, Olive's sister, remark that Dorothy was born in the same year as the Fabian Society (*TCB*, 27). The founding of the London School of Economics, under the direction of Sidney and Beatrice Webb with help from Charlotte Payne Townsend, Shaw's wife, appears on page 228. The "Fabian Crisis," precipitated by the "imperious ambition of H. G. Wells," informs page 530. The coed Cambridge Young Fabians are described on page 532, and the famous Fabian Summer Camps on page 607.

Additionally, historical Fabians, Wells, Shaw, Rupert Brooke, the Webbs, and others make cameo appearances in Byatt's historical montages. This inclusion of actual Fabian events and members lends credence to Byatt's description of attitudes attributed to the Fabians and their family values and position on current events. Faced with the background of cruel poverty endured by the newly arrived Phillip Warren, Dorothy, who considered herself exploited because she was the oldest child and a girl, "was forced, because she had been brought up in the Fabian atmosphere of rational justice, to admit that she had 'no right' to feel unhappy, since she was exceedingly privileged" (*TCB*, 27). Byatt also identifies the then-current ideas of child rearing of socialists and other intellectuals as Fabian and suggests, "The Fabians . . . saw, in a way that earlier generations had not, that children were people, with identities and desires and intelligences. . . . They saw, many of them, that children needed freedom, needed not only to learn, and to be good, but also to play and be wild" (434). As these children reached young adulthood, the children of Fabians "formed what became known as the Fabian Nursery, full of forward-looking idealistic young men, and determined young women" (527). Articulating a Fabian position on war, specifically the Boer War, proved contentious with "the Imperialists" advocating the spread of English democracy to other nations, while the 'gas-and-water' contingent believed in concentrating their efforts on issues closer to home." Byatt features Shaw in a speaking role in this debate: "G. B. Shaw argued that the Society should sit on the fence and wait till the war was won and demand nationalization of the Rand mines and good working conditions for miners" (257).

Byatt implants her fictional Fabians into the actual Society, thus strengthening the connection of novel to history. She has several prominent characters become members of the Society as part of their development as responsible, forward thinking socialists. Olive and Humphrey Wellwood join the Society soon after its founding in 1884 (*TCB*, 36). Several members of the younger generation of Wellwoods and their circle also become members. After enrolling in the London School of Economics, Charles/Karl Wellwood joins the Fabians, fulfilling the requirement of signing the Fabian Basis, and attending the camps (527, 606). Julian Cain also becomes affiliated in his postgraduate days, meeting the young Rupert Brooke and James Strachey (527). Other supporting characters identified as Fabians, such as Leslie and Etta Skinner (43) and Miss Patty Dace (130), provide the impetus for much of the "good works" performed in support of the more hapless and hopeless characters in the novel.

These Fabian elements combine to reinforce the primary connection with the Fabian Society in the novel: major characters based on the lives of actual Fabians whose lifestyles provide much to the X-rated, page-turning sizzle of the novel. Critics aver that Byatt does not judge her characters;[71] she does not need to do so because of the numerous historical accounts of the bohemian lifestyles, infidelities, and resulting blended families of several prominent Fabians. In principle, Fabians believed that parents should provide a happy home for children or have them removed by the State.[72] In fact, many children of Fabians grew up in unusual circumstances by most standards, as exemplified by the Nesbit-Bland arrangement. Byatt's parallel between "the personal lives of Nesbit and Olive Wellwood is certainly visible," contends Maltz, but the similarity does not extend to their writing of fairy stories, with Olive's tales being "far more traditional in style than Nesbit's."[73] However, Olive and Humphrey do follow Nesbit's and Hubert Bland's trajectory; both have children by other partners who are brought up as one family. For added spice, Byatt creates another female relative, Olive's sister Violet, who secretly bears two of the family's children, Phyllis and Florian (652). Olive, with secrets of her own, conceives Dorothy after a fling with a German puppeteer, Anselm Stern (381).

"Aunt" Violet manages the family home, Todefright, with efficiency and love and may resemble Alice Hodson, Nesbit's friend and adopted family member who raised the Blands' various children. And so, of the seven children reared as Olive and Humphrey's own, two are really Violet's and Humphrey's offspring and one is the daughter of Olive and Anselm Stern. Stating that things are not always as they seem, Byatt reveals these facts through a series of unraveling secrets that the children learn about by listening carefully through the walls of Todefright. Understandably, most of the children would rather not know these truths and allow things to go on as usual in the household. Yet the whole series of affairs produces an unmistakable "muddle," one of Byatt's favorite words to describe the atmosphere in the family. Byatt may not overtly judge the parents' morals, but the children suffer—and most live their lives desiring stability and order and a firm sense of identity. In a seemingly innocent discussion of cuckoo birds, Violet sets the stage for revelations to come: "It's surprising how many creatures don't know their real parents" (101).

Of all the characters involved in nefarious affairs and tangles, the one character scorned by Byatt is Herbert Methley, the New Lifer based on a composite of H. G. Wells and Hubert Bland.[74] Moreover, while Humphrey and Olive's story strongly resembles that of Edith and Hubert Bland, Byatt herself identifies Wells as the model: ". . . a lot of this is based on is H. G. Wells going to Newnham College and seducing a young lady. . . . She ended up pregnant with H. G. Wells' child."[75] The character Methley perpetrates the same scenario with Florence Cain, the daughter of Prosper Cain, friend and admirer of Olive and rescuer of several children and young adults caught in "the muddle." Throughout the story, Methley manages to seduce his women [including Olive herself] through a feminist rhetoric ("this is your right, this is your right"). Here Byatt's satire is at its most scathing, as Methley's much-used seduction line becomes tiresome and predictable, but not to him or to the women he preys upon.[76] Methley fathers several children throughout the novel, and Byatt suggests that his reputation as a scoundrel is well known, even by his common-law wife Phoebe Methley. Byatt reveals Phoebe's awareness of her husband's deplorable ways during the episode in which the "three good fairies" plan to aid Elsie Warren, pregnant with Methlely's child. Although Elsie never identifies the father of her unborn child, the women have their suspicions. Patty Dace questions if the father could be a member of the Fludd family with whom Elsie resides, and Phoebe firmly replies, "He is not . . . I am certain of that" (*TCB*, 351). Thus another secret is maintained and several blended families are formed as a result of Methley's philandering unfaithfulness, much like the blended families of Wells and Bland. Maltz concludes: "If progressive lifestyles give some characters license to behave intemperately and self-indulgently, then they also inform a new model of family obligation, serving as venues for virtue as well as excess. Nesbit knew this, as does Byatt."[77]

These blended families produced by the "progressive lifestyles" described above bring us back to Shaw, himself an inhabitant, if not a product, of a blended household and author of numerous works featuring "fascinating foundlings."[78] Dietrich elaborates:

> The question of Shaw's fatherlessness "has . . . intrigued biographers. . . . B.C. Rosset's *Shaw of Dublin* stirred up some fascinating speculation in 1964. Rosset's controversial thesis . . . is that George Bernard Shaw was named not after George Carr Shaw but after George Vandeleur Lee, the third party in the putative *ménage à trois* that lasted in the Shaw family from sometime shortly before Bernard's birth (1856) until Lee and Mrs. Shaw decamped separately leaving George Carr and George Bernard behind. This scenario has his mother and his 'real' father abandoning their 'love child' when he's sixteen, a possibility that seems unlikely."[79]

Dietrich continues that Shaw's fascination with "the orphan hero" becomes most likely a metaphor for "the homelessness of genius amidst the decay and death of the old Victorian father figures."[80] In the future of universal socialism, "we are all parents and children of one another," Shaw always insisted.[81] Holroyd offers a different analysis: "that Shaw may have had an unconscious wish to be the son of the remarkable George Lee and not of the miserable George Carr Shaw is possible" (I: 24). Holroyd avers that Shaw's seeking the certainty of his parentage was undertaken primarily in deference to his mother, but the theme of the search for the father recurs obsessively in his plays, although "the emotional independence of the woman is virtuously stressed" (ibid.). Because of the perennial confusion concerning the identity of his father, Shaw ultimately dropped the "ambiguous" Christian name that he shared with both men. "Don't George me" he often fumed at those who were not privy to the family situation (25). Interestingly, Byatt has one of her characters, Elsie Warren, remind the reader of the historical problem of parental identification. Remembering the deplorable conditions of the London slums, Elsie recalls "families in Burslem where someone's little brother or sister was generally thought to be really her child by her brother or father. They slept so close there, flesh to flesh" (*TCB*, 324). This perceived taint of the lower-class morality was well known at the time and must have haunted Shaw as well as the fictional Wellwood children, who wrestled with the truth of their own identities.

In sum, both Shaw and Byatt recognize "the Fabian atmosphere of rational justice" both in *The Children's Book* (27) and throughout Shaw's oeuvre. The preceding is no "anxiety of influence study";[82] rather, it concerns two writers absorbed in the same time and milieu (1895–1917), one who lived and helped to create it and the other who "fictialized" it. Bristow provides an assessment of *The Children's Book* that applies to Shaw as well: it is important to "see that a better future depends on knowing what happened to the radical possibilities of the past. By extension, there will be the discovery that this generation of late Victorians tried to establish a more open-minded world—one fired by the ambition of the Arts and Crafts, the New Life, and the Fabians—that we most probably have still yet to realize."[83] In critiquing these "radical possibilities," Byatt masterfully incorporates Bernard Shaw's life and work to weave her fictional account of the Fabians and the society and culture that led to their development. Byatt underscores Shaw's continuing relevance as a writer and thinker by emphasizing both the Fabian and Shavian message of the importance of releasing the individual from the blocking influence of societal ills.

NOTES

1. R. F. Dietrich, e-mail communication to International Shaw Society membership list, 21 April 2010.

2. A. S. Byatt, interview with Ramona Koval, *The Book Show*, ABC Radio National, 24 April 2009. www.abc.net.au/radionational/programs/bookshow/as-byatts-the-childrens-book/313.

3. Bernard Shaw, *Fanny's First Play*, in *The Bodley Head Bernard Shaw: Collected Plays with Their Prefaces*, 7 vols., ed. Dan H. Laurence (London: Max Reinhardt, 1970–74), 4:445. All references to the play are to this edition, with page numbers given parenthetically in the text. Subsequent references to *Collected Plays with Their Prefaces* will be as *CPP*, followed by volume and page numbers.

4. Byatt interview with Ramona Koval, 4. See note 2 above. Please note that Byatt's sister, the novelist Margaret Drabble, is married to Shaw biographer Michael Holroyd.

5. A. S. Byatt, *The Children's Book* (New York: Alfred A. Knopf, 2009).

6. Michael Holroyd, *Bernard Shaw, 1856–1898: The Search for Love* (London: Chatto and Windus, 1988), 22–27.

7. Joseph Bristow, "Introduction: What Happened? The Children's Book and the Question of History, 1805–1919," *Journal of Victorian Culture* 17, no. 1 (2012): 64 and 68.

8. A. S. Byatt, "True Stories and the Facts in Fiction," in *Essays on the Fiction of A. S. Byatt: Imagining the Real*, ed. Alexa Alfer and Michael J. Noble (Westport, Conn.: Greenwood Press, 2001), 178.

9. Lagretta Tallent Lenker, *Fathers and Daughters in Shakespeare and Shaw* (Westport, Conn.: Greenwood Press, 2001), 15.

10. Bristow, "Introduction," 66.

11. Anne Fremantle, *This Little Band of Prophets* (New York: Macmillan: 1960), 15–29.

12. Bristow, "Introduction," 65. Norman and Jean MacKenzie and other historians, however, note that the relationship between the Fabians and the Labour Party was often tenuous. H. G. Wells and others urged the founding of a separate political party that was more in keeping with Fabian precepts (335–36).

13. A. S. Byatt, interview with Maylin, "An Interview with A. S. Byatt on her new novel *The Children's Book*," The Dewey Divas and the Dudes, 20 May 2009. http://deweydivas.blogspot.com/2009/05/interview-with-s-byatt-on-her-new-novel.html.

14. Katherine Uhsadel, "The Continuity of Victorian Traces: A. S. Byatt's The Children's Book," *Journal of Victorian Culture* 17, no. 1 (2012): 73.

15. Diana Maltz, "The Newer New Life: A. S. Byatt, E. Nesbit and Socialist Subculture," *Journal of Victorian Culture* 17, no. 1 (2012): 80–81.

16. Kathleen Coyle Kelly, *A. S. Byatt* (New York: Twayne Publishers, 1996), 114–16.

17. Bristow, "Introduction," 68.

18. See Lenker, *Fathers and Daughters*, 2–5, for a discussion of Shaw as a feminist author.

19. Jane Campbell, *A. S. Byatt and the Heliotropic Imagination* (Waterloo, Ontario: Wilfrid Laurier University Press, 2004), 20.

20. Ibid., 21.

21. Edward R. Pease, *The History of the Fabian Society by Edward R. Pease Secretary for Twenty-five Years* (New York: E. P. Dutton, 1916). Downloaded through Project Gutenberg www.gutenberg.org/files/13715/13715-h.htm on 27 June 2012. I am indebted to Edward R. Pease, Ian Britain, Anne Fremantle, and Norman and Jean MacKenzie for their fine work on the history of the Fabian Society.

22. Pease, *History of the Fabian Society*, 12.

23. Ibid., 19.

24. Quoted in Ian Britain, *Fabianism and Culture: A Study in British Socialism and the Arts c 1884–1918* (Cambridge: Cambridge University Press, 1982), 19.

25. Britain, *Fabianism and Culture*, 16.

26. The Manifesto is recorded in Pease, *History of the Fabian Society*, on 21–23 and the Basis on 139–40.

27. Britain, *Fabianism and Culture*, 20–21.

28. Fremantle, *Little Band of Prophets*, 52.

29. Ibid., 155.

30. Ibid.

31. Britain, *Fabianism and Culture*, 12.

32. Ibid., 273.

33. Norman and Jean MacKenzie, *The First Fabians* (London: Weidenfeld and Nicolson, 1977), 214–17.

34. Holroyd, *Bernard Shaw, 1856–1898*, 1:163.

35. James Alexander, *Shaw's Controversial Socialism* (Gainesville: University Press of Florida, 2009), 18.

36. Charles A. Carpenter, *Bernard Shaw as Artist-Fabian* (Gainesville: University Press of Florida, 2009), 23.

37. Alexander, *Shaw's Controversial Socialism*, 18.

38. Carpenter, *Bernard Shaw*, 70.

39. R. F. Dietrich, *British Drama 1890–1950: A Critical History* (Boston: Twayne Publishers, 1989), 83–84.

40. Ibid., 84.

41. Tracy C. Davis, *George Bernard Shaw and the Socialist Theatre* (Westport, Conn.: Praeger, 1994), 37–38.

42. Carpenter, *Bernard Shaw*, 45.

43. Archibald Henderson, *George Bernard Shaw: His Life and Works* (Cincinnati: Stewart Kidd and Co., 1911), 399. http://openlibrary.org/books/OL20599000M/George_Bernard_Shaw_His_Life_and_Works. Accessed 11 August 2012.

44. Fremantle, *Little Band of Prophets*, 36–37.

45. Shaw, *Fanny's First Play*, CPP 4:341–449.

46. J. Ellen Gainor, *Shaw's Daughters* (Ann Arbor: University of Michigan Press, 1991), 182.

47. Ibid., 184.

48. Shaw, *Pygmalion*, CPP 4:653–823.

49. Arthur Ganz, *George Bernard Shaw* (New York: Macmillan, 1983), 179–80.

50. Shaw, *Heartbreak House*, CPP 5:9–197. Subsequent references to *Heartbreak House* are to this edition and are given in the text as *HH* with page number.

51. Eric Bentley, *Bernard Shaw 1856–1950* (New York: New Directions, 1947), 140.

52. Ibid., 140–41.

53. A. S. Byatt interview, "Nothing like the Dame," lifestyle.scotsman.com. www.scotsman.com/lifestyle/books/features/as-byatt-interview-nothing-like-the-dame. Accessed 17 April 2009.

54. Byatt, interview, the Dewey Divas and Dudes, 1.

55. Ibid.

56. Maltz, "Newer New Life," 80.

57. See Lenker, *Fathers and Daughters*, 2.

58. Campbell, *A. S. Byatt*, 20.

59. See Dietrich, *British Drama*, 123, for a discussion of the debunking of myth and fairy tales in *Pygmalion*.

60. Morna O'Neill, "'The Craftsman's Dream': Objects and Display in *The Children's Book*." *Journal of Victorian Culture* 17, no. 1 (2012): 88.

61. Shaw, CPP IV:394.

62. Gainor, *Shaw's Daughters*, 184.

63. Lenker, *Fathers and Daughters*, 84.

64. Bernard Shaw, *Man and Superman*, "Maxims for Revolutionists," CPP II:78.

65. Lenker, *Fathers and Daughters*, 98.

66. Maltz, "Newer New Life," 80.

67. A. S. Byatt, interview with Nichols A. Basbanes, "Blaming Nora," 1 May 2009, *The Guardian* 3–4. www.guardian.co.uk/stage/2009/may02/ibsen-a-dolls-house.

68. A. S. Byatt, interview with Sophie Rochester, "The Impact of Writing on Families," www.themanbookerprize.com/perspective/articles/1264, 2.

69. lifestyle.scotsman.com 1.

70. Maltz, "Newer New Life," 81.

71. Campbell, *A. S. Byatt*, 14–17; see also Richard Todd, *A. S. Byatt* (Northcote House in association with the British Council, 1997), 5.

72. Manifesto in Pease, *History of the Fabian Society*, 2.

73. Maltz, "Newer New Life," 79–80.

74. Ibid., 82.

75. ABC Radio, 2.

76. Maltz, "Newer New Life," 82.

77. Ibid., 84.

78. R. F. Dietrich, *Bernard Shaw's Novels: Portraits of the Artist as Man and Superman* (Gainesville: University Press of Florida, 1996), 169.

79. Ibid.

80. Ibid., 170. A. M. Gibbs presents an alternative view of Shaw's early life and its effect on his writing in *Bernard Shaw: A Life* (2005), especially chapters 1 and 2.

81. Ibid., 171.

82. Harold Bloom, *The Anxiety of Influence* (Oxford: Oxford University Press, 1973).

83. Bristow, "Introduction," 67.

Authorship and Shaw's *Shakes Versus Shav*

CHRISTOPHER WIXSON

The fact is, you look on an author as a sort of god. I look on him as a man I pay to do a certain thing for me. . . . Who and what is an author that he should be privileged to take liberties that are not allowed to other men?

—*Misalliance*[1]

I confess that though as a matter of business I wish my plays to be performed, as a matter of instinct I fight against the inevitable misrepresentation of them.

—Preface to Plays Pleasant[2]

In his final speech in *The Tempest*, Prospero, bereft of his "potent art" and the aid of his "demi-puppets," pleads with the audience to set him free.[3] Particularly in light of the Victorian sentimental tradition that elided the character with the retiring Shakespeare, the image of the magician ultimately subject to the pull of commerce is startling yet prophetic, given the industry the Bard would become in subsequent centuries, his works perpetually refinished to suit popular taste. Our last glimpse of the author/character is as a puppet trapped within his own text, the authority shifted from the producer to the consumers. Mortality's effects on authorial control were also on Bernard Shaw's mind late in his life when he concluded a 1949 op-ed piece about tax-code discrimination against writers with the questions: "Why is property in our creations communized after less than two lifetimes and that of simple distributors made perpetual? Why is property in turnips made eternal and absolute when property in ideas is temporary and conditional?"[4] In his published response, novelist Charles Morgan amplified its underlying concern that, "when Mr. Shaw's heirs are deprived of their power to prevent it, [any disreputable cad or political enthusiast] will be able, by garbling the text and adding his own introductions, to represent Shavianism as advocacy of almost anything on earth." Shaw's anxiety is not surprising, considering the playwright's prolific success at self-authorization and frequent skirmishes with theatrical adversaries for textual mastery. A few months after this piece, he wrote *Shakes Versus Shav*, which he believed in all "actuarial probability" to be his "last play" and "the climax of [his] eminence."[5] In it, playwrights are depicted as actual puppets, and their petty squabbles become Shaw's response to the fate of the late playwright, his charms o'erthrown, his image at the mercy of other hands.

Commissioned by Waldo Lanchester for the Malvern Marionette Theater, *Shakes Versus Shav* begins with Shakes out for revenge, angry that his authorial persona is being disparaged and his words appropriated by an upstart crow named Shav, whom he condemns as a "shameless fraud," an "infamous imposter" lost in an "ecstasy of self-conceit" in "[daring] to pretend / here to reincarnate my very self."[6] When Shav appears, they brawl, stage a bout between surrogates Macbeth and Sir Walter Scott's Rob Roy, and view a presentation of *Heartbreak House* in dramaticule. Following further heated charges of plagiarism and pessimism, Shav asks Shakes to "for a moment suffer / My glimmering light to shine." A light suddenly and mysteriously appears between them, to which Shakes responds by immediately "puffing out" the splendid torch, saying "out, out brief candle."[7] Treated as an eccentric one-off, *Shakes Versus Shav* is rarely performed and considered, at least by one midcentury scholar, "one of [Shaw's] dotages, a pathetic exhibition of nonagenarian *gaminerie*."[8] Taken more seriously, biographers have found it a rich mine of allusion, invoking (among other things) the playwright's interest in the infamous "long count" of the 1927 Tunney-Dempsey boxing match as well as purported genealogical links between the Shaws and Rob Roy and Macduff. Contemporary scholars have approached the play, which begins and ends with Shakespearean quotation, mainly within the context of Shaw's ongoing professional rivalry with his predecessor.[9] This essay seeks to reframe the grappling portrayed in *Shakes Versus Shav* within the larger idea of the uniquely vexed creative authority for playwrights, arguing that Shaw presciently muses over the ramifications for the Shavian text upon the death of the author.

Mechanic slaves
With greasy aprons, rules, and hammers, shall
Uplift us to the view.
—*Antony and Cleopatra*[10]

For Shaw, authorship was a source of tremendous aesthetic and economic autonomy, his plays, as Margot Peters contends, "a commodity over whose publication, distribution, and profit-taking he exercised more control than perhaps any other writer in history."[11] "I half suspect," he wrote in 1898, "that those managers who have had the most to do with me, if asked to name the main obstacle to the performance of my plays, would unhesitatingly and unanimously reply 'the author.'"[12] Shaw's preface to *Plays Unpleasant* details the struggle with managers and actors to produce an authentic representation of the author's artistic intent, a scuffle so disheartening that the playwright arrives at "the conclusion that his own view of his work can only be conveyed by himself[, that] he must fall back on his powers of literary expression."[13] The playwright's decision to "put [his] plays before the public in [his] own way"[14] enabled him to bypass the fiscal exigencies of the commercial stage, which foreclosed performance opportunities and in a larger sense constricted theater's possibilities as a "social organ."[15] Furthermore, transforming his plays into legal property, copyright protection secures textual borders so as to stave off the crisis in meaning that occurs when access to the territory is granted to all. That its authority is derived by a juridical system of economic privilege that Shaw the Socialist spent a lifetime attacking produces an intriguing friction.[16] Railing against what he called "the tragedy of private property," Shaw vehemently expressed his repugnance toward "our continual aspiration to possess property, our common hailing of it as sacred, our setting apart of the word Respectable for those who have attained it, our ascription of pre-eminent religiousness to commandments forbidding its violation, and our identification of law and order among men with its protection."[17]

Nonetheless, staking the playwright's claim, Shaw zealously policed his scripts against prospective poachers and squatters.

Authorship in the theater of course is never singular—rather, it is always collaborative, always negotiated, always fluid. The playwright's script is filtered through the interpretive gestures of a second group of artists made up of designers, performers, and the director before it reaches the audience. Even the paratextual apparati surrounding the *theatrical* text rebuke the playwright's exclusive control; the script is subject to the elements of performance (the varying intentional and accidental significations of body and language, audience and performer) that circumscribe the meaning of any theater event. On the printed page, Shaw is able to substitute his own *literary* paratext (prefaces, appendices, lengthy stage directions), that, as Katherine Kelly asserts, "[condition] the reader's reception of the play both before and after reading it,"[18] thereby consolidating his authority over its meaning. It is the paratextual material that makes reading a Shaw play feel curiously more like an experience with a writer than with a group of characters, creating an experiential disparity for the respective audiences. The published texts seek to displace theatrical elements that stand as the limits of the author's control, conferring upon the playwright an unusual degree of textual sovereignty. In addition to political motivations, then, Shaw's publication of his plays can be seen as a kind of coping strategy for the challenge theater itself presents to the writer's absolute dominance.

Those forces that the dramatist specifically strives to marshal are also those inherent to the theatrical text, ameliorated only by a translation to the printed page that sacrifices what is aesthetically distinctive about the stage. Shaw understood that consequence when he imagined published volumes of drama engendering a new hybrid genre of text. Similar to the puppeteering performance texts exalted by *Shakes Versus Shav*'s preface, these literary pastiches would be, according to Shaw, "part narrative, part homily, part description, part dialogue, and (possibly) part drama,"[19] its parts made whole through the solo performance of the master Author. As accurate a description of his own published volumes as that is, Shaw claimed he was not interested in producing them; rather, his goal was to write as a "practical dramatist[,] . . . to put down nothing that is irrelevant to the actor's performance and, through it, to the audience's comprehension of the play."[20] As Ian Clarke points out, though, "The lengthy passages of explicit analysis and commentary printed as stage directions have little direct tangible existence in the theatre."[21] While Shaw carefully adapts the theatrical material explicitly and self-consciously for a reader, his stage direction moves far beyond ordinary expository description, seeking to appropriate models of prose narration in order to determine more powerfully the theatrical text. In *Our Theatre in the Nineties*, for instance, he admits taking from Dickens a style of "description of the persons of the drama so vivid and precise that no actor with the faintest sense of character could mistake the sort of figure he has to represent."[22] The paratextual material seeks to solve the writer's dilemma, what Shaw refers to in one preface as "the actor's excess of power," which results inevitably in "the very originality and genius of the performers [clashing] with the originality and genius of the author."[23]

I could interpret between you and your love, if I could see the
puppets dallying.
                    —*Hamlet*[24]

The presence of GBS on the page as narrator/author is both direct and profuse;
on stage, it is less tangible and evasive, even as critics compulsively attempt
to pin it down, locate it in a single character or speech. Indeed, the critic is
another primary combatant in the interpretive field, attempting to replace the
writer as the text's origin in divining its intended meaning. Shaw wrote eight
plays while still working for the *Saturday Review*, and his published volumes
are expressions of the "critic-dramatist" codependence, "G.B.S." the nexus of
the mutual exegetical investment of the two roles. Donald Pease posits that
"[similar to] the division of industrial labor within the economic realm[,] what
alienated the author from his work's means of production . . . was not a factory
owner but the literary critic who claimed a power to understand it greater
than the author's own."[25] Harley Granville Barker attributes culpability to the
playwright, writing in 1934 about plays that "criticism will kill" as "full of fine
poetry, clever ideas, striking characters [and flawed only by] the failure of the
dramatist to eliminate himself from the play, [the audience] unceasingly conscious of the author, of his poetry, his ideas, his characters."[26]

To the writer, Barker prescribes self-effacement for the sake of the art
to stave off the cancerous critical invasion hellbent on interpolating the
author through the play. In light of Shaw's usual self-assertive strategy to
ward off misinterpretations, the preface to *Shakes Versus Shav* surprisingly
praises the inclination toward discretionary inconspicuousness in puppets
(and, by analogical extension, in playwrights), what Shaw describes as an
unfailing instinct to remain "invisible" when another performer is "speaking
or tumbling." The playwright adopted this tactic in his puckish conceal-
ment of *Fanny's First Play*'s authorship from its opening night audience so
as to provide "a measure of relief to those critics and playgoers who are so
obsessed by my strained legendary reputation that they approach my plays
in a condition which is really one of derangement."[27]

Indeed, a frequent assumption in both media reviews of productions and
academic scholarship on his plays is that a single character is simply the
author's mouthpiece, a premise that sometimes infuriated Shaw. In 1932, for
instance, Aubrey Bagot, *Too True to Be Good*'s notorious magician preacher,
was quickly interpreted as Shaw's "satirical self-portrait . . . [a] confession
of the bankruptcy of his own thought."[28] Shaw complained first in the
Malvern Festival Book about American critics who elided playwright and
character: "They annoyed me by . . . informing the world that I am finishing

my life in a condition of pitiable but theatrically very tiresome disillusion and despair, having recanted all my professions, renounced all my convictions, abandoned all my hopes, and demolished all my Utopias." Later, in the published version of *Too True to Be Good*, Shaw directly addressed the situation again in both the preface and the concluding stage direction, explicitly placing distance between himself and Aubrey. In spite of Shaw's protestations, reviewers and scholars seem as invested as he is in preventing the sundering of the play's language from a prescriptive authorial origin yet dedicated to situating themselves in that creative role.

Further challenging the playwright's textual sovereignty, new antagonists were on the horizon when *Shakes Versus Shav* is written. Methods of interpretative analysis emerging right around the time of Shaw's death sought to unshackle the reader from the author's control. In the mid-1940s, American scholars William K. Wimsatt and Monroe K. Beardsley influentially claimed that a poem or a story "is detached from the author at birth and goes about the world beyond his power to intend about it or control it," its meaning independent of all intention.[29] They go on to propose the intentional fallacy, after which the thread is taken up in the 1960s and 1970s by semiotic and poststructuralist theorists who conceptualize the Author as merely a shorthand rhetorical conceit, a figure of speech that, as Roland Barthes maintains, "[imposes] a limit on that text, [furnishes] it with a final signified, to close the writing."[30] For Michel Foucault, that restriction of expression performs an ideological function "by [impeding] the free circulation, the free manipulation, the free composition, decomposition, and recomposition" of the text.[31] The struggle to liberate prose and poetry from determinate meaning originating from an Author involves a kind of theatricalizing of the paged text, unlocking its potential for the unbounded play of signification.[32] Like the interference of theater artists, managers, and critics, the "death of the Author" paradigm dissolves any hope for the writer of agency over the work. Copyright only protects the text and the Author temporarily before the inevitable transformation of writer into puppet. Read in this context, *Shakes Versus Shav* is not only the culminating meditation on, but a final resolution to, a lifelong struggle for aesthetic autonomy.

> O excellent motion! O exceeding Puppet!
> —*The Two Gentlemen of Verona*[33]

According to the preface, *Shakes Versus Shav's* originated not in Shaw's imagination but in the puppets themselves. Lanchester constructed Shakes and Shav and sent them along with a "request for one of [his] famous dramas," a gesture that suggested to Shaw that he was "finished . . . as a playwright."[34] Neither that reaction nor his choice of this genre to explore the playwright's beleaguered lot is surprising, considering that one of the central conventions of the English puppet play is the lack of a fixed script. Like commedia dell'arte, the medium is resiliently antiliterary and vibrantly performative, rooted in an oral tradition in which scenarios are passed down through the generations, the performance texts "with each new generation . . . [evolving] to mirror events, personalities, and popular songs of the time."[35] Rendered irrelevant, the vulnerable playwright is displaced by a solitary storyteller who exerts an envious amount of dominance over the text. Not subject to the will of producers or actors, all of the scriptural and performance elements in theory are, as historian George Speaight asserts, the "direct projection of the performer's dramatic sense, and the show stands or falls by the personality of the man inside."[36] *Shakes Versus Shav*'s "Punch-and-Judy" idiom tacitly evokes the view that Shaw's dramaturgy was merely a puppet regime, populated by, as one of the critics in *Fanny's First Play* asserts, stand-ins "stuck up to spout Shaw."[37] The trend for marionette cabaret, newly resurgent during the late 1940s when Shaw wrote *Shakes Versus Shav*, was for the operating puppeteer to be clearly visible to the audience. Al Hirschfeld's famous artwork advertising the original production of *My Fair Lady* epitomizes this view of Shaw as puppet master manipulating Rex Harrison's Henry Higgins and Julie Andrews's Eliza Doolittle.

In *Shakes Versus Shav*'s preface, Shaw extols the virtues of puppets as performers, echoing his preference for single-handed characterization. Sally Peters finds the play's genre especially apt, considering "a puppet theater unhampered by the sensuous presence of flesh-and-blood actors more closely approximates the intellectual theater Shaw has long sought."[38] Exploiting the puppets' ability to "survive treatment that would kill live actors,"[39] *Shakes Versus Shav* provides a graphic illustration of a playwright's preference for bridled stage signifiers in its rendition of Macbeth's famously *offstage* decapitation. In the Shakespearean original, Macduff slays the Scottish king, carries the body out, and returns with his head. The logistical awkwardness of this sequence is a result of conventions of the early modern stage, particularly the lack of a curtain and of artificial lighting. Shaw demonstrates the superiority of puppets in not only solving the problem of representing a beheading but providing a creative solution to removing one of the only stage corpses in the Shavian canon. The headless Macbeth rises and comments, "I will return to Stratford: the hotels are cheaper there"; then he "picks up his head and goes off to the tune of the British Grenadiers."[40] The character's grotesque resurrection makes clear that, in essence, the puppet is a tool, an object whose animation solely and wholly is a function of the master's subjectivity. It is a writer's prop, lacking the live actor's body and subjectivity, which potentially disavows authorial direction.

Shaw's most brilliant sleight of hand, demonstrating ingenious dexterity at what manufacturers nowadays call branding, was his creation of GBS, a surrogate persona he conceives within the tradition of a commedia archetype. "It was as Punch," Shaw wrote, "that I emerged from obscurity ... to be the most humourously extravagant paradoxer in London."[41] In 1911, he deemed his successful authorial camouflage of *Fanny's First Play* during its first production a "secret de Polichinelle."[42] The impish puppet Shaw imagines the critic-dramatist to be seems far removed from the insecurities and impotencies of Shakes and Shav. Rather, his metonymic characterization gestures to the hand inside the glove, to what he calls "the actor" performing "a fantastic personality fit and apt for dealing with men."[43] As Sally Peters observes, the moniker suggests "someone famous enough to need only initials for identification [yet also] the absence of a name, veiling a secret name, even a secret self."[44] As such, "G.B.S." simultaneously obfuscates the author and asserts his total mastery, a puppet through which the master could ventriloquize his ideas and ward off those forces that threaten the integrity of the intended meaning. Shaw's page voice replicates this autocracy within his published volumes, in which he pulls all the strings, inside ("G.B.S.") and outside (Shaw) of the dramatic text simultaneously.[45] In stage practice, however, this unusual level of command for the dramatist is never realized, even in Shaw's only puppet play.

If, in *Shakes Versus Shav*, playwrights are on the ropes, the puppeteer's authority is also unexpectedly in crisis. Its preface opens on a note of trepidation that the evolution of "stagecraft into filmcraft" threatens to cause "the death of puppetry[, by taking away] its charm with its magic."[46] Shaw is apprehensive over the encroachment of technology on the genre, which will result in an audience distracted from appreciating the master's solitary technical skill and "completely illuded" by "simulations of live performers" against "scenic backgrounds of the cinema."[47] In other words, the theatrical text no longer proceeds from a stable, singular origin, a master synthesizing every element; instead, the live performance is at the mercy of ostentatious spectacle to which the master's real-time puppetry must conform. Shaw particularly laments the displacement by soundtracks of "the old puppet master [who] spoke all the parts himself."[48] As an example, the audience of the initial productions of *Shakes Versus Shav* experienced Macbeth's posthumous comment via prerecording, and the moment uncannily anticipates Samuel Beckett's *Rockaby* (1980) in its staging the splitting of the subject, the divorcing of voice and body. This dissociation of authorial voice from textual body is emblematic for what is at stake first at the writer's death and later at the end of copyright. Like all puppets, Shakes and Shav are objects posing as subjects, fitting emblems of the author's uncertain posthumous ontology, grasping in vain at artistic autonomy.[49] Circumscribed to a degree by a soundtrack, the puppet in performance is a more conflicted production element than the genre theoretically guarantees, one that, like a human actor, can potentially assert and undermine the playwright's authority.

As much as Shaw rhapsodizes about the genre's centrifugal authorial figure in its preface, *Shakes Versus Shav* deliberately departs from convention in other ways, seemingly self-aware of the impossibility of total authorial control. Pointedly, as written, it is impossible for a single master to perform. In a traditional puppet booth, "to keep the action going, and avoid leaving the stage empty, . . . the chief character [must]remain in sight of the audience . . . while a succession of other characters is introduced [so that] it is not possible to have more than two figures in view at a time."[50]

Shakes Versus Shav requires Shakes and Shav to behold the skirmish between Macbeth and Rob Roy as well as the *Heartbreak House* tableau, necessitating either multiple puppeteers or the very sort of intrusions of technology the preface denounces. The most puzzling dramaturgical feat for which the script calls is a "transparency suddenly lit up" that renders Captain Shotover and (presumably, since he oddly does not identify her by name) Ellie Dunn in tableau "as in Millais' picture called North-West passage."[51] The description, as well as the subsequent reference to the effect as a "picture," suggests a still life, yet the stage direction calls for Shotover to "raise his hand" as he "intones" his lines, eliminating the possibility of a projected slide image. The precise medium here is puzzling since, say, a puppet booth is not usually equipped with a scrim masking an inner stage. The possibility also exists that Shaw might have in mind a "televised" image accompanied by the recorded voices of "first-rate speakers."[52] In any case, though, *Shakes Versus Shav* itself fails to embody the dream of the master's unified text and mandates the kind of "reformer" puppeteering Shaw identifies as lethal to the form. The practical impossibility of total authorial mastery is already a foregone conclusion, and the playwright finds himself on equal footing with his characters, unable to own his words, to enforce the boundaries of his realm. The friction of *Shakes Versus Shav* proceeds from this central paradox of Shaw, as Sally Peters describes it, as "both puppet and puppetmaster, subject (acting) and object (acted upon)."[53]

Fie, fie! You counterfeit, you puppet, you!"
—*A Midsummer Night's Dream*[54]

The second half of *Shakes Versus Shav's* preface focuses on the Shakespeare authorship question whose persistent existence attests that vaulted acclaim does not dispel the exigencies of authorship. As Peters notes, in spite of the fact that "Shakespeare alone has the place in history that Shaw supposedly longs for," Shakes is "the aggressor" in the play, the "prosecuting plaintiff."[55] The dangers of open textual borders are nowhere more starkly realized than in the baleful trespasses against the work of that most institutionalized and idolized of playwrights. At times, Shaw objected to those who altered the plays, often as if their crimes were perpetrated against the man as well as the work. For instance, he characterized Henry Irving's *Cymbeline* as a "disemboweling," a word that conflates the author's body with the play's textual body, and more generally described the process of stage adaptation of Shakespeare's works as "one of debasement and mutilation," an "extremity of misrepresentation" from which only the "living author can protect himself."[56] By contrast, as Sonya Freeman Loftis remarks, "Shaw's sustained attack on Shakespeare's canon attempts to erase elements of Shakespeare's works with which Shaw disagreed,"[57] situating him within the long tradition of Shakespearean refashioning that he frequently repudiated. For instance, Shaw's 1937 revision of *Cymbeline* results in a last act that, as Joseph Wood Krutch put it, "all of the characters talk like Shaw rather than like themselves."[58] Reconceiving the fifth act "as Shakespear might have written it if he had been post-Ibsen and post-Shaw instead of post-Marlowe,"[59] Shaw's desire to fashion a post-Shaw Shakespeare masks a fantasy of producing the Author he wants as critic as well as the ability, writing as a "post-Shaw Shakespeare," of extending authorial control postmortem to craft his legacy.

A decade later, aiming to affirm the figure of the single author, Shaw in the preface to *Shakes Versus Shav* delivers a "knockout [to] Bacon-Shakespear and all the other fables founded on that entirely fictitious figure."[60] Destroying the image of the Bard, he argues, underwrites all rival claims, that of "an illiterate clown and poacher who could hardly write his own name,"[61] Shaw wishes to restore the authority of the "authentic" Shakespeare, a "well read grammar-schooled son in a family of good middle-class standing."[62] Yet the writing is mindful enough to realize that the latter, like characters in his *Cymbeline* revision, is a thinly disguised, self-serving Shavian simulacrum: "Nothing can extinguish my interest in Shakespeare [because his biographical details] are just like my own[,] Stratford-upon-Avon . . . a supplementary birthplace of my own."[63]

This identity-blending extends into the play as well in that the grappling authorial effigies are not as distinct as the binary title would suggest. Shakes's complaints against Shav, for example, sound awfully similar to GBS's early criticisms of Shakespeare when he accuses the Bard of being a "pretentiously platitudinous pilferer of other men's stories and ideas."[64] If Shakes is a self-caricature of the angry critic-dramatist, Shav is a version of his Stratfordian target, the reified author getting credit for other people's stories. Although the preface concludes with confirmation that Shaw and Shakespeare are separate, their surrogates embody their fortune as Time's puppets, when authors themselves become text and are not immune to refinishing. For Bernard Dukore, the protracted fray "concludes without a victor[, moving] from litigation to [an] accommodation between the disputants [that] places [Shaw] in Shakespeare's company, but not surpassing him."[65] What begins as a squabble over plagiarism and evolves into a contest of artistic superiority ends in the recognition of the irreversible succession of the future, replete with an ever-advancing army of ambitious younger playwrights and the promise of eventual self-extinction.

> Belike you mean to make a puppet of me.
>   *—Taming of the Shrew*[66]

If *Shakes Versus Shav* in the end is a reluctant concession to forces that seek to challenge the author's master control, the loss is offset by a more expansive perspective in the form of Shav's vision of the future, itself a patchwork repurposing of lines from three Shakespeare plays:

> Tomorrow and tomorrow and tomorrow
> We puppets shall replay our scene. Meanwhile,
> Immortal William dead and turned to clay
> May stop a hole to keep the wind away.[67]

Hamlet's musing on the irony of mortality is here applied to the death of the author, whose decayed body becomes the clay that seals the broken wall. For the deceased writer, copyright enables the same posthumous preserving of *textual* borders, protecting what is inside from what Hamlet calls "the winter's flaw."[68] William can thus be dead and immortal simultaneously.

As Shakes has discovered, though, any immunity of intrusion is short-lived, and the play portrays the successful annihilation of transgressive new dramatists to be perversely myopic. At its end, the Bard seems to emerge victorious, blowing out Shav's light, and the preface similarly concludes with

Shaw extinguishing the "feeling that the real Shakespear might have been myself."[69] But, rather than modeling a fantasy wielding of authorial authority in perpetuity, *Shakes Versus Shav* deftly undercuts what appears to be a triumph of the will.

Shakes Versus Shav is complicit with those literary scholars crafting the author's obituary in its satire of the quixotic vanity of playwrights and their futile mucking around for mastery. Shav's lines contain the distant echo of Othello's angry renunciation of his former self and faith, when he refers to cannons who "counterfeit . . . immortal Jove's dread clamours." Shaw's interpolation casts the overreaching authorial claims emerging from the "rude throats" of playwrights as the arrogant bounding of "mortal engines."[70] The poor author struts and frets his hour upon the stage and then is heard no more, his fury drowned out by the sound of his own swirling authorless language. Their vain short-sightedness is illustrated when Shakes's blowing out of the candle vanquishes *both* figures, not simply Shav, and quite literally ends the play with what Sally Peters refers to as a "[nihilistic] curse of darkness and final silence."[71] Within this genre, there is finally no room for playwrights. According to Speaight, puppetry produces "a drama that has no author, for—as every puppeteer knows—the puppets have a way of imposing their actions and their own personalities upon the performance."[72] Granville Barker argued that point about all theater, noting that "drama's peculiar and triumphant gift to us—that hour or so of complete illusion—is only to be gained by the dramatist's suppression of himself for the time being in favour of his characters and the actors of them."[73] Shaw's claim to have learned "part of [his] craft as conductor of rehearsals . . . *from* puppets" intimates that they embodied for him the rough magic of stage creation.[74] In *Shakes Versus Shav*, the puppets incorporate at once playwrights, critics, actors, character, and even audience, all the players with a stake in the theatrical text at and in play.[75] Conspicuously lacking Macbeth's sense of futility, Shav's forward reaching "tomorrows" suggest that the future of drama lies within the endless replaying of the puppets' scene, what Shaw calls, the "marvel that never pales."[76]

In the foreword to his revision of *Cymbeline*, Shaw reflects that he "[stands] in the same time relation to Shakespear as Mozart to Handel, or Wagner to Beethoven": "Like Mozart, I have not confined myself to the journeyman's 'additional accompaniments'; I have luxuriated in variations."[77] *Shakes Versus Shav* leaves behind the pretense of intact intention and implies that true durability lies within the theatrical encounter itself, the vital luxury of its infinite variations. It intimates that the erasure of living playwrights animates rather than inhibits textual play, sets the puppets in motion, and recasts individual mandate into collaborative and sundry meanings. As the plays enter the public domain in the twenty-first century, we are faced with the same question that confronted the playwright at the end of his life: What will Shaw look like post-Shaw? Rather than providing a specific answer, *Shakes Versus Shav* refuses to affirm the possibility of master control and instead celebrates contention itself. Without Shav's pilfering advances, Shakes and theater itself cease to endure. Forgoing the dead-end pursuit of hermetically packaged artistic texts, the play expresses a renewed faith in the political and artistic productivity of the wrangling revisions, in the vigorous acrobatics of stage signification. Put another way, as we ponder the implications and witness the contemporary permutations of "Immortal Bernard Dead," for Shaw, the thing's the play.

NOTES

1. Bernard Shaw, *Heartbreak House* and *Misalliance* (New York: Bantam, 1995), 38–39.

2. Bernard Shaw, "Preface" in *Plays Pleasant*, ed. Dan H. Laurence (New York: Penguin, 1993), 14.

3. Shakespeare, *The Tempest*, in *The Norton Shakespeare*, 2nd ed., ed. Stephen Greenblatt, Walter Cohen, Jean E. Howard, and Katharine Eisaman Maus (New York: W. W. Norton, 2008), 5.1.36, 50.

4. Bernard Shaw, "The Author's Gamble," in *The Times* (1/18/1949, Issue 51282), 5. In the letter, Shaw asks the Exchequer to either harmonize rates for all gamblers or restore an earlier arrangement in which authors were taxed based on averaged income and excused from a crippling surtax.

5. Bernard Shaw, *Shakes Versus Shav*, in *The Portable Bernard Shaw*, ed. Stanley Weintraub (New York: Penguin, 1985), 691. *Shakes Versus Shav* was first performed in August 1949 at the Malvern Festival, opening in London two years later for eight posthumous performances at the Riverside Theater in June 1951 and later at the Lyric Theatre in December 1953.

6. Ibid., 694, 693.

7. Ibid., 696. The allusion also slyly recalls Shaw's 1907 statement at Brighton: "Life's no 'brief candle' for me. It is a sort of splendid torch which I have got hold of for the moment; and I want to make it burn as brightly as possible before handing it on to future generations."

8. P. A. W. Collins, "Shaw on Shakespeare," in *Shakespeare Quarterly* 8, no. (Winter 1957): 1.

9. As examples, Bernard F. Dukore and John Bertolini both provide solid critical overviews of the short play; see Dukore, *Shaw's Theater* (Gainesville: University of Florida Press, 2005), 226–68, and Bertolini, *The Playwrighting Self of Bernard Shaw* (Carbondale: Southern Illinois University Press, 1991), 169–71. Sally Peters's thorough and articulate commentary posits *Shakes Versus Shav* as "the culmination of a

lifetime identification with Shakespeare" in which the earlier playwright "functions as an alter ego, a second self to Shaw the creative playwright." See Peters, "Shaw's Double Dethroned: *The Dark Lady of the Sonnets, Cymbeline Refinished*, and *Shakes Versus Shav*," in *SHAW 7: The Neglected Plays*, ed. Alfred J. Turco Jr. (University Park: Penn State University Press, 1987), 312, 302.

10. Shakespeare, *Antony and Cleopatra*, in *The Norton Shakespeare*, 2nd ed., ed. Stephen Greenblatt et al., 5.2.205–7.

11. Margot Peters, "*The Millionairess*: Capitalism Bankrupt?" in *SHAW 7: The Neglected Plays*, ed. Alfred J. Turco Jr. (University Park: Penn State University Press, 1987), 247.

12. Shaw, "Preface," in *Plays Pleasant*, 14.

13. Bernard Shaw, "Preface," in *Plays Unpleasant*, ed. Dan H. Laurence (New York: Penguin, 1946), 22.

14. Shaw, "Preface," in *Plays Pleasant*, 10.

15. Ibid., 11.

16. This ambivalence comes to govern Shaw's existence. Beginning with the American production of *The Devil's Disciple*, Shaw's economic success increasingly put him in a paradoxical position, having by the 1930s "acquired the position of a gentleman, and [living] very comfortably on other people's earnings." See Bernard Shaw, "Preface" to *The Simpleton of the Unexpected Isles* in *Plays Extravagant* (New York: Penguin, 1981), 139. As Margot Peters points out, Shaw "found himself living the profoundly contradictory life of the theoretical communist in a capitalist economy whose techniques he was exceptionally able to exploit." See Peters, "*The Millionairess*: Capitalism Bankrupt?" in *SHAW 7: The Neglected Plays*, ed. Alfred J. Turco Jr. (1987), 247.

17. Bernard Shaw, *Fabian Essays in Socialism* (New York: The Humboldt Publishing Company, 1891), 156, 129.

18. Katherine E. Kelly, "Imprinting the Stage: Shaw and the Publishing Trade, 1883–1903," in *The Cambridge Companion to George Bernard Shaw*, ed. Christopher Innes (Cambridge: Cambridge University Press, 1998), 50.

19. Shaw, "Preface," in *Plays Unpleasant*, 25.

20. Ibid.

21. Ian Clarke, *Edwardian Drama* (London: Faber and Faber, 1989), 96.

22. Bernard Shaw, *Our Theatres in the Nineties*, in *The Works of Bernard Shaw* (London: Wm. H. Wise and Company, 1930–38), 14:141.

23. Shaw, "Preface," in *Plays Unpleasant*, 21.

24. Shakespeare, *Hamlet*, in *The Norton Shakespeare*, 2nd ed., ed. Stephen Greenblatt et al., 3.2.225–6.

25. Donald E. Pease, "Author," in *Critical Terms for Literary Study*, ed. Frank Lentricchia and Thomas McLaughlin, 2nd ed. (Chicago: University of Chicago Press, 1995), 111.

26. Harley Granville Barker, *The Study of Drama* (Cambridge: Cambridge University Press, 1934), 60–61.

27. Bernard Shaw, *Fanny's First Play*, in *Shaw and His Contemporaries: Four Plays*, ed. Denis Johnston (Oakville, Ontario: Mosaic Press, 2001), 83.

28. Margery M. Morgan, *The Shavian Playground: An Exploration of the Art of Bernard Shaw* (London: Methuen, 1972), 261.

29. W. K. Wimsatt and Monroe C. Beardsley, "The Intentional Fallacy," in *The Verbal Icon: Studies in the Meaning of Poetry*, ed. W. K. Wimsatt (Kentucky: University of Kentucky Press, 1954), 5.

30. Roland Barthes, "The Death of the Author," in *Falling Into Theory: Conflicting Views on Reading Literature*, 2nd ed., ed. David H. Richter (New York: Bedford/ St. Martin's, 1999), 256.

31. Michel Foucault, "What Is an Author?" in *Language, Counter-Memory, Practice*, ed. Donald Bouchard (Ithaca: Cornell University Press, 1977), 119.

32. Many scholars have noted how Shaw anticipates poststructural notions of authorship and polyvalent textuality, always presenting himself self-consciously as, in Peter Gahan's words, "a paper author, a fictional shadow[,] . . . a product of his writing." See Gahan, *Shaw Shadows: Rereading the Texts of Bernard Shaw* (Gainesville: University of Florida Press, 2004), 22–23.

33. Shakespeare, *Two Gentlemen of Verona*, in *The Norton Shakespeare*, 2nd edition, ed. Stephen Greenblatt et al., 2.1.84.

34. Shaw, *Shakes Versus Shav*, 691.

35. Peter Fraser, *Punch and Judy* (London: B. T. Batsford, 1970), 7.

36. George Speaight, *Punch and Judy: A History* (Boston: Plays Inc., 1970), 116.

37. Shaw, *Fanny's First Play*, 141.

38. Sally Peters, "Shaw's Double Dethroned," 314.

39. Shaw, *Shakes Versus Shav*, 691.

40. Ibid., 695.

41. Shaw, "Preface," in *Plays Unpleasant*, 9.

42. Shaw, *Fanny's First Play*, 83.

43. Bernard Shaw, *Preface* to *Immaturity*, in *The Complete Prefaces*, ed. Dan H. Laurence and Daniel J. Leary (New York: Penguin, 1993), xlvii.

44. Sally Peters, "Shaw's Double Dethroned," 310.

45. In contemporary theoretical terms, Craig Owens notes that the brilliance of Shaw's paratextual material turns upon the deployment of "the Derridean *supplement*, the figure of speech and writing, and indeed the effect of language as a system, that allows the displaced to construct and maintain a kind of both-ness, an identity that oscillates between outside and inside." See Craig N. Owens, "Exorbitant Appartus: On the Margins with Shaw, Beckett, and Joyce," in *SHAW* 30: *Shaw and the Irish Literary Tradition*, ed. Peter Gahan (University Park: Penn State University Press, 2010), 192.

46. Shaw, *Shakes Versus Shav*, 692.

47. Ibid.

48. Ibid.

49. I borrow Andrew Sofer's phrasing when he reiterates in his essay the argument of his book *The Stage Life of Props* that the "ventriloquized skull on the Jacobean stage [is] an object posing as a subject." See Sofer, "'Take up the Bodies': Shakespeare's Body Parts, Babies, and Corpses," in *Theatre Symposium* 18 (2010): 136, 139.

50. Speaight, *History of the English Puppet Theatre*, 182.

51. Shaw, *Shakes Versus Shav*, 696.

52. Ibid., 691.

53. Sally Peters, "Shaw's Double Dethroned," 314.

54. Shakespeare, *A Midsummer Night's Dream*, in *The Norton Shakespeare*, 2nd ed., ed. Stephen Greenblatt et al., 5.1.36, 50.

55. Sally Peters, "Shaw's Double Dethroned," 314, 308.

56. Shaw, "Preface," in *Plays Unpleasant*, 20.

57. Sonya Freeman Loftis, "Shakespeare, Shotover, Surrogation: 'Blaming the Bard' in *Heartbreak House*," in SHAW 29: *The Annual of Bernard Shaw Studies* (University Park: Penn State University Press, 2009), 53.

58. Joseph Wood Krutch, *The Nation*, 11 October 1947), 388.

59. Bernard Shaw, "Foreword," in *Geneva, Cymbeline Refinished and Good King Charles* (London: Constable and Company, 1946), 136.

60. Shaw, *Shakes Versus Shav*, 693.

61. Ibid., 692.

62. Ibid.

63. Ibid., 692–93.

64. Charles A. Berst, "New Theatres for Old," in *The Cambridge Companion to George Bernard Shaw*, ed. Christopher Innes (Cambridge: Cambridge University Press, 1998), 61.

65. Dukore, *Shaw's Theater*, 228.

66. Shakespeare, *Taming of the Shrew*, in *The Norton Shakespeare*, 2nd ed., ed. Stephen Greenblatt et al., 4.3.102.

67. Shaw, *Shakes Versus Shav*, 696.

68. Shakespeare, *Hamlet*, 5.1.199.

69. Shaw, *Shakes Versus Shav*, 693.

70. Shakespeare, *Othello*, in *The Norton Shakespeare*, 2nd ed., ed. Stephen Greenblatt et al., 3.3.360.

71. Sally Peters, "Shaw's Double Dethroned," 314.

72. Speaight, *History of the English Puppet Theatre*, 183.

73. Barker, *Study of Drama*, 60–61.

74. Shaw, *Shakes Versus Shav*, 691.

75. Writing to Clunn Lewis in 1913, Shaw indicated that living actors should imitate the puppets' model of "suggestions and illusion" and avoid the "fatal" tendency to put forth "a too industrious effort to imitate and simulate every action or symptom of emotion instead of merely setting the audience to work to imagine it." This vision of theater necessitates the imaginary forces of the audience, something Shaw feels gets sacrificed in the dramaturgical turn toward cinema. See Stanley Kauffmann, "George Bernard Shaw, Twentieth-Century Victorian," in *Performing Arts Journal* 10, no. 2 (1986): 57.

76. Shaw, *Shakes Versus Shav*, 691.

77. Shaw, "Foreword," 137.

"Well, I'm Dashed!"

Jitta, Pygmalion, *and Shaw's Revenge*

PETER CONOLLY-SMITH

Jitta's Atonement, Bernard Shaw's 1922 adaptation of his German-language translator Siegfried Trebitsch's best-known play, *Frau Gittas Sühne* (1920), stands apart in the Shavian oeuvre as Shaw's only translation. Yet this twice-written tale of marital infidelity, death, mourning, and atonement commands little space in the volumes of Shaw scholarship, perhaps because, as Myron Malaw observes, "it is . . . the least known of Shaw's full-length plays."[1] The few critics to have considered the play all agree on the thrust of its metamorphosis, in Shaw's hands, from a bourgeois "Victorian melodrama" to a Shavian comedy characterized by irony, wit, and comic realism.[2] Shaw himself, in his introductory "Translator's Note," claimed he had produced a "comedic British version" of an originally "romantic tragedy" pervaded by a Viennese-inflected "melancholi[a]."[3] In addition to the play's often commented-upon move from tragedy to comedy, several critics have further noted Shaw's higher degree of emphasis on the erotic and especially the psychological dimensions of the play, the latter acknowledged by both Elisabeth Knoll in her German-language monograph, *Produktive Mißverständnisse*, and by Peter Gahan in his article, "*Jitta's Atonement*: The Birth of Psychoanalysis and the 'Fetters of the Feminine Psyche'"—works that respectively constitute the lengthiest analyses of the Shaw-Trebitsch collaboration, and of the play, to date.[4]

Yet no critic so far has examined *Jitta's Atonement* within the context of Shaw and Trebitsch's complex personal and professional relationship. "It is safe to assume that no text of Shaw's was written entirely disinterestedly," Gahan observes, noting that Shaw "was interested in the task quite apart from the challenge of translating the theatrical genre of romantic tragedy into that of serious Shavian comedy." Gahan's effort to explain Shaw's reasons for choosing to translate this of all of Trebitsch's plays considers *Jitta* in the context of Shaw's own work at the time, his interest in psychoanalysis (in which milieu the play is set), and his desire to examine this emerging science through a Shavian lens.[5] It is the concluding section of his analysis, however, in which Gahan sketches out the argument that Shaw's play represents an effort to perform a literary act of transgression (via translation) akin to Frau Gitta's marital transgression of infidelity, upon which the present essay seeks to build and expand.

Much as Gitta, in the play, cheats on her husband (a plot synopsis follows), so Shaw "cheats" on Trebitsch's original text by changing its ending. In so doing, this essay argues, Shaw exacted belated revenge on Trebitsch, whose own translation of *Pygmalion*, their last major collaboration prior to *Frau Gitta's Sühne*, had similarly changed the thrust of that play's ending. Indeed, the German-language *Pygmalion*, Shaw felt, obscured the fact that Eliza and Higgins part ways at play's end, instead leaving the audience at the 1913 Vienna world premiere with the impression of an impending romantic union.[6] This misperceived happy ending, which still haunts *Pygmalion* today, vexed Shaw for the rest of his life.[7] His analogous violation of *Frau Gittas Sühne*'s ending—from tragic to happy—evened the score. Moreover, *Gitta*, during the period of its translation and its later English-language production history, also served Shaw as a vehicle for vicarious revenge against others who, he felt, had wronged him in the context of *Pygmalion*. These wrongs ranged in magnitude from contractual disagreements over the film rights to *Pygmalion* to the greatest emotional affront he ever suffered: Mrs. Patrick Campbell's rejection of his romantic overtures during the rehearsals for the first English-language *Pygmalion*, in 1914.

Frau Gittas Sühne

At face value, little seems to connect the frothy *Pygmalion* and the maudlin *Frau Gitta*. Yet given the various violations Shaw felt his own play had suffered, *Gitta*'s themes of infidelity and breach of faith make the two plays interesting, if unlikely, companion pieces.

Set in an unnamed "major city ... [in] the present," according to Trebitsch's stage directions, *Gitta*'s Act I opens in the apartment psychologist Bruno Haldenstedt keeps for his secret trysts with Gitta, the wife of his colleague and collaborator Alfons Lenkheim.[8] The curtain rises on Frau Billiter, the landlady, as she tidies the place and wards off the nosy inquiries of a flower girl delivering roses that Bruno has ordered. Bruno himself enters moments later, out of breath from having taken the stairs in an effort to avoid the inquisitive eyes of the elevator operator. A "very distinguished" looking character in his "late forties," visibly shaken by the physical exertion—the stage directions repeatedly describe him "clutching his chest"—Bruno suffers from an unnamed heart condition (Trebitsch, 4, 5). Mrs. Billiter departs, and Gitta enters the scene: "a very beautiful woman of approximately thirty-three years of age, with large expressive eyes, a noble, almost tragic face" (Trebitsch, 6). The two lament the forced surreptitious nature of their love, yet while the childless Gitta is an unrepentant mistress whose marriage is so meaningless that she feels a closer connection to Bruno's daughter, Edith, than she does to her own husband, Alfons, Bruno feels guilt toward his family as well as his cuckolded friend and colleague.

To atone for his faithlessness, Bruno has devised a plan whose realization he entrusts to Gitta: a book he has completed, *Hemmungen der weiblichen Psyche* ("Fetters of the Feminine Psyche"), and which he expects to become an important contribution to psychology, he now plans to bequeath to Alfons after his own death, which Bruno feels is imminent. "The work has been completed. A typescript lies in my desk," its title page bearing Alfons's name. "I burned my hand-written manuscript, thus they will find *his* work among my papers: your husband's work" (11–12). Gitta is horrified and resists Bruno's morbid plan, but he insists: "Yesterday I felt rejuvenated upon having finalized and sealed the decision. I now feel that I have atoned for my debt to him, and am liberated and at ease" (12). After much remonstrating on Gitta's part, and much rationalizing on Bruno's—who points out that Alfons did in fact modestly contribute to his work, and will be inclined to accept the posthumous gift because of his desire to leave a mark in his field—Gitta reluctantly agrees. Bruno then reveals a second decision: that this is to be their last meeting. His health is so fragile that he can no longer risk seeing her, lest she find herself in a compromising situation with a dead body. More remonstrations, more noble resolve, but this time Gitta prevails. Dismissing his fatalism, she appeals to his physical desire: "We live still; your blood yet surges to mine. Let us . . . live—live." Carried away, Bruno "half deliriously" agrees to "hold [her] once more in [his] arms, drinking [her] gaze, feeling [her] kiss" (16, 15). As she leads the way offstage, however, he is overcome by his heart condition. Standing on the threshold of the boudoir, he slumps dead to the ground. Gitta returns, "sobs convulsively" over his body, then, gathering herself, flees the scene (16–17).

If the ending of Act I sounds melodramatic, the confrontation that concludes Act II approaches near-hysteria. Its opening finds Alfons Lenkheim,

Gitta's husband, at home in conversation with Dr. Fessler, Bruno's former assistant and also his daughter Edith's betrothed. While one level of dramatic irony has been achieved and awaits resolution (so far, only the audience knows the identity of Bruno's secret lover, whose flight from the scene of his death has become the subject of much gossip and speculation), another is now introduced. As the two men discuss the mysterious circumstances of their colleague's death, Fessler tells Alfons that these same circumstances have driven a wedge between Bruno's widow Agnes—his future mother-in-law—and her daughter, Edith. Unbeknownst to Agnes, Edith "knows or at least suspects the full truth," and is consequently hurt by her mother's failure to take her into her confidence (18). Gitta, who has taken ill for the few days that have passed in the interim, enters with tragic demeanor, followed soon after by the widowed Agnes, young Edith in tow, come to inform Alfons that Bruno has selected him to be the executor of his estate. Agnes hands over a mysterious package addressed to him, found in Bruno's desk. As she and Alfons retire to discuss estate-related matters, Gitta commiserates with Edith, but does not reveal her identity as Bruno's mistress. During the conversation, Edith confides her knowledge of the circumstances of her father's death and the extent of her alienation from her mother. She articulates her heartfelt desire to meet the mysterious woman who, she believes, gave her father a love he was unable to find at home.

After Edith leaves with her mother, Alfons, alone with Gitta, unwraps the package Agnes has left. He is aghast at its contents. As Gitta gently tries to persuade him to accept Bruno's bequest, it becomes clear that Alfons disagrees with the book's thesis: Bruno "knew perfectly well that I was only waiting to posit my own theories in challenge to his, to show that he erred" (37). As Gitta continues trying to persuade him despite his misgivings, he becomes suspicious at her persistence and, in a scene of intense verbal confrontation, realizes that she is the mystery lover: "It was you! Yourself! You sold me! And with that [he gestures toward his desk] he planned to pay for his sin. That thief!" (39). Gitta confesses, then announces her willingness to end the marriage. Alfons instead insists that they remain together for the sake of appearances, though he vows never to speak to her again: "There need be no spatial separation. One can be terribly separated, yet under the same roof. This is the separation I demand of you" (42). Gitta agrees, but only if he in turn promises to honor Bruno's will and take on the book as his own. With this agreement, the curtain falls.

Act III, finally, to varying degrees resolves the two levels of irony (will Agnes realize that her daughter knows? will Edith learn the identity of her father's lover? will anyone else?) by revealing parts of the truth to different characters. The act, set at Agnes's, opens with her obsessive desire to unmask Bruno's lover and her equally resolute refusal to let her daughter in on "the awful truth"—which Edith already knows. When Fessler (who of course *knows* she knows) helpfully suggests that he ease Edith into the circle of knowledge, Agnes responds hysterically, "no, no, no. She can and must never know any of this" (47). Equally intense is Agnes's desire to find the book Bruno claimed to have been working on during the last years of his life—little knowing that she has already handed it to Alfons. Its absence raises troublesome possibilities in Agnes's mind: "Where is it? What became of it?" And, if it does not exist: "what did he do with all those hours" supposedly spent working on it (45). When Edith reveals to her mother that she has known all along "where and how my father died," Agnes's distress is complete: "[sobbing]: . . . the child too is besmirched . . . This is the final straw" (53). Fessler, who plans to become a future member of the family and, as such, had hoped to reconcile mother and daughter in this matter, reproaches Edith: "You have robbed her of her last peace of mind" (53). Criticizing the manner in which Edith condemns her own mother yet idealizes a mistress she has never met, and who may yet turn out to have been unworthy of her father's love, he earns Edith's enmity. She breaks off the engagement, thereby ending Fessler's role in the play.

That same argument, however—that the mistress may have been unworthy—is what finally brings comfort to long-suffering Agnes. Both Alfons and Gitta assure her that it matters not who the mistress was, as she cannot have been deserving of Bruno's love (48–49, 59). To have "left [Bruno] in his hour of need," Gitta argues, to have chosen *not* "to be found at his side," casts aspersion on a mistress who, in Gitta's self-flagellating words, must have been a "woman of no consequence" to him (59). Finally at peace, and knowing Gitta's influence over Edith, Agnes asks that she persuade her daughter in like manner. Instead, in what is the play's emotional climax, Gitta—though she tries in vain to follow this line of argument—reveals herself to Edith as the mistress, and the two fall into each other's arms. The shared knowledge of this secret finally frees Edith to "be a comfort to my mother, and you [Gitta] now have a daughter too" (66). Thus Gitta brings peace to both mother and daughter: by telling one what she wants to hear; the other, the truth.

In a final twist, Alfons, having witnessed the scene, announces after Edith's exit that he no longer feels bound by their agreement. Nor Gitta, who, given these new circumstances, demands that he restore Bruno's legacy: "Give his heirs what is rightfully theirs" (67). Alfons instead threatens to burn the manuscript, but is prevented from doing so by Gitta as the reconciled mother and daughter enter arm-in-arm:

GITTA: I have joyous news. The book you have so desperately been
seeking has finally been found . . .

ALFONS: [*Looking hard at Gitta*] My wife has preempted me. Yes, dear
friend, you can put your mind at ease. (69)

As Agnes and Edith rejoice over this last turn of events, Gitta, in her final
sacrifice, asks Alfons to take her home, thereby accepting the prospect of a
lifelong, loveless marriage. Curtain.

The *Pygmalion-Jitta* Connection

As remote from one another in tone and subject matter as they are, there are
many odd parallels between the production histories of *Gitta* and *Pygmalion*.
Pygmalion had been the subject of Shaw and Trebitsch's correspondence
around the time of the outbreak of World War 1—whose "uncertain mail . . .
and . . . censor's knife" led to a prolonged hiatus in their communication—
while *Gitta* became its subject almost immediately thereafter. In one of his
earliest postwar letters, Shaw inquired, "what about your own plays?"[9] By May
1920, Trebitsch had sent him his recently premiered *Frau Gittas Sühne*, and
soon thereafter Shaw's translation work began.

Like *Frau Gitta's*, *Pygmalion's* world premiere had been at the Vienna
Hofburgtheater, seven years earlier, in 1913. It had been arranged, Trebitsch
believed, "as a token of [Shaw's] gratitude for the . . . services I had rendered
him" as his faithful translator of ten years' standing.[10] In fact, Shaw had
toyed with the notion of opening one of his plays in German translation for
some time, and consented to the Vienna premiere of *Pygmalion* in part to
snub the English critics who had long bedeviled him. "It is [their] custom . . .
when a play of mine is produced, to inform the public that it is not a play—
that it is dull, unpopular and financially unsuccessful," he explained (Weiss,
170 n. 3). Furthermore, Shaw recognized the potential boon of opening
on one of Europe's most prestigious stages and, hopefully, receiving positive reviews there. His gamble paid off. Successful at the Hofburgtheater,
Pygmalion went on to celebrate one hundred performances at the Lessing-
theater in Berlin, and was subsequently produced—still in translation—on
New York's German immigrant stage as well as in a number of other locales
before moving to London's His Majesty's Theatre in April 1914. And as Shaw
had hoped, the English newspapers, "knowing how successful the play had
been abroad, were less condescending . . . than they would have been."[11] Far
from it: *Pygmalion* disarmed Shaw's critics and once and for all established
his reputation as Britain's foremost living playwright.

Following *Frau Gittas Sühne*'s own premiere at the Hofburgtheater in 1920, it too had gone on to Berlin and (in Shaw's translation) to New York, before finally being produced in England. Despite these parallels in what Samuel Weiss calls this "neat reversal of roles"—Shaw translating his translator—*Gitta*, unlike *Pygmalion*, drew little positive attention; it played only seven nights in Vienna, less still in Berlin, then effectively flopped in both the United States and England.[12] Undoubtedly, Shaw had wished to help Trebitsch by translating *Frau Gitta*, but, as Myron Matlaw observes, the truth is that, although "it is the best-known among Trebitsch's works, it is perhaps the . . . poorest of Shaw's," failing both commercially and critically despite (and in part because of) Shaw's contribution.[13]

Pygmalion's success, in contrast, owed no small debt to Trebitsch. He had not only translated it, but, as Shaw's agent in the German-speaking realm, arranged for its productions in both Vienna and Berlin, which in turn consolidated the play's reputation, and Shaw's, worldwide. Inadvertently, however, Trebitsch may have incurred Shaw's resentment in the process, for the above-mentioned false assumption that the play's ending promised a Higgins-Eliza romance can be traced back to these earliest German-language productions. Both the Viennese and Berlin critics agreed that, though *Pygmalion*'s ending was ambiguous, Eliza and Higgins were undoubtedly destined for one another.[14] It was precisely such reviews that moved Shaw in his prose sequel to later inveigh (to little avail) against the "'happy endings'" that "misfit all stories." So strong was the presumption of a happy ending that even the 1914 English-language premiere, directed by Shaw himself, suffered the consequences of its foregone conclusion, as have most versions since (Shaw, 4:782, 787).[15]

Thus the success of *Pygmalion*, the play that marked "the climax of his career as a writer of comedies," according to Michael Holroyd, was based at least in part on a near-universal misunderstanding of Shaw's intent. "I have never been able to stop the silly and vulgar gag with which Eliza in Pygmalion, both here and abroad, . . . implies that she is going to marry [Higgins]," he complained.[16] Given what he took to have been Trebitsch's role in creating this false impression, Shaw may have relished the opportunity, one year after he penned the above lament to William Archer, to attach a happy ending of his own to a Trebitsch play, thereby changing, as he acknowledged in his introductory "Translator's Note," "the key in which it ends" (5:723).

The enduring resentment Shaw felt toward Trebitsch for his role in contributing to *Pygmalion*'s misunderstood ending survived in the context of another recurring tension between them: that over Trebitsch's repeated efforts as agent to strike deals that ran counter to Shaw's explicit contractual instructions.[17] Years later, after Shaw had purchased the rights to (the

English-language) *Jitta's Atonement* from Trebitsch, this recurring issue in their relationship came to a head when Shaw refused to agree to unfavorable terms Trebitsch had negotiated for an American film adaptation in 1937, a refusal Shaw justified because, he wrote, Trebitsch was "incapable of managing [their] affairs properly" (Weiss, 358).

While Trebitsch expressed bitterness over the failed negotiations ("I shall never forget Shaw this break of friendship," he wrote privately), the attentive reader of their correspondence will note that it was around the same time that they exchanged harsh words over a second film deal gone wrong (360): the 1935 German-language screen adaptation of *Pygmalion*. Like all cinematic versions of that play, the German film ended with the by-then universally assumed suggestion of a romantic union of Henry Higgins and Eliza Doolittle, an interpretation Shaw continued to oppose, and an ending his screenplay (translated by Trebitsch, of course) had explicitly denied (360).[18] For some time after the release of the film, which Shaw "detested," he had believed that sole responsibility for "falsify[ing] all the characters, put[ting] in everything I left out, and t[aking] out everything I had put in" lay with German producer Eberhard Klagemann. In a letter dripping with irony, Shaw wrote Klagemann that "there was really no need to put my name to [the film]" because, given its many departures from the original—"breaches of contract," every one—he really "had nothing to do" with it.[19] When Shaw later found out that Trebitsch had personally acquiesced to the objectionable changes, he was furious, accusing his translator of knowingly "deceiving me," not only "for the last thirty years"—evidence of Shaw's ability to bear a grudge—but also "for the last thirty weeks," during the period of negotiations and production of the German *Pygmalion*. It is important to add that much of Shaw's language in his voluminous correspondence with Trebitsch was tongue in cheek (including this letter's parting shot: "you . . . have no conscience whatever"). Still, the letter in its broader context provides one of many examples of Shaw's continued suspicion that Trebitsch was no more able to accurately translate his work than he was to enforce Shaw's famously strict contractual demands (354).[20] Perhaps, given his exasperation, it is no coincidence that he dashed Trebitsch's own hopes for a film deal for *Jitta* the following year.

The German-language *Pygmalion* and the controversy over its ending had also been on Shaw's mind at the time of his completion of the first draft of his translation of *Frau Gittas Sühne* some fifteen years earlier, in 1921. In the letter to Trebitsch enclosed along with the play, Shaw ended a lengthy reflection on character motivation, casting, staging, and other considerations with the following postscript: "I have just received . . . a copy of your translation of Pygmalion in Fischer's edition"—S. Fischer was Shaw's German-language publishing house, with whom Trebitsch was also under contract. "It is incomplete, lacking the prose sequel" (228). Trebitsch's omission must have irritated Shaw considerably. His prose sequel to *Pygmalion*, added to the English edition in 1916 along with a revised ending and a number of subtle but important changes to the play's dialogue, established more clearly that Eliza and Higgins do part ways at play's end, that Eliza marries Freddy, and that she does not return to her mentor-Pygmalion figure.[21] Thus Trebitsch's failure to add the sequel may have seemed to Shaw to constitute further evidence of their working at cross-purposes. Had he bothered examining the German edition more closely, he would have found that all his more subtle textual changes, and even the new ending, were also omitted from Trebitsch's version. While Trebitsch did add the sequel (and a later preface) to a special 1926 German-language edition timed to coincide with Shaw's receipt of the Nobel Prize, Shaw's various changes and revised ending remain absent from all extant versions of Trebitsch's translation, a circumstance that—had Shaw realized it—would surely have infuriated him.[22] Aware as he was, in any case, of the omission of his all-important sequel in 1921, Shaw now reciprocated, in his version of Trebitsch's play, with what, in their correspondence, he referred to as "tricks" and "outrages" enacted upon the text of *Frau Gitta*, and which, in his "Translator's Note," he acknowledged as nothing less than a "translator's treacheries"—a telling choice of words, given his own frustration over Trebitsch's past "crimes" (Weiss, 213, 233; Shaw, 723).

To repeat, Shaw surely wished his translator and oldest collaborator well, and was sincere in his efforts over the years to see *Jitta's Atonement* yield a profit, fruitless though those efforts remained. At the same time, however, the various "tricks," "outrages," and "translator's treacheries" he committed in the process of his translation—first and foremost changing Trebitsch's "tragic" to his own "happy ending"—mirror some of the offenses Shaw felt Trebitsch had committed against himself in the context of *Pygmalion*.

"Stella!"

As striking as the parallel between the ways in which the two plays' endings changed from those originally intended by their creators is a biographical parallel between the action of *Jitta's Atonement* and earlier events in Shaw's own life—a parallel that may in fact have drawn Shaw to *Frau Gitta*'s subject matter in the first place, and that may help explain his choosing it over *Ein Muttersohn* and *Gefährliche Jahre*, two earlier Trebitsch plays whose translation Shaw had considered but abandoned.[23] *Frau Gitta*'s main subject is infidelity and the penalty it incurs: Gitta's life sentence to a marriage on her unforgiving husband's terms, on which dismal note the play ends. Viennese tastes, Shaw later opined, were stuck in the nineteenth century, knowing "no gloom too deep to please the audience[;] . . . the more dreadful it all is the better it is liked"—all of which justified his changes, he felt, as "a play written under the tyranny of [such] a romantic audience . . . will miss its mark" on the English-language stage (5:722–23). Thus, in his version, the play ends both comically and on a note of compromise between the two estranged spouses. While a full reconciliation is unlikely, an understanding is hinted at; as in Trebitsch, theirs will likely be a marriage in name only, but perhaps one that is not of lasting mutual hostility: "In the original play Jitta lives miserably ever after," Shaw explained, and "her husband bears malice [whereas] . . . I could not help suggesting . . . that the ill-assorted pair settle down on reasonable human terms, and find life bearable after all" (723). This new ending was justified by virtue of what he believed to be "the fortunate circumstance that in real life the consequences of conjugal infidelities are seldom . . . so serious as they are assumed to be in romantic tragedy" (723).

Shaw knew whereof he wrote. His own infatuations were well known to his wife, Charlotte, and to their friends—sometimes even to the public. To Trebitsch, he wrote (as much in a comment on his recent completion of *Jitta* as in reference to his personal experience, it seems) that "nine-tenths of . . . adulterers end in reconciliations, and even in the connivance of the injured party at its continuation" (Weiss, 225). The latter was as true of Gitta's cuckolded husband's insistence on remaining married as it was of Charlotte's forgiving nature when it came to her own spouse's infidelities. As Shaw's friend and fellow Fabian Beatrice Webb observed of the Shaws' marriage at the time of his completion of *Pygmalion*, in 1912, "he and Charlotte are outwardly on the best of terms." Yet their marriage at that time, writes Michael Holroyd, was a mutual "conspiracy of denial," as Shaw emerged from the one infatuation that left his wife truly "devastated," and which may still have been on his mind eight years later, while working on *Jitta's Atonement*: his famous and highly public flirtation with Mrs. Patrick Campbell, who played Eliza in the London production of *Pygmalion*, and for whom Shaw had written the play.[24] The affair, albeit unconsummated, was erotic in that it placed them both—Shaw in particular—in a state of sustained sexual arousal that expressed itself in an outpouring of creativity, much of it channeled into their correspondence.[25]

Though Trebitsch in faraway Vienna may not have known of Shaw's personal feelings for Mrs. Campbell, he noted that *Frau Gitta* "made a strong impression" on Shaw "when he was told the plot," and that it "somehow fascinated him," if for reasons Trebitsch could or would not explain.[26] Certainly, he had been fully apprised of Shaw's plans to cast Stella Campbell in the role of Eliza as early as June 1913, three months prior to the Vienna premiere, when Shaw "quietly dropp[ed]" her name in correspondence (164 n. 2). By then, she was on the verge of ending their romance, a circumstance that complicated their collaboration on the London production the following year. Ironically, Mrs. Campbell had begun to feel jealous of Charlotte (the wife), as if she herself (Stella Campbell) were the wronged party—a dynamic Shaw later added to his version of Trebitsch's play.[27] Shaw himself, though angered when the liaison reverted to a purely friendly, creative partnership, was simultaneously plagued by guilt over the anguish he was causing his wife: it gave him "a sort of angina pectoris," he wrote Mrs. Campbell before the breakup. "It hurts me miserably to see anyone suffer like that."[28] Interestingly, Shaw in *Jitta* identified the mysterious heart condition afflicting Trebitsch's Bruno—another philandering husband—as precisely that ailment. When, in Act I of Shaw's *Jitta*, an out-of-breath Bruno is chastised by the landlady of his and Jitta's love nest—"How often have I begged you never to walk upstairs but always to take the lift? And now see the state you are in!"—he replies, "Don't look at me: it will only distress you. Angina pectoris is a horrible thing" (5:728).

That Mrs. Campbell was still on Shaw's mind while he was translating *Frau Gitta* years after the relationship is further indicated by his repeated, compulsive mentions of her in his letters to Trebitsch. On one occasion, indulging imaginary casting choices while negotiations for the American production of *Jitta* were under way, Shaw wrote to Trebitsch that "Mrs. Patrick Campbell . . . would have been a wonderful Gitta fifteen years ago" (Weiss, 232).[29]

Shaw and Trebitsch: Oedipus v. Pygmalion

If *Jitta's Atonement* reveals much about Shaw's unresolved feelings toward the women in his life—Charlotte and, especially, Stella Campbell, on whom more anon—it casts even more telling light on his conflicted relationship with Trebitsch, yet another Galatea to Shaw's Pygmalion. That Shaw identified with Higgins is so self-evident that few critics bother belaboring the point. Brilliant and admirable in many ways, yet dictatorial, vain, and immature, Shaw's most fully envisioned and engaging male character shares many personality traits with his creator. Higgins, writes Arnold Silver, is Shaw's "surrogate," turning Shaw, in turn, into Pygmalion. Thus

Mrs. Campbell becomes the likely stand-in for Eliza, Higgins's Galatea—who hasn't "an idea that I havnt put into her head or a word that I havnt put into her mouth . . . I have created this thing out of the squashed cabbage leaves of Covent Garden" (4:767)—a theory explored by Silver at length.[30] To limit the Galatea role to one person, however, is to miss the point that to Shaw, all the world was of his making. Confident to the point of vainglory, Shaw looked upon most (with the exception of great creative geniuses of his own caliber) as his intellectual inferior. Critics, actors, manager-directors, fellow socialists, enthusiasts of vegetarianism, boxing, and phonetics: all alike could learn from the master-teacher Higgins-Shaw, not least among them Siegfried Trebitsch. Indeed, from the outset, the Shaw-Trebitsch relationship bore all the hallmarks of a Pygmalion-Galatea, parent-child dynamic.

"Shaw's experience in professional, personal, and literary affairs, alongside Trebitsch's inexperience and naïveté," writes Knoll, "led to theirs resembling a teacher-student relationship. Shaw was from the start the counsel for all of life's situations, though he frequently trivialized his translator's personal problems and offered recommendations that often contained more irony and black humor than sound advice."[31] Most frequently, Shaw articulated his sense of superiority through scathing criticism of Trebitsch's occasionally faulty translations, in particular during the early years of their collaboration. The second source of major disagreement between them, however—Trebitsch's lax enforcement of Shaw's contractual demands— endured throughout their relationship, to be joined in later years, when Trebitsch was short of money, by disagreements over his reimbursement. "Again and again," Knoll observes, their correspondence "engaged in written combat, during the course of which Trebitsch, like a schoolboy," was subjected to Shaw's "tirades."[32] Indeed, in numerous letters to Trebitsch, including many that do not dwell on faulty translations, contracts, or financial disagreements, Shaw berates, ridicules, lectures, and in other ways patronizes his translator.

Of course, Shaw's perennial disgruntlement was an often-mocked mainstay of his public persona that often disguised the genuine affection he undoubtedly felt for Trebitsch and many others whom he subjected to the lacerations of his pen. Also, and despite his vanity, Shaw had a realistic sense of how insufferable he was, and cheerfully injected a dose of critical self-parody into his multiple public selves—much as he gave Higgins personality traits bordering on the ridiculous. Others, of course, criticized Shaw at their own peril, though the closer they were, the more truthful they were allowed to be. Trebitsch was unquestionably part of that privileged, inner circle. "Keep on reproaching me," Shaw encouraged him: "It . . . amuses me" (Weiss, 407).

Furthermore, Shaw publicly defended and praised Trebitsch on numerous occasions—most famously in the preface to the first German-language collection of Shaw's plays, in 1911, in an essay published in English under the title, "What I Owe to German Culture."[33] In their personal correspondence, however, Shaw would as often begin with praise ("your translations . . . have a certain charm of style and character that cannot be purchased for money or contrived by corrections & the like") before launching into blistering criticisms at times so lengthy that even he ran out of steam: "I have no room for more; but this is only the beginning" (26–27). In a variation of this epistolary game of carrot and stick, Shaw again and again encouraged Trebitsch's own literary efforts ("But why don't you write plays of your own?") knowing full well that the volume of work his translator faced made this nearly impossible (17).[34] Adding insult to injury, Shaw in 1913 let slip—albeit in reference to his French translator, Augustin Hamon, who was by far worse than Trebitsch—that he would have preferred to employ as translators only writers who were accomplished authors in their own right, but that, "whoever has something to produce himself doesn't translate" (166 n. 2). This comment must have hurt Trebitsch, who felt that he had given up a promising career to become, in what he considered "a horrible expression," merely "'Shaw's translator.'"[35] Shaw's reassurance to Trebitsch, following his 1913 quip regarding Hamon ("you have 'given your proofs' [i.e., published works of his own]: besides, I am going to translate a play of yours; so we shall both be tarred with the same brush") offers an early indication of the planned collaboration that was ultimately to come to fruition with *Jitta's Atonement* (166).

For all the long-contained resentment one discerns in Trebitsch's later memoir, published only after Shaw's death—"My name as a writer in my own right . . . faded away," he complained—the fact is, he willingly assumed the Galatea role.[36] As Judith Woodsworth observes in her analysis of Trebitsch's description of his and Shaw's first meeting, when the young Austrian arrived uninvited on Shaw's doorstep to propose that he become his translator, the starry-eyed Trebitsch felt that he had reached the destination of a "pilgrimage." Shaw, in turn, in his "Translator's Note," referred to young Trebitsch as his future "apostle."[37] Thus was established from the outset a dynamic that persisted for the duration of the two men's association: Shaw, the self-assured master-teacher, Trebitsch, the reverential disciple.

In September 1920, Shaw sent Trebitsch the first draft of Act I of *Jitta's Atonement*. Regarding its ending, when Bruno dies of a heart attack during the ill-fated rendezvous that opens the play, Shaw commented that he had been "horribly tempted to make [Bruno's corpse] sit up after Gitta's departure, and make [it] a comedy"—which is of course precisely what he did, if without bringing Bruno back from the dead (213). Despite the already foreseeable thrust of the adaptation Shaw had in mind, however, Trebitsch was delighted. It was a "great joy" reading Shaw's version of his work, he wrote back, surrendering his own claim to its provenance: "please do put your name on [it]." Immediately assuming his position as son to Shaw's father, he testified to his feeling "a childish delight reading Trebitsch in English." Shaw's version was "grand and again proves your stage-genious [sic]," everything about it being "much clearer [and] convincing" and indeed, "much better than the original" (217–18). In fact, Trebitsch appears to have internalized and in his correspondence reified his inferiority to Shaw. Some weeks later, after Shaw had sent him all three acts' worth of dialogue, now revealing the full extent of his revisions—which in addition to the altered ending included many farcical elements throughout—Trebitsch, though "puzzled very much reading your bold alterations," nevertheless swept aside any doubts he may have felt. Full of praise for Shaw's adaptation, which he found "clever" and "more comprehensible" than his own play, and which, with only minor exceptions, he "approve[d] . . . fully," he concluded that "your version is as much better than mine as you are the greater poet of the two of us" (228–29). His actual reservations ("the III. A[c]t is in your version almost a comedy!") were expressed to Shaw only this once, in passing, and were not articulated publicly until after Shaw's death, when, in his memoir, Trebitsch lamented how Shaw had made the play "more like a comedy than a drama . . . convinced that it was quite essential to brighten [it] up . . . for Anglo-Saxon audiences." Though one detects faint oedipal rumblings in his complaint that, in so doing, Shaw had taken "liberties that he himself would scarcely have forgiven his translator," he again, just a few sentences later (and even from the safety of this *post-mortem* vantage point) reverted to type, for, "as so often happens in life, once again Shaw turned out to be right"—an admission with which he surrendered once and for all to the dynamic Shaw had established between them in one of his earliest letters: "*I am never wrong. . . . I am omniscient and infallible*" (36).[38]

Jitta's Atonement

Though expressed in his trademark tongue-in-cheek manner, Shaw's sense of superiority over Trebitsch was in dead earnest, and to him justified the liberties he took with his translator's text. These seemed further justified by the poor reception the original *Gitta* had received in both Vienna and Berlin. The Viennese *Neue Freie Presse*, for example, faulted Trebitsch for his unnecessarily "baroque plotting," and observed that "the thirst for redemption displayed by sinful Gitta lacks all intellectual motivation," while her husband suffered "so many unsympathetic traits, such a glut of repellently nuanced defects, that the scales of Frau Gitta's own failings are unreasonably weighted in her favor."[39] Berlin's *Vossische Zeitung* was more damning still, following *Gitta's* opening there: its "plot resolves only in the most superficial manner, and only barely," the newspaper remarked. The kindest thing it could muster was that Trebitsch, "famous, if not always praised, for his translations of Shaw," had in this play wisely "withstood any temptation to fill [Shaw's] boots."[40] Such reviews render all the more pathetic Trebitsch's repeated claims, in his memoir, that "the first night . . . at the Burgtheater was a great success"—"a *real* success," as he emphasized elsewhere, compared to some of his even less well-received, earlier efforts— "as was also the Berlin first night."[41]

Shaw, if he was aware of these reviews as he worked on his translation, may have felt emboldened to change the play as he saw fit. Indeed, the worse the play fared on the Continent, the greater his license to change it in preparation for its hoped-for success on the English-language stage, a fate that would, in turn, have constituted a fitting repayment for Trebitsch having helped make *Pygmalion* a success ten years earlier, albeit with an ending other than the one Shaw had in mind. Not that Shaw waited until this play's final scene to depart from Trebitsch's intent: In *Jitta's Atonement*, completed in October 1922, he did so from the first sentence of his opening stage directions. The time in Shaw is "*1920*," already the recent past, rather than Trebitsch's "present"; the place, "*The drawing room in a flat in Vienna*," instead of Trebitsch's more generic "major city" anywhere (725). If indeed Shaw felt that Vienna suffered obsolescent tastes in theater, as he had written in his "Translator's Note," anchoring the play there in time and place may have signaled his condescension. As likely, he also wished to give *Jitta* a greater specificity of setting. Numerous other nods to the timeframe of the early 1920s reinforce this impression. Repeatedly, he has Agnes and Jitta (Shaw changed her name so that English-language audiences would not mispronounce it as having a hard "G") refer to Bruno's book as one destined to make its author's name as famous and great "as Einstein['s]"—recent winner of the Nobel Prize in Physics (773, 778). Later, in response to Agnes demanding that Edith tell her how she came to learn the truth about her father's death, Shaw has Edith exclaim, "Do you suppose any girl of my age nowadays does not know more than you were ever taught," thereby invoking two of the great cultural preoccupations of the early 1920s: the generation gap (though not yet so called) and young people's knowledge and interest in sexual matters (785).

Shaw's frank treatment of sexuality is apparent throughout. Whereas Gitta in Trebitsch offers to "cool [Bruno's] temples" to alleviate the guilt he feels over their affair (11), Shaw's Jitta more meaningfully *"draws him towards the bedroom"* (737). After having been persuaded against his better judgment to engage in one last tryst, Trebitsch's Bruno waxes romantic on the doorstep before slumping pathetically to his death (16); in Shaw, his heart attack is brought on by actions louder than words: *"He seizes her round the hips, and lifts her exultantly"* (744). When Jitta, having gone ahead, emerges from the bedroom to find his prone body, she responds with histrionics similar to those of her German-speaking counterpart, but does so in a state of dishabille, flashing a *"half-naked breast"* (745). Later, when Jitta's husband tries to appease Agnes's demand for the missing book by offering one of Bruno's unfinished lectures "on varieties of sleep," found among his papers, Agnes snaps, "I know the variety of sleep he learnt from her!" (782). At the same time, Shaw has Agnes indulge a hint of transgressive sexuality of her own: "I have had thoughts myself about the young men at our college sports"—a possibility Trebitsch never thought to entertain (791).

Shaw, in contrast, revels in the characters' sexuality, and as usual operates as much through dialogue as by way of description. Returning to his opening stage directions, typically Shavian in detail, he hints at the flat's purpose by way of its décor: the pictures on the wall are of an *"aphrodisiac character"*; the apartment itself, though *"elegantly furnished"* is *"not homelike,"* as it is not lived in at all; nor is it *"quite like a hotel sitting room; because there is very little furniture,"* although *"a bed with rose-colored hangings"* is conspicuously visible through an open door to the adjoining room (725). The landlady, Mrs. Billiter, who in Trebitsch has little to do but coo sympathetically over Bruno's poor health, in Shaw displays equal degrees of matronly concern and business acumen. A cross between *Pygmalion*'s Mrs. Pearce and the infamous Mrs. Warren, Mrs. Billiter's duplicity is also revealed by way of stage direction: *"Her hair, though not aggressively dyed, is still rather younger than her face"* (726).

Bruno, however, is made older, if subtly so: no longer in his "late forties" as in Trebitsch, he is in Shaw "on the verge of fifty" (728)—an odd distinction, unless one allows that Bruno might have been a stand-in for Higgins here, whom in 1912 Shaw had described as a "man of forty or thereabouts" (4:685). Thus Higgins would in 1920 indeed have been approaching his fifties, which had also been Shaw's general age at the time of his romance with Mrs. Patrick Campbell, as he repeatedly reminded her in his letters at the time.[42] Evidence that *Pygmalion*—and therefore his affair with Mrs. Campbell—was never far from Shaw's mind while completing *Jitta* is found not only in the frequency of his mention of her in correspondence with Trebitsch, but also in the text of the play itself. If, in Trebitsch, the otherwise inconsequential character of the nosy flower girl serves only to awaken Mrs. Billiter's sense of discretion, Shaw has her enact a knowing tribute to the scene in *Pygmalion* in which Eliza unsuccessfully attempts to gouge Pickering for some change. Eight years later, this flower girl too speaks *"in an accent* [that] *is not that of a lady,"* Shaw writes. She too hangs around waiting for a tip, and, having received one from Mrs. Billiter (after all, "the gentleman . . . promised"), tries to extract another from Bruno upon his arrival:

> *The gentleman enters. The girl ogles him. He recognizes her, and makes a gesture towards his pocket.*

> MRS BILLITER: [*very decisively*] Thats all right, sir, she's had what you promised. [*To the girl, sternly*] Good evening to you. [*She sails to the door so formidably that the girl, after an ineffectual grimace, has to go.*] (5:727)

Though subtle, a similarity to the analogous scene in *Pygmalion* is undeniable (4:682–83). Add to this Shaw's angina pectoris reference as well as Bruno's admission that it takes but "one throb of [Jitta's] breast" to break his "iron resolutions"—a reminder that Shaw had first fallen for Mrs. Campbell after "she took my hand [and] shook it so that it touched her bosom," as he liked to recount—and the notion that Shaw was projecting his own (alter-) ego into the scene becomes quite plausible (5:743).[43]

If Shaw identified with Bruno, however, he did not sugarcoat him. Indeed, in the same way in which he had once inserted an element of (self-) ridicule into Higgins, he also reveals some of Bruno's more ludicrous aspects: his morbid preoccupation with his imminent death is far more pronounced than in Trebitsch, for example, as is his vanity and self-importance in believing that he has "converted" Alfons (called Alfred by Shaw, perhaps to "avoid some of the original name's comic resonances"),[44] and that Alfred will therefore willingly claim Bruno's work as his own (735). In fact, unlike Trebitsch's Alfons, who merely disagrees with Bruno's thesis, Shaw's Alfred pronounces it "the most utter tommyrot that was ever put forward as a serious contribution to psychology," thereby significantly clouding our perception of the original Bruno's supposed brilliance (805). As for any pretense of nobility, Shaw's Bruno himself reveals the distasteful underpinnings of his bequeathing a book to Alfred in exchange for sleeping with Jitta, which, he concedes, represents merely "the price at which I buy his wife" (740).

In like manner, Shaw systematically inverts the play's other characters, recasting or at least adding to their personalities in ways that highlight how one-dimensional Trebitsch's characterizations had been in the first place. First and foremost, it is Jitta who is deconstructed. All noble self-sacrifice in Trebitsch, in Shaw she becomes

> *. . . one of those attractively refined women whose wistfully sensitive unsmiling mouths and tragic eyes not only make imaginative men fancy unfathomable depths in their natures, and something undefinably [sic] sad in their destinies, but actually force this conception on the women themselves, however commonplace their characters and circumstances may be. Jitta is nothing more extraordinary than the wife of a college don, and has done nothing more heroic than fall in love with another (also married).* (731)

Jitta is immediately revealed to be not only self-important and delusional, but spoiled, egotistical, and (incongruously) jealous of Agnes, as Shaw has her testify twice (730–31, 792), perhaps in an echo of Mrs. Patrick Campbell's earlier fits of jealousy in their own ill-fated affair. In a more positive inversion, Alfred, although described by Shaw as *"pompous"* and *"unctuous,"* not unlike Trebitsch's Alfons, is also at once jovial yet dignified, *"saved from being common, if not from being a little comic, by the stamp put upon him as a man of learning"* (763, 746). In fact, Alfred has some of the play's best lines (all of Shaw's own invention, and many departing significantly from Trebitsch's original). Fessler, a prig and a hypocrite in Trebitsch, is not only reunited with Edith for an over-the-top happy ending, in Shaw, but also displays a sense of humor and a knack for revealing uncomfortable truths (see especially 785–89).[45] Agnes, the wronged woman, yet also a nag and a drudge who in Trebitsch almost deserved to be cheated on, becomes a practical-minded hausfrau, whose obsession with unveiling Bruno's mistress is less motivated by jealousy, in Shaw, than by her conviction that said mistress must have stolen the book, which Agnes considers rightfully hers: "When she ran away she took that book with her . . . the book that [Bruno] said might be my best insurance policy. It was part of his provision for me" (780). Though still a somewhat ridiculous figure, as in Trebitsch, Agnes's status as a widow *"with a home to keep and a family to manage on a slender income"* makes her a distant cousin to *Pygmalion's* equally ridiculous but also sympathetic Mrs. Eynsford-Hill, another widow marked by the *"habitual anxiety of straitened means"* (5:753; 4:723).

Edith, meanwhile, the embodiment of adolescent rectitude in Trebitsch, is taken down a peg by Shaw. Though first introduced as *"young and ingenuous with a strong character,"* not unlike Oscar Wilde's ingénue characters or Shaw's own Vivie Warren, Edith, though she criticizes her mother for "positively wallow[ing]" in her sense of having been wronged, is herself more self-righteous than righteous, and not a little spoiled: "Oh bother," she exclaims, channeling Clara Eynsford-Hill as she stamps her foot when her mother interrupts one of Edith's private tête-à-têtes with Jitta. "Always spoiling everything" (759, 762); and to Jitta, who in one scene displays *the patronizing suavity of an older woman to a younger one*": "Oh these commonplaces! How you keep throwing them at me"; "You need not speak to me like that"; "Why do you treat me as if I were a little girl?"; and, "Please let us have no more of the 'poor child' business"—it is, Edith concludes angrily, "humbug" (756–59).

What becomes apparent, as one reads these lines, all added by Shaw, is the dual level on which they operate: as Edith and other characters, elsewhere, expose the shallow niceties of polite conversation, Shaw himself exposes the contrived nature of melodramatic conventions and their attendant stock phrases. Indeed, when he has Edith complain to Jitta about her use of "commonplaces," Shaw seems to be directing the comment as much at Trebitsch himself ("humbug"!). Likewise, Shaw's stage directions engage in a running meta-commentary on Trebitsch's original, which becomes increasingly obvious if one rereads them. In the scene in which the mourning Agnes and Edith first visit Jitta and Alfred to hand over the sealed manuscript, for example, Shaw describes the action as *"solemn, artificial, and constrained . . . All these movements are ridiculous; yet the mourning worn by the two visitors makes them seem, if not natural, at least becoming"* (753).

This meta-commentary becomes most apparent after Agnes and Edith have left, and Alfred for the first time examines Bruno's book, a scene that, as Gahan also observes, "may, on another level, be read as a burlesque of Shaw's own reading of Trebitsch's play."[46]

> *Turn[ing] over the cover [page] without looking at it, [Alfred] reads a bit, and makes a wry face. He disagrees intensely and contemptuously with every passage he reads, abandoning each with sniffs and pishes, only to be still more disgusted with the next . . . Finally he gives the book up as hopeless, shuts up the pages; and stares at the mass of manuscript as if wondering what he is to do with such trash.* (763–64)

In the end, Alfred, like Shaw, responds to the tommyrot-trash that has fallen into his lap by exposing its triteness and emphasizing its comic, over its tragic, elements. In this role, Alfred gets to articulate more Shavian ironies and utter more witticisms than any other character. Indeed, if in Act I Shaw identified with Bruno by casting the doomed love affair with Jitta as a nostalgic reimagining of his own with Mrs. Campbell, he now, in Acts II and III—following Gahan's characterization of the play as one "long series of displacements"—transfers his projected self-image to Alfred.[47] Wounded and angry upon learning the truth—as Shaw too had been after being jilted by Mrs. Campbell and, later, after her marriage to George Cornwallis West in the midst of the 1914 rehearsals for *Pygmalion*—Alfred bounces back (as did Shaw) and fully collects himself in time for the final curtain. There he has the satisfaction of confessing to Jitta that he too has had affairs—a kind of satisfaction Shaw never registered vis-à-vis Mrs. Campbell in real life, but here vicariously grants to this unlikely Lothario:

> ALFRED: Now dont begin imagining that I am a Don Juan [*a nod to Jack Tanner, another Shaw surrogate*]. To be precise I have kissed other women twice. I was drunk both times. And I had a serious affair with your dear friend Thelma Petersen. That lasted until she and her husband went back to Norway.

> JITTA: Oh, how disgraceful! . . . Alfred: I will never speak to you nor cross the threshold of your house again.

> LENKHEIM: (*more amused than ever*) Except when you call to tell me so. (803–4)

Alfred's last quip deliberately echoes an earlier exchange, after he has learned the truth about Jitta's affair with Bruno, in which only the first line (Alfred's) came from Trebitsch—"Not one word will I ever speak to you again when we are alone together"—while Jitta's witty rejoinder—"Oh, Alfred, you will tell me so ten times a day"—is pure Shaw (772; cf. Trebitsch 42). This most often-cited exchange from this rarely read play—Bernard Dukore wryly identifies it as "a realistic observation on married life"—is routinely listed as evidence of the way in which Shaw turned *Frau Gitta* into a Shavian comedy.[48] It is equally important as a setup for a much later punch line, however (Alfred's to Jitta, toward the end of the play, above; added by Shaw), with which Jitta's husband effectively turns the tables on her, and Shaw, in one fell swoop, vicariously turns the tables on Mrs. Campbell while at the same time ushering in the comic dénouement that was to vex *Jitta* throughout its inglorious performance history—much as he felt Trebitsch had saddled *Pygmalion* with a similar fate.

The unconvinced will remain so. Instead, therefore, of listing each of the remaining odd similarities, parallels, and congruencies between the contents and histories of *Gitta*, *Jitta*, and *Pygmalion*, I will simply conclude the present section as follows: At the end of Act II, Alfred, having unsealed the manuscript, having learned the truth, and having vowed never to speak to Jitta again, returns flummoxed to his desk, picks up the book, "*stares at it for a moment; and reads slowly* . . . 'By Professor Alfred Lenkheim, Doctor of Philosophy in the University of Vienna'" (774). Then Shaw—who, in a literary analogue to Freud's compulsion to repeat, himself believed in the importance of the strategic repetition of words[49]—has Alfred close out Act II of *Jitta's Atonement* with the following expression of bafflement and exasperation: "Well, I'm dashed!"—words last uttered, in the Shavian oeuvre, by Freddy Eynsford-Hill at the end of Act I of *Pygmalion*.[50]

Shaw's Revenge

Had *Jitta's Atonement* experienced anything even remotely close to *Pygmalion*'s success, Shaw's gratification would have been complete; not only would another play of his have succeeded in which he evened the score with Mrs. Campbell—as did the second work he completed during this period, *Back to Methuselah*, as well as a later play, *The Apple Cart*, all at a time during which he, in an ugly dispute, refused to grant her permission to publish his letters[51]—it would also have brought fame and fortune to Trebitsch, while simultaneously teaching him a lesson.

Sadly, there is no evidence of Mrs. Campbell ever having seen *Jitta*, or, therefore, that she even registered its possible nod to their affair. As for Trebitsch, though he took his medicine—"What could I do but agree," he later shrugged—*Jitta* never delivered the rewards he and Shaw had hoped for.[52] After a lackluster world premiere in Stamford, Connecticut, followed by a week in Washington, D.C., the play, plagued by mediocre reviews and bad luck, effectively flopped on Broadway, where it closed soon after the actor portraying Alfred died; no, "really, not dramatically," as Shaw explained to a bewildered Trebitsch: Francis Byrne collapsed one night after the show, having played Alfred for three weeks, and died of a heart attack the following morning (241). "The production, struggling on with two replacements, was withdrawn on 17 February [1923]," Weiss writes, after a total of only thirty-seven performances.[53]

The best the American press had to say was that Shaw appeared to have "remodel[ed]" Trebitsch's original and, in so doing, had "polish[ed] it up a bit, after his own fashion, manipulating the situations . . . and brightening them . . . with copious infusions of his own inimitable but totally irrelevant dialogue," according to the *New York Evening Post*.[54] Even less generously, the *New York Times* pronounced the play "an artificial comedy" with only "one or two situations, and occasional lines where the hand of Shaw is momentarily evident." Yet, alas, "the Shaw is only skin deep." Still, there were generally "capable performance[s]" all around, and at least the lead, an aging Bertha Kalich in an attempted comeback, was "superb in several moments of the play."[55]

A too strong star performance by the female lead, however, had been the one thing Shaw consistently warned of in his communications to Trebitsch and the few managers and producers who tried their hand at the play: such a star, he feared, "will go out of her way to find some worm [to play Alfred] whose powers will not enable him to compete with her," thereby spoiling the effect of Shaw's ending (235).[56] "What I want," he wrote elsewhere, "is . . . two first rate comedians for the widow and Jitta's husband, . . . and that their parts, and the part of the play that belongs to them, are not sacrificed to Jitta's heroics."[57] In vain: having pronounced *Jitta* "a failure under existing commercial conditions in New York," Shaw focused his efforts on a London production. After several false starts, the play was finally produced two years later with another fading star hoping for a comeback, Violet Vanbrugh, at the suburban Fulham Grand Theatre, from where Shaw hoped it might find its way to the West End. He helped rehearse the cast, then went on a trip to Madeira, sending his trusty secretary Blanche Patch to witness the premiere in his stead. "I thought it rather dismal," Miss Patch later recalled. "Can [Shaw], I wondered, see this as a West End success? It never was."[58] The critics amused themselves guessing which lines were Trebitsch's and which Shaw's, and found only the play's third act to offer any "'atonement,' as the *Daily News* put it, for [its] 'portentous dulness' [sic]" (quoted in Weiss, *Letters* 254 n. 2). Trebitsch, never one to allow the facts to cloud his memory, later wrote that the "the play was . . . a success, in London with Violet Vanbrugh and in New York with Berta Kalisch [sic], a success that . . . was even greater that that at the Vienna Burgtheater and that at the Berlin Residenztheater."[59]

When Shaw himself saw *Jitta's Atonement* (for the first time ever) in Leicester, upon his return from Madeira—having concluded an inglorious Fulham run, Miss Vanbrugh was now touring the small-town circuit—he had to admit that it was "still not right," and had suffered "a bad performance . . . I hardly know what to do about the play." Interestingly, he now blamed its failure on "Miss Vanbrugh . . . [who, though] a handsome woman and a lady . . . gathered from the book [i.e., from Shaw's version] that Jitta was an improper person and a hypocrite, and played her accordingly," while the actor playing Alfred had "clown[ed]" up the role—both portraying their characters exactly as Shaw had written them, in other words (255).

Later, Shaw himself conceded this point, in as close to an admission of his own failings as he ever allowed in the whole affair. His version was "Anglicized and vulgarized," he acknowledged. More important, he observed that only if Miss Vanbrugh were to receive "a literal translation of Gitta"—which Shaw now commissioned on her behalf—would she be likely to develop "a better notion of the part. I have spoiled the play horribly" (271). And later: "Unless she reads the original, she will misrepresent the character" (272). Years later still, in 1930, Miss Vanbrugh revived *Jitta*—unsuccessfully. Shaw wrote Trebitsch that the London *Times* "says that I 'have made the play a travesty of what it must have been and made the task of Miss Vanbrugh, as Jitta, quite impossible.' In short, that *I* have spoilt your play, which," he finally admitted unequivocally, "I am afraid is true." Yet in the same letter, Shaw indulged his habit of justifying one of his own faults by citing another he felt he had unjustly sustained. For the main subject of this particular missive was not *Jitta*, but Shaw's anger at Max Reinhardt for (again) taking liberties with one of his own plays—*The Apple Cart*, this time[60]—and his irritation with Trebitsch for (again) taking Reinhardt's side. Thus, even while admitting that his translation *had* "spoilt [Trebitsch's] play," he immediately added, "Serve[s] you right for letting M[ax] R[einhardt] spoil mine"; renewed proof that even at his most humble, Shaw never missed the chance to settle a score (315).

Although he certainly used his plays to exact vicarious revenge, trade swipes, and settle scores both old and new, Shaw, while adapting *Frau Gittas Sühne* from 1920 to 1922, could hardly have been punishing Trebitsch for any treachery committed against the not-yet-written *Apple Cart*. Rather, his self-admitted "tricks" and "outrages" were more likely in retribution for some of Trebitsch's own "past crimes" (213, 233, 354). That many of these were associated in Shaw's mind with *Pygmalion* and its odd road to worldwide success—a matter further complicated by that play's connection to one of his greatest personal humiliations, the unhappy affair with Stella Campbell—may have justified, in Shaw's mind, the liberties he took in *Jitta's Atonement*, liberties that further undermined what little chance the play may ever have had to succeed, as Shaw himself later acknowledged.

NOTES

1. Myron Matlaw, *Jitta's Atonement: Shaw's Adaptation and the Translation of Trebitsch's Original* (Ann Arbor: University Microfilms International), 1979, xvi; other, brief assessments of *Jitta's Atonement* can be found in Eric Bentley, *Bernard Shaw, 1856–1950* (New York: New Directions, 1957), 174; and Bernard Dukore,

Bernard Shaw, Playwright: Aspects of Shavian Drama (Columbia: University of Missouri Press, 1973), 203–11. Judith Woodsworth, "In the Looking-Glass: Bernard Shaw On and In Translation," *Translation, Translation*, ed. Susan Petrilli (New York: Rodopi, 2003), 531–51, considers the play in the context of the practice and theory of translation. The above-listed aside, *Jitta's Atonement*, and its source text receive more detailed consideration in the works listed in note 4 below.

2. Bentley, *Bernard Shaw, 1856–1950*, 174.

3. Bernard Shaw, "Translator's Note," *Jitta's Atonement*, in *Bernard Shaw: Collected Plays with Their Prefaces* (New York: Dodd, Mead All further references to Co., 1972), 5:723. All further references to Shaw's works are to this edition; page numbers (and, where necessary for clarity, volume) are given parenthetically in the text.

4. See Elisabeth Knoll, *Produktive Mißverständnisse: George Bernard Shaw und sein deutscher Übersetzer Siegfried Trebitsch* (Heidelberg: Universitätsverlag Carl Winter, 1992), esp. 189f.; Peter Gahan, "*Jitta's Atonement*: The Birth of Psychoanalysis and the 'Fetters of the Feminine Psyche,'" SHAW: *The Annual of Bernard Shaw Studies* 24 (University Park: Penn State University Press, 2004): 128–65, passim.

5. Gahan, "*Jitta's Atonement*," 130.

6. See Peter Conolly-Smith, "Shades of Local Color: *Pygmalion* and Its Translation and Reception in Central Europe, 1913–1914," SHAW: *The Annual of Bernard Shaw Studies* 29 (University Park: Penn State University Press, 2009), 127–44.

7. On Shaw's lifelong efforts to correct audiences' understanding of *Pygmalion*'s ending, see Peter Conolly-Smith, "Adaptations, Translations, Makeovers: Pygmalion's Journey, from Stage to Screen to *My Fair Lady* and Beyond," *Adaptation Theories*, ed. Jillian St. Jacques (Maastricht, Netherlands: Jan van Eyck Academie, 2011), esp. 184–90.

8. Siegfried Trebitsch, *Frau Gittas Sühne* (Berlin: S. Fischer, 1920), 1. Translation mine, as are all that follow. Further references to Trebitsch's original are to this edition and are given parenthetically in the text.

9. Samuel Weiss, *Bernard Shaw's Letters to Siegfried Trebitsch* (Stanford: Stanford University Press, 1986), 172–73, 182, 207. All further references to this work—both to the Shaw-Trebitsch correspondence and to Weiss's commentary—are given parenthetically in the text.

10. Siegfried Trebitsch, *Chronicle of a Life* (London: Heinemann, 1953), 173.

11. St. John Ervine, *Bernard Shaw: His Life, Work and Friends* (New York: William Morrow, 1956), 458. On the play's pre-London productions, see Conolly-Smith, "Shades of Local Color," 134–38.

12. Samuel Weiss, "Bernard Shaw's Further Letters to Siegfried Trebitsch," SHAW: *The Annual of Bernard Shaw Studies* 20 (University Park: Penn State University Press, 2000), 221.

13. Matlaw, *Jitta's Atonement*, xvi.

14. On *Pygmalion*'s reception in Vienna and Berlin, see Conolly-Smith, "Translations, Adaptations, Makeovers," 181–84.

15. On *Pygmalion*'s reception in London, see ibid., 184–90.

16. Michael Holroyd, *Bernard Shaw, Volume 2, 1898–1918: The Pursuit of Power* (New York: Random House, 1989), 325.

17. Unlike Trebitsch, whom Samuel Weiss has characterized as "eager for production, ready to accommodate and compromise," Shaw himself was famously "inexorable in his terms, and scrupulously attentive to contractual detail." Weiss, "Further Letters," 221.

18. On the German-language screen adaptation of *Pygmalion*, see Bernard Dukore, *The Collected Screenplays of Bernard Shaw* (Athens: University of Georgia Press, 1980), 43–49.

19. Quoted in Dukore, *Collected Screenplays*, 49; letter to Klagemann, quoted in Dukore, ed., *Bernard Shaw on Cinema* (Carbondale: Southern Illinois University Press, 1997), 96–97.

20. Trebitsch himself maintained that the additions and deletions to Shaw's screenplay constituted but "small changes and improvements." Trebitsch, *Chronicle*, 351. Dukore, in *Collected Screenplays*, answers the question, "Why did not Trebitsch interfere [with Klagemann's efforts] or at least tell Shaw what was happening," by observing that, "[a]s a Jew in Nazi Germany, Trebitsch was in no position to register an effective complaint" (49).

21. See Conolly-Smith, "Adaptations, Translations, Makeovers," 184–90.

22. For Trebitsch's sequel, see *Pygmalion*, trans. Siegfried Trebitsch (Zurich: Coron Verlag, 1926), 165–80; cf. *Pygmalion*, trans. Siegfried Trebitsch (Berlin: S. Fischer Verlag, 1920), to which edition Shaw referred. On the various issues raised by Trebitsch's translation of *Pygmalion*, see Conolly-Smith, "Shades of Local Color," 127–44.

23. See Gahan, "*Jitta's Atonement*," 133.

24. Holroyd, *Bernard Shaw, Volume 2, 1898–1918*, 322, 313, 311.

25. See Alan Dent, ed., *Bernard Shaw and Mrs. Patrick Campbell: Their Correspondence* (New York: Alfred A. Knopf, 1952), passim.

26. Trebitsch, *Chronicle*, 184.

27. For Mrs. Campbell expressing jealousy, see, for example, Dent, ed., *Bernard Shaw and Mrs. Patrick Campbell*, 70, 82, 87, 120.

28. Ibid., 128.

29. Shaw indulged in this idle imaginary casting of Mrs. Campbell as Jitta elsewhere, too (see, for example, Weiss, *Letters*, 226); around this same time (1921–22, in the midst of the translation of *Jitta*), he also casually commented to Trebitsch that Mrs. Campbell "has published a lot of my letters in her autobiography" (232), on which, see note 51 below.

30. Arnold Silver, *Bernard Shaw: The Darker Side* (Stanford: Stanford University Press, 1982), 257 and passim, 253–59.

31. Knoll, *Produktive Mißverständnisse*, 30–31. Translation mine, as are all that follow throughout this essay.

32. Ibid., 31. For examples (which, Knoll writes, can be found in "virtually every letter"), see those she cites (from Weiss, *Letters*) on 31 n. 39.

33. "With all due respect to Herr Trebitsch's correctors and biographers," Shaw wrote, "there is no man in Europe to whom I am more deeply indebted or with whom I feel happier in all our relations, whether of business, or art, or of personal honor and friendship." Shaw, "What I Owe to German Culture," *Complete Prefaces*, ed. Dan H. Laurence and Daniel J. Leary, vol. 1 (New York: Penguin, 1993), 344.

34. See also Weiss, *Letters*, 18, 22, 207.

35. Trebitsch, *Chronicle*, 272; see also 97, 125, 144; Trebitsch's sacrifice of his own career is a recurring theme throughout the memoir. However, his sense of the merit of his writing was inflated, Knoll points out; see Knoll, *Produktive Mißverständnisse*, 44–45.

36. Ibid., 273.

37. See Woodsworth, "In the Looking-Glass," 538.

38. Trebitsch, *Chronicle*, 264.

39. *Neue Freie Presse* [Vienna], 4 February 1920, 7; Knoll, 191–92.

40. *Vossische Zeitung* [Berlin], 18 December 1921, 3.

41. Trebitsch, *Chronicle*, 263, 168.

42. See Dent, ed., *Bernard Shaw and Mrs. Patrick Campbell*, 19, 55, 57, 90, 104.

43. Ibid., 59.

44. Dukore, *Bernard Shaw, Playwright*, 203n7. Gahan suggests that Shaw might have changed Alfons to Alfred because the latter name serves as a near anagram for Freud. Gahan, "*Jitta's Atonement*," 152.

45. See Dukore, *Bernard Shaw, Playwright*, 206.

46. Gahan, "*Jitta's Atonement*," 154.

47. Ibid., 160.

48. Dukore, *Bernard Shaw, Playwright*, 205.

49. For Shaw lecturing Trebitsch on the importance of repeating key phrases at key moments of a play, see Weiss, *Letters*, 36.

50. See Bernard Shaw, *Androcles and the Lion, Overruled, Pygmalion* (Brentano's: New York, 1916). This, the original text of *Pygmalion*, published prior to Shaw's later sequel and preface and his various changes, contains Freddy's line, which was among those later amended. At the time of *Jitta's Atonement*, however, the line stood. See 126.

51. See Silver, *Bernard Shaw: The Darker Side*, 261–70; cf. Dent, ed., *Bernard Shaw and Mrs. Patrick Campbell*, 251, 254, 256, 261ff.

52. Trebitsch, *Chronicle*, 264.

53. Weiss, "Further Letters," 241, n1.

54. *New York Evening Post*, 18 January 1923, 7.

55. *New York Times*, 18 January 1923, 16.

56. Interestingly, Shaw had once given Mrs. Campbell near identical casting advice regarding *Pygmalion*. See Dent, ed., *Bernard Shaw and Mrs. Patrick Campbell*, 15–19.

57. Quoted in Lawrence Langner, *G.B.S. and the Lunatic: Reminiscences of the Long, Lively and Affectionate Friendship between George Bernard Shaw and the Author* (New York: Atheneum, 1963), 95.

58. Blanche Patch, *Thirty Years with G.B.S.* (London: Victor Gollancz, 1951), 58.

59. Trebitsch, *Chronicle*, 264.

60. The dysfunctional Reinhardt-Shaw relationship—"the inevitable clash of [a] playwright-genius and [an] acclaimed creative director"—is traced by Weiss in "Further Letters," 244n6.

Taking Sides and Affixing Blame

Polish Stage Productions of Shaw's
Mrs Warren's Profession, 1907–1952

BARRY KEANE

Mrs Warren's Profession is both drama and crypto-pamphlet, wherein high-pitched disputes morph into hyperbole speech asking about prostitution and its causes; the capitalist foundations upon which prostitution is organized, and the rights of women to earn a livable wage. The play's eponymous heroine is a Madame of several continental brothels who began at the inauspicious bottom of society's ladder. The self-management of her business affairs, however, is a Victorian success story, built as it was on the virtues of industriousness, astuteness, thrift, and the ability to make good connections and surround oneself with the right sort of people. What is more, Mrs. Warren has selflessly tended to the upbringing of her only daughter, Vivie, who has grown up to become a brilliant mathematician and who, as the play begins, is contemplating a bright future after having achieved top honors at Cambridge. But if the play commences where mother and daughter have every reason for self-congratulation, their felicity is short-lived. Both are due to spend a pleasant weekend together in their country cottage, but as events transpire the house ends up playing host to a gathering of Mrs. Warren's associates and admirers, both past and present, whose loose-tongued ways will reveal to Vivie the truth about her mother's ill-gotten wealth. However, it is not so much Mrs. Warren's past as her refusal to give up her business interests that will fatally compromise her in the eyes of her daughter.

Shaw wrote this, his self-professed greatest play, in 1893 at the outset of his career as a dramatist. Nevertheless, hardly before the ink had dried on the manuscript, it was refused a licence for performance by the

Lord Chancellor. The play mostly remained in the drawer for another decade before it was briefly staged to a mixed reception at the New Lyric Club on 5 January 1901.[1]

The first night's performance was triumphant, whereas the second and last performance the following afternoon, staged for the benefit of critics and luminaries of the theatrical world, was largely denounced for having attacked the ideals upon which British society was built. *Mrs Warren's Profession* had its first public performance in the United States on 27 October 1905, in the Hyperion Theatre in New Haven, Connecticut, but the production was immediately closed down, having been described as a whole rotten mess of immoral suggestions, and was wished a speedy exit from the boards there and elsewhere.[2] While *Mrs Warren's Profession* was receiving such negative banner headlines stateside, in partitioned Poland the early critical response to the play was entirely positive. And while an errant production almost irreparably distorted this fact, as we shall see the play continued to hold a fascination for Poland's theatrical world, which attempted to grapple with both the issues that underpinned the play and the motivations of its lead characters.

Preempting the play's German premiere by several months, on 2 August 1907 *Mrs Warren's Profession* had its Polish premiere in Warsaw's Mały Teatr [Little Theatre], the city's first private theater of the new century. Run by Marian Gawalewicz, the theater itself had no permanent home but took the chamber room of Warsaw's Philharmonic, which could seat four hundred patrons.[3] With the translated manuscript provided by Wiktor Popławski, the play opened to largely favorable reviews. However, one critic, Jan Lorentowicz, suggested that the play could have been cut down from four to two acts and should have focused entirely on how Vivie absorbs the truth about her origins and upbringing.[4] In turn, Lorentowicz felt that Shaw might have explored better the dogged reasoning behind Mrs. Warren's decision to carry on running her business, particularly when she realizes that this decision will definitively end her relationship with her daughter. The critic regarded these preponderances as largely unanswerable and concluded that both mother and daughter were in fact archetypes of intransigence in a melodrama that was simply hard to fathom. In this respect, Lorentowicz thought that the public had been fed laughter and intrigue, when in fact they had been seeking to be better informed by the issues that Shaw had been looking to raise.[5] Yet for all the expressed doubts as to the perceived inconsistencies of the play, Lorentowicz did contend that the play's realism would ensure it a long life in Poland, and at least in the immediate term his prediction proved correct. Elsewhere, a review in *Tygodnik Ilustrowany* [*The Illustrated Weekly*], initialed J. Kl., hailed the premiere as a de-masking of England's puritanical mores and its exposure of amoral capitalist practices. Indeed, the critic was not surprised in the slightest that the play had been banned in Shaw's adopted homeland, as few in England, he assumed, would have been prepared to hear that they would move heaven and earth to "sell to the highest bidder."[6]

The play was soon taken up by the foremost theatrical director of the age, Tadeusz Pawlikowski, who first staged the play in Kraków's Teatr Miejski [Municipal Theatre]. Pawlikowski's Kraków production, which premiered on 5 October 1907, boasted a new translation (although the preserved manuscript is unsigned).[7] It was unquestionably the most successful of the three stagings of the play in Poland during this era, and the run was extended for a number of performances due to popular demand. Although critic Konrad Rakowski greatly admired both the play and the Kraków production, he was keen to impress upon readers that the play's loose ends should be ascribed to the fact that it was not a new play, but a precursor to greater works by Shaw.[8] What is more, Rakowski contended that in their condemnation of the play, the English had only exposed their ignorance of Continental courtesan drama. Here he gave as an example Victorien Sardou's *Odette*— although one wonders if Rakowski was aware that Shaw had dismissed the French playwright years earlier with the coined term "Sardoodledom,"[9] implying that his plays were empty of ideas.

Two years later, Pawlikowski brought the play to Lwów, where its two performances turned out to be memorable for all the wrong reasons. A late and colorful recounting of the Lwów production can be found in an article that was featured in theater programs from productions of the play staged in the cities of Wrocław (in 1952) and Elbląg (in 1954). The author of this account was actor and director Wiktor Biegański, who, at the time of the Lwów premiere, had been an apprentice member of the cast.[10] Interestingly, Biegański thought that the Lwów performance had been the Polish premiere, indicating either the extent to which Gawalewicz's 1907 production had perhaps already become a forgotten event or simply the degree to which it was unknown to a wider audience at the time.

This production also boasted a new translation, and the annotations on one of the two surviving theater manuscripts show that, months prior to the premiere of the play, the theater manager Ludwik Heller had complimented the translator during a read-through on a job well done.[11] Vexingly, the two extant manuscripts are unsigned, but comparison does indicate that it is a different translation from the Kraków manuscript.

Coming to the performance of the play, which took place on 17 February 1909, it seems that problems began with the cast, who took a very burlesque approach to their characterizations.[12] Ferdynand Feldman, who played Crofts, Mrs. Warren's business partner, conceived his character as a coarse, larger-than-life pimp. Indeed, Biegański suggested that such low-life was all too common on the streets of the city at the time, and that some people in the audience assumed that Feldman had been trying to make an unsubtle point. Indeed, everything the play offered grated on the sensibilities of sections of the audience, who were in any case generally disgruntled about what they regarded as Pawlikowski's hitherto decadent French-leaning repertoire.[13] The audience was unsettled by the way that Frank addressed his father, and also by the fact that the play impugned the reputation of a cleric. All in all, Biegański thought that Pawlikowski had failed to come to grips with the play and, by giving his actors free rein, had lost sight of the values or challenging issues that were central to the play.

The tumult that ensued during the second performance two days later stemmed principally from the fact that some sections of the audience had been spoiling for a fight, particularly right-wing sympathizers who had been stirred up by a review of the play in the conservative newspaper *Słowo Polskie* [*The Polish Word*], which had decried the play's immorality.[14] This same group grew noisy and agitated in the third act when Mrs. Warren and Crofts pay the pastor a visit to his home, and are then guided toward the church. This trampling over sacred ground proved too much for a schoolteacher, a certain Michalski: sitting in the front row, he stood up and demanded that the curtain be brought down on a play that was an offense to the most basic notions of human decency, shouting, "It's a disgrace that such plays are performed on a Polish stage."[15] Others in the rows immediately behind Michalski soon joined him in facing down the stage. But these protesters were not to have it all their way, as students from the university and the polytechnic in the galleries came to the defense of the play and were joined in their out-shouting of the protesters by a strong Jewish contingent associated with the newspaper *Dziennik Polski* [*The Polish Daily*] and who were members of socialist organisations.[16] The commotion that followed lasted twenty minutes and pitched "respect for freedom and free thought" against a determination to defend social norms at all costs.[17] By the time the police had arrived, agitators and defenders were squaring up to each other in isolated pockets of the theater. The police somehow managed to restore order and remove Michalski from the premises. As a gesture of solidarity, some of his supporters followed him out of the theater. However, once order had been restored, the actors carried on—despite a police request that the performance be terminated. However, the cast threw their all into the final act, and Biegański fondly remembered the night as a great piece of theater in every respect. In spite of a full house, with many more having sought entry, the city authorities demanded that all performances cease. Nobody could have predicted that this mini riot would bring the curtain down on *Mrs Warren's Profession* in Poland for the next thirty years.

This long hiatus is explained perhaps by the fact that theaters in the intervening years could choose from the many plays of Shaw's oeuvre, and that Shaw's licensed translator, Florian Sobieniowski, simply never got around to translating *Mrs Warren*. However, his exclusive rights to Shaw's works meant that the other existing manuscripts were effectively confined to their respective archives for posterity.[18]

In celebration of Shaw's eightieth birthday, the play was revived in 1936 and at Teatr Malickiej [Malicka's Theatre], a small theater located on Warsaw's Karowa Street. Vivie was played by the theater's founder and artistic director, Maria Malicka. Historically, this production is important, as it attracted separate reviews from two of Poland's foremost literary figures of the era, fellow Skamander poets Antoni Słonimski and Kazimierz Wierzyński. Słonimski was possibly the first Polish theater critic to ponder Vivie's not fully explainable stance in respect of her mother.[19] He wondered, for example, if Vivie would have been so similarly moved had she discovered that her mother was the owner of a colliery, where every day men sacrificed their health and risked death for a pittance. Słonimski also suggested that Vivie was not at all motivated by moral or societal concerns, and doubted whether the profits derived from her new actuarial profession would be put toward alleviating the lives of the fallen women whose labor had funded her education and hitherto privileged life. Wierzyński, in turn, understood that Mrs. Warren and Crofts were by necessity extreme archetypes who served to illustrate the workings of the capitalist world, whereas Vivie's decision to strike out on her own showed how the pursuit of a fulfilling occupation for people of her sphere negated the need to make moral compromises.[20]

It was perhaps fitting that Lwów, the city that had seen off *Mrs Warren's Profession*, should also play a part in its revival. The production was directed by Wilam Horzyca and came at the end of his turbulent tenure as director of Lwów's municipal theater. In 1924, Horzyca had co-founded with Leon Schiller in Warsaw the Teatr im. Bogusławskiego [The Bogusławski Theatre], where he was content to work as a low-profile literary director and sounding board for Schiller. Both men believed in a literary theater wherein a drama's words were understood as possessing a poetic magic that acted on intuition and the imagination. Horzyca and Schiller proposed, in turn, a monumental theater that would harness the grandiose visions and ideals of Poland's Romantic tradition.[21] In 1931, when Schiller lost his position as director of Lwów's municipal theater due to his left-wing sympathies, Horzyca promptly reemployed Schiller and his team.[22] This arrangement also suited Horzyca, since he did not have to direct plays himself and could pursue his own artistic vision. However, six years after his appointment, and with his tenure coming to an acrimonious end following a protracted run of unsuccessful productions, Horzyca chose to take the directorial helm of Shaw's *The Black Lady of the Sonnets*, which was immediately followed by *Mrs Warren's Profession*. Working on these two plays led Horzyca to write about the staging of Shaw in the programs for all of Horzyca's future productions of *Mrs Warren's Profession*.[23] For Horzyca, insofar as Shaw's characters think and act within the parameters of a given problem or idea, *Mrs Warren's Profession* depersonalises the characters in order to serve a higher purpose. In this respect, the director saw a link with morality plays, with Crofts, for example, as the embodiment of Vice, becoming for Horzyca a more authentic figure within the confines of the play's reality because the problems of the play are so real and current. What is more, for Horzyca, Shaw had found a way of turning the world on its head by mixing congenial speech with weighty sermonizing, an approach that amounted to selling truths that in turn become part of public discourse.[24]

The play had its first performance on 17 April 1937 in Lwów's Teatr Wielki [Great Theatre], and enjoyed a run of thirteen performances. One perspicacious review featured in *Gazeta Lwowska* [*Lwów Gazette*][25] declared that *Mrs Warren's Profession* was different than many of Shaw's other plays because it proposed heavy moralizing without the distraction of pleasant goings-on and beautiful ladies, and could only offer the distressing tragedy of a young girl who suffers the kind of earth-shattering shock that few could come to terms with. However, this opinion was clearly formed by the fact that the actress playing Vivie, Zofia Życzkowska, had become more and more visibly upset as the play's action revealed itself, and was something of a nervous wreck by the time the curtain was brought down on the evening. That being said, the critic was left most affected by Mrs. Warren's cries of the heart: "We feel that from the stage there speaks a profound authority on the human soul."[26]

If Horzyca had wished to put the seal on his time in Lwów with an artistic and commercial success, he had clearly managed to achieve his aim. Moreover, the success of the play may also have persuaded skeptics on the board of the National Theatre of Warsaw to offer him the position of Artistic Director, although many were surprised at his appointment. Indeed, an editorial in the newspaper *Dziennik Narodowy* [National Daily] wondered how it was that someone who had made such a mess of things in a provincial theater could have been gifted with a position of such national prominence.[27]

After the war, *Mrs Warren's Profession* was staged by Leon Schiller, now artistic director of Łódź's Teatr Powszeczny [General Theatre]. The play, which premiered on 26 June 1947, was directed by Stanisław Daczyński, who also played the part of Praed. In all, the production enjoyed a run of thirty-five performances and played to fourteen thousand theatergoers, a figure confirming in no uncertain terms that Shaw would continue to have an enduring appeal in the new era. To celebrate Łódź's relaunching of Shaw in postwar Poland, the pamphlet *Łódź Teatralna* [*Theatrical Łódź*] dedicated an entire issue to Shaw. The pamphlet included an excerpt from G. K. Chesterton's 1909 essay "G. B. Shaw" on Shaw's determination to speak of "useful attitudes," which certainly had a nation-(re)building aspiration probably not lost on people still moving about among the city's bombed-out ruins. The remaining pieces featured Shaw's eulogy of communist Russia (delivered in Malvern in 1929), praising the Soviet Union as a great Fabian experiment. This extract was complemented by an article written by critic Anatoly Vasilyevich Lunacharsky, who hailed Shaw's revolutionary power and speculated that had Shaw lived in Shelley's time, he would have shared the poet's fate in being forced out of the country by England's bourgeoisie. Lunacharsky also gleefully recalled meeting a Scottish socialist who had proclaimed that Shaw's extravagances in offending every sacred English ideal could be put down to the fact that he belonged to "the lesser race of the Irish." As we may deduce, much of what appeared in the pamphlet was presented so as not to give England an iota of credit, and to toy with the idea of Poland and the Soviet Union as being Shaw's natural homes.

Horzyca reentered this story when he staged *Mrs Warren's Profession* in Poznań's Teatr Dramatyczny [Drama Theatre] in February 1950. Two years later, he took the play to Warsaw's Teatr Współczesny [Contemporary Theatre] in a production, which premiered on 31 November 1950, that proved the apex of Horzyca's directorial career. The administrative director of the Contemporary Theatre was Erwin Axer, who had done much since the theater's founding that year to blind-side any potential Russification policies with regard to the proscriptive directives for the staging of social realism. Instead, Axer had posited the artistic aims of the theater as those that entailed the staging of contemporary European drama that was socially engaged and that would help people to overcome the difficulties posed by everyday life.[28] The theater had also placed its activities on a commercial footing and chose to focus on a small repertoire wherein plays were expected to run for several months. Though not a contemporary play, *Mrs Warren's Profession* was regarded as being so provocative that it was greeted as a new and exciting work that reflected tumultuous times. It was also hailed as a celebration of the new political system in Poland, one that had done away with a capitalist world that had allowed vice to cripple human life.[29]

By this time, Horzyca had managed to attune the play more to his vision of drama as morality play. For example, the way in which Vivie absorbed and reacted to the series of revelations was shown as evidence of her own flawed nature. In other words, she had always been a victim of her own illusory existence, albeit still perhaps not cognizant of this fact by the end of the play. However, it seems that this "depersonalizing" of the cast was ultimately undermined by the powerhouse performance delivered by the acclaimed actress Irena Eichlerówna.[30] Indeed, Horzyca must have known that by allowing his star actress to upstage the rest of the cast, he had contravened Shaw's rejection of perfect plays written around popular performers.

Understandably, reviewers were particularly intrigued by the character of Vivie and were keen to discuss her character as a critique of the capitalist system. This question was most notably taken up by critic Alfred Degal. Writing for the weekly *Nowa Kultura* [*New Culture*], Degal averred that Mrs. Warren was a negative character because her justifications for continuing to run brothels were hollow, and because she flung accusations at the very capitalist system that she herself had wholly embraced.[31] However, Włodzimierz Lewik, writing in the same journal the following week, asserted that Vivie was deserving of little praise, as she had only thought about her future in terms of money and the stock markets.[32] This debate between Degal and Lewik did much to set in train a circular debate among reviewers of the play as to the rights and wrongs of the stances taken by mother and daughter. Perhaps in realization of this fact, Jan Alfred Szczepański, writing for *Teatr* [*Theatre*], concluded that this level of confusion and ambiguity was what Shaw had had in mind all along, and that he had neither been looking to deal solely with prostitution nor to pull heart strings and ask theatergoers to take sides.[33]

Aside from the commercial success that the play enjoyed with its ultimate run of 244 performances, Horzyca was very gratified to learn from Erwin Axer that Bertolt Brecht had attended the play and had been greatly impressed with Horzyca's interpretation of *Mrs Warren's Profession* as a morality play. Brecht told Axer that the production should be shown in Berlin, although he also quickly added that a new stage set design would have to be conceived, while also recommending that some members of the cast be replaced. Axer relayed these comments to Horzyca, who repeated them in a joyful letter his wife. It is easy to discern from Horzyca's letter that such generous praise was a rarity in his world: "Just look! It took Brecht to come from abroad for them to see that once again [my] Warren is not so nonsensical."[34] Sadly, Horzyca was unable to bask in this success for long. Before the play had even completed its run, Horzyca began rehearsing Alexander Ostrovsky's The Forest for the National Theatre of Warsaw. But Horzyca's mystical interpretation did not sit well with the new directors of the theater, Bohdan Korzeniewski and Marian Meller, who had been tasked with implementing the principles of social realism. They sat in on the rehearsals and offered suggestions that were little more than couched warnings. Horzyca tried to dismiss such interference and thought he could steer the course, but when they moved against him, no quarter was shown: Korzeniewski fired Horzyca just weeks before the opening of the play and took over as director, and Horzyca's name was removed from the poster.[35] Fortunately, Horzyca was offered the directorship of Wrocław's Teatr Dramatyczny [Drama Theatre], a position he held from 1952 to 1955.

Horzyca's continued determination to adhere to his monumental style in defiance of social realism made him the constant target of attacks from those bent on bowing to the egregious demands of the genre. And even his decision to stage Mrs Warren's Profession couldn't rescue him from his travails. Initially reluctant to restage the play, he was swayed by the persuasions of Irena Eichlerówna, who wanted to reprise the role of Mrs. Warren. However, if she had put the Warsaw cast in the shade, she strode like a colossus on the stage in Wrocław. It was soon evident that compared to Eichlerówna the cast was third rate. Equally bothersome was the casting of Vivie. Although the part had been given to Renata Fiałkowska, Horzyca had wanted the role to go to his assistant, Halina Dzieduszycka, whom he wished to relaunch as an actress. Initially, Eichlerówna did not agree to such a change, but then Fiałkowska, who was heavily pregnant, began to show signs of her condition. Life truly encroached on art when the audience began to suspect that Frank had had his way with Vivie, and that the bump was part of the plot! And so it was agreed to release Fiałkowska and replace her with Horzyca's protégée.[36]

The story of Mrs Warren's Profession in Poland in the first half of the twentieth century spans three eras, and the play's translation, production, and reception bring together a dazzling array of Poland's literary and theatrical greats. But perhaps what stands out most from the narrative presented here is the extent to which Shaw's play generated impassioned debate about its literary conundrums, while also reaffirming for each era that Poland occupied the moral high ground in terms of its treatment of women and the working classes. Whether this was an illusory contention or not, *Mrs Warren's Profession* gave Polish galleries a great deal to cheer about.

NOTES

1. See Archibald Henderson, *George Bernard Shaw: Man of the Century* (New York: Appleton-Century-Crofts, 1956), 462.

2. See L. W. Conolly, ed., *Bernard Shaw, Mrs Warren's Profession* (Peterborough, Ontario: Broadview Press, 2005), 13–17.

3. The Little Theatre actually managed to turn a tidy profit in its first season and enjoyed a reputation for serious theater with productions of Ibsen, Goethe, and Polish dramatists. Gawalewicz took much personal credit for the theater's achievements, stating, "Jeżeli się teatr dobrze prowadzi, to powodzenie jest niewątpliwe" ["If a theater is well run, then success is assured"]. See *Kurier Warszawski* 134 (1907), cited in Roman Taborski, *Warszawskie teatry prywatne w okresie Młodej Polski* [*Warsaw's Private Theatres during the Era of Young Poland*], (Warsaw: PWN, 1980), 38.

4. Jan Lorentowicz, *Dwadzieście lat teatru* [*Twenty Years of Theatre*], vol. 2 (Warsaw: Hoesick, 1930), 194–96.

5. Ibid., 194.

6. ["Sprzedawać temu, kto da najwięcej"]. J. Kl. (Kleczyński), "Z teatru" ["From the Theatre"], *Tygodnik Ilustrowany* 32 (1907): 658.

7. The manuscript is held in the Archive of the Słowacki Theatre in Kraków, call no. 2032.

8. "Pani Warren [. . .] ulega jeszcze w znacznej części wymaganiom współczesnego sobie *teatru*, jest niejako surowym dopiero materiałem prawdziwej rzeczywistej komedyi, której stylu mianem, jest: Bernard Shaw" ["Mrs. Warren [. . .] whilst conforming to the requirements of modern theater, is still raw material for the kind of comedy whose style is: Bernard Shaw"]. Konrad Rakowski, "Z teatru. *Profesja pani Warren*, komedyja w 4 aktach Bernarda Shawa" ["From the Theatre. *The Profession of Mrs Warren*, a comedy in four acts by Bernard Shaw"], *Czas* 230 (1907): 1.

9. Bernard Shaw, *The Saturday Review*, 1 June 1 1895.

10. Quoted in Wiktor Biegański, "Polska Prapremiera Profesji Pani Warren" ["The Polish Premiere of Mrs Warren's Profession"]. Theatre Program for *Profesja Pani Warren*. The Theatre of Stefan Jaracz. Osztyn-Elbląg (1954), 12–14.

11. The manuscript is held in the Library of Silesia, call no. 3710. "12/4 1908 była czytana próba, na sali p. d. L. H. i równocześnie składano tłumaczowi gratulacje!" [12/4 1908 the read-through took place in the theater p. d. (Mr Director) L. H., who also extended his congratulations to the translator]. The other manuscript is held in the archive of Warsaw's Teatr Współczesny [Contemporary Theatre], call no. 6.

12. It is important to note that at the beginning of the twentieth century, municipal theaters in cities like Warsaw, Kraków, and Lwów were subsidized by the city, and very often their remit or program, as defined by the theater manager, was to present as many plays as possible. As a consequence, this meant that theaters would very often stage up to three plays a week, placing almost impossible demands on the actors and often impacting negatively on the quality of their performance. See Adam Grzymała-Siedlecki, *Tadeusz Pawlikowski i jego krakowscy aktorzy* [*Tadeusz Pawlikowski and his Krakovian Actors*] (Kraków: Wydawnictwo Literackie, 1971), 153–60.

13. See Alfred Wysocki, "Tadeusza Pawlikowskiego czasy lwowskie" ["The Lwów Era of Tadeusz Pawlikowski"], *Pamiętnik Teatralny* 1 (5) (1953): 145; see also Antoni Dębnicki and Ryszard Górski, "Bernard Shaw na scenach polskich. Okres Pierwszy 1903–1913" ["Bernard Shaw on the Polish Stage: The First Period, 1903–1913"], *Pamiętnik Teatralny* 2 (22) (1957): 232–33.

14. See Z. Wasilewski, *Słowo Polskie* 84 (1909). Dr. M. Thullie summarized Wasilewski's standpoint as follows: "Więc sztuka o treści zbyt drażliwej, aby o niej napisać w gazecie, napisana w sposób cyniczny, ale z wielkim talentem, można działać umoralniająco na audytorium teatralne?" [And so the play is too awful to be written about in the newspaper, it's been written in a cynical manner, but with great talent, may affect the morals of those in the theater auditorium?"] "Tumult w Teatrze Miejskim we Lwowie" [Tumult in Lwów's Municipal Theatre], *Przegląd Powszechny* 101 (1909): 482–83.

15. ["Wstyd, że takie sztuki przedstawia się na scenie polskiej."] See Thullie, "Tumult w Teatrze Miejskim we Lwowie," 482–83; and Biegański, "Polska Prapremiera Profesji Pani Warren," 14. See also Stanisława Kumor, *Polskie debiuty Bernarda Shaw* [The Polish Debuts of Bernard Shaw], (Warsaw: Wydawnictwo Unwiersytetu Warszawskiego, 1971), 135–36.

16. See Biegański, "Polska Prapremiera Profesji Pani Warren," 14; and Thullie, "Tumult w Teatrze Miejskim we Lwowie,"483.

17. ["wzywające do poszanowania wolności i swobody myśli"]. Biegański, "Polska Prapremiera Profesji Pani Warren," 14.

18. In a 1936 article in the journal *Teatr*, which had put together an issue dedicated to Shaw, Florian Sobieniowski recalled having traveled to London in 1912 to meet with Shaw in order to discuss the possibility of translating his recent plays for the newly opened Teatr Polski (Polish Theatre) of Warsaw. What followed was an awkward meeting that lasted three hours, whereby Shaw pressed Sobieniowski on his literary qualifications and suitability for the task of translating his plays. Shaw would have been impressed with Sobieniowski's educational path, having earned a degree in fine arts from Krakow University and having completed postgraduate stints in both Vienna and Paris. Whether or not Shaw thought he was taking a gamble on a translator with no significant successes to his name, at the end of the interview he presented Sobieniowski with wrapped proofs of the as-yet-unpublished plays *Pygmalion* and *Androcles and the Lion*. The subsequent staging of *Pygmalion*, which arose from Sobieniowski's translation, would cement Shaw's stellar reputation in Poland. As a result, Shaw gave Sobieniowski exclusivity over the translation

of his plays in Poland. See Florian Sobieniowski, "Wspomnienia tłumacza" ["The Recollections of a Translator"], *Teatr*, 9–10 (21–22) (1936): 17–18.

19. Antoni Slonimksi, "Profesja Pani Warren" ["Mrs Warren's Profession"], *Wiadomości Literackie* 27 (1936): 6.

20. Kazimierz Wierzyński, *Wrażenia teatralne* [*Theatre Impressions*], (Warsaw: Państwowy Instytut Wydawniczy, 1987), 312.

21. See Wilam Horzyca, *Polski teatr monumentalny* [Polish Monumental Theatre] (Wrocław: Wiedza i Kultura, 1994).

22. See Lidia Kuchtówna, "Wilam Horzyca (1889–1959): kronika życia i działalności" ["Wilam Horzyca (1889–1959): A Chronicle of His Life and Activities"], *Pamiętnik Teatralny* 2–4 (150–52) (1989): 213–14. See also "Dyrektor Horzyca obejmuje jutro Teatry Lwowskie: specjalny wywiad *Słowa Polskiego*" ["Tomorrow Horzyca Takes Charge of Lwów's Theatres"], *Słowo Polskie* 5 (1932).

23. The article was also published in the monthly journal *Teatr*. See Wilam Horzyca, "O Profesji pani Warren. Uwagi rezysera" ["On 'Mrs Warren's Profession': Director's Comments"], *Teatr* 2 (1952): 222–23.

24. " . . . aby więc trafić do uszu słuchacza, musi treść tę ubrać w kształt możliwie najbardziej nieoczekiwany i zaskakujący. Tylko w ten sposób można sprzedać prawdy. które jeszcze nie przemijają." [" . . . so in order to reach the ears of the listener, he has to dress his message up in a form that is both unexpected and surprising. Only in this way may he sell truths that retain some sort of permanence."], ibid., 223.

25. Article signed with "zastępca" [replacement]), "Profesja pani Warren" ["Mrst Warren's Profession"], *Gazeta Lwowska* 88 (1937).

26. ["czujemy, że ze sceny przemawia głęboki znawca duszy ludzkiej"]. Ibid.

27. See Lidia Kuchtówna, "Wilam Horzyca (1889–1959)," 225.

28. See Zygmunt Hübner and Jerzy Rakowiecki, *Rozmowy o teatrze* [*Conversations about Theater*], (Warsaw: Wiedza Powszechna, 1955), 187.

29. One critic went so far as to say that people should go and see the play in order to witness why Poland had done so well to free itself from the tyranny of capitalism. See L. M., "Profesja pani Warren" ["Mrs Warren's Profession"], *Głos Pracy* 294 (1952).

30. Many reviewers hailed Eichlerówna's performance as being one of the most memorable of recent times. See, for example, Edward Csato, "Eichlerówna," *Teatr* 3 (1952): 11–12.

31. Alfred Degal, "Filozofia pani Warren" ["The Philosophy of Mrs. Warren"], *Nowa Kultura* 4 (1952): 8.

32. Włodzimierz Lewik, "Czy Wiwia jest pozytwnym bahaterem?" ["Is Vivie Warren a Positive Protagonist?"], *Nowa Kultura* 5 (1952): 10.

33. Jan Alfred Szczepański, "Dwie Wiwie Warren" [The Two Vivies Warren], *Teatr* 3 (1952): 12–13.

34. ["Popatrz się! Trzeba było aż Brechta z zagranicy, by zobaczyli, iż znowu Warren (moja), to nie taki nonsens"]. Letter from Wilam Horzyca to Stanisława Horzyca dated Warsaw, March 1952, in: *Listy Wilama Horzycy* [*The Letters of Wilam Horzyca*], (Warsaw: Instytut Sztuki Polskiej Akademii Nauk, 1991), 246–47.

35. See Wojciech Dudzik, *Wilama Horzycy: dramat niespełnienia: lata 1948–1959* [*Wilam Horzyca: a drama of unfulfillment: the years 1948–1959*] (Warsaw: Uniwersytet

Warszawski, Katedra Kultury Polskiej, 1990), 141; see also Magdalena Raszewska, *Teatr Narodowy 1949-2004* [*The National Theatre 1949-2004*], (Warsaw: Teatr Narodowy, 2005), 38–39.

36. See Tadeusz Lutogniewski, "Shaw i Eichlerówna na scenie wrocławskiej" [Shaw and Eichlerówna on the Wrocław Stage"], *Sprawy i Ludzie* 92 (1952): 2; see also Irena Bołtuć, "Z wrocławskich wspomnień" ["Wrocław Memories"], *Pamiętnik Teatralny* 2–4 (1989): 359–67.

A Country Bumpkin in Cosmopolitan Shanghai

John Woo's My Fair Gentleman and the Evolution of Pygmalion in Contemporary China[1]

KAY LI

This article explores how stage and film productions of *Pygmalion* in contemporary China present the image of a country rising to affluence and international importance. Chinese adaptations of *Pygmalion* keep featuring Elizas who are country bumpkins moving to the huge metropolitan centers of Shanghai and Hong Kong. Their training by the Western-educated Chinese Higgins is an analogy of how China adapts to intense cross-cultural encounters as it enters the global arena. As we shall see, gender reversals in two of the four Chinese adaptations of *Pygmalion* highlight how China is moving from the shadows of imperialism and the foregrounding of the West to a more egalitarian recognition of the complex interchanges between Chinese and Western cultures.

My focus will be on John Woo's 2009 film adaptation of *Pygmalion*, *My Fair Gentleman* (*Yao Tiao Shen Shi*),[2] and on its portrayal of the newly affluent Chinese entrepreneurial peasants. This is an important concern in China, where numerous entrepreneurial peasants moved from the impoverished countryside to the metropolis and became actively engaged in economic, social, and cultural exchanges. Likewise in Woo's film, the entrepreneurial peasant Charles Zeng Tian-gao, the Eliza Doolittle figure, moves to metropolitan Shanghai and amassed his wealth. His transformation by Candice Wu Jia-qian, the Higgins figure, from country bumpkin to gentleman, is an analogy for how the country quickly emerged from the devastating poverty caused by the Cultural Revolution to the affluence resulting from China's modernization. Above all, *My Fair Gentleman* shows how intricately Shaw wove his theory of the Life Force and Creative Evolution into *Pygmalion*.

SHAW, Vol. 33, 2013 | Copyright © 2013 The Pennsylvania State University, University Park, PA

Pygmalion is the Shaw play most frequently adapted by the Chinese, and with each adaptation the roles of Eliza Doolittle and Henry Higgins acquire new meanings that reflect the country's current social and political situation. In each there is a movement from countryside to large cosmopolitan city. In the 1988 film *Gongzi Duoqing* (*The Greatest Lover*),[3] Locomotive Fat (Eliza), played by Chow Yun-Fat (of *Crouching Tiger, Hidden Dragon* and *The Killer* fame),[4] is an illegal immigrant sneaking away from his village in Southern China to Hong Kong. The role kept evolving as China increasingly took center stage in the international arena, with the Chinese Elizas becoming richer and more socially powerful. The 1997 Hong Kong stage production of *Pygmalion* featured a flower girl dressed in country garb speaking the Toishan country dialect,[5] in contrast to a Higgins dressed in Western clothing speaking perfect Cantonese and English. The 2003 film, co-produced by Hong Kong and mainland China, *Pao Zhi Nu Peng You* (*My Dream Girl*),[6] featured Zhang Nin, a country girl newly reunited with her rich industrialist father living in Shanghai. As I have covered previous adaptations in my *Bernard Shaw and China: Cross Cultural Encounters*,[7] I will focus here on the latest adaptation of *Pygmalion* in China, *Yao Tiao Shen Shi* (*My Fair Gentleman*), produced by John Woo, Terrance Chang, and Michelle Yeoh, and show how this 2009 version is much more significant than previous Chinese ones. We will see that Shaw's play, set in London in 1912, is so versatile as to be easily adapted to any time and place in China.

Shanghai: Marketing in a Big Cosmopolitan City

The Eliza Doolittle in *My Fair Gentleman* is the rich Charles Zeng Tian-gao, an entrepreneurial peasant developing his farming business in Shanghai. Such a protagonist reflects the success of the city's marketing economy and its rapid developing consumerism. *My Fair Gentleman* is dominated by the city of Shanghai; in fact its working title was *Dirt Rich in Shanghai*. The first shot of the film is the Oriental Pearl TV Tower, a futuristic landmark emblematic of the city's history. According to the Shanghai government website, the population of Shanghai in 2009 was 19,213,200 and according to the *China Daily* may have topped 23 million in more recent years.[8] The city continues to play an important role in the economic and social development of the country. Although only 0.06 percent the size of China, it accounts for 1 percent of the country's population, one eighth of the nation's financial income, one-eleventh of the flow of goods, and 25 percent of the import and export of commercial products.

The entrepreneurial peasant in *My Fair Gentleman*, therefore, plays an important role in the development of the Shanghai economy, as the marketing of farm produce is significant. In 2009, its total value was 28.313 billion yuan (about U.S. $4 billion). In particular, the city's emphasis on the development of branded farming industries produces a rapid development of farm products: 370 enterprises with 800 certified farm products. In 2009, the export of farm products totaled 1.291 billion yuan (U.S. $183 million) and these were sold to Japan, Korea, Southeast Asia, the United States, and Europe. There were also 419 leading farming enterprises, with sales totaling 41.95 billion yuan (almost U.S. $6 billion).[9]

Therefore, *My Fair Gentleman* is not just a simple story of a country bumpkin's comic blunders in a cosmopolitan city and how he becomes a gentleman by taking image-consulting lessons. The transformation of the protagonist in the film is also emblematic of the rise of the entrepreneurial peasants and their adaptation to a globalized Chinese economy.

The Significance of *My Fair Gentleman*

Without a doubt, the adaptation of *Pygmalion* into *My Fair Gentleman* is more significant than previous Chinese adaptations because in highlighting the contribution of the entrepreneurial peasants to keeping the nation's economy thriving, *My Fair Gentleman* has become part of the myth of nation building.

The appearance of *My Fair Gentleman* was timely. Produced between June 2006 and August 2009, it premiered in Beijing on 21 September 2009 and was released on the 28th throughout China. The film was also featured at the Shanghai Film Festival, the cast and crew attending high-profile press conferences throughout the country to promote it. This was a very bold move because 28 September 2009 was the eve of the sixtieth anniversary, on 1 October, of the establishment of the People's Republic of China. To commemorate the occasion, a long and important film was made in 2009: *Jian guo da ye* (*The Founding of a Republic*),[10] co-produced by the China Film Group, the China Central Television (CCTV) Movie Channel, and the Shanghai Film Studio. The state-owned China Film Group Corporation had a film monopoly prior to China's accession to the World Trade Organization. It is still the only importer of foreign films and is responsible for overseeing and managing all Sino-foreign film co-productions.[11] China Central Television is the major state broadcaster in China. Supervised by the State Administration of Radio, Film and Television (a subsidiary of the State Council of the People's Republic of China), CCTV is one of the major official media and is comparable to the *People's Daily* and the Xinhua news agency. *The Founding of a Republic* runs 138 minutes and traces the founding of the People's Republic, providing a veritable portrait gallery of modern Chinese political leaders. It allegedly has the largest number of film stars of any other major film and features Jackie Chan, Jet Li, Zhang Ziyi, Donnie Yan, and Andy Lau, among others—although some play minor roles, speak only a line or two, or make only silent cameo appearances.

Previous Chinese adaptations of Shaw's *Pygmalion* had appeared at critical times: *The Greatest Lover* (1988) on the countdown to the handover of Hong Kong to Chinese sovereignty, the stage production *Pygmalion* (1997) right after the handover, and *My Dream Girl* (2003) as Hong Kong was recovering from the Asian financial crisis. But *My Fair Gentleman* topped them all: it premiered in Beijing during the height of the celebrations marking the sixtieth anniversary of the founding of the People's Republic.

My Fair Gentleman, despite powerful competition from *The Founding of a Republic*, had an extremely successful opening. On the first day of screening in Beijing, it ran second only to *The Founding*,[12] and many cinemas increased the number of showings to satisfy the audience's needs. The film was screened nationwide, deliberately making use of the holiday week to reach the largest audience. The film's budget was 20 million yuan (U.S. $2.83 million) covered by production companies in China, Hong Kong, and Taiwan. Director/screenwriter Gui Yuen Lee had spent four years raising money—until he met one of the producers, Terence Chang. Within a fortnight of the opening, *My Fair Gentleman* (*Yaotiao Shenshi*) had earned a respectable 13 million yuan (U.S. $1.84 million).[13] Given that the cost of a ticket to a domestic film in China is about 2 to 3 yuan,[14] 13 million yuan means a potential audience of 4.3 to 6.5 million. In 2011, *My Fair Lady* was performed in the Festival Theatre at the Shaw Festival at Niagara-on-the-Lake, Ontario. As the Festival Theatre contains 869 seats, the Chinese audience attending *My Fair Gentleman*, within only the first two weeks, could fill almost five thousand to seventy-five hundred Festival Theatres. It was an enormous opening audience, perhaps the largest for any Shaw play in China. The film was so successful that many extra copies were officially made and delivered to cinemas screening the film. This is significant, as China had only about 6,000 screens in 2011, while the United States has about 6,100 cinemas and 37,700 screens.[15] In 2009, the overall movie box-office return in China was U.S. $1 billion[16] and that of *My Fair Gentleman* alone was U.S. $1.84 million.[17] Thus *My Fair Gentleman* remains by far the most significant Chinese adaptation of any Shaw play.

Why was this particular adaptation so successful? Thanks to the prolific social media reporting on the premier, the response of the Chinese audience to the film was captured very vividly. Although the launch of the film was reported nationwide in various newspapers and their online versions, very few realized the film was a reversal of Alan Jay Lerner's *My Fair Lady* and none at all mentioned Shaw's *Pygmalion*, let alone the underlying Greek myth. *My Fair Gentleman* attracted a huge Chinese audience for three reasons: it had a Hollywood crew, it was a romantic comedy with a stellar cast, and it was a reflection of the rise of the entrepreneurial peasants and the Chinese economy.

A Hollywood Crew

The promotion of the film relied much on its Hollywood cast and crew. All online media reports and social media discussions focused on the Hollywood crew and stellar cast. Although *My Fair Gentleman* was a domestic film, "Made in China," the producers were Hollywood veterans and the Chinese media advertised the film as if it were a Hollywood production, adding with national pride that it had a Chinese Hollywood crew. Shaw's films, or adaptations of his plays, had enjoyed great success in Hollywood: *Pygmalion* (1938)[18] won the Oscar for "Best Writing, Screenplay" in 1939 and *My Fair Lady* (1964)[19] garnered eight Oscars. Yet there have been few recent Hollywood productions of Shaw's plays. It is noteworthy that the three producers of *My Fair Gentleman*, John Woo, Terence Chang, and Michelle Yeoh, are, respectively, a Hollywood director, producer, and actress. Woo is famous for his Hollywood films, such as *Face/Off* (1997), starring John Travolta; *Mission Impossible: II* (2000), starring Tom Cruise; *Paycheck* (2003), starring Ben Affleck; and of course the very popular films starring Chow Yun-Fat, such as *A Better Tomorrow* (1986) and *The Killer* (1989). Terence Chang is Woo's longtime collaborator and the executive producer of *Paycheck*, *Face/Off*, and *Anna and the King* (1999). Michelle Yeoh starred in Ang Lee's *Crouching Tiger, Hidden Dragon* (2000) and in the James Bond thriller *Tomorrow Never Dies* (1997). The director and screenwriter of *My Fair Gentleman*, Gui Yuen Lee, had worked for years with Ang Lee, who won Oscars for Best Director with *Crouching Tiger, Hidden Dragon* and *Brokeback Mountain* (2005).[20]

A Romantic Comedy Played by a Stellar Cast

As in *The Greatest Lover*, gender is reversed in *My Fair Gentleman* with promises of a romantic ending. The plot traces the transformation of a man low in social status into a gentleman and ends with romantic prospects between the student and his trainer. The major interest of the film, however, is the cast. Genders are reversed, with actor Honglei Sun playing Zeng Tian-gao as the Eliza Doolittle figure and actress Kelly Lin playing Candice Wu Jia-qian, Higgins. These two are among the most popular film stars in China. Sun, a graduate of the prestigious Central Academy of Drama, worked with top directors, among them Zhang Yimou, and has won nationwide best-actor awards. Lin, born in Taiwan, graduated with a B.S. in economics and comparative literature from the University of California. Her role in *My Fair Gentleman* is very close to her real background, as Candice is a marketing consultant educated at an American Ivy League university, and she wears a Harvard jersey at the end of the film. The film's gender reversal took the audience by surprise, for Sun is usually featured in strong masculine roles and Lin plays beautiful leading ladies. But now Charles (Sun) is the student trained by Candice (Lin).

Media reports and online discussions reveal that the main attrac-tion of *My Fair Gentleman* was its being a romantic light comedy, quite a contrast to the solemn official celebrations and the rhetoric of the Chinese National Day. Moreover, watching the play is a very comfort-able experience, since much of the pressure is removed because the Eliza Doolittle figure, Charles, has already made his money. He takes lessons from Candice for a very trivial reason: to attract the supermodel and actress Fang Na, who has slighted him publicly. But as Fang Na is played by new actress Xiao-ling Hong, the audience knows that she cannot compete with Candice, played by Kelly Lin. Thus the audience is literally invited to see how the romance works out between Charles and Candice, and the film becomes a relaxing light comedy suitable for the National Day holiday.

The media also promoted the film as fashionable and updated in that it showcases luxurious lifestyles and accessories popular in the great cities in China today with the opening of huge flagship stores in Beijing of such luxury brands as Louis Vuitton, Burberry, Dior, and Armani.[21] *My Fair Gentleman* had an extensive promotional campaign. The cast and crew traveled everywhere in China to hold high-profile promotional events, which were not merely press interviews but were accentuated by show-pieces such as the cast and crew brewing coffee on stage or baking and eating mooncakes. The symbolism is significant because the promotion combined the iconic hot drink of the West, coffee (Starbucks plans to increase its cafés in China to fifteen hundred by 2015), with the iconic pastry of the East, mooncakes, a Chinese baked delight, made with ingredients such as lotus seed paste and salty duck eggs, that can be traced as far back as the Ming Dynasty (1368–1644).

A Reflection of the Rise of the Entrepreneurial Peasants and the Chinese Economy

Like a Shavian sugar-coated pill, there is serious matter behind light comedy. *My Fair Gentleman* is perfect for the National Day weekend also because the film showcases Chinese national pride. It shows the rise of the entrepreneurial peasants who played a great role in the emergence of China's modern economic success. Their move from countryside to cosmopolitan city is an analogy for China's move from its impoverished state following the Cultural Revolution to its present affluence. *My Fair Gentleman*, which premiered at the same time as *The Founding of a Republic* and came second at the box office, was successful because John Woo's film features national pride on an everyday level, while the latter film exhibits national pride on the institutional, historical level. Much of the online media and social media appreciated how *My Fair Gentleman* provided light romantic comedy needed for a relaxing and entertaining holiday week in the midst of all the solemn national celebrations.

In addition to light comedy, however, *My Fair Gentleman* showcases the social and economic successes of the nation, while *The Founding of a Republic* captures the country's political ones. The arrival of the entrepreneurial peasants in the city is not accidental. *My Fair Gentleman* explores two important topical issues: the success of the market economy and the rise of the entrepreneurial peasants. Beginning in 1982, China adopted a policy of "reform and opening": the reform of the economic system and the opening of the country to foreign trade. It is a socialist economy with Chinese characteristics, moving rapidly from a centrally planned economy to a market economy. China's economy is the second largest in the world (after the United States), with an average GDP growth of 9.31 percent from 1989 to 2010.[22] The International Monetary Fund's forecast for China's 2012 economic growth was 8 percent.[23]

Shaw's 1912 play was made topical. In China, a significant change took place among the peasants, as the commune structure was largely dissolved and replaced by the responsibility system, with their economic responsibilities falling under townships and villages. Possibilities of free markets for farm produce, increasing marketing possibilities and rising productivity,[24] created many rich entrepreneurial peasants. According to Yasheng Huang, "Tens of millions of peasants began home-grown private businesses, from small-scale manufacturing to service delivery."[25] Huang believes that "China owes its astonishing economic expansion to hundreds of millions of entrepreneurial peasants. . . . Small-scale rural businesses created China's miracle [and] that nation's recovery from the global recession."[26] According to the latest census, China's population in 2011 was 1.37 billion, with more than 674 million categorized as rural population.[27]

Consequently, *My Fair Gentleman* presents Eliza and Higgins as two Chinese modern stereotypes evolved from the modern Chinese economy: Charles Zeng Tian-gao (Eliza) is a "土大款" a millionaire entrepreneur first making his money as a peasant, and Candice Wu Jia-qian (Higgins) is a "白骨精" a member of the white-collar hard-working elite. Together they capture the confrontation between the rural and urban populations in cosmopolitan Shanghai. The Eliza Doolittle figure is the entrepreneurial millionaire peasant Charles, who first makes his fortune as a peasant before proceeding to acquire companies in Shanghai. This dichotomy is significant and reflects such Chinese stage stereotypes as the Xiangsheng (相聲), sometimes translated as crosstalk, which is a traditional Chinese comedic performance often in the form of a quick and witty dialogue between two performers, so-called cross talks, featuring the uneducated and comic peasants and an educated city dweller. The coming together of Charles and Candice at the end of the film is symbolic of the new trend in advocating the brotherhood between peasants and city-dwellers, especially bearing in mind the important role of peasants in modern Chinese history.

Never had any Chinese Eliza been so fabulously rich as Charles. The 1997 stage production of *Pygmalion* is closest to Shaw's text, featuring a poor Chinese flower girl, To Lan-heung as Eliza, who is proud to go home in a rickshaw. The 1988 film *The Greatest Lover* showcases Locomotive Qian Jin Fat as Eliza, a Chinese illegal immigrant swimming across the border to Hong Kong with only the clothes on his back. Zhang Nin in *My Dream Girl* (2003) is a Mainland Chinese country girl newly reunited with her rich industrialist father Zhang Tin, a Shanghai manufacturer of Buick automobiles.

In *My Fair Gentleman*, the transformation of Charles is the result of marketing and consumerism, both pervasive in cosmopolitan Shanghai, while in earlier films it was presented merely as image consulting. According to a Reuters report by David Randall in 2012, China's premier called "expanding consumer demand" one of his priorities for the upcoming year.[28] Consumerism is pushed by branding and marketing. According to a 2009 KPMG study: "Luxury brands are investing large sums of money in heavy marketing to not just promote their brand and products but also to inform Chinese consumers about 'luxury' and why they should pay a premium for products offered by luxury brands. Brand building is occurring on a massive scale, not only through print and television advertising, but also through luxury events and shows and customised lifestyle publications."[29] *My Fair Gentleman* highlights the "heavy marketing" occurring in Shanghai. Candice says: "Everything begins with marketing," and *Pygmalion*'s linguistic strategies are translated into various kinds of marketing strategies. In Shaw's play, speaking a refined English is a skill that can hide one's humble origins; in *My Fair Gentleman*, it is a marketing strategy. The film opens with the expatriate English teachers: Candice can speak perfect English and her expatriate friends can speak perfect Chinese. Yet Candice hires a Canadian to present his marketing plan in English while she provides the Chinese translation. She assumes that her Chinese clients will value her proposals more if they are presented in English by a Westerner.

In actuality, Shanghai develops the branding of farming products and traditional goods are repackaged to facilitate world export. Likewise, in the film, Charles initially wants Candice to market through branding his newly acquired "Magic Dragon Wine," which is literally a lizard soaked in a bottle of wine. This traditional Chinese rice wine "has a history going back centuries and has been a 'luxury export' from China for decades. A greenhued, brandy-like liquor, it is produced by fermenting rice wine in a cask with a generous helping of geckos and ginseng. Drinking the wine is said to help ward off evil and to improve vision."[30] Candice suggests repackaging it to make it a high-end consumer good.

Other marketing strategies include bundle sales and advertisements. Once jilted by Fang Na, Charles presents the marketing contract as a bundle that includes himself and the "Magic Dragon Wine" and wants Candice to market them together. Candice turns Charles into a famous brand by a "software upgrade": she repackages him not only in expensive suits but also by teaching him how to appreciate the fine arts, asking him to take lessons in English conversation, playing golf, and coffee making. She even introduces him to the work of Leonardo da Vinci and to Verdi's opera *Rigoletto*. Whereas in *Pygmalion* and *My Fair Lady*, Eliza Doolittle's lessons consist mainly of phonetics and genteel manners, Charles's classes include the gamut of classical Western art and expensive pastimes. Employing the marketing strategy of "news value," Candice the ex-socialite makes use of the paparazzi by passing Charles off as her new boyfriend, and Charles becomes famous overnight. Fang Na becomes attracted to Charles and Candice fulfills her contractual agreement.

However, Charles's education does not end with merely copying the West. The film is aware of the complex cultural exchanges and joint productions between China and the West, and Candice makes Charles memorize background material and art criticism related to da Vinci and *Rigoletto*. The moment of truth—which parallels the ambassador's garden party in *Pygmalion*—is Candice taking Charles to a performance of *Rigoletto*, where he is asked whether the *Turandot* directed by Zhang Yimou is a Western or Chinese production. This is an important topical reference because Zhang Yimou, the famous film director who directed Puccini's *Turandot* in Florence and at the Forbidden City, Beijing, was producing his own version of *Turandot* on 6 and 7 October 2009 at the Bird's Nest Stadium in Beijing. This is the very stadium that had hosted the 2008 Beijing Olympics, a seminal moment of Chinese national pride, and whose opening and closing ceremonies Zhang had also directed. Neither Candice nor Charles can answer the question as to whether *Turandot* is Italian opera, as Zhang's *Turandot* exemplifies the interactive cross-cultural processes taking place in the creation of art: a story about a Chinese princess written by an Italian composer and directed by a Chinese, with Italian soprano Raffaella Angeletti playing a Chinese princess (Turandot) and a Chinese tenor, Dai Yuqiang, playing the foreigner Prince Calaf. The production was conducted by an Italian (Janos Acs) and the orchestra comprised members of China's National Opera House.[31] The production came complete with a one-thousand-square-meter LCD scroll displaying an animated movie telling the story.[32] (LCD had also played a prominent role in the opening ceremony of the 2008 Beijing Olympics.) This combination of East and West produced fascinating new cultural fusions. Significantly, both Charles and Candice fall asleep during the conventional stage production of *Rigoletto*. As with Higgins and Eliza, there are limits to what Candice can teach Charles. Marketing strategies cannot change human nature.

Life Force and Creative Evolution

The central question remains: Why is *Pygmalion* such an effective play to showcase a successful Chinese economy? Paradoxically, *My Fair Gentleman* turns out to be an examination of Shaw's theories of the Life Force and Creative Evolution, a philosophy of will adapted from Schopenhauer. The film begins where *Pygmalion* ends and rewinds backwards to the beginning, thus foregrounding the moment of transformation of Charles and his attainment of his self-will, and also highlighting the agent behind that transformation, Candice.

Although the Higgins figure is Candice Wu Jia-qian, a graduate of an American Ivy League university, she also has nuances of Eliza, who asks Higgins after the ambassador's party:

LIZA: [*pulling herself together in desperation*] What am I fit for? What have you left me fit for? Where am I to go? What am I to do? Whats to become of me?[33]

Higgins suggests his mother will find a rich man for her:

HIGGINS: [*a genial afterthought occurring to him*] I daresay my mother could find some chap or other who would do very well.

LIZA: We were above that at the corner of Tottenham Court Road.

HIGGINS: [*waking up*] What do you mean?

LIZA: I sold flowers. I didnt sell myself. Now you've made a lady of me I'm not fit to sell anything else. I wish youd left me where you found me.[34]

In a similar vein, Candice is introduced as an ex-socialite who was about to marry into a rich, prominent family in Hong Kong but was jilted at the last minute. Like Eliza opening her own flower shop, Candice has just opened her own marketing company in Shanghai. Eliza proclaims to Higgins that she will teach phonetics, and indeed Candice is offering her own training classes to Charles, in this instance an Eliza-turned-Higgins.

The Eliza in *My Fair Gentleman* has reversed the social climbing. In *Pygmalion*, Eliza asks Higgins:

LIZA: [*crushed by superior strength and weight*] Whats to become of me? Whats to become of me?[35]

But the male Eliza of *My Fair Gentleman*, Charles, like Zhang Nin in *My Dream Girl*, does not have this problem. He has already made his fortune and finished climbing the social ladder from peasant to millionaire. His problem in the film is how to repackage his products: the lizard wine company he has just acquired, and himself, in order to pass himself off in high society as a gentleman (for the sake, mind you, of seducing a film star who despises him). The situation is reversed, since it is Candice who wants to climb the social ladder, while Charles has already made his fortune. To Lan-heung, in the 1997 stage play, is considered the illegitimate daughter of a peer newly returned from England. Locomotive Fat, in *The Greatest Lover*, passes himself off as the Cambridge-educated son of a rich Chinese-American businessman at the Fancy Ball of the Foundation for Indian Retarded Children, and Zhang Nin becomes the genteel daughter at her father's upscale party. But *My Fair Gentleman* begins with a dinner party for Lung Cancer Awareness. Like some fairy-tale prince, Charles is dressed in all white but is publicly shamed by actress and supermodel Fang Na, which drives him to ask Candice to transform him. After a totally successful transformation, Fang Na mistakes him for an accomplished gentleman. Charles then reveals to her that he is the peasant she once despised: his attainment of self-will coincides with his reconciliation to his peasant origins.

In effect, *My Fair Gentleman* examines Shaw's theories of the Life Force and Creative Evolution. In shifting the adaptation from the image consulting in earlier adaptations of the play to marketing, the focus shifts from appearance to the fundamental human being and the assertion of his inner will. In *The Perfect Wagnerite* (1898), Shaw regards Siegfried as "the type of healthy man raised to perfect confidence in his own impulses by an intense and joyous vitality which is above fear, sickliness of conscience, malice and the makeshifts and moral clutches of law and order which accompany them."[36] In *My Fair Gentleman*, Charles possesses the most free will of all the Chinese Elizas. Shaw's Eliza wills to take lessons from Higgins, and so does the Eliza in the 1997 Chinese stage play, but they still have a concern for social class at the beginning of the play. Previous Chinese Elizas have been passive. Locomotive Fat in *The Greatest Lover* is forced to take lessons from the image consultant Anita by the rich Hong Kong businessman Big Mouth Sze, who wants to revenge himself on Fiona, the daughter of a shipping magnate who jilts him, by making her fall in love with the poor and ugly Locomotive Fat. In *My Dream Girl* (2003), Zhang Nin's father wants her to take image-consulting lessons so that she can acquire upper-class taste and manners.

But Charles in *My Fair Gentleman* is like Siegfried. He is fearless, and the catchphrase he uses to laugh at people is "too scared." It is significant that this catchphrase (also his first line in the film) was not in the original script. The actor Honglei Sun arrived at this line after living through the role, which shows how intrinsic the Siegfried spirit is to the character of Eliza Doolittle. Charles asks Candice to change his image just because he wants to chase Fang Na, the supermodel and actress. Charles trusts his impulses, disregards rules, and goes for everything he wants with vitality.

Therefore, the film moves from marketing to focus on the inner will and undirected Life Force within Charles, who, as a peasant entrepreneur, has a lot of energy but lacks a meaningful direction. In *The Perfect Wagnerite*, Siegfried stands for the will to live, the unhindered thrusting of the life energy of the world toward ever-higher organization. Charles has recently acquired the lizard wine company and reminds us of Old Bill Buoyant in *Buoyant Billions*: both are at the stage at which the Life Force struggles blindly in its fight for new ground and wastes its will on speculation. Candice helps Charles by putting his will to better use. She provides better direction for the Life Force to guide it toward Creative Evolution by enabling Charles to know himself and follow his will. Although she does not advise him to give up the starlet, her training makes him aware of his folly in chasing her. He realizes he should give her up, be himself, and go back to his roots.

At the end of the film, Charles finds his direction and goes back to the people. The first shot of the play is of the top of the 1,535-foot Shanghai Oriental Pearl TV Tower, the tallest building in China from 1994 to 2007, and the last shot is of Charles and Candice dancing the cha-cha with the ordinary people in Shanghai at the Bund, a riverbank. This dancing is not Bollywood, but a very realistic reflection of life in Chinese cities, where it is normal to see ordinary people dancing in groups as morning exercise. It is also a display of Charles reconciled with his peasant roots, as he first learned to dance in the countryside. This scene contrasts with the elitist dance to which Charles took Candice and reverses the ambassador's ball in the filmed version of *Pygmalion* and later in Shaw's play, when Eliza the flower girl becomes the Duchess Eliza. The Chinese Elizas are empowered by their Chinese cultural roots. In *The Greatest Lover*, it is eventually Qian Jin-fa's ability to speak Putonghua that impressed the governor of colonial Hong Kong. In *My Dream Girl*, Zhang Nin's ability to recite traditional Chinese poetry by Wang Guo Wei attracts the ambassador's son. In *My Fair Gentleman*, Charles leaves his luxury condo, taking only the works of Xu Zhi Mo, a Chinese poet famous for his advocacy of love and life. Significantly, as Charles finds his own self-will, *My Fair Gentleman* affirms Shaw's theory of the Life Force and Creative Evolution. Although the film makes no reference to the underlying Greek myth, the Pygmalion story is still present. In the myth, Pygmalion the sculptor falls in love with his own a statue, Galatea, praying to Aphrodite to turn the statue into a real woman. The goddess of Love grants his wish. The climax of *My Fair Gentleman* is the awakening of Galatea, when Charles brings Fang Na to his luxurious condo, which is decorated with expensive sculptures, and proclaims that the greatest work of art is himself. He then changes into the white suit in which he had first scared Fang Na away, and now is paradoxically driven away by Fang Na herself, this time from his own home. But this is of no consequence, as he is determined to reject Fang Na, and Candice is the real choice he makes in his newly enlightened state. He dons his casual clothes, mounts a bicycle, and joins the crowd of commoners outside.

Despite the stellar cast and the romantic comedy, the film maintains the ambiguous ending in Shaw's play without committing to a coming marriage between Eliza and Higgins. At the Bund, Charles, riding an ordinary bicycle instead of traveling in his luxury car, meets Candice, who happens to be half drunk and also riding a bicycle. By the time Charles declares his love for her on one of the Bund garden benches, she is fast asleep and never hears his profession of love. The film ends with Charles and Candice dancing with the common people, instead of the solo fairy-tale dance between Cinderella and the Prince.

Gender Reversals: Woo's *Pygmalion* Effect

Yao Tiao Shen Shi (*My Fair Gentleman*) explores the idea of male transformations as analogies for the empowerment of China. There are two male Chinese Elizas, both played by actors famous for their macho roles: Locomotive Fat played by Chow Yun-Fat and Charles played by Honglei Sun. The film again features the gender reversal found in *The Greatest Lover*, in which Chow Yun-Fat plays a male Eliza—Locomotive Fat—at the height of his fame, having starred in the John Woo gangster films *A Better Tomorrow* (1986), *A Better Tomorrow II* (1987), and *The Killer* (1989). Similarly, Honglei Sun in *My Fair Gentleman* is an actor famous for his macho roles, and his casting as Charles, who needs to be trained by a woman, surprised the first audiences because of his former roles The producer of *My Fair Gentleman*, Woo is famous for his creation of macho roles. Indeed, the male Elizas who are asked by a Western-educated female Higgins to perform ridiculous training tasks feel emasculated, thus furthering the China/West, female/male, powerless/powerful paradigms. Remembering the symbolic significance of the male Elizas as representing China under the threat of imperialism and colonialism, the gender reversals highlight the former disempowerment of the nation.

The transformations that the male Chinese Elizas go through are symbolic of the rise of modern China. Politically, Locomotive Fat is Mainland China about to resume sovereignty over the British colony, and economically Charles is the entrepreneurial peasant contributing much to the rising Chinese economy. Image consulting and marketing make them stronger, and these male Elizas highlight the agency restored to these characters after their transformation. Candice is also a symbol: she shows the empowered role of strong, educated women in contemporary China, showcasing a better balance of power between genders under Chinese communism in its market economy phase. Compared to Songlian (Gong Li) in Zhang Yimou's *Raise the Red Lantern* (1991),[37] featuring an appalling, toxic gender relationship, Candice's female agency is dramatic. While she was rejected by her first love because she was a social climber, the film shows her determination to resort to hard work and professionalism to establish her career.

My Fair Gentleman, therefore, is the culmination of previous Chinese productions of *Pygmalion*. It has resonances in other John Woo films with the empowerment of macho male protagonists by female characters. It was made simultaneously with Woo's *Red Cliff* and *Red Cliff II* (allegedly the most expensive Chinese films ever made, with an estimated budget of U.S. $80 million). These two expensive films are, based on the Chinese classic *Three Kingdoms*, depicting the battle between Cao Wei led by Cao Cao (曹魏), Shu Han (蜀漢) led by Liu Bei, and Dong Wu or Eastern Wu led by Sun Quan. The three rulers are classic macho figures in Chinese history and literature. But in *Red Cliff II*, Woo adds a new perspective by showing how the three men are redeemed by the female protagonists, one of which is played by Vicki Zhao Wei, who also played the female Eliza Doolittle in the 2003 *Pygmalion* adaptation, *My Dream Girl*.

The producers of *My Fair Gentleman*, John Woo and Terence Chang, went on to produce *Reign of Assassins* (2010),[38] starring Michelle Yeoh, who is the third producer of *My Fair Gentleman*, and Kelly Lin, who played Candice–Higgins. This film features elements of *My Fair Gentleman*, showcasing transformations of identities and the empowerment of a male protagonist by a female one. The female assassin Drizzle (Michelle Yeoh) plans to assassinate the prime minister and his son Renfeng to secure a treasure for the head of the Black Stone assassin gang, Wheel King, who turns out to be a eunuch of the emperor. Drizzle kills the prime minister but is then reformed by a monk, has plastic surgery, and lives in seclusion as Zeng Jing. Renfeng also has plastic surgery, changing his identity to Ah-sheng so that he can avenge his father's murder. Finding the reformed Zeng Jing, Ah-sheng falls in love with her and marries her. When Drizzle discovers Ah-sheng's true identity, both realize that their real enemy is Wheel King and defeat him—whether or not Wheel King is killed remains unknown, probably opening the way for a sequel. The film was featured at the Venice Film Festival and won best director and film of credit at the Hong Kong Film Critics Society Awards.

The Entrepreneurial Peasant in Cosmopolitan Shanghai

Significantly, the appearance of *My Fair Gentleman* coincided with celebrations of the sixtieth anniversary of the founding of a nation. The transformations featured in Shaw's *Pygmalion* show the adaptation of the entrepreneurial peasant to cosmopolitan Shanghai, a huge metaphor of the economic success of China and its people. As Shaw built his theory of the Life Force and Creative Evolution into the character of Eliza Doolittle, the character of the successful entrepreneurial peasant showcases the vital and willful Shavian Superman. In 1937, Shaw presented an album, with a letter pasted on the front page, to Wang Tjo-ling, one of the principal stage and film directors in Shanghai, when Wang was still a student in London. The letter ends with these words: "Up, China. Nothing can stop you in the Eastern world. Go ahead with your plays—only don't do mine."[39] These words ring true in *My Fair Gentleman* featuring how the entrepreneurial peasant is reconciled to cosmopolitan Shanghai. Shaw is not mentioned, of course, but this newest adaptation of *Pygmalion* shows that his influence remains strong and vital in China.

NOTES

1. A draft of this paper was read at the Fourth International Shaw Society Conference, "Shaw Without Borders/Shaw sans frontières," at the University of Guelph, Guelph, Ontario. I would like to thank Stanley and Rodelle Weintraub for their continuous support of my work on Shaw and China. I am also grateful to the ingenious advice of Leonard Conolly and Dick Dietrich, Suzanne Merriam and Christopher Innes, on the Sagittarius–ORION–Shaw project. Michel Pharand's revisions to this paper are deeply appreciated.

2. *Yao tiao shen shi* (*My Fair Gentleman*). Dir. Gui Yuen Lee. Perf. Honglei Sun, Kelly Lin, and Xiao-ling Hong. Lion Rock Productions, Mighty Media, Sil-Metropole Organisation, 2009.

3. *The Greatest Lover*. Dir. Clarence Fok. Perf. Chow Yun-Fat, Anita Mui, and Eric Tsang. Universe, 1988.

4. *Wo hu cang long* (*Crouching Tiger, Hidden Dragon*). Dir. Ang Lee. Perf. Chow Yun-Fat, Michelle Yeoh, and Ziyi Zhang. Asia Union Film & Entertainment Ltd., China Film Co-Production Corporation, Columbia Pictures Film Production Asia, 2000. *Dip huet seung hung* (*The Killer*). Dir. John Woo. Perf. Chow Yun-Fat,

Danny Lee, and Sally Yeh. Film Workshop, Golden Princess Film Production Limited, Long Shong Pictures, 1989.

5. *Yaotiao Shunu*. (*Pygmalion*.) Dir. Clifton Ko Chi-sum. Perf. Tse Kwan-ho and Chiu Woon. Springtime Film Productions, 1997.

6. *Pao Zhi Nu Peng You* (*My Dream Girl*). Dir. Raymond Yip Wai-Man. Perf. Ekin Cheng Yee-Kin, Vicki Zhao Wei, Vincent Kok Tak-Chiu, and Richard Ng Yiu-Hon. People's Productions, Universe Entertainment Company and Shanxi Film Production Company. Assisted by the China Film Co-Production Company, 2003.

7. Kay Li, *Bernard Shaw and China: Cross-Cultural Encounters*. Gainesville: University Press of Florida, 2007.

8. Online at www.shanghai.gov.cn Shanghai Municipal Government website and *China Daily* at www.chinadaily.com.cn/china/2011-02/23/content_12060936.htm.

9. Ibid.

10. *Jian guo da ye* (*The Founding of a Republic*). Dir. Sanping Han, Jianxin Huang. Perf. Guoqiang Tang, Guoli Zhang, and Qing Xu. China Film Group, CCTV Movie Channel, Shanghai Film Studio, 2009.

11. Andy "Chinese Cinema Finally Breaks Through (Part 2)?" www.chinastartupjobs .com/?p=150 March 14, 2011.

12. Online at ent.163.com.

13. Online at www.enbar.net.

14. "On Development of the Film Publishing Market in China," online at www .wypaper.com "wypaper."

15. Andy "Chinese Cinema Finally Breaks Through (Part 2)?" www.chinastartupjobs .com/?p=150, March 14, 2011.

16. Online at www.cnielts.com.

17. Foreign Exchange Calculator at www.hsbc.ca. Rates on 11 July 2011.

18. *Pygmalion*. Dir. Anthony Asquith, Leslie Howard. Perf. Leslie Howard, Wendy Hiller, and Wilfrid Lawson. Gabriel Pascal Productions, 1938.

19. *My Fair Lady*. Dir. George Cukor. Perf. Audrey Hepburn, Rex Harrison, and Stanley Holloway. Warner Bros. Pictures, 1964.

20. *Face/Off*. Dir. John Woo. Perf. John Travolta, Nicolas Cage, and Joan Allen. Permut Presentations, Touchstone Pictures, Paramount Pictures, 1997. *Mission: Impossible II*. Dir. John Woo. Perf. Tom Cruise, Dougray Scott, and Thandie Newton. Paramount Pictures, Cruise/Wagner Productions, Munich Film Partners & Company (MFP) MI2 Productions, 2000. *Paycheck*. Dir. John Woo. Perf. Ben Affleck, Aaron Eckhart, and Uma Thurman. DreamWorks SKG, Paramount Pictures, Davis Entertainment, 2003. *A Better Tomorrow*. Dir. John Woo. Perf. Lung Ti, Leslie Cheung, and Chow Yun-Fat. Cinema City, Film Workshop, 1986. *The Killer*. Dir. John Woo. Perf. Chow Yun-Fat, Danny Lee, and Sally Yeh. Film Workshop, Golden Princess Film Production Limited, Long Shong Pictures, 1989. *Anna and the King*. Dir. Andy Tennant. Perf. Jodie Foster, Chow Yun-Fat, and Ling Bai. Fox Movies, 1999. *Wo hu cang long* (*Crouching Tiger, Hidden Dragon*) (2000). Dir. Ang Lee. Perf. Chow Yun-Fat, Michelle Yeoh, and Ziyi Zhang. Sony Pictures Classics, Kinowelt Median AG (German), 2000. *Tomorrow Never Dies*. Dir. Roger Spottiswoode. Perf. Pierce Brosnan, Jonathan Pryce, and Michelle Yeoh. Danjaq,

Eon Productions, Metro-Goldwyn-Mayer (MGM), 1997. *Brokeback Mountain*. Dir. Ang Lee. Perf. Heath Ledger, Jake Gyllenhaal, and Michelle Williams. Alberta Film Entertainment, Focus Features, Good Machine, 2005.

21. Chen Yang, "Starbucks faces more competition in China," *Global Times* (26 October 2011). Online at www.globaltimes.cn,

22. Online at www.tradingeconomics.com "Trading Economics."

23. IMF Survey Online, "IMF Sees China Growth Around 8% in 2012," online at www.imf.org. Online at www.mongabay.com/ "mongabay."

24. Online at http://mitworld.mit.edu/ "MIT Video."

25. Ibid.

26. Online at www.chinatoday.com/ "China Today."

27. David K. Randall, "HOW TO PLAY IT: Targeting China's consumers as growth slows," online at www.reuters.com/article/2012/03/06/chinaconsumers-idUSL2E8E6AFV20120306, and Nick Debnam and George Svinos, "Luxury Brands in China," online at www.forbes.com "Forbes."

28. Online at www.chinasuccessstories.com/ "China Success Stories"; "Refined Strategies: Luxury Extends Its Reach Across China." Online at www.kpmg.com/CN/en/IssuesAndInsights/ArticlesPublications/Documents/Luxury-extends-its-reach-across-China-201005.pdf.

29. "What's your poison? The world's weirdest drinks: Lizard wine, China and far east Asia" Online at travel.uk.msn.com.

30. Online at www.china.org.cn/.

31. Online at www.haosi.com.cn/ "Haosi International."

32. Bernard Shaw, *Collected Plays with Their Prefaces*, ed. Dan H. Laurence. 7 vols. (London: Max Reinhardt, 1970–74), 5:749.

33. Ibid., 750.

34. Ibid., 748.

35. Bernard Shaw, *Major Critical Essays* (Harmondsworth: Penguin, 1986), 240.

36. *Da hong deng long gao gao gua* (*Raise the Red Lantern*). Dir. Zhang Yimou. Perf. Li Gong, Jingwu Ma, and Saifei He. Beijing: ERA International, China Film Co-Production Corporation, Century Communications, 1991.

37. *Jianyu* (*Reign of Assassins*). Dir. Chao-Bin Su. Perf. Michelle Yeoh, Woo-sung Jung, and Kelly Lin. Beijing Gallop Horse Film & TV Production, Media Asia Films, Zhejiang Dongyang Dragon Entertainment Venture Investment, 2010.

38. Quoted in Rubeigh J. Minney, *Next Stop, Peking: Record of a 16,000-Mile Journey through Russia, Siberia and China* (London: George Newnes, 1957), 144.

Shaw in "Sallust's House"

STANLEY WEINTRAUB

Just to stir things up seems a great reward in itself.

—Caius Sallustius Crispus

Caius Sallustius Crispus is a mysterious and subtle signifier in Bernard Shaw's writings. As *Sallust*, the Roman political philosopher appears in only one early work, Shaw's last completed novel—and there only as the hideaway address of the hero. Shaw's fifth novel was *An Unsocial Socialist*, an apparently foreshortened effort suggesting that he had found more congenial avenues for his ideas. Originally titled *The Heartless Man*, the novel was drafted in Pitman shorthand at a desk in his informal university, the domed Reading Room of the British Museum, which he later claimed offered all the writerly benefits of socialism—public access to its facilities. Largely dialogue-based, *An Unsocial Socialist* foreshadows his plays, especially *Man and Superman*, which also focuses upon an attractive, compulsive and moneyed young gentleman given to radical polemics and susceptible to the wiles of women.

Shaw finished his rewrite, in 336 handwritten pages, in December 1883. He had intended a longer and more polemical work, he later claimed, but possibly he had wearied of the split personality hobbling his hero, who is both reformer and charlatan, vagabond and mountebank, wooer and hermit. Publishers, each in turn as Shaw's packet of manuscript was returned by the post, rejected the novel. One critic, John Morley, better known later as a Liberal politician, described it as "paradoxical, absurd and impossible." The author, Morley conceded, "knows how to write; he is pointed, rapid,

forcible, sometimes witty, often powerful and occasionally eloquent."
Yet he questioned the sustained irony—whether readers would wonder
whether the author "was serious or was laughing at them." Shaw seemed
to seek both reactions, simultaneously—to Victorian publishers a suicidal
commercial strategy. *An Unsocial Socialist* appeared as a low print-run book
only after it was first serialized, a year later, for no payment, in the monthly
Socialist magazine, *To-Day*.

Through the Zetetical Society, a debating circle of politically radical
young men in London, Shaw had become friendly with the scholarly young
Sidney Webb, who apparently gave his name, although not his personality, to
the novel's flamboyantly heartless socialist, Sidney Trefusis. Almost immediately on meeting Webb, Shaw considered the dumpy, scraggly bearded
but surprisingly learned Colonial Office clerk the most brilliant mind in
England. Appearances seldom deceived Shaw. Forcing his friendship on the
mumbling cockney who looked like a caricature of a nineteenth-century
German professor, Shaw augmented at second-hand his own Dublin drop-
out education.

It is possible that Shaw learned of Sallust (86–34 BCE) from the widely
read Webb, and followed up hints about the Roman worthy from the capa-
cious shelves of the Reading Room. An aristocrat and a senator, Sallust had
called himself a *novus homo*—a "new man." (The term echoes in Shaw.)
Attacking Cicero as an upper-class demagogue, Sallust espoused the causes
of the plebs—the common people. Attaching himself to Julius Caesar, Sallust commanded a legion in North Africa. Returning to Rome in 44 BCE, he
was accused of plundering his conquered province, but through Caesar's
intervention was never brought to trial. (A later accusation of immorality, scurrilous gossip at odds with his writings, may have originated in the
confusion between him and his adopted son, Sallustius Crispus, a minister of Caesar Augustus, and known for great wealth and luxurious tastes.)
The end of Sallust's public career and his retirement to his garden and to
writing apparently came after Caesar's assassination. Shaw's pithy remarks
attributed to Julius Caesar in *Caesar and Cleopatra* may owe something to
Sallust's writings about Roman politics. (A "Sallust of Perusia" appears as a
betrayer of Emperor Julian the Apostate in Ibsen's turgid *The Emperor and
the Galilean*, and is mentioned once in Shaw's *The Quintessence of Ibsenism*,
in 1890. The character bears no relation to the earlier Sallust.)

An Unsocial Socialist is set in 1875. Sidney Trefusis, the possessor of
inherited manufacturing wealth about which he feels guilty, and wed to an
attractive heiress, runs off after six weeks of marriage. Henrietta, whom he

professes to love, is devastated, but Sidney nevertheless returns to a country cottage he calls *Sallust's House*. The retreat, complete to a library, where he masquerades improbably as the plebeian "Jeff Smilash," is close to Manchester, where much of his late father's mill-based income was generated. Marriage was an impulsive mistake. Trefusis claims to need freedom from his new and unexpectedly restrictive conjugal yoke to work at political proselytizing. He predicates his flight with flattery. "The first condition of work with me is your absence," he explains to the baffled Henrietta. "When you are with me I can do nothing but make love to you. You bewitch me." Two millenia earlier Sallust had written, "No mortal man has ever served at the same time his passions and his best interests."

Pursuing Sidney into the provinces, Henrietta returns without her husband, who sweet-talks her, and sends her home. Ill from exposure in the bleak December weather, she dies, two days before Christmas, of pneumonia, misdiagnosed by expensive doctors summoned by her father. Back in London too late to matter, Trefusis rails against fashionable but ignorant physicians in one of Shaw's earliest tirades against members of the medical fraternity who, like other professionals, protected each other. One of the specialists who had been called in when Henrietta's suffering seemed beyond the skills of the family's general practitioner explains, "Everything was done that could be done, Mr. Trefusis."

"Professional etiquette," Trefusis feels, but leaves unspoken, "bound [the physician] so strongly that, sooner than betray his colleague's inefficiency, he would have allowed him to decimate half of London." A citation from Sallust would have confirmed that. "It is in the nature of ambition to make men liars and cheats, and hide the truth in their breasts, and show, like jugglers, another thing in their mouths."

"The glory of riches and of beauty is frail and transitory," Sallust had also written. Henrietta's mother assures Sidney that there had been no neglect of his wife. "What have I to complain about?" he responds coldly, in his most extreme political vein, although he had wept, to his own surprise, at her deathbed. "She had a warm room and a luxurious bed to die in, with the best medical advice in the world. Plenty of people are starving and freezing to-day that we may have the means to die fashionably." Adding to his outrageous treason to his class, Trefusis also opts—to his father-in-law's horror—for a "common" tombstone by a journeyman stonecutter rather than an extravagant and florid one, for the lifeless remains of Henrietta were beyond appreciating the superfluous art of a Royal Academician. ("No grief reaches the dead," Sallust had observed.) Sidney's apparent brutality—his aversion from extravagant show—sustains the alleged heartlessness of the novel's original title. Henrietta is interred in Highgate Cemetery, where Karl Marx would be buried in the year Shaw wrote *An Unsocial Socialist*.

As a widower not given to mourning, Sidney Trefusis remains easily bewitched. Again in *Sallust's House*, he indulges only briefly in what he misdescribes as his "lonely ascetic hermit life," surrounded by a library of "dry books" that spurs his "Socialist propagandism." By novelistic coincidence, the Sallustian hermitage happens to be close to Alton College, an exclusive academy for well-to-do young women. For Trefusis, finding the burden of his plebeian alter ego as a workman-for-hire increasingly difficult to maintain credibly in the lively feminine ambience, the opportunities afforded by the finishing school are, for him, like netting goldfish from a bowl.

One of the Alton maidens is the high-spirited Agatha Wylie, who by mid-novel is expelled for misbehavior. (The college's petty rules are rigid.) By no coincidence, she is the niece and ward of the late Henrietta's father, a banker. The compulsively social Socialist, with an obviously faked humble bearing, conceals himself much too visibly at *Sallust's House*—itself a rather odd name for his cottage unless Sallust had some unexplained significance. Trefusis could have christened it, for example, *Marx's House*. Or left it unnamed.

"Jeff Smilash" fancies the lively girls, especially Agatha, but claims to be beyond their pale as an uneducated day laborer seeking work at the College. (Sidney Trefusis actually has a Cambridge degree.) As Smilash, he also goads workmen in the area to claim various political rights, including a public right-of-way through such private land as the school's "pleasure ground." At any opportunity he pours Marxist scorn on the commercialization of music, dance, painting, fiction and the other arts so important to the school's curriculum.

Just after Sidney's flight from marriage, Agatha had written to Henrietta—prompting his wife's chase after him, and her death—that she had recognized him despite his pseudo-cockney talk and his corduroy workman's garb. While also attracted by Jeff Smilash, the other girls fail to see through him as a moneyed crank and adventurer as well as a philandering provocateur—a very social Socialist. Smilash's inherited wealth as Trefusis is unknown to all of the girls but Agatha, yet her classmate Gertrude Lindsay describes his exotic *Sallust's House*, along the Riverside Road, with its "cinnamon-colored walls and yellow frieze," as suggesting "a foreign air"—much unlike a laborer's rude cottage and more, to Gertrude, "like a toy savings bank."

Wary from the start, Miss Wilson, the headmistress, is further suspicious of Smilash once she recognizes through his absurdly phony dialect "a scrap of Euclid." When Miss Wilson offers Smilash all of ninepence to roll the lawn, he offers his gratitude, praying, "May your ladyship's goodness sew up the hole which is in the pocket where I carry my character, and which has caused me to lose it so frequent. It is a bad place for men to keep their characters in; but such is the fashion." He explains that "words don't come natural" to him—that he has "more thoughts than words," and that what words he summons up "don't fit his thoughts." Yet they do, and playing the fool with radical ideas beyond those of an unlettered laborer is a continuing risk that he cannot resist.

The classical slip is not Sallustian, but the Roman would resonate through Shaw's writings. Smilash's wry cynicism belying his pose apparently derives from Sallust. The christening of the cottage cannot be accidental. Rescued from beneath centuries of volcanic ash, and known in Shaw's time, a House of Sallust survives, with portions of its frieze, in Pompeii, on the Via Domitiana. According to *The Buried Cities of Campania* (1872) by archaeologist W. H. Davenport Adams, the pages of which Shaw could have turned in the British Museum, the house and garden walls "are gaily painted . . . with a whimsical frieze above," and its stuccoed panels evidence, still, "different and strongly-contrasted colours."

No Sallust, despite the uncanny echoes of the house in Pompeii, Smilash retorts loftily to the upper-class Gertrude, who claims to be "an unprotected girl" in a man's world, "Why, you are fenced around and barred in with conventions, laws, and lies that would frighten the truth from the lips of any man whose faith . . . was less strong than mine." Sallust had written, succinctly, "The higher your station, the less your liberty." Floodlighting his bizarre guise as "Smilash," from which he is soon fully outed—undermined throughout by his witless frivolity—Trefusis turns the maxim into ponderous Marxism. Despite the plethora of paradoxes in *Das Kapital* and associated writings, one would have to hunt hard to find any gaiety in Karl Marx.

It has long been assumed that Voltaire or La Rochefoucauld—the French refer to Sallust as the Roman Rochefoucauld—were behind Shaw's ironic aphorisms in his plays, prefaces and especially the "Maxims for Revolutionists" pamphlet ostensibly by John Tanner in *Man and Superman*, whom Sidney Trefusis foreshadowed. Friedrich Nietzsche, already familiar to Shaw, had credited Sallust for his own epigrammatic bent. "My sense of style, for the epigram as a style, was awakened almost instantly when I came into contact with Sallust." Nietzsche also praised the Roman political chronicler for his "cold sarcasm."

"I am honest when well watched," Smilash concedes, and in a foreshadowing of Alfred Doolittle of *Pygmalion*, agrees with a parson that overpaying him for a job would only set him drinking, and that less cash would keep him drunk until Sunday morning, which is all he requires before religion, and pub closings, intervene. Trefusis (or Smilash) seems to have read, in his *Sallust's House* and earlier at Cambridge, the apothegms of Sallust, whose keen sense of sarcasm and anticlimax seems to have appealed to Shaw. Later characters who are in part spokespersons for GBS continue to echo the paradoxical Sallust, who wrote, "Few prize honor more than money," and "By the wicked the good conduct of others is always dreaded." Or the wry "He that will be angry for anything will be angry for nothing," and "To have the same desires and the same aversions is assuredly a firm bond of friendship."

The GBS who wrote in the preface to *Man and Superman* of "the true joy in life" as being used up in causes beyond one's self appears to have read (with allowances for the translations he encountered) Sallust's "He only may be truly said to live and enjoy his being who is engaged in some laudable pursuit, and acquires a name by some illustrious action, or useful art." In *Maxims for Revolutionists*, an appendix to the play, appears the maxim, "Liberty means responsibility. That is why most men dread it." Sallust in its counterpart had written, "Few men desire liberty. The majority are satisfied with a just master."

One can imagine *The Devil's Disciple* in Sallust's "Those moved to tears by every word of a preacher are generally weak, and rascals when the feelings evaporate." And *Arms and the Man*, where Captain Bluntschli's comment about the inadvertent heroism of Major Sergius Saranoff suggests Sallust's "In battle it is the cowards who run the most risk; bravery is a bulwark of defense." The brazenly utopian ventures of Andrew Undershaft, the multi-millionaire armaments czar in *Major Barbara*, explained in his sharp paradoxes, are scorned by Lady Britomart, his scheming, estranged wife, as "That's Andrew all over. He never does a proper thing without giving an improper reason for it." The pithy Sallust had written, "By the wicked the good conduct of others is always dreaded." Undershaft had already built his industrial empire and green company towns for his workmen on a premise described in Sallust as, "To someone seeking power, the poorest man is the most useful."

Oswald Spengler recommended, in his *Decline of the West*, perhaps thinking of *Major Barbara*, that Shaw, the "prime exponent of capitalistic socialism," should "read Sallust on *Catiline* and *Jugurtha*." Apparently Shaw already had. Samplings of Sallust after a perusal of Shaw suggest that GBS himself dwelt, metaphorically, in *Sallust's House*.

Sources

No allusion to Sallust seems to appear in Shaw's published writings after *An Unsocial Socialist* (London: Sonnenschein, 1887; first serially in *To-Day*, 1884); yet the central image of *Sallust's House* cannot be accidental. Painted on the outer wall of the Pompeiian villa is "C. Sallust." A full description of the excavated house is in W. H. Davenport Adams, *The Buried Cities of Campania* (London and Edinburgh: T. Nelson, 1872), 217–18, a discovery made by Michel Pharand. A full text is online via the Getty Research Institute Library. Quotations from Sallust above are from his *The Conspiracy of Catiline*, *The Jugurthine War*, and surviving fragments of his *Histories*, as translated online. The quotation from Nietzsche is from his *Twilight of the Idols*. Spengler is cited from vol. 2 of *The Decline of the West*.

Shavian Elements in the *My Fair Lady* Film

DEREK MCGOVERN

It seems temporally appropriate that George Cukor's screen version of *My Fair Lady* should have been released in 1964, since it neatly concluded a half-century of attempts by actors, directors, and adapters alike to romanticize Bernard Shaw's *Pygmalion*. From the very moment, in fact, that Herbert Beerbohm Tree and Mrs. Patrick (Stella) Campbell—in their respective roles of phonetician Henry Higgins and Cockney flower seller Eliza Doolittle—had improvised lines and stage business to imply to their opening-night London audience in 1914 that a romantic union between their two characters was inevitable, Shaw was embroiled in a perpetual struggle to control his conception of the play.

To Shaw, the culminating point of *Pygmalion* was that Eliza achieves independence from the bullying Higgins. An Eliza-Higgins marriage, he declared, would have been "a revolting tragedy."[1] To that end, Shaw appended a prose sequel to the first (1916) English-language publication of *Pygmalion* in book form, in which he outlined Eliza's married life with the youthful Freddy Eynsford Hill, a minor character in the play. However, the public, in general, "went on preferring its own version."[2] The advent of talking pictures offered Shaw an opportunity to reassert his wishes, and to this end he wrote his own screenplay adaptation in 1934 for the first (German) film version of *Pygmalion* (Erich Engel, 1935), making it a contractual requirement that the filmmakers adhered to his (translated) scenario, in which any suggestion of a Higgins-Eliza romance had been carefully removed. Without having seen the resulting film, Shaw also granted screen adaptation rights on the same condition to Dutch- and English-language productions (*Pygmalion*, Ludwig

Berger, 1937; *Pygmalion*, Anthony Asquith and Leslie Howard, 1938), revising his 1934 screenplay for the latter.[3] However, the makers of these film versions ignored their contractual obligations, and to varying degrees implied a romantic resolution between Higgins and Eliza.

All three films were domestic commercial successes, but it was almost certainly the international popularity of the *British* film, with its worrisome potential to influence future stage productions of the play, that compelled Shaw to revise his published stage text twice in 1939 (for, respectively, his 1939 and 1941 editions), on both occasions emphasizing (again) that Eliza did not marry Higgins.[4] Following Shaw's death in 1950, the executors of his Estate—ignoring their late client's often-stated opposition to the musicalization of *Pygmalion*—granted the musical adaptation rights to the play to Gabriel Pascal, producer of the 1938 film version. The resulting Broadway musical, *My Fair Lady* (Frederick Loewe and Alan Jay Lerner, 1956) was essentially an adaptation of the 1938 film, rather than the play, while the subsequent *screen* version of the musical eight years later was *in some respects* more faithful to Shaw than its stage counterpart, notwithstanding its continuation of the romanticization of the Higgins-Eliza relationship.

This essay examines the 1964 *My Fair Lady* film, addressing the following questions: (1) to what extent is the film a faithful adaptation of its stage musical counterpart? (2) In what specific ways do the film's aesthetics convey the likelihood of a Higgins-Eliza romance? (3) In what respects is the *My Fair Lady* film more faithful to the stage version(s) of Shaw's play than the 1938 film version of *Pygmalion*?

I

In spite of its inclusion on the American Film Institute's list of 100 Greatest American Films in 1998 (at No. 91) and its ranking at No. 8 on the same organization's list of the 25 Greatest Musicals in 2006, the screen version of *My Fair Lady* has received scant attention from film scholars. Gerald Mast attributes this neglect to a perception that the film is "too reverential for a 'real movie musical'—giving up the clever game between stylized song and credible movie storytelling."[5] Its fidelity to its stage source has been overstated, however. In his adaptation of his own stage libretto,[6] screenwriter Alan Jay Lerner makes numerous changes to the musical, rearranging the order of songs, deleting certain scenes and adding new ones, while incorporating a considerable amount of new dialogue material drawn from *Pygmalion* (the play) and the 1938 *Pygmalion* film (non-Shavian dialogue).

Lerner makes nine principal changes in his screenplay:[7]

1. The acrobatic "Street Entertainers" performance by three buskers that begins the stage musical is deleted.
2. Eliza returns to Covent Garden the morning after her first encounter with Higgins instead of going directly to Higgins's flat in Wimpole Street.
3. The order of Alfred Doolittle's songs "With a Little Bit of Luck" and "I'm an Ordinary Man" is reversed, so that the latter now precedes the former.
4. A bathroom scene, in which a terrified Eliza is forced to bathe by housekeeper Mrs. Pearce and two maids, is added.
5. Doolittle's reprise of "With a Little Bit of Luck" (Act I, Scene 4 in the stage musical) is deleted.
6. Most of *My Fair Lady*'s Act I, Scene 6 ("Near the race meeting, Ascot") is deleted, together with a portion of Act I, Scene 10 ("The promenade of the Embassy"); these deletions amount to approximately two pages of non-Shavian dialogue by Lerner.
7. A brief scene involving Higgins and his mother is added after Eliza's faux pas at the Ascot Races (see Shavian additions below).
8. The Intermission/Entr'acte is brought forward so that it now precedes the Embassy Ball scene rather than following it.
9. Higgins sings a new twelve-line verse in the ensemble number "You Did It."

Cukor asserts that the film version of *My Fair Lady* employed "even more of Shaw's screenplay than the stage version [of the musical] did."[8] It would be more accurate to state that the film is closer to the (third and final) 1941 edition of *Pygmalion* than Shaw's 1934–38 screenplay, since in two instances (both of which are asterisked on the following page) Lerner features dialogue in his screenplay that appears only in the stage editions of *Pygmalion* (all versions), and not in Shaw's screenplay, together with material that is unique to the 1941 version. Accordingly, all subsequent quotations from the stage version of *Pygmalion* are taken from the 1941 edition of the play.[9]

The additional Shavian material in the *My Fair Lady* film comprises the following:

1. Mrs. Eynsford Hill's interaction with Pickering from Act I is restored—"Oh, sir, is there any sign of [the rain] stopping?"[10]
2. Mrs. Pearce's Act II remonstration ("It's no use talking to her like that, Mr. Higgins. She doesnt understand you") and her attempt to retrieve

Higgins's handkerchief from Eliza—"Here, give that handkerchief to me! He give it to me, not to you!"*

3. The aforementioned Bathroom Scene (Optional Scene #2 from the 1941 version).

4. Higgins's brusque treatment of Mrs. Eynsford Hill in Act III ("Ive seen you before somewhere. Oh it doesn't matter. Youd better sit down").

5. Mrs. Higgins's Act III objections to Higgins's "experiment" on Eliza.[11]

6. Higgins's insistence to Pickering in Act IV that he had not been nervous during the Ambassador's reception ("Werent you a little bit nervous once or twice?" / "No, not when I saw we were going to win hands down. I felt like a bear in a cave, hanging about with nothing to do").

7. Eliza's exchanges with Freddy in Wimpole Street after her row with Higgins: e.g., "Eliza, where are you going?" / "To the river." / "What for?" / "To make a hole in it." / "Eliza, darling, what do you mean?" (from Optional Scene #5 in the 1941 version).

8. Part of Doolittle's first speech in Act V—"Who asked him to make a gentleman out of me? I was happy. I was free. . ... Now I'm tied neck and heels and everybody touches me. . . . . Oh, I have to live for others now, not for meself. That's middle-class morality."

9. Mrs. Higgins's scolding of Higgins and Pickering for not praising Eliza sufficiently after her performance at the Ambassador's reception (Act V).[12]*

The non-Shavian material drawn from the 1938 *Pygmalion* film comprises just three brief instances: Pickering's insistence that Higgins give up the experiment with Eliza after the fiasco of her appearance at Mrs. Higgins's at-home day; the Ambassador's wife's exchange with Higgins regarding her curiosity about Eliza—"Such a faraway look, as if she's always lived in—in a garden" / "So she has; a *sort* of a garden"—and the Queen of Transylvania's request that Eliza dance with her son.

Lerner's new (original) dialogue comprises approximately fifty exchanges of minor significance. One-third of these involve Doolittle in his Covent Garden milieu in scenes corresponding to Act I, Scene 2 and Act I, Scene 4, respectively, of the stage musical. The majority of Doolittle's new exchanges are with his cronies, as the former extols his carefree ways and rationalizes his parental neglect of Eliza—"I give her the greatest gift any human being can give to another: life. . . . Then I disappears and leaves her on her own to enjoy it." Lerner provides Eliza with a number of new lines in the interpolated bathroom scene as she struggles with Mrs. Pearce and two maids,[13] and also adds several exchanges to the Embassy Ball scene,[14] increasing the element of suspense as the Ambassador's wife dispatches Karpathy (Nepommuck in Shaw's 1941 edition) to discover Eliza's identity.

Thematic consequences of Lerner's changes. Lerner's Shavian additions in his screenplay principally bolster the transformation theme as regards both Eliza and her father by following the structure of *Pygmalion's* Act III more closely in the first instance and restoring dialogue from the elder Doolittle's Act V appearance in the second. In respect of the former, whereas the Ascot Races scene in the stage musical concludes with Higgins's roars of laughter at Eliza's "Move your bloomin' arse!,"[15] the film version includes an additional scene at Ascot utilizing material adapted from the end of *Pygmalion's* Act III in which Mrs. Higgins remonstrates with Higgins over his experiment on Eliza[16]—"Youre a pretty pair of babies playing with your live doll."[17] Although Lerner does not include Mrs. Higgins's concerns regarding the potential social consequences of transformation on Eliza,[18] the addition is significant nonetheless in that it underscores Higgins's inability to consider Eliza as a fully developed person—a point that is further emphasised by the restoration of his Act III line, "It fills our whole lives: teaching Eliza, talking to Eliza, listening to Eliza, dressing Eliza."[19] The terseness with which Mrs. Higgins addresses her son in this scene also underlines Shaw's point that, of all the characters in *Pygmalion*, she and Mrs. Pearce possess the most common sense.

As regards Doolittle's transformation, the restoration of eight sentences from the first of his (Act V, *Pygmalion*) speeches emphasizes the comic irony of his plight to a much greater extent than in the stage musical. While the stage version fails to clarify why Doolittle objects to his new status as a middle-class gentleman, the film Doolittle identifies the essence of his distaste for "middle-class morality"—"Oh, I have to live for others now, not for meself." To a greater degree than the stage version of *My Fair Lady*, the film also emphasizes Doolittle's loss of freedom—"Who asked him to make a gentleman out of me? I was happy. I was free"—while also conveying his realization that his predicament constitutes a form of retributive justice: "I touched pretty nigh everyone for money when I wanted it, same as I touched [Higgins]. Now I'm tied neck and heels and everybody touches me. A year ago I hadn't a relation in the world, except one or two who wouldn't speak to me. Now I've 50, and not a decent week's wages amongst the lot of them."

Significantly, however, Lerner does not restore any dialogue from Doolittle's more serious second (Act V) speech, in which he reveals his fear of the workhouse. This omission is consistent with the overall tone of Lerner's screenplay, which in many respects is a more comic work than his stage libretto.

II

In this section, I examine the film's various aesthetic elements, concluding with a discussion of how these encourage the expectation of a romantic relationship between Higgins and Eliza.

Shot composition and editing. Not surprisingly, given that *My Fair Lady* and the 1938 *Pygmalion* film share the same cinematographer in Harry Stradling, there are striking visual similarities at times between the two films. In the opening Covent Garden scenes of both films, high camera angles are employed on Wendy Hiller and Audrey Hepburn—the actors portraying Eliza in the 1938 and 1964 films, respectively—to underline Eliza's fear and vulnerability when she discovers that Higgins is transcribing her conversation. Moreover, the similarity in the appearance, clothing, and grouping of the onlookers in both scenes is remarkable.[20] In the Embassy Ball scene, the arrival of Eliza occurs in an almost identical manner,[21] as she emerges from a door and walks toward the camera, while earlier in both films Cukor emulates Asquith's use of low angles in the 1938 film to emphasize Higgins's dominance over Eliza as he stands on a staircase. In both films, the use of shadow and contrast on Eliza is also very similar in the scene corresponding to that of Act IV in the play. The films differ significantly, however, in the degree of fluidity of their respective directors' approach, with Cukor employing none of the long panning and tracking shots that Asquith uses in *Pygmalion*, nor any of his montage work. Moreover, unlike *Pygmalion*, much of *My Fair Lady* is filmed in either medium or medium-long shot, with few medium close-ups, and virtually no close-ups.

Cukor's camera is mostly static, particularly during the film's equivalent to Acts II, IV, and V in the play, with only the occasional panning shot.[22] Reaction shots are minimal, and consequently assume greater significance than usual when they do occur, such as a cutaway to Eliza (to reveal her interest) when Higgins (Rex Harrison) boasts to Pickering (Wilfrid Hyde-White) that he "could pass her off as a duchess at an embassy ball." During Doolittle (Stanley Holloway)'s first long speech at Higgins's home, the camera remains entirely static. This composition style, coupled with the widescreen Super Panavision 70 format,[23] reinforces the theatricality of the film, with the viewing perspective often akin to that of being seated in an ideal position in the circle of an auditorium. This is evident during some of the musical numbers involving characters other than Higgins, Eliza, or Doolittle. In "You Did It," for example, there are no close-ups—or even medium close-ups—on Pickering while he is singing; instead, he is filmed mainly in profile with cutaways to Higgins for spoken comments and to Eliza for reaction shots. When Doolittle makes his first appearance in Higgins's study, and Higgins identifies Doolittle's origins as "Brought up in Hounslow, mother Welsh," Cukor retains the camera on Higgins after this line rather than cutting to a (presumably surprised) Doolittle for his reaction.

At other times, the editing is highly effective. Examples include the rapid cutting of shots taken from both low and aerial angles in the opening scene to convey the scurrying of people in Covent Garden during the sudden downpour, and the wittiness with which Cukor conveys the clipped speech of the British upper classes by cutting to a different shot of its members after each word—"Pulses/rushing/faces/flushing"—during the Ascot Gavotte, an ensemble number mocking the reserve of British high society.

Visual motifs and color. Cukor begins *My Fair Lady* with rapid dissolves of still photographs of flowers in bloom, and these constitute virtually the only close-ups in the entire film. The flowers remain throughout the ensuing credits and eventually dissolve into flowers on the banisters of the entrance to the Royal Opera House, as its elegantly dressed patrons descend the stairs. They subsequently reappear throughout the film: at the Covent Garden market the morning after Eliza's first encounter with Higgins—again in close-up—presumably symbolizing not only a new day, but also the beginning of Eliza's transformation, and in the blurred foreground on both the left and right sides of the screen during Freddy (Jeremy Brett)'s serenade to Eliza, "On the Street Where You Live," and its reprise. Thus, flowers are associated with Eliza as both a metaphor for the blooming of her character—or its transformation—and as a symbol for the transformation she effects in others. Freddy accordingly "blooms" in her presence. But as Mast observes, when Eliza abruptly leaves Wimpole Street, as she does after Freddy's reprise of "On the Street Where You Live," by the following morning "the same street has become drab and autumnal—with gray tree trunks and limbs barren of leaves, brownstone houses devoid of color,"[24] thus emphasizing the drabness of Higgins's life without her as he sings his soliloquy of self-discovery, "I've Grown Accustomed to Her Face."

As Mast goes on to observe, Cukor also uses color to distinguish between the natural environments of his two main protagonists: "If Higgins's habitat is the cavelike indoors, saturated in deep browns, Eliza's natural habitat is outdoors, blazing with color."[25] As depicted here, however, the vibrant colors of Eliza's pre-transformation environment of Covent Garden overpower any real sense of the squalor of her habitat. This is presumably deliberate on Cukor's part, for his motive is not one of social realism, but rather one of irony, for by associating the spirit of Eliza with color, he is able to contrast her character with that of the upper classes whom she would aspire to join. Accordingly, "Covent Garden's fashionable antithesis is the Ascot racetrack, where the 'Ascot Gavotte' takes the themes of Art and Nature, monochrome and color into a daytime outdoor world." Here, the 'proper' grays of the men's attire and the blacks and whites of the women's symbolize a world "that . . . is inhabited by people who aren't flowers."[26] Cukor also uses color in this scene to signify that Higgins, in his conspicuously inappropriate light-brown rustic-looking suit, is as much an outsider as Eliza, with her socially inappropriate behavior.

Use of music. In comparison with the Broadway and London original cast recordings of *My Fair Lady*, both of which use the 1956 production's orchestrations by Robert Russell Bennett and Phil Lang, the film features a much larger orchestra and opulent new arrangements that emphasize the romantic and sentimental elements of the score, particularly in the greater use of strings. The chorus is also considerably larger than that of the original production. When four costermongers farewell Eliza at the end of her melancholy "Wouldn't It Be Loverly?," it is not the voices of four men that we hear but a full choral ensemble. Similarly, at the end of Doolittle's valedictory ode to unmarried life, "Get Me to the Church on Time," the extensive use of angelic-sounding high soprano voices in the choir differs markedly in impact from that of the earthier, leaner-sounding chorus in the original production. The greater romanticism of the film score is also emphasized by conductor André Previn's slow tempi, and the frequent use of the melody from Eliza's romantic "I Could Have Danced All Night"—a song in which she both alludes to her celebratory dance with Higgins after conquering her speech problems and implies that she is in love with him—which features not only in both the Overture and the Intermission/Entr'acte, but is reprised throughout the film from the aftermath of the Ascot Races scene onward. Cukor uses the melody to convey Eliza's contrasting moods; for example, the exultation of the Embassy Ball (where she dances with Higgins for the second time) and, later, the bitter aftermath of her fight with Higgins, as she searches for her ring that Higgins has flung into the fireplace.

Music is also used to indicate moments of impending significance. When Eliza wanders through Covent Garden the morning after her first encounter with Higgins, a sustained note from a violin precedes Higgins's overlaid dialogue on the soundtrack ("You see this creature with her kerbstone English?"). As Eliza continues to wander, the music becomes agitated, reflecting her inner conflict, and we again hear Higgins tell her that she is a "disgrace to the noble architecture of these columns." The melody then finds its partial resolution in a reprise of a single line from "Wouldn't It Be Loverly?" ("All I want is a room somewhere"), thus providing reassurance through the use of a familiar tune, as Higgins intones, "I could even get her a job as a ladies' maid," before changing to a major key and a new straightforward melody as Eliza stands up, indicating that a decision has been made.

Romance. Unlike the 1938 *Pygmalion* film, Cukor's *My Fair Lady* presents Freddy as a credible romantic alternative to Higgins, eschewing its predecessor's caricature-like depiction of this character. Much of this is arguably due to Brett's naturalistic performance as Freddy. Whereas David Tree overacts in the 1938 film and portrays Freddy as a slow-witted and ineffectual would-be suitor, Brett is consistently understated in a performance that suggests a "much less foolish Freddy."[27] Brett's Freddy is still clearly infatuated with Eliza, but not ludicrously so. At no time does he appear "*frightened*" of the more assertive Eliza, as Lerner's libretto states in the stage version of *My Fair Lady* (146); instead he is merely startled by her unpredictability. A contributing factor to this impression is Brett's relative maturity. Thirty years old at the time of filming, he is seven years older than the 1938 film's Tree—an age difference that de-emphasises Freddy's callowness.[28] Brett's more worldly and passionate Freddy does not faint, as Tree's Freddy almost does, when presented with the opportunity to kiss Eliza.[29] Moreover, there is arguably a romantic chemistry between Hepburn's Eliza and Brett's Freddy in their Ascot Races and Wimpole Street scenes—a quality that is absent in the equivalent scenes with Hiller and Tree in the 1938 film. As Sara Martin observes, "When Hepburn/Eliza sings 'Show me' to [Brett/Freddy], openly asking for love, it is evident that Hepburn and Brett make an attractive couple."[30]

One important aspect of Freddy's greater impact in *My Fair Lady* is due to a change that Lerner makes in his screenplay, which treats Freddy more respectfully than in his libretto. In the stage musical, Act II, Scene II ends with Eliza ridiculing Freddy by "*crowning him with [her suitcase]*" at the conclusion of her declamatory song "Show Me." However, in the film, Eliza does not strike Freddy; she merely rebuffs his attempts to embrace her during the song. Moreover, at the completion of this song, Lerner restores dialogue from the equivalent scene in Shaw's 1941 version (optional scene 5) that emphasizes a much more perceptive Freddy than that of the 1938 film. Instead of emulating Tree's stuttering bewilderment when Eliza informs him that she is "going to the river . . . to make a hole in it," Brett/Freddy—clearly comprehending Eliza's distraught and possibly suicidal state of mind—grasps her arm and asks her quietly but seriously, "Eliza, darling, what do you mean?"

In further examples of Freddy's romantic aggrandisement in Cukor's *My Fair Lady*, the Overture, which plays during the opening credits of the film, begins with Freddy's "theme" ("On the Street Where You Live"), and continues for two and a half minutes, replacing "You Did It" and other melodies from the stage version of the Overture. It is then followed by the melody of Eliza's "I Could Have Danced All Night," thereby linking Freddy and Eliza (musically) to each other from the outset. This symbolic partnering is further emphasized by the fact that, of all the characters in the film, it is Freddy (in medium shot) whom we first see (together with his mother), followed in the next shot by Eliza. This cinematic device recalls Shaw's visual linking of Freddy and Eliza in his screenplay, in which he introduces the *"good-looking"* Freddy to the audience *before* Higgins is seen, and then subtly links him to Eliza when, caught in a heavy shower, Freddy *"rushes off,"* followed by Eliza, who *"disappears in [his] footsteps."*[31]

Moreover, Brett/Freddy's manners toward Eliza are impeccable in their first scene together, and immediately imply a romantic and sensitive man, as opposed to Tree's haughty indifference. While in the 1938 film Tree/ Freddy mutters a cursory "Sorry!" when he upsets Eliza's basket of flowers and then continues on his way, Brett/Freddy is no more culpable than Eliza when they collide, yet apologizes profusely to her and attempts to help her in gathering the violets. In an action that minimizes the class differences between them (or perhaps suggests that such differences are not important to him), he also maintains eye contact with Eliza as he kneels (smilingly) to help her. In short, *My Fair Lady* suggests that Freddy is both charming and lacking in snobbery—arguably important qualities if we are to believe that Eliza would consider him matrimonially.

For her part, Hepburn/Eliza is attentive to Freddy and appreciative of his interest when the two meet again in the Ascot Races scene, gracefully acknowledging his gift of the bet on a horse. Freddy's impact in this scene is undermined, however, by the absence of reaction shots, close-ups, or medium close-ups on him and by the fact that, in comparison with Eliza, he is shown mostly in profile. For the remainder of the film, Freddy is similarly distanced from the audience. When he performs "On the Street Where You Live" and its reprise, he is filmed mostly in medium shot (and never closer); when he sings to Eliza at the beginning of "Show Me," Cukor focuses his camera on Hepburn while Brett is afforded only a quarter profile. Freddy's visual marginalization in these scenes thus suggests a deliberate attempt on Cukor's part to undermine the former's romantic eligibility with respect to Eliza. At the same time, it is possible that commercial considerations may have influenced Cukor's decision to emphasize Hepburn, a major Hollywood star at the time, over the then virtually unknown Brett.

Irrespective of Freddy's visual marginalization in the film, the juxtaposition of Brett's amorous portrayal of the character with that of Harrison's Higgins, who at fifty-five is clearly a much older man, is in stark contrast to the 1938 film, in which "the sexual competition for Eliza's favors between Leslie Howard as Higgins and David Tree as Freddy is won hands down by Howard's smooth Higgins."[32] Harrison's performance, in any event, is arguably much closer to Shaw's conception of Higgins than Howard's. In contrast with Howard's soft-spoken Higgins, Harrison delivers his lines *"explosively"* where Shaw's stage play (and Lerner's libretto) requires him to do so. As Lerner observes,

> I personally believed that brilliant as he was in the film, Howard was not the complete Higgins. We all ran the film together and I said to Rex [Harrison] that my entire argument could be based on the reading of one line. The line occurs in the scene after the ball when Higgins is "humbly" taking full credit for Eliza's triumph. When they are alone together, there is a moment when Eliza cries out: "What is to become of me?" Higgins looks at her and says: "Oh! That's what is worrying you, is it?" To me, when Leslie Howard delivered the line one could tell he knew full well what she was talking about. You could almost see in his eyes that he was aware of her pain and of strange stirrings within himself.[33]

Harrison, in contrast, portrays Higgins in this scene as a man who is oblivious to any romantic "stirrings"—either within himself or Eliza—delivering the line in an almost-offhand, dismissive manner. Yet although Harrison's Higgins avoids any implication that he considers himself a "Romeo"—as Shaw had complained of Howard's interpretation of the role[34]—an earlier scene in the film suggests that he is already aware of his feelings for Eliza. This occurs immediately before Eliza makes her appearance on the staircase at Wimpole Street dressed for the Embassy Ball. In a line written by Lerner that also features in the stage version of *My Fair Lady*, Higgins tells Pickering that Eliza "matters immensely," and then appears to reflect on the significance of his acknowledgment. By leaving his camera on Harrison for several seconds after he has spoken these words, Cukor subtly emphasizes that the moment is one of self-revelation for Higgins.

Elsewhere in the film, Cukor employs a variety of means to imbue the film with suggestions of romance between Higgins and Eliza. At the end of the "Rain in Spain" scene, Cukor cuts from a shot of Higgins and Pickering, as they are discussing where best to "test Eliza in public," to a medium close-up of Hepburn, who appears to be gazing at Harrison/Higgins in adoration. When minutes later Eliza sings "1 Could Have Danced All Night," Cukor cuts to a rare close-up of her singing virtually into the camera as she begins the lines "I only know when he / began to dance with me." By framing Eliza in this way, Cukor creates the sense of a confessional release on her part to the audience. Later, when Eliza appears at the top of the staircase at Wimpole Street in her Embassy Ball gown, the melody to "1 Could Have Danced All Night" is heard softly on the soundtrack as Higgins peruses her appearance, reaching its climax as Higgins takes Eliza's arm and leads her from the room in a manner suggestive of a prince escorting his princess. When Eliza subsequently dances with Higgins at the Embassy Ball, Cukor cuts to a shot of Pickering and Mrs. Higgins beaming with contentment, thus suggesting parental approval of the younger couple.

Notwithstanding this romantic ambience, Cukor refrains from conveying the impression that Higgins and Eliza will ultimately marry. When Eliza— as in the 1938 *Pygmalion* film and the stage version of *My Fair Lady*—returns to Wimpole Street in the film's non-Shavian final scene, she tentatively approaches Higgins,[35] who is seated on the other side of the room, after he utters the (enigmatic?) closing line, "Where the devil are my slippers?," but then stops halfway. As she stands there, looking over at a slouching Higgins whose hat is pulled down over his face concealing his expression, she appears slightly rueful. The film ends.

This is a more ambiguous conclusion than that of the 1938 film, which depicts an assertive Eliza standing against the door of Higgins's laboratory with a knowing half-smile on her face. Although Cukor's ending does not rule out an Eliza-Higgins marriage, the subdued nature of the scene implies a decidedly bittersweet resolution in which only Higgins is the real beneficiary. While Eliza's return underscores the continuation of her friendship with Higgins—presumably on a more equal footing than before—her abrupt halt as she approaches him symbolizes her realization that, in terms of intimacy, their relationship cannot proceed beyond this point.

III

In several significant respects, the film version of *My Fair Lady* is closer to Shaw's *Pygmalion* than either its stage musical counterpart or the 1938 *Pygmalion* film. First, it does not dismiss the notion of Freddy as a plausible future husband for Eliza. While the 1938 film undermines Shaw's attempts in his screenplay to create a romantic chemistry between these two characters—portraying Freddy as too callow and insipid to be worthy of Eliza's attention—and the stage version of *My Fair Lady* ultimately implies a symbolic rejection of the former through Eliza's "*crowning*" of him with her suitcase, the film version of *My Fair Lady* neither ridicules Freddy nor undermines his romantic eligibility. Moreover, in contrast to the 1938 film, in which David Tree's stammering Freddy is never a serious rival in Eliza's affections to Leslie Howard's youthful-looking and implicitly sensual Higgins, the juxtaposition in *My Fair Lady* of Jeremy Brett's more mature, gallant, and self-assured Freddy with Rex Harrison's visibly older and strongly paternalistic Higgins represents the differentiation between these two characters that Shaw had desired in the screen version of *Pygmalion*.[36] Consequently, the contrast in the *My Fair Lady* film between "Brett's dandy looks and romantic performance [and] Harrison's fatherly bachelor" creates uncertainty for the audience as regards Eliza's motivation for returning to Wimpole Street in the final scene.[37] As Martin asks rhetorically, "Why, indeed, would Hepburn/Eliza feel an overwhelming 'biological' attraction for Harrison/Higgins, preferring him over Brett/Freddy?"[38]

One could add that, in comparison with Hiller's more expectant and assertive demeanor in the final scene of the 1938 *Pygmalion* film, Hepburn's return implies a sense of sadness on her character's part at the possible realization that the romantic feelings she had expressed so ecstatically at the conclusion of "I Could Have Danced All Night"—"when all at once my heart took flight"—will never be reciprocated by Higgins. As Martin observes, the 1938 film principally differs from the film version of *My Fair Lady* in that while the former suggests that, "Higgins and Eliza may come to an eventual understanding," "Harrison's mordant Higgins and Hepburn's Eliza make peace between [the two characters] less certain."[39] In short, the ending to the *My Fair Lady* film is carefully ambiguous. As in its stage counterpart, it concludes with the melody to "I Could Have Danced All Night"—a reprise that seemingly supports the inference that romance will ensue. In the film, however, Cukor's employment of the same melody can be regarded as ironic given not only the physical distance between Eliza and Higgins that exists in the scene, but also the former's distinctly subdued demeanor.

My own interpretation of the 1964 film's ending is that it indicates that the relationship between Eliza and Higgins has reached an impasse. As such, it is faithful to Shaw's sequel, in which further (if disharmonious) contact between Eliza and Higgins does indeed ensue. Moreover, in accordance with the sequel, the film ending is more Shavian than either the

1938 *Pygmalion* film or the stage version of *My Fair Lady* in that it does not preclude Eliza's future marriage to Freddy.

In other respects, the *My Fair Lady* film is closer to Shaw's 1941 version than its stage musical counterpart. It restores the optional bathroom scene, together with the revelation of Eliza's suicidal thoughts to Freddy in the optional Wimpole Street scene (and Freddy's concerned response), and an exchange from Act V between Higgins and Eliza in which the latter elaborates on her reasons for wishing to marry Freddy. Thematically, the film version is also closer to all printed editions (and Shaw's screenplay) of *Pygmalion* than the stage version of *My Fair Lady* through its emphasis on the irony of Doolittle's transformation, clarifying (where the stage musical obscures) the predicament of the once-incorrigible sponger who becomes the sponged upon.

Judged purely on its cinematic merit, however, the *My Fair Lady* film generally conforms to Thomas Schatz's observation that Hollywood musical adaptations in the 1950s and 1960s suffer from "uninventive direction."[40] Cukor's curious decision to distance audiences from the film through the constant use of medium shots and a largely static camera imbues the film with "an impersonal, oddly perfunctory quality."[41] Moreover, if one compares the visual aesthetics of the screen version of *My Fair Lady* with those of the 1938 *Pygmalion* film, the former emerges as being more akin to a photographed play than a work that has been reconceived for a different medium. As a cinematic representation of the characters of Higgins and Freddy, however, *My Fair Lady* is undoubtedly the more Shavian of the two works.

NOTES

1. Dan H. Laurence, *Bernard Shaw: Collected Letters IV: 1926–1950* (London: Max Reinhardt, 1988), 311.

2. Michael Holroyd, *Bernard Shaw. Volume II: 1898–1918: The Pursuit of Power* (London: Chatto and Windus, 1989), 332.

3. Shaw's 1934–38 *Pygmalion* screenplay was first published in Bernard F. Dukore, *The Collected Screenplays of Bernard Shaw* (London: Prior, 1980).

4. The 1938 *Pygmalion* film concludes with Eliza returning to Higgins's Wimpole Street flat, in clear defiance of Shaw's screenplay (which he modified for the 1938 film). In Shaw's version, Eliza departs from Mrs. Higgins's flat with her suitor, Freddy Eynsford Hill, leaving behind an amused Higgins, who then contentedly visualizes Eliza's future married life with Freddy, declaring it "a happy ending."

5. Gerald Mast, *Can't Help Singin': The American Musical on Stage and Screen* (Woodstock: Overlook, 1987), 310.

6. Alan Jay Lerner, *My Fair Lady: A Musical Play by Alan Jay Lerner* (New York: Coward-McCann, 1956).

7. Lerner's 1964 *My Fair Lady* screenplay has not been published. All quoted dialogue relating to it has been transcribed in this essay directly from the film.

8. Gavin Lambert, *On Cukor* (New York: G. P. Putnam's, 1972), 244.

9. Bernard Shaw, *Androcles and the Lion, Overruled, Pygmalion* (London: Constable, 1941).

10. Mrs. Eynsford Hill also interacts with Higgins (as she does in the stage and screen versions of *Pygmalion*), but the new exchange is based on Clara's response to Higgins in Shaw's text(s). Clara's rebuke in *Pygmalion*—"Will you please keep your impertinent remarks to yourself"—is transferred to her mother in *My Fair Lady*: HIGGINS: "I don't know whether you've noticed it, madam, but it's stopped raining. You can get a motor bus to, er, Hampton Court. Well, that's where you live, isn't it?" MRS EYNSFORD HILL: "What impertinence!" Mrs. Eynsford Hill also addresses one line (written by Lerner) to Eliza—"Go about your business, my girl."

11. In a curious change, however, Mrs. Higgins says of Eliza in the same (film) scene: "She's ready for a canal barge." In Shaw's play, by contrast, it is *Higgins*'s language that his mother deems appropriate only "on a canal barge"—thus underscoring her point that "as long as [Eliza's] in Henry's hands" the experiment will fail. This point is obscured in Lerner's adaptation, with Mrs. Higgins merely stating that "[Eliza's] ready for a canal barge," to which Higgins replies, "Well, her language may need a little refining."

12. Mrs. Higgins's lines are transferred, however, to Eliza, who now recounts the two men's behavior to the former: "They just sat there congratulating each other on how marvellous they had been, and the next moment on how glad they were that it was all over and what a bore it had been."

13. No maids accompany Mrs. Pearce in either Shaw's play or in the 1938 *Pygmalion* film.

14. Shaw had written this scene in 1938 for the British *Pygmalion* film, and subsequently retained it as an optional scene in his 1941 stage edition.

15. Lerner, *My Fair Lady*, 108.

16. Although Pickering is also the target of Mrs. Higgins's criticism in Shaw's play, here he is absent.

17. Shaw, *Pygmalion*, 156.

18. Nor does Mrs. Higgins draw any comparison between Eliza and Mrs. Eynsford Hill, whose genteel poverty in Shaw's play is not apparent here.

19. Shaw, *Pygmalion*, 155.

20. The black-and-white photography of the 1938 *Pygmalion*, however, in contrast with the vibrant color of *My Fair Lady* does help to create a dirtier, more realistic Covent Garden.

21. The only difference is that Higgins and Pickering are positioned on reverse sides of the screen.

22. For example, when the camera follows Eliza at the beginning of the film, thus alerting the audience to the fact that she is a character of some significance.

23. This process uses 65mm-width film, as opposed to the standard 35mm.

24. Mast, *Can't Help Singin'*, 312.

25. Ibid.

26. Ibid.

27. Sarah Martin, "Resistance and Persistence: *Pygmalion* and *My Fair Lady*, Two Film Versions of G.B. Shaw's *Pygmalion*," *Enter Text* 1, no. 2 (Spring 2001): 56.

28. The choice of a thirty-year-old actor may have been prompted by the fact that Audrey Hepburn was thirty-four at the time (although she appears younger than her years). *My Fair Lady* producer Jack Warner may have been concerned at the possibility of a younger actor accentuating the age difference between Freddy and Eliza.

29. In *My Fair Lady*, Freddy attempts to kiss Eliza, but is prevented from doing so by an iron fence that separates the two characters during Eliza's rendition of "Show Me."

30. Martin, 56.

31. Dukore, *The Collected Screenplays of Bernard Shaw*, 226.

32. Martin, "Resistance and Persistence," 55–56.

33. Alan Jay Lerner, *The Street Where I Live* (New York: W. W. Norton, 1978), 58.

34. Dukore, *The Collected Screenplays of Bernard Shaw*, 84.

35. In a curious technical lapse, Eliza's return is marred by a shadow moving across the room that precedes her arrival. Since audiences may incorrectly assume that the shadow is Eliza's, her actual appearance seconds later loses much of its element of surprise.

36. Shaw's preferred choice for the role of Higgins in the 1938 film was Charles Laughton, an actor whose unheroic physicality and persona he believed would discourage romanticization.

37. Martin, "Resistance and Persistence," 56.

38. Ibid. One could add, however, that this question may not necessarily have occurred to Cukor, whose intention here has not been established. It is possible that, given the number of popular films starring Audrey Hepburn during the previous decade in which she had been successfully wooed by much older men—e.g., Humphrey Bogart (thirty years her senior) in *Sabrina* (Billy Wilder, 1954), by Fred Astaire (thirty years her senior) in *Funny Face* (Stanley Donen, 1957), and by Cary Grant (twenty-five years her senior) in *Charade* (Stanley Donen, 1963)—Cukor simply assumed that audiences would not regard the twenty-one-year age gap between her and Harrison as an impediment to a romantic relationship.

39. Ibid., 54.

40. Thomas Schatz, *Hollywood Genres: Formulas, Filmmaking, and the Studio System* (New York: McGraw-Hill, 1981), 197.

41. Patrick McGilligan, *George Cukor: A Double Life* (New York: St. Martin's, 1991), 292.

Shaw by the Numbers

GUSTAVO A. RODRÍGUEZ MARTÍN

Every question may be conceived as capable of being reduced to a pure question of numbers.
—Auguste Comte, *Cours de Philosophie Positive*

Numbers captivate our imagination because of their dual nature. They are the representation of the abstract concepts upon which a vast share of human knowledge rests. In addition, they are one of the most useful tools for the daily tasks of life ever since man's relationship with nature necessitated calculation. Regardless of pragmatic necessity, numbers have transcended mere arithmetic, hence their use as symbolic representations of spiritual, artistic, and emotional concepts. In this respect, they began to be assimilated into ceremonial rituals early in history, as they became progressively detached from the natural or the stochastic. Why we do something in synchronization on the count of three, why a boxer loses a bout after a count of ten, or why our weeks last exactly seven days, are contemporary remnants of the formulaic usage of numbers.

This particular function of numerals and number words is nearly ubiquitous in all the cultures that have reached a certain stage in abstract thinking.[1] What is more, there seems to be a handful of numbers that have been bestowed this symbolic function virtually in every period of history, virtually everywhere.[2] Bernard Shaw was familiar with the underlying meaning of these numbers and did not hesitate to grant others a prominent place in his plays, either.

There exist several sources for Shaw's acquaintance with the cultural centrality of numbers. For example, he was keenly interested in economic science. For him, "Marx was a revelation. His abstract economics, I discovered later, were wrong, but he rent the veil."[3] Furthermore, he did not consider economics a merely auxiliary science, necessary for his socio-economic criticism, as can be seen from his role in the founding of the London School of Economics and of the Fabian Society. All this cannot conceal the fact that—at least in theory—Sidney Webb played the role of the "the man of numbers," whereas Shaw remained "the man of letters."[4] In truth, Shaw never mastered complex equations or differential calculus. His grasp of economics and its mathematical scaffolding had an inevitable tilt toward literature and history, which prevented economics from "succumbing to rigor mortis" for him.[5] This scholarly bias helped him, nevertheless, to get acquainted with numbers and their key role in a variety of canonical texts.

On a more pragmatic scale, Shaw was "always scrupulous in financial affairs,"[6] which allowed him to act as his own literary agent and, on occasion, editor. However, he would sport a disdainful attitude toward simple arithmetic, partially due to his alleged incapacity for calculation: "my own incapacity for numerical calculation is so marked that I reached my fourteenth year before I solved the problem of how many herrings one could buy for elevenpence in a market where a herring and a half fetched three halfpence."[7] It is thus surprising that some of his characters display brilliant argumentation based on mathematical calculation. Anastasia (in *The Fascinating Foundling*), for example, is in awe before the disparity between the earnings of the Lord Chancellor and his clerk, Mercer: "ANASTASIA. One-fifty into £10,000 goes about 66 times. Why does he get 66 times as much as you? Is he sixty-six times as good?" (IV, 772).[8]

Shaw's unorthodox appeal for numbers was unquestionably influenced by his early readings of the Bible, especially the Old Testament and "the scores of ones, twos, threes, fours, sevens, and all the tens, forties, and even richer numbers in which the scriptures abound."[9] Although Shaw possessed a vast biblical scholarship—faulty as it was, at times[10]—it is no secret that he discarded the religious significance of Scripture to some extent. This religious flippancy stemmed, in part, from his peculiar upbringing,[11] and also from his inborn critical attitude toward established institutions. The verbiage of religion, out of which numbers represent a major fraction, remained deeply embedded in his dramatic style—a natural consequence of his habit to display conventional wisdom in his canonical form prior to showing it wrong by means of (un)subtle literary distortion. By and large, Shaw's exploitation of the religious symbolism of numbers can be seen as another manifestation of "his penchant for appropriating to his own uses traditional religious phraseology, and infusing it with heterodox Shavian meaning."[12]

Whatever Shaw's personal attitude toward each number-related area of knowledge, his use of numbers in his literary production, particularly in the plays, is significant. In view of the prominent place numbers occupy for Shaw, it is worth making a systematic analysis of this phenomenon. Thus, the purpose of this essay is to analyze the stylistic and symbolic function of number words in Shaw's plays: their role in specific plays, in the speech of particular characters, and over his entire dramatic canon. I will discuss in the next section those stylistically prominent numbers that are related to Shaw's socioeconomic critique. The second section will be devoted to numbers whose literary function relies on some sort of religious significance.

Numbers and Socioeconomic Critique

Bernard Shaw is often remembered for his insightful treatment of social and economic inequality, whether in his essays, speeches, or plays. It is not surprising, then, that in the present global economic crisis—resulting in social turmoil in many countries—readers frequently encounter his words quoted by all sorts of journalists, especially in the economic press. Notwithstanding the unequivocal fact that most of Shaw's economic sagacity comes in the form of extensive analyses and powerful quips, it remains nonetheless true that numbers aid his train of thought and resourceful expression when he deals with human economics. In particular, large round numbers are the usual arithmetic conveyor of Shaw's unorthodox ideas on economic issues,[13] albeit with a variety of uses that underscore the different topics he deals with. For example, the "idle rich class" is one of the inequities Shaw is most outspoken about, because the members of that class would not "take their proper places as drones in the hive," and because "what they consume in luxury and idleness is not capital and helps to sustain nothing but their own unprofitable lives."[14] In dramatic terms, Shaw resorts to exorbitant figures spent on childishly luxurious items to emphasize the kind of erratic behavior he describes in his economic essays.

Take, for instance, Miss Mopply's jewels (in *Too True to Be Good*), a necklace that "must be worth about twenty thousand pounds," and a diamond ring "worth four thousand pounds if it's worth a penny" (IV, 648); or Mrs. Hushabye's (in *Heartbreak House*) spending five hundred pounds in "barely four months," a "monstrous extravagance" (I, 528) for which her own father remonstrates her. Even when someone uses common sense to prevent extravagant expenses or bets, it is no match for the spoiled young aristocrats in *Arms and the Man*:

CATHERINE: [*hastily interrupting him*] Dont be foolish, Paul. An Arabian mare will cost you 50,000 levas.

RAINA: [*suddenly coming out of her picturesque revery*] Really, mother, if you are going to take the jewellery, I dont see why you should grudge me my Arab. (III, 170)

Sometimes, however, this flamboyant display of wealth through the counting of a character's assets is taken to the utmost extreme with the intention of reversing the moral and social outlook of material prosperity. This is especially the case when one social status achieved by means of hereditary nobility is confronted with another obtained from free enterprise. When Bluntschli (in *Arms and the Man*) proposes to become Raina's official suitor instead of Sergius, he is not taken seriously at first because "the Petkoffs and the Saranoffs are known as the richest and most important families in the country. Our position is almost historical" (III, 194). Despite this initial drawback, he decides to join the game of showing off his economic and social stature by counting among his possessions "two hundred horses," "seventy carriages," and "four thousand tablecloths." But he does not stop there:

BLUNTSCHLI: . . . I have nine thousand six hundred pairs of sheets and blankets, with two thousand four hundred eider-down quilts. I have ten thousand knives and forks, and the same quantity of dessert spoons. I have six hundred servants. I have six palatial establishments, besides two livery stables, a tea garden and a private house. I have four medals for distinguished services; I have the rank of an officer and the standing of a gentleman; and I have three native languages. Show me any man in Bulgaria that can offer as much. (III, 195)

If the overwhelming numerical evidence is not enough to humble Sergius's familial pride, the final humiliation materializes in view of the opposite political models each suitor embodies. Sergius is aristocratic and reactionary, whereas Bluntschli, when asked if he was "the Emperor of Switzerland," replies: "my rank is the highest known in Switzerland: I am a free citizen" (III, 195).

Charity and almsgiving are other pragmatic aspects of microeconomics that Shaw always rejects, believing that the alleged "deserving poor" are only "people who have discovered that it is possible to live by simply impudently asking for what they want until they get it, which is the essence of beggary."[15] The third of the *Farfetched Fables* provides a conspicuous example of a "Tramp" who would rather "live from hand to mouth" than be given a head start of "five guineas," on the grounds that it "would be robbing." He prefers wearing rags because "who would give alms to a well-dressed man? It's my business to be in rags" (VI, 501). Again, most Shavian beggars and tramps are delineated with the aid of numbers in the form of sums of money. These serve the dramatic trick of presenting the audience with familiar monetary situations whose ethical implications turn out to be the exact opposite of what conventional thinking would dictate. Take Doolitle, Eliza's father, in *Pygmalion* as an example. We witness what seems a happy ending for a secondary plot of the play—Doolittle's financial struggles—once Ezra D. Wannafeller bequeaths him "a share in his Pre-digested Cheese Trust worth three thousand a year on condition that I lecture for his Wannafeller Moral Reform World League." Higgins and Pickering agree that this should be "a safe thing" for Doolittle. However, he begs to disagree because,

> [w]hen I was a poor man and had a solicitor once when they found a pram in the dust cart, he got me off, and got shut of me and got me shut of him as quick as he could. Same with the doctors: used to shove me out of the hospital before I could hardly stand on my legs, and nothing to pay. Now they finds out that I'm not a healthy man and cant live unless they looks after me twice a day. In the house I'm not let do a hand's turn for myself: somebody else must do it and touch me for it. A year ago I hadnt a relative in the world except two or three that wouldnt speak to me. Now Ive fifty, and not a decent week's wages among the lot of them. I have to live for others and not for myself: thats middle class morality. (I, 264)

The fact that talking about money raises some social taboos makes it a valuable dramatic tool for creating Shaw's trademark uneasiness in the audience.[16] If the moral question at stake is complicated as well, as is Mrs. Warren's profession in the homonymous play, the effect is heightened. In this particular case, the repeated use of Crofts's investment on Mrs. Warren's enterprise ("forty thousand pounds") produces some of the finest moments of tension in the play. First, when Vivie discovers that her mother's occupation is not "wound up"; then the fact that Croft has been Mrs. Warren's "business partner" for many years, since he "put not less than £40,000 into it, from first to last." The situation proves too much for Vive, who has to "put her hand on the sundial to support herself," "her color quite gone" (III, 81). Later on in the play, when Vivie is on the verge of exhaustion due to social shame,[17] she manages to sublimate the social taboo of prostitution by underscoring the taboo of talking about money, hence isolating the entrepreneurial dimension of her profession:

VIVIE: Here: let me draft you a prospectus. . . . You shall see. [*She writes*].
"Paid up capital: not less than £40,000 standing in the name of Sir
George Crofts, Baronet, the chief shareholder. . . . Premises at Brussels,
Ostend, Vienna, and Budapest. Managing director: Mrs Warren"; and
now dont let us forget her qualifications: the two words. (III, 94–95)

Shaw also looks into the institution of marriage from an economic angle. In
that respect, he believes that the root of most evils is the economic slavery of
women. This means that "to a woman without property or marketable talent a husband is more necessary than a master to a dog," the husband being
"her only means of livelihood."[18] Numbers and sums of money enable the
dramatist to emphasize the economic component of marriage. Thus, the
reification of a social taboo by means of technical discourse fittingly serves
the purpose of promoting Shavian ideology under the disguise of farcical
humor. Thus Skyes (in *Getting Married*) does not hesitate to appoint himself as the sole provider and economic leader of the family once he marries
Edith, hastily reminding her that "when we are married I shall be responsible for everything you say," because her caustic public speeches may have
cost him "a thousand pounds damages apiece from me for that if we'd been
married at the time" (IV, 431). When the time comes, Edith hoists the rogue
with his own petard and argues that "if Cecil wishes any of the children to
be his exclusively, he should pay a certain sum for the risk and trouble of
bringing them into the world: say a thousand pounds apiece."

The textual role of numbers in Shaw's plays is not only semantic but can
also be structural. Perhaps the clearest leitmotif in *The Millionairess* is the
"fifty thousand pounds" that Epifania's suitors must make to marry her. The
phrase occurs eleven times, not to mention another three times in which
the "pounds" are omitted because they have already been mentioned. One
may even summarize the first part of the play by means of the sentences in
which this sum appears:

If within six months he had turned that hundred and fifty pounds into
fifty thousand, I was his. If not, I was never to see him again." . . . "Alastair
came back to me after six months probation with fifty thousand pounds
in his pocket instead of the penal servitude he richly deserved" . . . "this
imbecile made fifty thousand pounds and won Epifania Ognisanti di
Parerga for his bride." . . . "At all events, the net result was that instead
of his being fifty thousand pounds to the good I was four hundred and
thirty pounds to the bad. Instead of bringing me the revenues of a prince
and a hero he cost me the allowance of a worm. (VI, 210, 211, 222, 228)

Among the many heads of Shaw's critical hydra, the advances of the hard sciences also get their share of disparagement. The number of scientific and technological breakthroughs that Shaw witnessed in his lifetime was beyond the factual comprehension of the scientific layman. In addition, a mystic—as Shaw at times considered himself—saw the same leap of faith in religion as in geological dynamics or in the study of atomic particles. In fact, he could not understand "why the men who believe in electrons should regard themselves as less credulous than the men who believed in angels."[19] As a consequence, Shaw mocks what he considers scientific hairsplitting because, at best, it cannot answer the key philosophical questions of life, and, at worst, it becomes pure dogma.[20] It should come as no surprise that this critical attitude is sometimes derisively directed against the quintessential totem of modern science: numbers. Newton (in *In Good King Charles's Golden Days*) exemplifies this type of mockery particularly well:

NEWTON: . . . [*To Sally*] Youre from Woolsthorp, are you? So am I. How old are you?

SALLY: Twentyfour, sir.

NEWTON: Twentyfour years. Eight thousand seven hundred and sixty days. Two hundred and ten thousand two hundred and forty hours. Twelve million six hundred and fourteen thousand, four hundred minutes. Seven hundred and fiftysix million eight hundred and sixtyfour thousand seconds. A long long life. (VI, 14)

Newton, as Shaw notes in his preface to the play, is the incarnation of a rectilinear universe consisting of "right" (straight) lines. This is, by itself, a perfect metaphor of the sometimes dogmatic nature of scientific thought, which is also rendered useless when it turns simple things into unintelligible hocus-pocus. Sometimes a straight line is the shortest distance between two points, but "the line of beauty is a curve." This is especially true in the case of linguistic expression, as is the case with drama, since the beautiful curves of idiom and hyperbole fall flat when contrasted with pure figures:

NEWTON: I mean that the number of occasions on which Mr Rowley could possibly be unfaithful to you is ten thousand two hundred and twenty plus seven for leap years. Yet you allege one hundred thousand occasions, and claim to have lived for nearly three centuries. As that is impossible, it is clear that you have been misinformed about Mistress Gwynn. (VI, 25–26)

When the Duchess of Cleveland (Barbara) claims that Charles has been unfaithful to her "a hundred thousand times" with Nell Gwynn, Newton's phlegmatic response does not serve as an anticlimactic counterpoint but, on the contrary, stresses the tension in the scene. Dealing with such delicate matters in purely statistical terms irritates Barbara, who thinks she is being laughed at. In sum, it can be said that Shaw's critical attitude necessitates numbers both as one of the basic tools of his villains and as the foundation of many of the intellectual evils of humankind.

Religious Symbolism

Most of the symbolic numbers that Shaw employs in his plays have a religious origin. However, it is necessary to establish a clear distinction from the outset between those numbers that comply with traditionally sanctioned religious semantics and those that simply draw on traditional religious symbolism to construct Shaw's New Religion.[21] In truth, both functions overlap to a great extent, but the fact that the predominant role of a particular number is either one, tells us much about Shaw's dramatic purpose.

Numbers that follow a pattern of meaning in connection with traditional religious texts of the Judeo-Christian canon abound in the speech of characters with a clear religious background. It is, therefore, far more likely to find those numbers out of the mouth of priests, soothsayers, oracles, and members of the clergy in general. Such is the case of Ftatateeta, the Egyptian priestess, who curses Belzanor thus:

FTATATEETA: [*savagely*] Touch me, dog; and the Nile will not rise on your fields for seven times seven years of famine. (III, 372)

In the case of *Caesar and Cleopatra*, this is not an isolated usage of number seven as a marker of soothsaying or superstition in the play. In fact, seven is one of the most salient numbers in terms of its magical and spiritual symbolism.[22] It should come as no surprise, given that ancient texts from the Pythagorean School include a musical scale with seven intervals and record a striking parallelism between the magic of music and the seven planets of the known universe.[23] The classical civilizations also grouped many totemic items in sevens, such as the Seven Sages of Greece and the Seven Wonders of the Ancient World. In addition, the sacred Jewish texts—and subsequently the Bible—also grant seven a special role among the multitude of numbers with a nonreferential meaning in them, whether it is the seven days of creation, the seven deadly sins, the 777 days of Lamech's life,[24] or the seven angels with seven vials containing seven plagues.[25] To name but a few other instances from the play, Cleopatra tries to prevent Caesar's victory with "a cake with my magic opal and seven hairs of the white cat baked in it"; Belzanor is afraid of the Romans because legend has it that "they have each man seven arms, each carrying seven spears"; and there is even a reference to the burning of the library of Alexandria when Theodotus cries, "the first of the seven wonders of the world perishes." In this sense, number seven adds to the overall tension attached to the events of the play, and also to the "curious historical relevance that artistic nonhistory can achieve."[26]

As it was mentioned before, a wide array of members of the clergy are prone to using this type of numerical phrases. The Bishop in *Getting Married*, for example, has a peculiar numerical conception of reality, to the extent that his chronological counts are made "by sevens":

THE BISHOP: . . . those whom we in our blindness drove out of the Church will be driven out of the registry office; and we shall have the history of Ancient Rome repeated. We shall be joined by our solicitors for seven, fourteen, or twenty-one years—or perhaps months. Deeds of partnership will replace the old vows. (IV, 437)

The fact that the use of the number seven in this passage obeys metaphorical patterns is underscored by the indifferent reference to "years" or "months." In addition, the germane discussion about the former sanctity of marriage makes the applicability of this number symbolism more than plausible, especially if one takes into consideration the ubiquity of the phrase "seven years" in the Bible.[27]

The dramatic power of number symbolism when used by religious characters is often reinforced by the religious nature of their discourse. When Keegan (in *John Bull's Other Island*) poses an outrageous version of the Holy Trinity, his speech fittingly pivots around number three:[28]

KEEGAN: In my dreams it is a country where the State is the Church and the Church the people: three in one and one in three. It is a commonwealth in which work is play and play is life: three in one and one in three. It is a temple in which the priest is the worshipper and the worshipper the worshipped: three in one and one in three. It is a godhead in which all life is human and all humanity divine: three in one and one in three. It is, in short, the dream of a madman. (II, 611)

Keegan is an asocial former priest whose first words in the play are uttered in conversation with a grasshopper. The early realization that Keegan is insane or, to say the least, eccentric, makes him the perfect character to introduce such subversive speeches, and much more so when the topic is religion. In this case, one of the popular mottos of the trinity doctrine serves the alleged "madman" as a pattern to substitute elements of human existence (work, play, life, religion) for the three persons of God. As a result, it is easy to draw a parallelism between this metaphorical substitution and Shaw's theological ideal, in which people should be able to say "I am God and here is God, not as yet completed, but still advancing toward completion, just in so much as I am working for the purpose of the universe, working for the good of the whole of society and the whole world, instead of merely looking after my personal ends."[29]

The religious nature of discourse does not necessarily stem from the occupation of the characters involved in the conversation. The philosophical background of the situation sometimes suffices to provide the appropriate setting for the exploitation of number symbolism rooted in religion. Anyone would think of "Don Juan in Hell" as the perfect realization of a suggestive setting; first, because it brings to mind all the literary and musical versions of the myth of Don Juan,[30] deeply embedded in the folklore of spiritualism and the afterlife; and second, because hell is a literal and metaphorical crucible in which to forge a dialectical synthesis of the multiple religious visions that Shaw entertained, hence the differentiated personalities of the Devil, Don Juan, Ana, and the Statue. Take, for instance, Don Juan's manipulation of one of the best-known "seven-phrases" of traditional Christianity:

DON JUAN: No; but there is justice in hell: heaven is far above such idle human personalities. You will be welcome in hell, Senora. Hell is the home of honor, duty, justice, and the rest of the seven deadly virtues. All the wickedness on earth is done in their name: where else but in hell should they have their reward? (III, 604)

The seven deadly sins become the seven deadly virtues, a few of which are listed ("honor, duty, justice") as the sources of "all the wickedness on earth." The blow to conventional moralistic views is phenomenal and, although Shaw had expressed similar views in other plays,[31] the phraseological kernel "seven deadly" highlights the strong foundations of the ideological institution he is challenging. It should be noted that in the nineteenth and early twentieth century, studies on the seven deadly

sins exhibit "a tendency to examine their subject from structural and
historical perspectives in which the content of the sins is imagined to
be relatively stable."[32] In the above example and some others, the fact
that the action takes place in hell provides the appropriate setting for
a reversal in morality and ethics, in which numbers play a major role
again. In particular, one of the Devil's long speeches contains most of
the symbolic, characterizing, and foreshadowing effects that numbers
may have in Shaw's dramatic language (III, 619–21). To begin with, the
Devil introduces one of Shaw's recurring topics: longevity and long-term
human evolution. Although I will discuss this in greater detail later on,
it suffices to say for now that the use of high round numbers ("hundred,"
"thousand"), especially in time phrases,[33] is again a trademark sign of
this Shavian concern. Hence, the Devil complains about how little certain aspects of humankind have changed in "ten thousand years," or
"a thousand centuries." This hyperbolic phraseology is strengthened
by other large figures regarding the irrational expenditure of modern
warfare ("hundreds of millions of money in the slaughter"). Furthermore,
the notion of infinity that pervades much of this speech finds a syntactic
parallel in Shaw's abuse of enumeration throughout it.

However, when the Devil expresses his admiration at how rapidly
human destructive abilities have developed, he again resorts to the use of
symbolism-laden numbers, especially but not exclusively number seven.
Hence, years and centuries become "a score of weeks," and he recounts
the tragic death of a London bricklayer with "seven children" who "left
seventeen pounds club money" and whose wife "would not have spent
sevenpence on her children's schooling."

Since "Don Juan in Hell" contains references to the religious symbolism
of numbers and to Shaw's obsession with the Life Force and human evolution, it is only logical that he should also exploit the semantic properties
of number twelve.[34] Indeed, twelve is ever present in scripture,[35] and it is
usually associated with genealogies (e.g., the twelve tribes of Israel). That
is also the case in this section of *Man and Superman*. After feeling that her
chastity is being affronted, Ana claims to have done a huge favor to "the
earth which I replenished" by having borne twelve children out of her marriage, instead of having "twelve husbands and no children," an option that
the dissolute Don Juan hints at. In the end, Don Juan comes to the conclusion that "twelve children by twelve different husbands would have replenished the earth perhaps more effectively." There is additional substantiation
that number twelve symbolizes reproductive strategies in this debate, for
Don Juan insists in using it to express another point of view: "Twelve lawful

children borne by one highly respectable lady to three different fathers is not impossible nor condemned by public opinion" (III, 632–33).

Although, as can already be seen, symbolic numbers with a religious meaning abound in Shaw's dramatic discourse, there are two plays that encompass most of this arithmetical representation: *Back to Methuselah* and *Saint Joan*. These two plays lean heavily toward the creative kind of numerical symbolism; after all, these two plays are the canon of Shavian "Scripture" for his New Religion and the Life Force. As Richard F. Dietrich succinctly puts it,

> Shaw set about more explicitly than ever to create such an iconography—an imagery and a narrative that would compel belief in the Life Force's dominion over the Death Force, that would give a reason to prefer life to death, and to prefer a moral life. Immodestly no doubt, but desperately, Shaw began to write a new Bible: *Back to Methuselah* (1918–1920), subtitled a Metabiological Pentateuch, constituting a new Old Testament, and *Saint Joan* (1923) providing a new New Testament.[36]

In general, *Back to Methuselah* contains the most intricate network of symbolic numbers of any of Shaw's plays, to the extent that in the latter parts of the play numbers become so embedded in some characters' speech that we are given layer over layer of numerical symbolism. This is especially successful in accentuating the uncanny effect of the character's words, since the specific allusions are harder to grasp. Take, for example, the following words of the She-Ancient:

> THE HE-ANCIENT: I also came to understand such miracles. For fifty years I sat contemplating this power in myself and concentrating my will.

> THE SHE-ANCIENT: So did I; and for five more years I made myself into all sorts of fantastic monsters. I walked upon a dozen legs: I worked with twenty hands and a hundred fingers: I looked to the four quarters of the compass with eight eyes out of four heads. Children fled in amazement from me until I had to hide myself from them; and the ancients, who had forgotten how to laugh, smiled grimly when they passed. (II, 252)

Shaw could have described the character's monstrous transformations in myriad ways, each of them highlighting a sense of disgust, ugliness, mockery, or scorn. However, despite the vast array of descriptive techniques at his disposal, Shaw chooses to depict the She-Ancient's bestial conversions with numbers; the number of extra limbs, head, or eyes she grew. If the mere choice of numbers over other stylistic contrivances has a powerful signification, the symbolic nature of each of them and their mythological reminiscences add up to it. Indeed, different mythological creatures and deities, both from classical pantheons and from biblical tradition, share features with the above description. Scylla, the sea monster, had twelve tentacle-like legs and four dog heads ringing her waist. "The eight eyes out of four heads" may easily be connected with the biblical text of Ezekiel's vision of four cherubs.[37] This link can be established both because Shaw was familiar with the scriptural narrative and because he must have been substantially influenced by Blake's pictorial re-creation of the passage.[38] In addition, Blake's representation is dominated by linear angularity and evenly apportioned spaces,[39] thus also hinting at the "four quarters of the compass."

Notwithstanding the general use of number symbolism in *Back to Methuselah*, Shaw used it most often in this play to illuminate the importance of longevity, aging, and the passing of generations in the evolution of humankind. Likewise, numbers play a major role in the construction of the allegorical scaffolding of Shaw's new man, who undergoes new fall and redemption that re-create the biblical story. This new man is a universal project, and so it is symbolically related to number twelve, like in the previous example from *Man and Superman*. As a symbol of ancestral phylogeny, "the twelve busts" of the ancients that Arjillax presents at the Festival of Arts epitomize the recurrent conflict between the old and the new, between the evolution of man toward the superman, and traditionalism. This dialectical tension is summed up in the argument between the sculptor and Ecrasia, a self-appointed critic:

ECRASIA: Yes, ancients. The one subject that is by the universal consent of all connoisseurs absolutely excluded from the fine arts. [*To Arjillax*] How can you defend such a proceeding?

ARJILLAX: If you come to that, what interest can you find in the statues of smirking nymphs and posturing youths you stick up all over the place? (II, 222)

It is interesting to note that a fundamentally philosophical argument can also be expressed from an aesthetic point of view. The "twelve tribes of Israel" are not the young offspring of Jacob but the busts of ancients, which are not only old, but dead marble instead of living flesh. Furthermore, as

Ecrasia suggests, the beauty of youth was seen by some as a more suitable theme for art, an idea that Shaw challenges throughout his works.

If number twelve lays the foundations of Shaw's inklings on longevity by means of genealogical allusion, number forty epitomizes a set time span that is characterized by toil and struggle; in all, a necessary step in the improvement of the new breed of humans. For instance, Mrs. Luthering complains that the youth are spoiled because they "have no conception of the dread of poverty that hung over us then, or of the utter tiredness of forty years' unending overwork and striving to make a shilling do the work of a pound" (II, 120).

Even when the Life Force has had its way with humans and the consequences of the evolutionary process in the play are clear, number forty is a strong symbolic reminder of former life conditions:

> PYGMALION: . . . In those days they were very ignorant of the differences between things, because their methods of analysis were crude. They mixed up messes that were so like protoplasm that they could not tell the difference. . . . Why, the Newly Born there already knows by instinct many things that their greatest physicists could hardly arrive at by forty years of strenuous study. (II, 230)

Religious symbolism aside, these words clearly allude to his personal doubts about certain scientific advances; hence his provocative ideas on issues such as vaccination or vivisection.

In creating his new theological opus, Shaw resorted to certain numbers to signify the origin of his chosen people ("twelve") and to establish conventional time spans that would summarize the inevitable toil until men supersede the limitations of the flesh ("forty"). The most central numbers in *Back to Methuselah*, however, are those with which the author can dwell on the superficial theme of the play: longevity. Unless people live long enough that they are afraid to be blamed for the consequences of their actions for years on end, humankind will see little improvement, especially from the political scene. The numerical equivalent of this curious argument in textual terms has a twofold manifestation: the symbolic number for the average age of the primitive humans ("short-lived") and a parallel symbolic age for the followers of the Life Force ("long-lived).

The first of these two figures is "three score and ten," which is a clear reminiscence of the biblical psalm stating that "the days of our years are threescore years and ten."[40] This number phrase takes a deliberately archaic form, which plausibly stems from its dramatic link to equally archaic—for

Shavian standards—social structure. That is what one can collect from Conrad's words, for "three-score-and-ten, though it may be long enough for a very crude sort of village life, isnt long enough for a complicated civilization like ours" (II, 72). The derisive tone toward the "shortlived" is even clearer when Franklyn pities those who "could hardly count on three score and ten years of life" (II, 77). This median age of the "shortlived" becomes the canon against which the product of Creative Evolution is measured, to the extent that Barlow ("The Elderly Gentleman") attempts to fight off the discouragement that often kills the "shortlived" when they visit Ireland—now inhabited by the "longlived"—by accepting his three score and ten years: "If they are filled with usefulness, with justice, with mercy, with good-will: if they are the lifetime of a soul that never loses its honor and a brain that never loses its eagerness, they are enough for me, because these things are infinite and eternal" (II, 192). The allegorical counterpart to these three-score-and-ten years is three hundred years. In fact, this round figure is arguably the main leitmotif of the text, since the exact phrase is repeated thirty-six times over the five parts of this "Metabiological Pentateuch." This count does not include periphrastic allusions such as "a third of [Methuselah's life]" (i.e., approximately three hundred and thirty years), or "three centuries," which occur nine times.

Once (Conrad) Barnabas states the goal of extending human life expectancy to three hundred years in the opening scene of Part II ("The Gospel of Brother Barnabas"), this number of years becomes a constant topic of discussion throughout the play. At first, it is gauged against the background of present life conditions, with the ever-present contrast with the three-score-and-ten years of ordinary lives. This perspective allows Shaw to throw in some social denunciations. For example, Lubin—the quintessence of political corruption and disregard for the public—wonders: "Oh! Are the citizens to live three hundred years as well as the statesmen?" (II, 82). Other characters refuse to believe that such an age can be reached by sheer "force of will." On being asked whether he was convinced that such a thing was possible, Haslam retorts: "our being able to live three hundred years? Frankly no" (II, 87–88). Part III, with the self-explanatory title of "The Thing Happens," portrays many of the changes in everyday affairs that the new life length results in. The Archbishop, for example, confesses to having married only once because "you do not make vows until death when death is three hundred years off" (II, 113). But many social differences still remain in a world of "shortlived" and "longlived." As a consequence, the people with an ordinary life span complain that a few "draw a pension for three hundred years" (II, 123).

In the end, as we witness in Part IV, both *breeds* remain separated in different geographical areas, and the British Isles are inhabited exclusively by "longlived" people. Zoo, one of the leading *longlived* characters, summarizes the superiority of her race: "the extension of life to three hundred years has provided the human race with capable leaders, and made short work of such childish stuff" (II, 161). Still, the "princes of this world," such as Napoleon, want to consult "a man three hundred years old, who has had the capacity to profit by his experience" in order to be assisted with his mundane matters (II, 176). However, it is not until the closing speech of the play that we realize that this extended longevity is not aimed at a slightly altered existence, but to the most perfect manifestation of humankind. Lilith, the creator, the mother of Adam and Eve, decides to spare the existence of her kinfolk because, despite having solved the problem of longevity, she wishes to see humans supersede the limitations of the flesh, and achieve the ultimate goals of the Life Force: "The pangs of another birth were already upon me when one man repented and lived three hundred years; and I waited to see what would come of that. . . . And though all that they have done seems but the first hour of the infinite work of creation, yet I will not supersede them until they have forded this last stream that lies between flesh and spirit, and disentangled their life from the matter that has always mocked it" (II, 261). Therefore, the phrase "three hundred years" becomes the Shavian symbol for longevity and for the next step in civilization, becoming one of the defining elements by which Shaw intends to confront his audience with a critically distorted version of themselves. Consequently, the whole play can be taken as "a hall of mirrors directed upon human nature from many angles and all distorting in various ways."[41]

Perhaps the most perplexing reflection of this number phrase in this hall of mirrors strikes the audience in the fifth part of the play ("As Far as Thought Can Reach"). In the opening stage direction, it is a "summer afternoon in the year 31,920 A.D."—that is, exactly thirty thousand years after it was written. Shaw's precise connection with his lifetime in choosing a date with such obvious reminiscences poses multifold implications for the play, especially in light of the author's ideas on Creative Evolution and what Henri Bergson termed the *élan vital*; for he came to believe that humankind was driven toward higher, more perfect forms.[42] Therefore, first of all, Shaw is making an explicit connection between his play—and himself— and the origin of this alleged leap forward in evolution. Furthermore, as we have already seen, the number of years elapsing until "the clever ones have inherited the earth" and "they have accepted the burden of eternal life" is thirty thousand; in other words, 100 times 300. As noted before, three hundred years is the first greater life span achieved by the "longlived" when they decide that "the term of human life shall be extended." Consequently, one hundred generations have passed since the dawn of the new man until the caste of the "longlived" is the only surviving one. This fixed pattern of one hundred generations is akin to that of the Bible, in which another hundred generations are needed to fill the chronological gap between the creation of man and the birth of Jesus, the first superman.[43] Chronologically speaking, according to biblical data, four thousand years elapsed since creation until Jesus was born. Since forty years, as we have seen, is the average span for a biblical generation, it is easy to see that four thousand years account for one hundred generations. Although these calculations have always been rough approximations,[44] Shaw was certainly aware of the theological controversies brought about by the discoveries of British geologist Charles Lyell, who "spread the idea that the age of the earth was far greater than the conventional 6,000 years."[45] Furthermore, he explicitly mentions "Archbishop Ussher's Biblical estimate of the age of the earth as 4004 B.C. plus A.D." and the fact that, in dating the Earth's age "the laugh may not be with Lyell quite so uproariously as it seemed fifty years ago."[46] Therefore, the parallelism is blatant: mankind awaits the coming of an improved, supreme version of itself for a long period of intermission that is to last for a hundred generations, regardless of what the average generation lives.

Although, as mentioned earlier, the symbolic meaning of "three hundred years" is codified primarily in *Back to Methuselah*, it is also found in other plays. This proves the ubiquity and importance of longevity, social evolution, and their symbols in Shaw's plays. In fact, several of the momentous steps of the advancement of the Life Force are also measured by "three hundred years" with respect to the previous state of affairs. So, for example, the new discoveries in the hard sciences imply that (in *Too Good to Be True*) "the universe of Isaac Newton, which has been an impregnable citadel of modern civilization for three hundred years, has crumbled like the walls of Jericho before the criticism of Einstein" (IV, 694–95). Queen Elizabeth (in *The Dark Lady of the Sonnets*) also concedes that certain improvements in culture and the fine arts will also take time, as a necessary action toward intellectual purity: "it will be three hundred years and more before my subjects learn that man cannot live by bread alone, but by every word that cometh from the mouth of those whom God inspires" (II, 663). On a more curious note, Shaw makes a deliberate effort to mark his chronological separation from Shakespeare—inaccurately—at exactly three hundred years:

SHAKES: . . . Younger you are
By full three hundred years, and therefore carry
A heavier punch than mine; but what of that? (V, 23–24)

In view of the significance of this number of years, the passage could be taken as further evidence that Shaw sees himself as the next step in the evolution of literature, at least in the tongue-in-cheek discourse of this puppet play. In sum, here we have another round in the everlasting rivalry of Shav versus Shakes.

If *Back to Methuselah* is the Shavian Old Testament, and ultimately "Shaw's aesthetic coming of age as the fabulist he basically always was,"[47] *Saint Joan* is the Gospel of his pinnacle as a playwright. Within this rhetorical framework, numbers again play an invaluable role in Shaw's discourse. In fact, the literary superiority of this play can also be seen in the intricate subtlety of number symbolism, often diverting from traditional metaphor. At times, Shaw makes a deliberate effort to strengthen the atmosphere of the play by means of numerical symbolism, even if it means relegating historical accuracy. For instance, he dates an ill-omened event by resorting to "unlucky thirteen" when Cauchon recollects about another man who was burnt at the stake for heresy in *Saint Joan*: "The man Hus, burnt only thirteen years ago at Constance, infected all Bohemia with it" (II, 365). The use of number thirteen in this particular case is a premeditated exploitation of its connotations as a foreshadowing device, since Jan Hus was executed in 1415, that is, fourteen years before the date of the scene, not thirteen.[48]

The vast majority of symbolic numbers in *Saint Joan*, however, are directly related to Joan herself, a character of messianic proportions in the eyes of Shaw. In this sense, it is not difficult to find overt links between crucial episodes in Joan's life and biblical history. Particularly significant are the numbers milestoning Joan's trial, recantation, execution, and final appearance as a ghost. The importance of these events is paramount, especially if we look at them as a literary parallel of the passion and resurrection of Christ—i.e., the personification of human redemption. To begin with the symbolic numbers marking Joan's legal tribulations, let us look into the following conversation between Courcelles and The Inquisitor, during which the latter informs the former that the articles on which the prosecution bases the case against Joan have been cut down:

COURCELLES: My lord; we have been at great pains to draw up an indictment of The Maid on sixty-four counts. We are not told that they have been reduced, without consulting us.

THE INQUISITOR: Master de Courcelles: I am the culprit. I am
overwhelmed with admiration for the zeal displayed in your
sixty-four counts; but [. . .] I have thought it well to have your
sixty-four articles cut down to twelve—(II, 389)

In his depiction of the trial, "Shaw was determined to remain faithful to
French history,"[49] his primary source being T. Douglas Murray's translation of Jules Quicherat's French and abridged version of the records of the
trial. A "meticulous comparison of Murray to the shorthand manuscripts of
Saint Joan shows how faithful Shaw was to the French records."[50] Whereas
it is certainly true that the articles against Joan were reduced to twelve, the
original articles were not sixty-four, but seventy.[51] Why, then, did Shaw
state three times—plausibly a symbolic repetition as well—that sixty-four
was the initial numbers of articles the Inquisition brought against Joan?[52]
Although it may well be that Shaw occasionally nods, one must consider
the only other occurrence of number sixty-four in Shaw's plays, which is
related to another of Shaw's major interests: music. Thistle (in *Farfetched
Fables*) describes the limitations of the musical notation of the nineteenth
century, thus: "their keyboards had only twelve notes in the octave instead
of our sixty-four" (VI, 508). The parallelism that can be drawn goes as follows: sixty-four items (charges or notes) would do a richer and more precise
job than twelve of them. However, a larger set of notes or charges only work
well for learned people like Courcelles[53] or Thistle[54]—it would be tempting
to include Shaw in the list—whereas pragmatic people like The Inquisitor
or the rest of us are better off with the simpler version of things. It is up
to the reader to decide to what extent this is a product of sheer coincidence, intentional numerical parallelism, or a subconscious poetic symbol.
Whatever the cause, the concurrence of both numerals remains striking.

Far more blatantly symbolic numbers occur when Joan initially abjures
from her alleged sins and Ladvenu congratulates himself that "the lamb has
returned to the flock; and the shepherd rejoices in her more than in ninety
and nine just persons" (II, 406). The reference to the biblical "sheep gone
astray" that has been found by its shepherd has a conspicuous numerical
component,[55] apart from the fact that Joan is compared to a lamb, an animal traditionally associated in Christianity with sacrifice—as well as being
a representation of Christ.[56] Both allegorical links befit the ideological strategy Shaw had for his new theology, in which Joan plays a major role as a
subversive messiah, as suggested earlier.

Once again numbers serve as textual milestones in Joan's tribulations
when Joan eventually refuses recantation. On that occasion, she claims that

abjuring would "keep from me everything that brings me back to the love of God," and that would be "worse than the furnace in the Bible that was heated seven times" (II, 407).[57] The allusion to this particular passage has several stylistic implications, although it seems fit to begin by the reiteration of number seven as a basic religious symbol. In addition, the semantic parallelism between the men who were burnt in the furnace by Nebuchadnezzar and the Maiden who was to be burnt at the stake is clear. In fact, Joan establishes that comparison herself by previously defying tribunal members: "Light your fire: do you think I dread it as much as the life of a rat in a hole?" (II, 407), in a similar vein to which the four Jews defied the Babylonian king ("be it known unto thee, O king, that we will not serve thy gods, nor worship the golden image which thou hast set up.")[58]

The summit of numerical symbolism in the play comes about in the epilogue. In this particular scene, numbers do not even have to be mentioned explicitly to cast their symbolic shadow over the dramatic text. The specific number of characters on stage is enough to bestow the scene the deepest symbolic meanings of such number, at times a complex intertwinement of cultural layers relying on aspects other than numerical. Let us look first at the actual words of the collection of characters who witness the apparition of Joan in the epilogue of the play:

JOAN: My sword shall conquer yet: the sword that never struck a blow. Though men destroyed my body, yet in my soul I have seen God.

CAUCHON: [kneeling to her] The girls in the field praise thee; for thou hast raised their eyes; and they see that there is nothing between them and heaven.

DUNOIS: [kneeling to her] The dying soldiers praise thee, because thou art a shield of glory between them and the judgment.

THE ARCHBISHOP: [kneeling to her] The princes of the Church praise thee, because thou hast redeemed the faith their worldlinesses have dragged through the mire.

WARWICK: [kneeling to her] The cunning counsellors praise thee, because thou hast cut the knots in which they have tied their own souls.

DE STOGUMBER: [kneeling to her] The foolish old men on their deathbeds praise thee, because their sins against thee are turned into blessings.

THE INQUISITOR: [*kneeling to her*] The judges in the blindness and bondage of the law praise thee, because thou hast vindicated the vision and the freedom of the living soul.

THE SOLDIER: [*kneeling to her*] The wicked out of hell praise thee, because thou hast shewn them that the fire that is not quenched is a holy fire.

THE EXECUTIONER: [*kneeling to her*] The tormentors and executioners praise thee, because thou hast shewn that their hands are guiltless of the death of the soul.

CHARLES: [*kneeling to her*] The unpretending praise thee, because thou hast taken upon thyself the heroic burdens that are too heavy for them. (II, 427)

There are nine characters on stage who kneel to Joan in this scene and who represent more than a mere selection of her worldly enemies. I believe that Shaw is depicting here a dramatic re-creation of the nine orders of the angelical hierarchy, over whom Joan rules in her heavenly majesty after her death and ascension to heaven. Evidence to support this claim is not scanty and is based on two principles: that Joan is regarded as an angel throughout the play, and that the characters in the scene above have more in common with the angelical hierarchy than meets the eye.

The fact that Joan resembles an angel both for her contemporaries and for Shaw himself is well documented in the text. For example, we can read in the preface that the Maid "had to depend on those who accepted her as an incarnate angel."[59] Several characters also call her "an angel" and "an angel dressed as a soldier" because of her military prowess and the alleged miracles she works.

LA HIRE: Yes, an angel. She has made her way from Champagne with half a dozen men through the thick of everything: Burgundians, Goddams, deserters, robbers, and Lord knows who; and they never met a soul except the country folk. I know one of them: de Poulengey. He says she's an angel. (II, 334–35)

The Archbishop and Bluebeard, however, are in disbelief as regards her divine status and set up a ruse to "easily find out whether she is an angel or not." They finally have to believe their own eyes when Joan "finds the blood royal" and recognizes the Dauphin without having met him before.

Twenty-five years after Joan's execution, once it is known that "the sentence on her is broken, annulled, annihilated, set aside as non-existent, without value or effect" (II, 416), she appears as a ghost before many of the main characters in the above scene. In addition, another ghostly apparition—a soldier from the twentieth century—announces that she has been canonized. It is in that moment that the nine characters "kneel to her" and "praise her" for all Joan did in her lifetime. This scene becomes the moral and spiritual restitution from the past that gives a sense of closure to the play, together with the recently announced canonization. As a saint, Joan enters heaven according to Catholic dogma. For her to do so, angels must play a key role, for it has been believed since medieval times that "they helped canonized saints (particularly by escorting the departed soul into heaven)."[60] That is exactly the role these nine characters play, because, much like the nine hierarchies of angels, each of them stands for either some theological virtue or any of the ministries medieval theologians ascribe to them.[61] In this respect, we can see characters who are close to God because of their love or knowledge, others who represent "ordained power," and others who are "active in human affairs." This angelological vision of the scene includes other intricate layers of meaning. For example, the seraphim—the highest ranking beings in the angelical hierarchy— "burns with the love of God and never leaves His presence."[62] The syn-esthetic allusion to Joan's burning can be taken as another playful way to "get rid of the notion that the mere physical cruelty of the burning has any special significance,"[63] a notion that finds a punning wording later on in the preface of the play: "The question raised by Joan's burning is a burning question still."[64]

Despite not ranking particularly high among the features of Shaw's dramatic style, numbers are an unquestionably rich toolkit in the Shavian stylistic repertoire. Their multiple semantic nuances cater to a wide range of dramatic situations, typifying in the process certain characters as well as their speech. Much of this stylistic trait is connected with classical and biblical idiom, which has been broadly recognized as an integral part of Shaw's discourse. However, the numerical element of this intertextual connection has been generally overlooked. In addition, these linguistic segments sharpen Shaw's plays not only because of the relevant information they provide in their own right, but because of the numerous exegetical possibilities they evoke. In short, it is hoped that the foregoing study of numbers and number words will make a small contribution toward a fully articulated description of Shaw's dramatic language.

CHART			
	Years	**Pounds**	**Total Occurrences**
Hundred[i]	67	21	300
Thousand	27	35	291
Million[ii]	2	0	66
Billion	0	0	1

[i] This chart only counts the exact combinations in the phrases "hundred years," "hundred pounds," "thousand years," and "thousand pounds." Ordinals (e.g., "hundredth") or plurals ("thousands") are not included. There are other equivalent combinations that were not taken into consideration, such as "hundreds of years" or money phrases with different currencies, like dollars.

[ii] Million and billion have been included for comparative purposes only. However, it must be noted that "million" is often used with reference to money as well, but without an explicit mention of the currency. Take, for instance, Sempronius's words in the opening scene of *The Apple Cart*: "My father might have made millions in the theatres and film studios."

NOTES

1. Although the study of the differences between numerals (i.e., number symbols such as 1 or 37) and number words (such as seven or thirteen) has produced a relatively vast literature, these terminology issues are omitted in this essay. Therefore, the terms "number" and "number words" will be used interchangeably to refer to both concepts. After all, numbers are hardly ever expressed other than verbally in drama.

2. "Nothing in the history of number symbolism is so striking as the unanimity of all ages and climates in regard to the meaning of a certain few number symbols." Vincent Foster Hopper, *Medieval Number Symbolism: Its Sources, Meaning, and Influence on Thought and Expression* (Mineola: Dover Publications, 2000), 3.

3. Hesketh Pearson, *Bernard Shaw: A Biography* (London: MacDonald and Jane's, 1975), 68.

4. Michael Holroyd, *Bernard Shaw: The One-Volume Definitive Edition* (New York: Random House, 1998), 102.

5. E. Ray Canterbery, *A Brief History of Economics* (Singapore: World Scientific Publishing, 2011), 3. In fact, Shaw's mathematical remarks regarding any economic issue were normally limited to currency figures or income comparison. See, for instance, Bernard Shaw, *Essays in Fabian Socialism* (London: Constable, 1961), 232.

6. Holroyd, *Bernard Shaw: The One-Volume Definitive Edition*, 230.

7. Pearson, *Bernard Shaw: A Biography*, 24.

8. All quotations from Shaw's plays are from *Bernard Shaw: Complete Plays with Prefaces*, 6 vols. (New York: Dodd, Mead and Company, 1962). Numbers in parentheses at the end of every quotation correspond to volume (roman) and page (arabic).

9. Eric Temple Bell, *The Magic of Numbers* (New York: Whittlesey House, 1946), 288.

10. Bernard Shaw, *The Religious Speeches of Bernard Shaw* (University Park: Penn State University Press), 103.

11. If Shaw's father claimed that the Bible was "the damndest parcel of lies ever written," his uncle Walter made "controlled, deliberate, fastidiously chosen and worded" efforts to "destroy my incalculated childish reverence" for religious diction (Pearson, *Bernard Shaw: A Biography*, 12, 27).

12. Sidney P. Albert, "The Lord's Prayer and *Major Barbara*," SHAW: *The Annual of Bernard Shaw Studies* 1 (1981), 107. See also Gustavo A. Rodríguez Martín, "'I Often Quote Myself' (And Others): Modified Quotations in the Plays of Bernard Shaw," SHAW: *The Annual of Bernard Shaw Studies* 31 (University Park: Penn State University Press, 2011), 192–206.

13. See the chart at the end of this essay. Shaw's interest in economics and longevity can be seen in these numbers' most frequent companions: the words "pounds" and "years."

14. Shaw, *Essays in Fabian Socialism* (London: Constable, 1932), 277.

15. Ibid., 109.

16. It should be noted that "the rules underlying deeply held social prohibitions are often best revealed when people violate these rules. . . . [V]iolations of the money taboo subject people to personal discomfort and even criticism." Robert Wuthnow, *Poor Richard's Principle: Recovering the American Dream Through the Moral Dimension of Work, Business, and Money* (Princeton: Princeton University Press, 1996), 144.

17. "VIVIE. . . . The two infamous words that describe what my mother is are ringing in my ears and struggling on my tongue; but I cant utter them: the shame of them is too horrible for me" (III, 94).

18. Shaw, *The Complete Prefaces of Bernard Shaw* (London: Paul Hamlyn, 1965), 23.

19. Ibid., 629.

20. Ibid., 887–88.

21. Shaw, *The Religious Speeches of Bernard Shaw*, 29–37.

22. For further information on the cultural echoes that each number carries, and on the historical processes that may have brought about the association of specific meanings with specific numbers, see Eric Temple Bell, *The Magic of Numbers* (London: McGraw-Hill, 1946); Graham Flegg, *Numbers: Their History and Meaning* (Harmondsworth: Penguin, 1984); Karl Menninger, *Number Words and Number Symbols: A Cultural History of Numbers* (New York: Dover, 1992); and Tim Glynne-Jones, *The Book of Numbers: From Zero to Infinity* (London: Arcturus, 2007).

23. Mercury, Venus, Mars, Jupiter, and Saturn had been identified by Babylonian astronomers as early as the second millennium BCE. Those five planets plus the sun and moon integrated the seven heavenly bodies that orbited around the earth, considered the center of the universe. See Michael Hoskin, *The History of Astronomy: A Very Short Introduction* (Oxford: Oxford University Press, 2003).

24. Genesis 5:31.

25. Revelation 15.

26. Charles Berst, *Bernard Shaw and the Art of Drama* (Chicago: University of Illinois Press, 1973), 76.

27. The phrase appears a total of forty times in the Bible, thirty-nine of them in the Old Testament.

28. See Martha F. Black, *Shaw and Joyce: The Last Word in Stolentelling* (Gainesville: University Press of Florida, 1995), 401–2, on the importance of this speech and its influence on other Irish writers, especially Joyce.

29. Shaw, *The Religious Speeches of Bernard Shaw*, 19.

30. Shaw may have been influenced by the first impersonation of Don Juan in Tirso de Molina's *El Burlador de Sevilla y Convidado de Piedra* (c. 1620), and perhaps more so by the other classical Spanish re-creation of the story by José Zorrilla (1844). However, the presence of operatic elements from *Don Giovanni* cannot be overlooked, especially given Shaw's use of the critical elements of Mozart's opera ("an uncommon share of wisdom, beauty, and humor"). Bernard Shaw, *Shaw's Music, Vol. 3, 1893–1950*, ed. Dan H. Laurence (London: The Bodley Head, 1981), 196.

31. Take, for instance, *Fanny's First Play*, where Duvallet disparages "that stupid quality of military heroism which shews how little we have evolved from the savage: nay, from the beast."

32. Richard Newhauser, "Introduction," *The Seven Deadly Sins: From Communities to Individuals*, ed. Newhauser (Leiden: Brill, 2007), 7.

33. See the chart at the end of the essay and note 13 above.

34. Twelve has been tremendously important in the development of arithmetic since its earliest stages: Babylonian spoken numbers and written numerals, the "great hundred" in Old Norse (made of ten twelves), Roman duodecimal fractions, which account for present-day 12 ounces/inches to the pound/foot, or Charlemagne's monetary standard. See Menninger, *Number Words and Number Symbols*, 155 passim.

35. Twelve is such a remarkable number in the Bible that not only does it appear 164 times, but its multiples also share its mysticism. A notable example occurs in the Book of Revelation, in which John had the following vision: "a Lamb stood on the mount Sion, and with him an hundred forty and four thousand, having his Father's name written in their foreheads." It requires no special mathematical ability to realize that 144,000 can also be rendered as 12x12x1000.

36. Richard Farr Dietrich, *British Drama: 1890 to 1950* (Boston: Twayne Publishers, 1989), 132.

37. Ezekiel 1:5–6. "Also out of the midst thereof came the likeness of four living creatures. And this was their appearance; they had the likeness of a man. / And every one had four faces, and every one had four wings."

38. Although Shaw's indebtedness to William Blake is primarily philosophical, it also "extends quite unmistakeably [sic] through the entire range of speculation by both men in regard to art, science, literature, religion, and virtually every question of human nature and human destiny." Irving Fiske, "Bernard Shaw and William Blake," in *G. B. Shaw: A Collection of Critical Essays*, ed. R. J. Kaufmann (Englewood Cliffs, N.J.: Prentice-Hall, 1965), 171.

39. It should not be forgotten that some scholars make a wholly Blakean reading of the play. See Valli Rao, "*Back to Methuselah*: A Blakean Interpretation," SHAW: *The Annual of Bernard Shaw Studies* 1 (University Park: Penn State University Press, 1981), 141–82.

40. Psalm 90:10.

41. Margery Morgan, "*Back to Methuselah*: The Poet and the City," in *G. B. Shaw: A Collection of Critical Essays*, ed. R. J. Kaufmann (Englewood Cliffs, N.J.: Prentice-Hall, 1965), 131.

42. As Shaw would put it when addressing his audience at Kensington Town Hall: "Just think about yourselves, ladies and gentlemen. I do not want to be uncomplimentary, but can you conceive God deliberately creating you if he could have created anything better?" Bernard Shaw, *The Religious Speeches of Bernard Shaw*, 17.

43. The NT genealogies of Jesus starting from Abraham number forty-two generations (Matthew 1:1–17), or seventy-seven generations starting from Adam (Luke 3:23–38). These seventy-seven generations, however, are once again a symbolic number; first because number seven is closely connected with perfection and divinity, and also because Luke expresses Jesus' genealogy with eleven lists of seven names.

44. See G. Brent Dalrymple, *The Age of the Earth* (Stanford: Stanford University Press, 1991), 13 passim.

45. A. P. Stanley, "The Religious Aspects of Geology (Funeral Sermon on Sir Charles Lyell)," in *Religious Controversies of the Nineteenth Century: Selected Documents*, ed. A. O. J. Cockshut (Lincoln: University of Nebraska Press, 1966), 241.

46. Shaw, *The Complete Prefaces of Bernard Shaw*, 512.

47. Dietrich, *British Drama: 1890 to 1950*, 134.

48. Shaw knew much about Hus and his dissident religious group, and he comments on Joan's "projected crusades" against the Husites in the preface of the play. Therefore, this can hardly be a chronological mistake.

49. Michel Pharand, *Bernard Shaw and the French* (Gainesville: University Press of Florida, 2000), 154.

50. Ibid., 155. Pharand is describing the systematic comparison in Brian Tyson's *The Story of Shaw's "Saint Joan"* (Kingston: McGill-Queen's University Press, 1982).

51. Daniel Hobbins, trans. and intro., *The Trial of Joan of Arc* (Cambridge, Mass.: Harvard University Press, 2007), 4.

52. Stanley Weintraub is also puzzled by the disparity in these numbers ("why does Shaw speak of sixty-four?"). *Saint Joan. Fifty Years After: 1923/4–1973/4* (Baton Rouge: Louisiana State University Press, 1973), 53.

53. The Inquisitor acknowledges Courcelle's "great learning" and admits that "all the members of the court are not so subtle and profound as you."

54. Thistle is a scholar at the Genetic Institute of the Isle of Wight.

55. Matthew 18:12–3 and Luke 15:4–7.

56. George Ferguson, *Signs and Symbols in Christian Art* (London: Oxford University Press, 1961), 21.

57. Daniel 3:19.

58. Daniel 3:18.

59. Shaw, *The Complete Prefaces of Bernard Shaw*, 627.

60. David Keck, *Angels and Angelology in the Middle Ages* (Oxford: Oxford University Press, 1998), 44.

61. Ibid., 58–65.

62. Ibid., 59.

63. Shaw, *The Complete Prefaces of Bernard Shaw*, 621.

64. Ibid., 624.

Carolina Gold

Discoveries in the Archibald Henderson Scrapbooks at the University of North Carolina

ISIDOR SASLAV

[On 8 January 2013, less than three weeks before his death, Isidor Saslav emailed me a draft version of an article I had accepted for publication in this volume of the SHAW. He noted: "I've spent some time going over my 2011 speech (at the Shaw Symposium at Niagara-on-the-Lake) about the Henderson scrapbooks (which you so kindly read to our colleagues) as the basis for my article. I plan to fully cite the sources of the excerpts in the scrapbooks as well as to fully cite the collative works in the endnotes. Plus I plan to find further items to cite between 1921 and 1931, which I've found subsequent to the speech." I hope Isidor's findings will entice others to follow his path to Chapel Hill in search of "Carolina gold."

—MICHEL PHARAND]

My article is about the Archibald Henderson scrapbooks at the Louis Round Wilson Library of the University of North Carolina, Chapel Hill. But before I describe this astonishing collection, I wish to say a word about another significant collection, the scrapbooks kept by Shaw himself collecting all of his published music criticism (also held at Chapel Hill). These scrapbooks begin with the anonymous, unsigned articles that the young Shaw ghostwrote starting in 1876 for George John Vandeleur Lee, Mother Shaw's one-time conductor and vocal coach in Dublin. Having previously moved to London, Lee commissioned the recently arrived Shaw to write anonymous music criticisms for him in a magazine called *The Hornet*.

When it came time for the much maturer Shaw to collect all his music criticisms into four volumes for the Collected Edition in the 1930s, Shaw deliberately chose to omit all those jejune criticisms that had appeared in *The Hornet*. Yet it was thanks to those scrapbooks and the presence in them of all those unsigned articles that Dan Laurence was able to establish their authenticity and to create, finally, a truly complete edition in 1981 of *Shaw's Music*, as Laurence called his collection. But it was only in 1991, when the paperback version of *Shaw's Music* was published, that the collection became truly complete. Shaw had written one final review of a concert given by the Bach Society in 1894, a review so scathing that the editor of *The World*, Shaw's official employer at the time, refused to print it. Shaw thereupon resigned his position, thus ending his official status as a full-time music critic, though he continued to write music criticisms occasionally from that year until the year of his death in 1950. Thus it took until 1991 for this Shaw critique to be finally published.

When I arrived in Chapel Hill in the fall of 2007 for a concert performance, I was cordially greeted by the staff of the Rare Book Collection of the Wilson Library. They knew of my interest in Shaw and in that longtime North Carolina resident and UNC faculty member, Archibald Henderson. The Wilson Library holds almost four hundred different works by Henderson alone. Aside from his work on Shaw, Henderson's fields of expertise extended beyond mathematics (whose department at UNC he had headed for many decades) and into the fields of theater, American history, and cultural history in general.

In the course of showing me and Mrs. Saslav through their collections, the staff came in their stacks to a wide filing cabinet. They pointed to the bottom drawer and asked me to open it. In that drawer were seventy-six scrapbooks, assembled by Henderson (and no doubt by his helpers), each containing about eighty to ninety double-sided paste-in pages of newspaper and magazine articles from the 1880s to the 1950s. Naturally, the subject of all these clippings is Bernard Shaw: articles and letters by and about him, reviews of his plays' performances, reviews of books about him, etc. Henderson had obviously collected these items for use in creating his three Shaw biographies: *Life and Works* (1911), *Playboy and Prophet* (1932), and *Man of the Century* (1956). The vast nature of Henderson's undertaking was sensed even by Shaw when he quipped to the press upon meeting Henderson for the first time at a London railroad station in 1907, "Since it will take Henderson a quarter century to finish the job he is imploring me to do nothing more until he catches up with me."

Faced with such a treasure trove of Shaviana, I thought up a request to view something in particular. The staff informed me, however, that this would not be possible. For you see, they said, nobody knows what's in these scrapbooks, because they've never been catalogued! Impossible, I thought. Such a goldmine of Shaw artifacts inaccessible to anyone? This situation must be remedied, I thought. So for the last five years I have been traveling back and forth to Chapel Hill to go where no one has gone before: to catalogue the Archibald Henderson scrapbooks. So far my work has extended to fourteen volumes, taking me to the year 1931.

If I could only bring these volumes back to Texas, where I live, the work would go much faster. But no: these rarities can never leave the premises of the Wilson Library. While in Chapel Hill, I spent eight hours each open day at the library's study tables reading, describing, and summarizing the nature of each item. But that's just the beginning of my labors. Bringing my descriptions home to Texas, I had to collate each item with a three-foot-wide collection of reference books, including the Laurence and J. P. Wearing bibliographies, various reprint volumes such as *The Matter with Ireland, The Theater Observed, Shaw's Music, Practical Politics, Shaw on Religion, The Religious Speeches of Bernard Shaw, The Letters of Bernard Shaw to "The Times," Platform and Pulpit, Interviews and Recollections*, the four volumes of collected letters, Mander and Mitchenson's *Theatrical Companion to G. B. Shaw, The Road to Equality, Bernard Shaw: Theatrics, Agitations*, etc, etc, etc.

No doubt much of what's in these scrapbooks has found its way into the three Henderson biographies, and many of the articles are now published in those various reprint volumes. But the interesting part of my research, besides creating a guide to what's in these scrapbooks, is to ascertain what, if anything, has *not* found its way into any sort of reprint or catalogue. And rest assured there are a vast number of such items in the scrapbooks.

The greatest opportunities for discovery lie in two areas: that of secondary sources and of chronology. We all know the three-volume Wearing catalogue of secondary sources published by Northern Illinois University Press in 1986–87. But within the scrapbooks are countless other articles from British provincial, and even London, newspapers and magazines that were *not* gathered up by Wearing and his subsequent collaborators into the NIUP volumes. These would form the stuff for a greatly expanded edition of Wearing et al. Another work that could be vastly expanded by research into the scrapbooks is A. M. Gibbs's admirable *A Bernard Shaw Chronology*. Speech after speech, meeting after meeting, which Shaw either gave or attended, and his whereabouts thus documented by those reports in the scrapbooks, would find a welcome home in a new and expanded edition of Gibbs's indispensable work.

The contents of the Henderson scrapbooks can be divided into seven categories, all of them mixed together, as the individual items follow one another in usually chronological order. (But there are plenty of out-of-place howlers as well.) First, there are Shaw's letters published in newspapers and magazines. Second, Shaw's articles in newspapers and magazines. Third, reviews of Shaw's works, both play performances and books. Fourth, reviews of books about Shaw (including several of Henderson's own first Shaw biography—often not flattering, I assure you). Fifth, reports of Shaw's speeches, including religious, political, and on the arts. Sixth, reports of various meetings that Shaw attended and at which he spoke. And seventh, miscellaneous articles that include gossip, anecdotes, Shaw quotations, parodies, etc.

The first category, Shaw's letters to newspapers and magazines, can be divided into two parts: Shaw's letters to the London *Times* and Shaw's letters to every other periodical. In 2007, Ronald Ford collected and republished all of Shaw's letters to *The Times*, so that category is for practical purposes taken care of (although if I come across any such letters in the Henderson scrapbooks overlooked by Ford, I'll let you all know). The second part of this category, Shaw's published letters to other periodicals, was dealt with, but only selectively, in the collection entitled *Agitations* (1985), edited by Dan Laurence and James Rambeau. There are a good number of Shaw's published letters to the press in the Henderson scrapbooks that were not selected for *Agitations*. One example among many is "A Letter from a patient man" (Laurence, *Bibliography* II, item C1478), dated 15 April 1905, a letter addressed by Shaw to the editor of the *Daily News* taking that gentleman to task for using "damd" instead of "damned" in Shaw's quoting of Shakespeare. A later abashed Shaw had to admit that he had sent the letter to the wrong newspaper, the offending publication having been the *Daily Chronicle*. But the *Daily News* letter, which also includes the editor's retort claiming innocence, does not appear in *Agitations*.

The second category, Shaw's articles in various newspapers and periodicals, have likewise been much collected and reprinted in the collections cited above. However, an example of a Shaw article in the Henderson scrapbooks that seems never to have been reprinted is Shaw's article in *The Academy* of 29 June 1907, "The solution of the censorship problem" (Laurence, *Bibliography* II, item C1590), which discusses the hypocrisy and absurdities of the censorship and "Comstockery" vilified in its danger to art. This article was collected neither in *Agitations*, *Theatrics*, nor in *The Drama Observed*, and deserves to be reprinted somewhere.

The third category, reviews of Shaw's play performances and books, was dealt with by T. F. Evans in his *Shaw: The Critical Heritage* (1976), although Evans devoted himself largely to reviews of plays and their performances, while books were only marginally represented. For example, he included only one review of Shaw's novel *The Irrational Knot*, and that as it appeared in Dixon Scott's article, "The Innocence of Bernard Shaw," in the *Bookman* in September 1913. In contrast, the Henderson scrapbooks contain about four or five reviews of that novel in various newspapers and magazines when *The Irrational Knot* was reprinted in small format by Constable in 1914. Even among play reviews there are a large number of these in the scrapbooks uncollected by Evans that could go into a second edition of *The Critical Heritage*.

There is a whole subseries of reviews and articles by William Archer uncatalogued by Wearing. Here is an example from page 16 of the fourth Henderson scrapbook: "The Morning Leader/London 4 Nov. 1908," "AMERICA AND 'MRS. WARREN.'—By William Archer." [My summary: The Anglo-Saxon has never lost his tendency to be shocked by "immorality." But at least *Mrs Warren's Profession* gets *performed* in America, so the public can at least judge it. Not like in England, where but one man, the censor, Mr. Redford, gets to make the decision.]

Many of the missing items in Wearing from the Henderson scrapbooks belong to the fourth scrapbook category, reviews of works *about* Shaw, category K in Laurence's *Bibliography*, which includes Henderson's own Shaw biography. In my opinion, a whole new reprint collection could be created devoted to this one Henderson category alone (such a collection has never been created, as far as I know), or at least a large new section devoted to this category could be inserted into a new edition of *The Critical Heritage*. For example, there are about three reviews of Joseph McCabe's book, *George Bernard Shaw: A Critical Study* (1914), pasted into the scrapbooks, but only the one from *The Socialist Review* of July 1914 appears in Evans.

Then as the fifth scrapbook category there are the reports of Shaw's speeches, many of them collected in the specialized reprint collections mentioned above. But even in this carefully mined area, there still show up in the Henderson scrapbooks several speeches that have yet to be reprinted; for example, a Shaw speech at Shrewsbury dated by Henderson "November 24, 1909." Almost every item in the scrapbooks, with a few exceptions, has been supplied a handwritten notation of the name of the source, the city of publication, and a date. (If the name of the publication appears in the source, it is usually omitted from Henderson's notation.) The dates noted in the scrapbooks are often at variance with those

Laurence supplied for these items. I try to deal with these discrepancies in my bibliographical notes. Thus if Henderson's date of 24 November 1909 for Shaw's Shrewsbury speech is correct, then Shaw could perhaps have spoken on 23 November or shortly before. (By the way, this speech is full of astute and very up-to-date political and economic assessments that could apply equally well to ourselves in our current economic crisis.) This speech is catalogued neither by Laurence nor Wearing and is not reprinted in *Platform and Pulpit, Practical Politics*, or *The Road to Equality*; nor is the trip to Shrewsbury noted in *A Bernard Shaw Chronology*. If any of Shaw's speeches deserved reprinting, it's certainly this one.

Then as the sixth scrapbook category are the reports of Shaw's attendance at various meetings, often noting his comments. One example is a meeting of the Society of Authors, presumably on 20 March 1907 (the article in the *Daily Chronicle* describing the meeting is dated by Henderson "March 21, 1907"). The Society discussed the pros and cons of the recently launched Times Book Club, with Shaw very much in favor. (He even issued one version of the joint publication of *John Bull's Other Island, How He Lied to Her Husband, and Major Barbara* in a special Times Book Club edition in 1907.) Shaw wrote a letter to *The Times* a few days later (published on 25 March) reporting the amusing goings-on at this meeting.

In scrapbook category seven are countless shorter squibs, often very amusing, whose brevity has prevented their being collected anywhere. One example: When *Arms and the Man* was made into the operetta *The Chocolate Soldier* by Oskar Straus (much against Shaw's will), there appeared in the *London Opinion* on 6 June 1908 an ironical and rather vulgar ten-line verse, supposedly sung by Shaw himself, entitled "TO BE SHAW!" Henderson also collected similar items from *Punch*.

Also in the area of parody are the following two clippings: In the fourth Henderson scrapbook (p. 15), we find: "Pall Mall Magazine/London/ Nov. 1908," "PERCIVAL./HE TAKES CELIA TO SEE SHAW./BY ELLIS ROBERTS./ILLUSTRATED BY G. MORROW." (There follow two fantastic parodies of supposedly "Shaw" plays, the second of which turns *Man and Superman* into "*Overwoman*," who proposes to eight men in succession. Four cartoons with captions, plus a devilish-looking head of Shaw floating in the sky, accompany the article.) And on page 78 of the same scrapbook, we find headed as "The New Age London 13 Jan. 1910" a satirical poem, signed "ERIC DEXTER," referring to many events to come in 1910, including Shaw's being made prime minister after the election, twice-a-day performances of *Man and Superman*, and censor Redford having to sit through fourteen days' worth of performances of the *Shewing-up of Blanco Posnet*—and then dying! Quite amusing.

Yes, the Henderson scrapbooks are great fun to explore for this kind of unusual Shaviana. Here is another example of the kind of orphan event, speech, or report that I'm trying to discover in the scrapbooks. "The Liverpool Daily Courier/13 Nov. 1908," "THE SUPER-DRAMATIST.—A Study of Mr. Bernard Shaw.—BY CHRIS HEALY." This newspaper article, an insightful interview with Shaw in which he is quoted on many topics at great length, runs to no fewer than three and a half columns. It is not in Wearing or in Laurence, although Laurence does record a verbatim report of a Shaw speech, but not an interview, in that same Liverpool newspaper four days later (*Bibliography* II, item C1656). This Shaw interview with Healy is not in *Interviews and Recollections*; *A Bernard Shaw Chronology* (p. 182) does not report a Shaw trip to Liverpool; and the name Chris Healy appears nowhere in Wearing. This article certainly deserves to be reprinted and catalogued somewhere.

Here is another Shaw speech, in the fourth Henderson scrapbook (p. 82), that runs two and a half columns: "Eastern Morning News/Kingston-on-Hull 25 Feb. 1909 [*recte* 1910]," "MR. BERNARD SHAW.—Entertaining Lecture at the/Assembly Rooms.—IMPRESSIONS OF HULL." (The ferocity of the middle class when cornered; socialization of bread; the government should collect royalties on lapsed copyrights and inventions; case of Shakespeare brought forth.) This article is not in Laurence or Wearing, nor in *Platform and Pulpit*, *Bernard Shaw: Practical Politics*, or *Bernard Shaw: The Road to Equality*. Other than in the old files of the *Eastern Morning News* in Kingston-on-Hull, it doesn't seem to be anywhere except in the Henderson scrapbooks. Time for a reprint!

Here's another example, this one from the sixth Henderson scrapbook, 1911–13 (p. 3): "Liverpool Daily Post and Mercury 30 Dec. 1911," "'G.B.S.' IN LIVERPOOL.—Straight Talk at the Art Gallery.—SOCIAL UTILITY OF PICTURES/AND THE DRAMA.—COMMERCIAL PROFITS/ CONDEMNED.—LIVERPOOL'S STUPID POLICY." (An abundance of fine arts keeps young people from destroying their lives with those wayward impulses that Dr. Horton imagines occur only in theaters, libraries, galleries, etc. Profit on municipal enterprises was a crime and diverted money to the rich. Huddersfield babies referred to: the mayor gave a pound extra to every family whose baby reached a certain weight by a certain date. Policemen should be on the lookout not for criminals but for hungry children who should be sentenced to two meals a day. Municipal theaters should be established which should present only plays that didn't make a profit. Art and artists are inspired like religion used to be inspired.) This article is also not in Laurence, Wearing, *Platform and Pulpit, Practical Politics*, or *The Road to Equality*. Other than in the old files of the *Liverpool Daily Post and Mercury*, it doesn't seem to be anywhere except in the Henderson scrapbooks. Again: time for a reprint!

And how about this one: "Coventry Herald/16 Mar. 1912," "MR. BERNARD SHAW AT COVENTRY.—SOME CRITICAL LOCAL REFERENCES-/'THIS DIRTY, SMOKY PLACE.—/LABOUR UNREST, IDLE RICH, AND POOR/ WORKERS." This is a lecture sponsored by the Fabian Society, with chairman P. E. T. Widdring's opening remarks quoted at great length, followed by a verbatim report of Shaw's discussion of the recent railroad workers' strike, the threatened coalminers' strike, and the suffragettes breaking windows in London. (The up-to-dateness of this speech staggers the imagination: the outsourcing of capital to foreign countries; tax the rich idlers and give the money to the poor: bailouts of big banks and millions for CEOs but no money directly to the people, etc.) Again, this speech is missing from the expected collections of Shaw's political speeches.

My examples from the Henderson scrapbooks have been selected only from the years 1885 to 1931 because that's as far as I've gotten in my cataloguing work. If anyone would like to see this process speeded up, kindly refer me to some generous granting agency so that I might spend more of my time at the Wilson Library of the University of North Carolina!

REVIEWS

Bringing About Change: New Contexts for *Mrs Warren's Profession*

Bernard Shaw. *Mrs Warren's Profession*. Edited by Brad Kent. London: Methuen Drama, 2012. 1 + 173 pages. $14.95.

With every new critical edition of a literary work, the greatest challenge is usually trying to find something new and relevant to say about the text and its author, rather than simply reworking the same familiar ground. This is particularly true for a work such as *Mrs Warren's Profession*, one of the most notorious works from one of the world's most famous playwrights. So much has been written about both the play and the playwright that it is difficult to imagine creating a fresh approach to the play, making it both astonishing and delightful that the New Mermaids edition, edited by Brad Kent, manages to do just that.

In presentation, the volume incorporates the textual features with which New Mermaids readers are familiar. Some of these—the numbered lines and the running heads that identify the acts—are welcome and helpful improvements over other scholarly editions. The one that continues to rankle is the decision to treat Shaw's preface as an adjunct, rather than as an important aspect of the reader's encounter with the text as Shaw formulated it. This seems particularly indefensible for *Mrs Warren's Profession*, as the lengthy stage censorship of the play made Shaw particularly acutely aware of the play's literary presence; and yet in this edition, Shaw's special preface to the play lies buried in the midst of the appendices.

Nonetheless, the editorial decisions and additions are otherwise superb. Kent's real accomplishment derives from the freshness and originality of his perspective on the text and its context, even, in some cases, when he addresses familiar subjects. Kent begins his introduction with the obligatory biographical note; however, in his account of Shaw's rises to and falls from greatness, Kent manages to account for the entire Shavian dramatic oeuvre, and even names Shaw's most significant dramatic collaborators, with easy efficiency, to offer a more comprehensive and satisfying snapshot of Shaw's career than others might do with twice the space.

Even more innovative is Kent's account of the play's origins and influences. While other editions have noted that Shaw himself acknowledged the play's genesis in Janet Achurch's recounting of Guy de Maupassant's novella *Yvette*, Kent is the first, to my knowledge, to examine this connection at great length in his introduction, even including an excerpt from that work in one of the appendices. Kent goes even further in examining the play's influences by placing it within the larger literary context of "prostitute literature," a genre, he points out, that "traces its British origins back to royalist pamphlets in the seventeenth century" (xix). Kent notes that Shaw would have been drawn to the genre's original focus on prostitution as an economic phenomenon, used to "explore the changing relationships between people in an increasingly mercantile and urban culture" (xix–xx). By the time Shaw wrote *Mrs Warren's Profession*, Kent points out, the prostitute had reemerged as a focus in litera-ture and drama, "indicating a millennial hysteria for changing sexual mores in the wider society and a desire to question and push those boundaries" (xx).

In focusing so extensively on the topic of prostitution and the context of prostitute literature, Kent diverges from other editors, many of whom tend to focus more on the economic aspects of Shaw's argument, and approach prostitution more or less as the vehicle by which Shaw delivers that argu-ment. Shaw's choice of prostitution to facilitate his economic thesis is commonly attributed to his acute awareness of the pervasive social prob-lem caused by the sex trade from his work as a vestryman and from a few awkward personal encounters with prostitutes. Clearly, however, prosti-tution was an integral, not merely incidental, aspect of Shaw's argument. He was acutely aware that turning Mrs. Warren into a thief, a Fagan-like character, would leave the economic argument intact and allow the play to be licensed for production; however, while he made those modifications to enable a copyright performance (coincidentally protecting *his* economic interest), he refused to let them stand, even at the risk of making his play unproduceable in England for decades. Kent provides a new perspective on this decision by reminding us that Shaw was simultaneously positioning his play in the new dramatic form of the social-problem play, but also in the more familiar and highly marketable genre of prostitute literature.

Another welcome addition in Kent's approach to the play's origins is his methodical accounting of Shaw's edits, additions, and omissions during the process of writing *Mrs Warren's Profession*. Frequently these are offered as annotations within the text of the play itself; additional variant scenes are reproduced in one of the appendices. For the scholarly reader, these revisions provide an intriguing glimpse into the evolution of Shaw's thinking about the characters and the circumstances that bind them together. Another salient perspective on the play's evolution is offered in Appendix 5, which reproduces the readers' reports commissioned by the Lord Chamberlain's Office from 1916 to 1924 in response to repeated (and mainly unsuccessful) requests brought forward by hopeful theater producers to license the play for production. This rare behind-the-scenes look at the workings of the Lord Chamberlain's censorship process culminates in its own dramatic climax with the last report by the Lord Chamberlain himself in 1924, which finally acknowledged that "times have however greatly changed since 1898 when this Play was first stopped by Mr [George A.] Redford. . . . It would therefore be absurd to go on refusing a Licence to this Play, ignoring the march of time and the change it brings about in public opinion" (150).

Given the notoriety around staging *Mrs Warren's Profession*, any critical edition would be incomplete without some discussion of the play's production history and audience reactions to it, and here again Kent covers some familiar ground while managing to provide some new insights, including a fuller narrative context for the production requests that the Lord Chamberlain's readers are responding to in Appendix 5. His account of later productions demonstrates the same concise and efficient delivery of a broad scope of information as his earlier biographical content.

Inevitably, not all is perfection. Kent's attempts to offer some insights into relative cash-conversion values—by his own admission a "notoriously difficult" task—is hard to follow. While his intent is to provide some sense of the characters' relative lifestyles, he compares absolute incomes without satisfactorily taking into account the generation that separates Vivie's sisters from her daughter, or offering any clue what those incomes signified in terms of the costs of living across those decades. There is also the odd lapse in proofreading in the introductory and editorial matter, resulting in some typos, omissions, and improperly constructed sentences. While the annotations to the play are generally useful for their rich insights into its historical context and Shaw's composition and production decisions, they are copious enough without the addition of annotations that merely offer the kind of information that could easily be gleaned from a dictionary.

For the most part, though, these issues are minor in comparison to the wealth of helpful, fresh, and relevant context offered by this New Mermaids edition. Times may have greatly changed since Shaw's play was written, but this edition offers ample evidence that *Mrs Warren's Profession* will continue to keep pace with them.

D. A. HADFIELD

Morse Code

Robert E. Wood and Anthony Wynn. *Valiant for Truth: Barry Morse and His Lifelong Association with Bernard Shaw.* Portland, Oregon, and Calgary, Alberta: Planet Publications (Lulu), 2012. 219 pages. $23.95 paper.

In 1995, Robert Wood and Anthony Wynn worked with Barry Morse when he co-starred with June Lockhart in A. R. Gurney's play, *Love Letters*, which gave them the opportunity to listen to one of the consummate professionals tell wonderful stories about his amazingly busy and varied career in theater, television, film, and radio, which added up to more than three thousand roles. It undoubtedly added up to considerably more than three thousand words to tell the story of that career or provide acting venues for it, as Wood and Wynn did in the ensuing years in a variety of ways, from the co-authoring with Morse of books such as the autobiographical *Pulling Faces, Making Noises* (2004) and the theatrical memoir *Remember with Advantages* (2007), to scripts for television, radio, the stage, audio recordings, CD projects, etc., in which Morse displayed his art in all its fantastic range.

Although the world knew Barry Morse as Police Lieutenant Gerard, "the most hated man in America" as he relentlessly pursued the innocent Dr. Kimble in the hit 1960s TV series *The Fugitive*, Wood and Wynn discovered that there was a sort of "Morse code" operating in Morse's life which signaled the fact that he was more the pursued than the pursuer, that from the age of fifteen on G. B. Shaw was always "on his case" in the sense of often being on his mind as a guide to life in and out of the theater. In 2009, at a symposium sponsored by the International Shaw Society at the Shaw Festival in Niagara-on-the-Lake, Ontario, Wynn delivered a talk entitled "Shavianism—A Morse Code: The Lifelong Dedication of Barry Morse to George Bernard Shaw," in which was begun the revealing of that code that has resulted in this book, a book that is chock-full of Shaviana (including a collection of rare photographs), much of which will not be found anywhere else.

Born in 1918 and raised in London's Shoreditch area, ironically the locus of much of the vibrant life of the Elizabethan theater, but despised in the early twentieth century as a slum to escape from, Barry Morse exited that world when he underwent a Pygmalion-like transformation after luckily receiving at the age of fifteen a scholarship to learn acting at RADA, the very same Royal Academy of Dramatic Art that Shaw had helped establish financially (and continues to benefit through his will) and helped to lead with advice to its board. At Morse's RADA audition, Shaw was already in his life in spirit, as he chose for one of his audition pieces the Chaplain's recantation of the burning of Joan of Arc in Shaw's *Saint Joan*. The actual Shaw materialized later with visits to RADA, some with administrative purposes primary, but occasionally to visit with the students and teach acting. How to play the lion in *Androcles and the Lion* was Morse's most amusing lesson from Shaw, taught by illustration as Shaw got down on the floor and impersonated a lion having its belly rubbed. Would that there had been a smartphone camera around to capture that!

At RADA, Morse soon learned precisely what Eliza Doolittle had learned under similar tutelage: that you could play royalty if you could speak the part. So Morse's cockney accent disappeared, replaced by the King's English and whatever other dialect was called for by the role. The kindly ministrations of Shaw to the young actor changed him in other ways too, partly as it encouraged the reading and playing of the playwright's works, leading gradually to such total absorption of Shavian ideas about life and theater that he found himself in numerous Shaw roles as his career developed because they had become second nature to him. And so it came to pass that, after the young Morse's eventual move to Canada, it seemed only logical and natural, in 1966, that he should become the Artistic Director of the Shaw Festival in Niagara-on-the-Lake, Ontario, just across the lake from Toronto. The 1966 season was the one that, under Morse's enthusiastic and indefatigable direction, transformed that struggling young theater festival into one much better situated to become a worthy rival of Ontario's Stratford Festival. He opened that season with *Man and Superman*, the role of Tanner (ironically a man hotly pursued!) being one he knew well from having performed it under Jerome Kilty's direction in Boston.

Barry Morse played a role in every Shaw play (more than fifty) and directed many, a feat and a dedication to a single author that was obscured by his busy, usually more commercial work in countless other television, film, radio, and stage productions that had nothing to do with Shaw. An actor with a family to support, he was one of the lucky few who seemed never to be out of work because it was love of the work that ruled his life, not the lusting after awards and prizes or star roles; and although he had plenty of those along the way, the quiet constant in it all was Shaw.

Fig. 1 | Nancy Wickwire and Barry Morse in Group 20's Boston production of *Man and Superman* at Theater on the Green, directed by Jerome Kilty, 1957. (Photo courtesy of the Morse Estate.)

By the end of his life in 2008, Barry Morse may have known Shaw better than anyone else ever has because he knew him inside and out, as a recipient of Shaw's friendship and teaching, a reader of all Shaw's works, an actor of the words and director of the plays, and as someone who tried to live up to the noble intentions of the words, knowing Shaw so well that he could easily pass for Shaw when impersonations were needed, never mind the shorter stature. The impersonation that's most relevant here was Morse's playing of Shaw in Anthony Wynn's play, *Bernard and Bosie: A Most Unlikely Friendship*, which dramatizes the relationship, mostly in correspondence form, between Shaw and Lord Alfred Douglas, the "Bosie" who enticed Oscar Wilde into the disastrous suing of Douglas's father, the Marquess of Queensberry, for slander, with Morse's son Hayward playing the part of "Bosie" in the 2004 production on a branch campus in Sarasota of the University of South Florida at the first Shaw conference sponsored by the International Shaw Society. This also began an expanding relationship between the ISS and the original Shaw Society in London that was fostered by the latter's president, whose name was Barry Morse, which in 2013 culminated in the co-hosting of the two societies, with the National Trust, of a Shaw Conference at Ayot St. Lawrence—although, alas, too late for Barry.

In the preface to this book, entitled "Shaw and SuperShaw," Morse acknowledges Shaw as a fellow actor, his thesis being that although Shaw had had to invent a fantastic personality for himself "fit and apt for dealing with men" (as Shaw put it), the jesting "SuperShaw" known as G.B.S., Morse thought that the best and truest role that Shaw played was one that Shaw himself had expressed admiration for, that of "Valiant-for-Truth" in *The Pilgrim's Progress*, who upon his passing speaks lines of no regret for his life that were read at Shaw's cremation in 1950, attended by Morse. That Wood and Wynn find this role of "Valiant-for-Truth" appropriate to Morse as well accounts for their using it as the perfect title for a book that details the relationship between Shaw and Morse and of the passing of the sword from one to the next.

The reading of this book will of course do more justice to the richness of Morse's life than has been hinted at here. This book is best found online at http://www.lulu.com/shop/search.ep?keyWords=Valiant+for+Truth& categoryId=107101.

R. F. DIETRICH

Shaw and the Sacred Cows: A New Look at the Plays

Bernard F. Dukore. *Bernard Shaw: Slaves of Duty and Tricks of the Governing Class.* University of North Carolina at Greensboro: ELT Press, 2012. viii + 139 pages. $60. Also an E-Book, UPCC Collection, Johns Hopkins University Press.

As this lively new study of Shaw's plays reminds us, the word "duty" in the nineteenth century covered a wide spectrum of social and personal moral obligations. In Lord Nelson's famous exhortation to his fleet at the beginning of the Battle of Trafalgar, "England expects that every man will do his duty," the term no doubt signified an obligation loyally to serve and, if necessary, die for, King and country in the cause of defeating the forces of the enemy. But of course it was not only in the military sphere that the concept of duty held sway as a regulator of conduct in Shaw's lifetime. In some cases, the concept was supported by the dictates of law and religion; in others, it was simply part of generally accepted assumptions about what constitutes proper human behavior. The codes of conduct included: the duty of children to honor and obey their parents; the duty of wives to honor and obey their husbands, and to perform their tasks as housewives and mothers, as well as the more subtle obligations to behave in womanly ways; the still-continuing duty of members of Parliament in England and the Commonwealth to swear allegiance to the English Crown, and the more general duty of citizens to show loyalty to their country. As Dukore argues, the concept of duty is often also invoked by politicians as one of the tricks of governing classes to lend a mask of respectability to projects fundamentally driven by acquisitive and power-seeking motives.

The ideal of duty was one of the many sacred cows that Shaw, as playwright and activist, was fond of ridiculing. In *The Admirable Bashville*, Shaw has his pugilist hero, Cashel Byron, parody Nelson's immortal message by saying that every man "Shall twaddle / About his duty," and declare that the two things he hates are "my duty and my mother." In the Dream in Hell scene of another Edwardian play, *Man and Superman*, Don Juan calls duty "one of the seven deadly virtues." Dukore rightly identifies Henrik Ibsen as a major influence on Shaw's radical questioning of widely accepted ideals of duty. In *A Doll's House*, Nora astounds her husband and the rest of the world by renouncing her duty both as wife and mother, and declaring that she has discovered a prior duty—to herself. In *Ghosts*, Mrs. Alving, as encouraged by the counseling of a sanctimonious pastor, comes to endure the dreadful consequences of being a dutiful wife to her debauched husband.

The twin themes announced in the subtitle of this book are remarkably pervasive in Shaw's drama. Dukore argues that in one form or another they appear in about two-thirds of his dramatic output of more than fifty plays and playlets. Several early plays lend themselves well to analysis under the "slaves of duty" rubric. In *Mrs Warren's Profession*, Vivie Warren is presented from early in the play as a young woman who has emancipated herself from Victorian stereotypes of what constitutes "womanly" behavior. The denouement of the play depends on her final refusal, after a titanic struggle, to follow the rules of loyalty and obedience that Victorians expected from daughters in relation to their mothers. In the first of their two long quarrels, Mrs. Warren describes Vivie as "a bad daughter and a stuck-up prude." In the second, she rails at Vivie's refusal to do her "duty as a daughter."

Like Nora Helmer, the wife/mother figure in *You Never Can Tell*, Mrs. Clandon (as she now calls herself, having discarded her married name of Crampton) is a woman who has renounced her duty to her husband; unlike Nora, she has taken her children with her when she walks out. After the children have grown up, there is an accidental family reunion at a seaside hotel. The father, the embittered and irascible Crampton, is a stickler for proper behavior and is aghast at the merry cheekiness of his twin children and the haughtiness of their older sister. They do not behave in the manner of dutiful children. As the play develops, however, we see a thawing-out of Crampton's crabbiness and moral rigidity, and a revised view of parent-child relationships: as Dukore aptly puts it, the "comedy dramatizes the emancipation from slavery to duty ... and its replacement by freely bestowed affection" (109). In *Man and Superman*, nice dramatic ironies are created when Ann Whitefield demurely professes her daughterly duty to follow the terms of the will of her deceased father and the wishes of her mother. These dutiful professions, however, mask her real motivation: the pursuit and capture of the attractive, voluble (and rich) Socialist, Jack Tanner.

In one of the speeches of Napoleon in *The Man of Destiny*, Dukore finds a satirical view of duty that links with his account of the "tricks of the governing class." "Shaw's Napoleon," Dukore writes, "expresses the view [that] the English, who act in their own interests, do so after they have convinced themselves that what they do derives from a moral and religious duty, which they use to justify exploitation: colonizing backward nations, employing religion as a tool for creating overseas markets, and enslaving the children of their own poor" (112). He examines various ways in which Shaw treats the trickery and humbug practiced by members of the governing class in a number of plays, including *Major Barbara, John Bull's Other Island, Augustus Does His Bit, Heartbreak House, The Apple Cart, On the Rocks, Buoyant Billions*, and other late works. In *John Bull's Other Island*, Broadbent provides a classic example of the way in which members of the governing class, in this case a capitalist entrepreneur, tend to dress up self-interested designs as worthy, public-spirited projects. Dukore takes the second part of his subtitle from a speech by Undershaft in Act III of *Major Barbara*. Shaw's highly articulate and shamelessly unscrupulous tycoon is an appropriate focal point for further exploration of governing class tricks in this study.

Ambitiously, Dukore sets out in this one hundred and thirty-nine page book to survey the entire corpus of Shaw's dramatic works. His treatment of the plays is always based on careful and intelligent reading; but this whirlwind tour of the Shavian canon involves treating some of the plays and related subjects in very summary fashion. One related subject that comes to mind concerns Shaw's rather blinkered view of the tricks of the governing class. His principal targets in this regard were the governing classes in England, with occasional side swipes at America, both representative of the capitalist system he denounced. In many ways, the tricks being played in other countries, such as Germany, Italy, and Russia, in the second quarter of the twentieth century, made those in England and America look like parlor games. In retrospect, it is clear that Shaw was far too generous in some of his earlier statements about Hitler and Mussolini (though he was not the only contemporary outside observer to be impressed by them), and his admiration for Stalin remained virtually unwavering. In an interview during World War II in answer to the question "Whom do you think is the greatest man this war has yet produced?" Shaw replied "Stalin, of course." Such was the effectiveness of Russian propaganda that Stalin continued to be widely regarded, throughout World War II and beyond, as the benevolent figure affectionately known as "Uncle Joe."

Dukore might reasonably argue that investigation of the complex subject of Shaw's attitude to twentieth-century totalitarian leaders was outside his brief. But in reading a book about Shaw's treatment of "tricks of the governing class," it is difficult not to be reminded of the painful (to Shaw admirers) subject of his failure adequately to condemn the brutality and political deceptions that characterized the totalitarian regimes that flourished in the last three decades of his life. The distance between Shaw, the creator of delightfully witty and humane comedies and writer of wonderfully entertaining, kindly, and generous letters, and the sometimes disturbingly callous commentator on world affairs in his later years remains mysterious.

Whatever might be said about that enigma, this new book is certainly to be welcomed as an insightful, well-written, and valuable contribution to Shaw studies. Dukore has explored two rich seams of thematic interest in Shavian drama, and his succinct discussions show many of the plays in a new light.

A. M. GIBBS

NOTE

1. Bernard Shaw, "Democracy is Indestructible—Says Bernard Shaw," interview in *Cavalcade*, 28 March 1942. Repr. in A. M. Gibbs, ed., *Shaw: Interviews and Recollections* (London: Macmillan, 1990), 467–69.

Abiding Love: Shaw and Russia

Olga Soboleva and Angus Wrenn. *The Only Hope of the World: George Bernard Shaw and Russia.* Bern: Peter Lang, 2012. 11 black-and-white illustrations. 231 pages. $64.95.

Bernard Shaw's 1931 trip to the Soviet Union, and his increasingly vociferous public endorsements of Stalin and the Soviet experiment that issued from his pen after the trip, are well known. Not so well known, but captured brilliantly by Olga Soboleva and Angus Wrenn in their new book, *The Only Hope of the World: George Bernard Shaw and Russia*, is Shaw's long-standing love affair with Russian culture, which goes back at least to the 1880s, when he was moving in the same circles as émigré Russian revolutionaries Sergius Stepniak, Prince Peter Kropotkin, and Esper Serebriakov. The book chronicles those heady times in 1880s London, and traverses all the way to Shaw's last years, but it has the additional advantage of surveying a few especially interesting Soviet productions of Shaw's plays, and of ending with a detailed history of a play about Shaw and his relationship with Mrs. Patrick Campbell, *Dear Liar*, which has had a remarkable stage life within Russia from the time shortly after it was written in the late 1950s right up to the present day.

The book is comprised of a brief introduction and six chapters, each one detailing an aspect of Shaw's relationship with Russia. The first chapter, "Admirals and Amiable Gentleman: Shaw and the Russian Anarchists," provides brief but fascinating biographies of the Russian anarchists mentioned above, especially Stepniak and Kropotkin, and makes for compelling reading on that score alone. We learn that it was Sergius Stepniak's poignant expatiation on the deplorable conditions in Russia under the Czars that converted William Morris to socialism, and he exerted an equally strong influence on Sidney Webb as well. The authors contend that these highly educated, debonair anarchists, who stressed the necessity of strong leadership and an elite class of revolutionaries to bring about change, likely had a deep influence on Shaw, and that the "negative attitude toward democracy which Shaw had encountered early in the work of Carlyle, within a British context, would have been augmented in the 1880s, as Shaw began to come into contact with the Russian émigrés in London, from middle and upper-class, even aristocratic backgrounds" (38).

In Chapter 2, "'All Art at the Fountainhead Is Didactic': Shaw and Lev Tolstoy," the authors claim that Shaw found in the great Russian not so much a mentor as "an explicit validation of his own thoughts" (52). Much of the chapter covers both Shaw's and Tolstoy's negative views of Shakespeare, which went further with Tolstoy than with Shaw. (Shaw actually came to Shakespeare's defense when he felt that Tolstoy unjustly berated Shakespeare for his style, although he agreed with Tolstoy that Shakespeare lacked philosophical purpose.) Much of the rest of the chapter is spent comparing *The Shewing-up of Blanco Posnet* to Tolstoy's *The Power of Darkness*, which Shaw claims inspired the play. Soboleva and Wrenn show how the play took the form it did as a result of Tolstoy's criticism of *Man and Superman*. Tolstoy admired the earlier play, but felt Shaw's brilliant writing was an obstacle to his didactic message. *Blanco Posnet*, on the other hand, expresses the same theme as *Man and Superman*, but with "clarity and simplicity," as Tolstoy recommended, so that it was "accessible even for an unsophisticated audience" (64). Tolstoy may have served as an explicit validation of Shaw's own thoughts, but also clearly influenced Shaw more than that statement implies—or so the authors appear to suggest.

In Chapter 3, "'A Fantasia in the Russian Manner': Shaw and Maxim Gorky," the authors argue that Gorky was the strongest influence behind *Heartbreak House*, rather than, as is usually thought, Chekhov. Most of the chapter consists in an illuminating and incisive analysis of *Heartbreak House* alongside Gorky's *Summerfolk*, which was interpreted at the time of its 1904 premiere as "a postscript to *The Cherry Orchard*, in which Lopakhin's dream had found its most wicked and cynical realization" (85). Like Gorky's *Summerfolk*, *Heartbreak House* dramatizes, within an English setting, the Russian literary theme of the Superfluous Man. The chapter also details the decades-long friendship between Shaw and Gorky and their similarities as modern, twentieth-century didactic playwrights.

Chapter 4 brings us to the first of Shaw's plays written in reaction to the tumultuous changes in Russia that began in 1917, "'Mr Shaw Has Always Had a Weakness for Shrews': Shaw and *Annajanska, the Bolshevik Empress*." Here Soboleva and Wrenn begin to wrestle with Shaw's enduring support of the Bolshevik Revolution, which they regard in many ways as antithetical to his philosophy of Fabian gradualism. Space prohibits an account of the vicissitudes of the Revolution and its aftermath and the close attention that Shaw gave to it, but suffice it to say that, from this chapter to the end of the book, the authors do a fine job of chronicling Shaw's attitude toward events in postrevolutionary Russia, which culminates in the next and longest chapter in the book, where they detail Shaw's 1931 visit to the Soviet Union. They argue here that Shaw only gave his unequivocal support to the Bolsheviks in 1921, when "Lenin's New Economic Policy created an effective bridge-passage to Fabian reformist gradualism" (128). Shaw wrote *Annajanska, The Wild Grand Duchess* (as the playlet was originally titled) at actress Lillah McCarthy's request, and it opened in January 1918 as part of a triple-bill that included short plays by J. M. Barrie and John Galsworthy. Inspired by the ongoing events in Russia, the authors believe the protagonist, the "Grand Duchess," was inspired by Kropotkin's daughter Aleksandra Kropotkin-Lebedeva, otherwise known to Shaw as Princess Sasha, who in his opinion was "a perfect example of an active revolutionist—decisive in her actions and persuasive in her views (all the qualities manifested in Annajanska)" (108). The chapter also touches on other relevant Shaw works, such as *Arms and the Man*, *Great Catherine*, and *Common Sense About the War*.

In the penultimate chapter, "'Russia Is All Right and We Are All Wrong': Shaw's Trip to the USSR," the authors have managed through diligent research to put together as comprehensive an itinerary of Shaw's trip to Russia in 1931 as is possible. Shaw was unusually reticent about his trip, staving off questions about his more than two-hour-long meeting with Stalin, for example, with quips such as, "He has a black mustache." In addition to recounting Shaw's trip step-by-step as well as they can, the authors discuss Russia's propagandistic strategy of having Western intellectuals visit the country, how the trips were stage-managed by Soviet authorities, and how Shaw was clearly disingenuous in his remarks to the press when he asserted that Soviet authorities in no way mitigated harsh conditions for his perusal. One of Shaw's traveling companions, Lord Lothian, "who was given exactly the same tour of the country, did not turn a blind eye to the crisis" and wrote about it on his return (161). The chapter provides an excellent overview of Shaw's relationship with the Soviet Union, the abuses Shaw hardened his heart to (and why he may have done so), and details the specific ways his enthusiasm for the USSR and its leader were manifested right up until his death in 1950.

The final chapter, "'Dear Liar': Shaw's Last Plays," is divided roughly into two parts. The far longer first part provides short but cogent analyses of some of the plays Shaw wrote after his trip to the Soviet Union, such as *Geneva*, *Too True to Be Good*, and *The Millionairess*, but the fullest treatment is reserved for the play Shaw wrote before his trip, *The Apple Cart*, a favorite in the Soviet Union, although, oddly enough, not produced there until 1972 (despite his high status, we learn that Shaw was more read than staged). That celebrated 1972 production, ingeniously staged (by Vadim Golikov) as a chess match, is given extensive attention by the authors. The last third of the chapter is devoted to Jerome Kilty's play *Dear Liar*, about Shaw and Stella Campbell, in particular to Soviet film director Grigorii Aleksandrov's brilliant production, which originally starred his wife, Soviet movie star Liubov Orlova.

This is, in short, an excellent book: well researched, clearly written, and difficult to put down. Given the dramatic changes that Russia underwent in the first half of the twentieth century, and given what Shaw, writing to Maxim Gorky, called his "life-long passion for the 'strange intensive culture of the Russian soul'" (212), this book is long overdue.

MATTHEW YDE

Shaw and the "isms"

Shaw and Feminisms: On Stage and Off. Edited by D. A. Hadfield and Jean Reynolds. Gainesville: University Press of Florida, 2013. xvi + 234 pages. $74.95.

Bernard Shaw often proves difficult to pinpoint definitively on any subject, as anyone who has dealt with his socialism, Fabianism, pacifism, and especially feminism has no doubt discovered. The editors and contributors experience this same dilemma in *Shaw and Feminisms: On Stage and Off*, a much welcomed volume that considers the always-complex Shaw and his favorite topic, women—literal and fictional—from multiple perspectives. The aptly titled work (*Feminisms*) studies Shaw's various approaches to feminist thinking, playwriting, and personal actions, for good or ill, with the stated goal of collecting "materials covering various aspects of Shaw's work and influence and put[ting] them into dialogue with contemporary feminist thinking." Shaw's long life and career saw changes and evolutions in his positions, and the book's contributors explore these developments. The editors praise Shaw as the first British playwright to stage serious debates about the "woman question" and as the creator of extraordinary female characters. However, several of his personal relations with women, especially would-be women playwrights, are called into question.

Much of the book's considerable strength derives from several chapters that feature *au courant* literary theory, never-before-published Shaw letters, seldom-discussed Shavian female characters, and Shaw as a multinational figure. For example, in an exemplary essay, Tracy J. R. Collins considers the body as portrayed in drama a major topic in contemporary theory and in the works of Shaw himself. Shaw's athletic women characters use their bodies to advantage in their relations with other characters and generally prove to be women of action in the quest to describe the New Woman that fascinated society during Shaw's early playwriting years.

Leonard Conolly presents never-before-published letters from Shaw to the actress Mary Hamilton not only to shed light on Shaw's relationships with women but also to introduce a previously overlooked addition to Shaw's large collection of female friends and acquaintances. Fresh Shaw material is always valuable, and in this essay Conolly uses these letters to aptly demonstrate how Shaw could "speak openly and freely about the Life Force, playwriting, acting, morality, love, marriage, and happiness."

Brad Kent fills a void in Shaw studies by addressing the paucity of commentary devoted to Irish women and focuses on the treatment of female characters in *John Bull's Other Island* by "situating them in a broad literary history." Kent posits that Shaw's ambivalence toward women in the play results from his conflicted relationship with his native land, but suggests that Shaw also offers hope for transformation of traditional roles for women into positive agents of progress and change.

Kay Li identifies Shaw as a writer of multinational importance and relays the stage history of the first Chinese performances of *Mrs Warren's Profession* (1920), a talky, immoral play by Chinese standards. Nevertheless, according to Li, the play proved useful to Chinese intellectuals in their "slow march toward equality for women."

In a timely and important interview with D. A. Hadfield, Jackie Maxwell, artistic director of the Shaw Festival in Niagara-on-the-Lake, Ontario, tells of her desire not only to produce stellar productions of Shaw plays featuring his dynamic and energetic women characters, but also to discover and give voice to female playwrights of the Victorian and Edwardian eras. Maxwell surmises: "There's no doubt that his [Shaw's] plays are still provocative . . . because the status quo is so hideously unchanged in so many ways."

The book closes with Michel Pharand's bibliography of writings by and about Shaw concerning love, sex, marriage, women, and related topics, which will be of great value to those wishing to continue and further the study of Shaw and feminisms.

However, despite these and other stellar contributions, puzzling aspects of the book emerge. The editors aptly describe the various waves of feminist activism that Shaw lived through and participated in yet never define *feminisms* or clarify the standard(s) to which Shaw is being held by the various contributors. Instead, the volume focuses on the broader concept of the Woman Question that fueled discussion, often led by Shaw, in the late 1890s and early 1900s. Some definition of or standard for the stated topic would help to unify the work. In the Introduction, the editors suggest that Feminism and Shavian thinking coalesce around three postmodern themes: identity, ambivalence, and incompleteness. Without a clear definition of terms, the volume shares the latter two of these characteristics in examining Shaw's feminism(s).

In addition, the collection suffers from an unfortunate lack of balance in representing Shaw's many works. The editors and contributors rely heavily on two plays to construct their arguments, with *Mrs Warren's Profession* and *The Philanderer* appearing in five of the book's ten chapters. Brad Kent and John McInerney provide refreshing exceptions with their treatments of *John Bull's Other Island* and myriad Shaw plays, respectively.

The chapter entitled "Shaw and Cruelty" examines the strain of theatrical cruelty that supposedly runs from Henrik Ibsen to Shaw to Bertolt Brecht and Antonin Artaud. Lawrence Switzky posits that the largely feminist antivivisection movement gave Shaw the language of cruelty with which to inflict pain upon the audience as he created his own dramaturgy. Switzky believes that Shaw learned from Ibsen how to construct the "crucial shift from watching and judging pain to experiencing pain," using this technique in his *Plays Unpleasant* "to inflict audience suffering by exposing the complicity of spectators in slum-landlordism, prostitution, and the systematic corruption that licenses these practices." Shaw's method presumably reveals the tendency toward cruelty in human nature but is "justified by the promise of social benefit." While Switzky's thesis is intriguing, even tempting, his emphasis on Shaw's use of "cruelty" perhaps exaggerates and overstates (a favorite Shavian tactic) Shaw's stated practice of "sharpshooting at the audience" to help them recognize themselves in the so-called stage "vivisectionists," such as Sartorius, Crofts, and Charteris, and to make those who did so *uncomfortable* with their own positions, thereby achieving an effect very different from cruelty. Many critics conclude that in launching his social barbs, Shaw, an avowed meliorist, eschewed "audience vivisection," even in dealing with unpleasant social practices in great need of reform, in favor of humor.

The theme of possible cruelty continues as three contributors employ never-published material to reveal a potential flaw in Shaw's feminism. D. A. Hadfield questions Shaw's efforts to liberate women and avers that his creation of celebrated women characters "may have largely served a desire to constrain and confine them . . . within the ones he himself defined." She concludes that Shaw's success as a writer of women was built on his success in keeping them from writing themselves; this theory is based on letters that Shaw exchanged with the celebrated Shavian actress and close friend Janet Achurch, letters in which Shaw discouraged her from continuing to write her unpublished play *Mrs. Daintree's Daughter* (Hadfield includes excerpts), based on the same de Maupassant play as Shaw's *Mrs Warren's Profession*. While Shaw may have desired to thwart Achurch's playwriting career in order to save her time and energy to star in his own plays, the next two essays feature women would-be playwrights who sought Shaw's endorsement of their work for their own advancement. Margaret Stetz presents unpublished material, including sections of a play by George Egerton (Mary Chavelita Dunne, wife of Reginald Golding Bright, Shaw's dramatic agent), to supplement her discussion of Shaw's supposed blocking access of Egerton's work to the Court Theatre. In addition, Virginia Costello offers unpublished material from the Emma Goldman archives to reveal Fabian Shaw's refusal to support Goldman's anarchist causes, contending that Shaw only supported women's causes when he had the "upper hand." Costello further asserts that many of Shaw's female acquaintances felt that in his personal life, Shaw did not live up to the radical philosophy expounded in his plays. One wishes that these charges leveled against Shaw had been set in a stronger context than a few personal letters and reported conversations. Opinions of other contemporaries that these works are worthy of performance and publication would have given more weight to these complaints. Based on the evidence provided in the book, Janet Achurch may have had legitimate grounds for resenting Shaw's refusal to acknowledge her playwriting talents, while Goldman and Egerton may have attempted to use the famous author to promote their own purposes, a ploy that Shaw would no doubt have recognized.

Nevertheless, despite these omissions and missteps, *Shaw and Feminisms* provides valuable material in the quest to place Shaw's multivalent attitudes toward women and gender issues within the debates of his era. The editors and contributors attempt to present various aspects of Shaw, the tireless Fabian fighter for women's rights in his essays and speeches; the would-be world betterer who preached his message of social justice to female audiences and through dazzling New Woman characters; and the inspirer of "actresses and agitators." The editors quote Lillah McCarthy extensively to underscore this point: "I played Ann Whitefield in 'Man and Superman.' She was a 'new woman' and she made a new woman of me . . . she set the world of women free.'" Shaw fought tirelessly for equal rights among the sexes but, according to some, fell short of his own ideals in his personal relationships with women. Yet because the depiction of Shaw as a stalwart feminist is juxtaposed with the implied portrait of a controlling, sometimes cruel, chauvinist (although the term is never used), a clear picture of Shaw and feminism(s) never emerges—and perhaps there isn't one. Undoubtedly, however, this work offers helpful updates and fresh assessments in the continuing study of Shaw and his favorite subject: women. As Rodelle Weintraub states in her foreword, "I learned lots and had to expand my thinking about Shaw," thus fulfilling one of the main purposes of scholarship: a basis for further study.

LAGRETTA TALLENT LENKER

PASSINGS

In Memoriam: Sidney P. Albert

Sidney P. Albert died peacefully on 9 January 2013; he was ninety-eight years old. Born in Syracuse, New York, Sid received an A.B. from Syracuse University in 1935 and a Ph.D. in philosophy from Yale in 1939. After serving in the military, he did postdoctoral study in drama and theater under the G.I. Bill at Carnegie Tech, Northwestern, Stanford, the University of Illinois, and Columbia. He was a founding member of the International Shaw Society and helped organize and run several Shaw organizations. His extensive collection of Shaw manuscripts, books, and correspondence, the Sidney P. Albert–Bernard Shaw Collection, is now housed at Brown University. He is survived by his sister, Beverly Cooper Silvers; his former wife, Lucy Ann Albert, and their thee children, Vivian, Alan, and Laurence; four grandchildren; and his longtime friend, Elaine Amromin.

A professor emeritus of philosophy at Cal State LA, Sid published his magnum opus, *Shaw, Plato, and Euripides: Classical Currents in "Major Barbara,"* in 2012 with the University Press of Florida as part of its Bernard Shaw Series. According to the series' editor, R. F. Dietrich, "The sort of grit and determination that saw Sid through to the finishing of the book was typical of him. And I learned in the process an even greater admiration for his scholarship and his scholarly integrity, for, despite the urgency of an author in his 90s, there was no cutting of corners in the research and writing of this book. And what came out at the end was a work of philosophical discourse rare in his clarity and ground-breaking in showing very concretely how Shaw had borrowed Greek thought but modernized it. *Major Barbara* stood revealed at last as a step forward, an evolutionary growth, from ancient wisdom." According to Dietrich, "I'm sure it was Sid's experience in this that led to his strong support for me when, at the 2000

SHAW, Vol. 33, 2013 | Copyright © 2013 The Pennsylvania State University, University Park, PA

Shaw Conference at Marquette University in Milwaukee, I proposed the founding of the ISS, which has borne promising fruit and seems likely to last, but which would be much stronger by now if I had known how valuable Sid would have been as a partner had we founded it ten years earlier. I am delighted, however, that the ISS was able to take advantage in 2007 of another Sid Albert obsession, the collecting of works on and by Shaw. The second ISS conference just happened to be at Brown that year, and what a rare privilege it was to see the display of Sid's wonderful collection. I've heard since that Sid has a *second* collection of Shaviana that rivals the first, and I only hope that a suitable home can be found for it."

In many ways, Sid's life amounted to a sort of "Quintessence of Shavianism" in both work and deed—a legacy and an inspiration for his family, friends, and colleagues.

MICHEL W. PHARAND

In Memoriam: Isidor Saslav

Isidor Saslav, violinist, musicologist, Haydn scholar, and longtime concertmaster for the Longview Symphony, died on 26 January 2013 in the Tyler East Texas Medical Center in Tyler, Texas, twenty miles from his home in Overton. He was seventy-four. He is survived by his wife of fifty years, pianist Ann Heiligman Saslav, with whom he concertized for more than thirty years, and by their children, David and Leanora, both of San Francisco.

Born in Jerusalem and raised in Detroit, Michigan, Isidor began studying the violin at the age of seven, and by seventeen was a member of the Detroit Symphony Orchestra. He graduated from Wayne State University and received a doctorate in music from Indiana University. He went on to enjoy a distinguished career as concertmaster of numerous orchestras, including the Buffalo Philharmonic, the Minnesota, Baltimore, and New Zealand symphony orchestras, and the Indiana University, Dallas, Kennedy Center, Terrace Theater, and Baltimore opera orchestras, and was a member of the Detroit and Chautauqua symphonies and the Orchestra of the Festival Casals in Puerto Rico. He also taught at the Peabody Institute of Johns Hopkins University, the Eastman School of Music, and SUNY Buffalo. He established, and for more than a decade headed, the strings program at Stephen F. Austin State University in Nacogdoches, Texas.

Isidor's second passion was Bernard Shaw. Beginning in 1960, with the purchase of a first edition of Shaw's first play, *Widowers' Houses*, he amassed an impressive collection of more than eight thousand items of Shaviana. With characteristic generosity, he displays and talks about his treasures at http://libra.appso1.yorku.ca/virtual-tour-of-the-isidor-saslav-shaw-collection/ and at http://libra.appso1.yorku.ca/the-saslav-collection/.

In addition, during the last five years, Isidor made numerous trips to the University of North Carolina at Chapel Hill to examine the extensive collection of scrapbooks kept by Shaw biographer Archibald Henderson. Isidor's intention was to catalogue and publish his findings, some of which are delineated in his article in this issue. Perhaps his account of what he calls "Carolina Gold" will inspire others to make the trek to one of the world's greatest Shaw archives and to continue, perhaps even complete, Isidor's groundbreaking research. His enthusiasm was palpable, and when listening to him speak of his Shavian discoveries, one could not help but be equally galvanized.

Just prior to his untimely death, Isidor was in the midst of planning a unique performance that would have combined his musical and Shavian pursuits: a recital of Shaw's favorite music at the June 2013 Shaw conference at Ayot St. Lawrence. The evening's music making was dedicated to Isidor's memory, and we raised our glasses to his indomitable spirit.

MICHEL W. PHARAND

A CONTINUING CHECKLIST
OF SHAVIANA

JOHN R. PFEIFFER[1]

I. Works by Shaw[2]

Shaw, Bernard. *Arms and the Man*. Mineola, New York: Dover Publications, 2012. Not seen. Amazon: Kindle. Price: $0.95.

———. Autoreply Postcard for Unsolicited Mail. 9 February 1948. 5 November 2012 <webspace.utexas.edu/allicia36/Shaw2FullSize.jpg>. The photograph presented at this URL is of a modified printed postcard the ninety-two-year-old Shaw sent to order 150 more "copies as amended." It reads in part: "Mr. Bernard Shaw's readers and the

---

1. Thanks to Richard W. Winslow III for discovering and supplying page copies for a number of entries in this list. As SHAW bibliographer, I welcome information about new and forthcoming Shaviana: books, articles, pamphlets, monographs, dissertations, films, videos, audio recordings, electronic publications, and the like, copies of which may be sent to me at the Department of English Language and Literature, Anspach Hall, Central Michigan University, Mt. Pleasant, MI 48859; e-mail pfeif1jr@cmich.edu; fax 989-774-1271.

2. The number of e-book editions of Shaw works for the longer term remains undiminished. The listings here in most cases represent at least one for each publisher. This section of the Checklist, as well as Section II. Books and Pamphlets, below, includes entries of reprints, "exact" reproductions, and scanned reproductions of early twentieth-century books about Shaw, as offered on Amazon.com. Increasingly, no postal address is available for many of these electronic publishing entities. Such listings here try to provide the names of the publishers and dates of 2012 or 2013 publication.

spectators at performances of his plays number many thousands. The little time remaining to him at his age is fully occupied with his literary work and the business it involves; and war taxation has set narrow limits to his financial resources. He has therefore to print the following ~~warnings~~ [add "intimations"]. He cannot engage . . . advise . . . discuss . . . receive. . . . He will not send messages. He begs to be excused accordingly. Ayot Saint Lawrence, Welwyn, Herts."

———. *Candida*. Lenox, Massachusetts: HardPress Publishing, 2013. Not seen. Many Shaw titles and out-of-print titles about Shaw are available in print-on-demand form from HardPress.

———. *Cashel Byron's Profession*. London: John Murray, 2012. Not seen. Also issued by John Murray in 2012 are *Unsocial Socialist* and *Love Among the Artists*.

———. *Common Sense About the War*. Tyger Valley, South Africa: Ulan Press, 2012. Not seen. Ulan publishes other Shaw titles in Spanish (*César & Cleópatra*) as well as English.

———. *The Complete Plays of George Bernard Shaw . . . 34 Complete and Unabridged Plays. . . .* Braeside, Victoria, Australia: Oxford City Press, 2012. Not seen.

———. *The Dark Lady of the Sonnets*. Loki's Publishing, 2013. Not seen.

———. *The Dark Lady of the Sonnets*. Luxembourg: CreateSpace Independent Publishing Platform, 2013. Many Shaw titles are available as print-on-demand paperbacks from CreateSpace.

———. *Don Juan in Hell*. Mineola, New York: Dover Publications, 2012. Not seen.

———. *The Essential Bernard Shaw Collection*. Amazon: Kindle, 2012. Not seen. Forty-two "books" are listed as included, in 4,917 electronic pages. Price in April 2013: $1.99, which includes free wireless delivery.

———. Excerpt from *Man and Superman*. In *Classically Speaking*. Raleigh, North Carolina: LuLu.com, 2013. A two-page "practice text" to provide an exercise for British pronunciation.

———. *Great Catherine: Whom Glory Still Adores*. ReadHowYouWant [no postal address], 2012. Not seen. ReadHow advertises other Shaw titles.

———. *The Intelligent Woman's Guide to Socialism, Capitalism, Sovietism and Fascism*. Alma Books (London: Hesperus Press, 2013). Not seen.

———. *The Intelligent Woman's Guide to Socialism, Capitalism, Sovietism and Fascism*. New York: Welcome Rain, 2013. Not seen.

———. Letter, previously unpublished, to Shaw's French translator, Augustin Hamon. "Un inédit de George Bernard Shaw" in *Langues de l'histoire, langues de la vie. Mélanges offerts à Fañch Roudaut*, Brest Les Amis de Fañch Roudaut, 2005. pp. 387–98.

———. Letter to Mark Twain of 3 July 1907. In *Mark Twain Anthology: Great Writers on His Life and Works*. New York: Library of America, 2010: 113–14.

———. *Man and Superman and Three Other Plays* [*Candida, Mrs Warren, Devil's Disciple*]. Edited by John A. Bertolini. Amazon: Kindle, 2013. Not seen. Texts and introduction are from Bertolini's Barnes & Noble print edition.

———. *Manual de socialismo y capitalismo para mujeres inteligentes*. Introduction by Margaret Walters. Translated by Dolors Udina. Barcelona: RBA LIBROS, 2013. Not seen. Spanish translation of *Intelligent Woman's Guide. . . .* See substantial excerpt of Walters's "Introduction" online at www.elboomeran.com/upload/ficheros/obras/bernard_shaw_adelanto.pdf. See review by Tereixa Constenla in section III. Periodicals, below.

———. "Morris as I Knew Him." Introduction to *William Morris: Artist Socialist*. Volume 2. By May Morris. Cambridge: Cambridge University Press, 2012. Paper. Originally published in 1936.

———. *Mrs. Warren's Profession. The Norton Anthology of English Literature*. Ninth edition. Edited by Stephen Greenblatt and M. H. Abrams. New York: W. W. Norton & Co., 2012. Not seen.

———. "One of Your Calculating Fits." *A Wealth of Numbers: An Anthology of 500 Years of Popular Mathematics Writing*. Edited by Benjamin Wardhaugh. Princeton: Princeton University Press, 2012. Not seen.

———. *Plays Pleasant and Unpleasant*, Volume I. Berkeley to Santa Cruz: University of California Libraries, 2012. Not seen. "Libraries" refers to a ten-university group.

———. *Pygmalion*. Amazon: Kindle, 2013. Not seen. Many Shaw titles are offered by the Kindle reader. The editions offered by Kindle are from many Internet and traditional publishing entities (Balefire Publishing, Dover Publishing, Start Publishing LLC, etc.)

———. *Pygmalion*. Berlin: Suhrkamp Verlag, 2012. A German-language edition, with commentary in German. Not seen.

———. *Pygmalion*. Translated by Arezo Shojaei. Iran: Qatreh Publications, 2012. A Persian-language edition. Not seen.

———. *Pygmalion* (illustrated). Amazon: Kindle, 2013. Not seen. Offered as including 11 illustrations by Yuan Shi.

———. *Pygmalion and Three Other Plays* [*Major Barbara, Doctor's Dilemma, and Heartbreak*]. Edited by John A. Bertolini. Amazon: Kindle, 2013. Not seen. Texts and introduction are from Bertolini's Barnes & Noble print edition.

———. *Pygmalion: The Original Classic.* Ruislip, Middlesex: Tebbo, 2012. Not seen. Many Shaw titles are available as print-on-demand paperbacks from Tebbo.

———. Quoted in *Best Thoughts and Quotes of the World: Lead an Inspired Life.* By Shashikant Nishant Sharma. Luxembourg: CreateSpace, 2012. Not seen. Eight items.

———. Quoted in *Inspirational Being.* By Cornelius D. Jones. Lulu.com, 2012. Not seen. A book of "inspirational quotes." Nine items.

———. *The Revolutionist's Handbook and Pocket Companion: A Companion to Man and Superman.* Auckland: The Floating Press, 2012. Not seen. Floating Press also offers *Superman.*

———. *You Never Can Tell.* Charleston, South Carolina: Nabu Press, 2012. Not seen. Many Shaw titles are available as print-on-demand paperbacks from Nabu.

II. Books and Pamphlets

Ajtony, Zsuzsanna. *Britain and Britishness in G. B. Shaw's Plays: A Linguistic Perspective.* Newcastle upon Tyne: Cambridge Scholars Publishing, 2012. "The main body of the plays analysed in this book reveals a series of cultural and ethnic differences and the plays' constitutive elements, comprising oppositions on the basis of which the plays are structured. *Arms, Devil's Disciple, John Bull, Caesar and Cleopatra* [*Pygmalion*] are works in which ethnicity is directly present." See also, Ajtony, in Section IV. Dissertations and Selected Theses.

Allis, Michael. *British Music and Literary Context (Music in Britain, 1600–1900).* Woodbridge, Suffolk: Boydell Press, 2012. Several references to GBS, some of which recognize his authority as a music critic.

Alonso, Harriet Hyman. *Yip Harburg: Legendary Lyricist and Human Rights Activist.* Anderson, Indiana: Wesleyan, 2012. Harburg loved Shaw, especially *Androcles* and its comic proposition that "Christians are such radicals." Seven other references to Shaw.

Appleton, Victor. *Adolf Hitler and His Submarine: Adolf vs. the Mafia Part of the Hitler Chronicles.* Luxembourg: CreateSpace, 2012. Two references to Shaw as a co-conspirator of formal eugenics planners—this time in Canada. Shaw stays to collect his royalties as a eugenics propagandist. Shaw is the top achiever.

Bauer, Ingeborg. *Auch Am Rand Ist in Der Mitte—Eine (Nicht Nur) Literarische Reise Durch Irland.* Stoughton, Wisconsin: Books on Demand, 2013. Seven references to Shaw and a short chapter, "Garinish Island and Bernard Shaw." Not seen.

Bertolini, John A. "Over the Falls in Golden Barrel: The Shaw Fest Celebrates (*The Shaw Festival: The First Fifty Years* by L. W. Conolly)." *SHAW: The Annual of Bernard Shaw Studies* 32 (2012): 187–89.

Blackstock, Alan R. *The Rhetoric of Redemption: Chesterton, Ethical Criticism, and the Common Man.* New York: Peter Lang, 2012. Thirteen references to GBS. Not seen.

Broich, John. *London: Water and the Making of the Modern City (Pittsburgh Hist Urban Environ).* Pittsburgh: University of Pittsburgh Press, 2013. "The contestants over London's water supply matched divergent strategies for administering London's water with contending visions of modern society. . . . The struggle . . . was joined by some of the most colorful figures of the late Victorian period, including John Burns, Lord Salisbury, Bernard Shaw, and Sidney and Beatrice Webb." Ten references to Shaw. Not seen.

Brown, Craig. *Hello Goodbye Hello: A Circle of 101 Remarkable Meetings.* Chicago: Simon and Schuster, 2012. Includes three famous GBS meetings: With John Scott-Ellis (4), Harpo Marx (170–73), and Bertrand Russell (174–76).

Caddy, David. *Cycling After Edward Thomas and the English.* San Gabriel Valley, California: Spout Hill Press, 2013. Three references to Shaw. Not seen.

Carpenter, Charles A. "Undershaft as Platonic/Euripidean/Shavian Life Force (*Shaw, Plato, and Euripides: Classical Currents in Major Barbara* by Sidney P. Albert)." *SHAW: The Annual of Bernard Shaw Studies* 32 (2012): 177–81.

Charlton, James. *The Military Quotation Book, Revised for the 21st Century: More than 1,100 of the Best Quotations about War, Leadership, Courage, and Victory.* New York: St. Martin Press, 2013. Ten items for Shaw. Not seen.

Clare, David. "Bernard Shaw's Irish Characters and the Rise of Reverse Snobbery." In *The European Avant-Garde: Text and Image.* Edited by Selena Daly and Monica Insinga. Newcastle upon Tyne: Cambridge Scholars Publishing, 2012: 138–53. Not seen.

Coates-Smith, Michael, and Gary McGee. *The Films of Jean Seberg.* Jefferson, North Carolina: McFarland, 2012. Reviews the low opinion of Seberg's role in the film of Shaw's *Saint Joan* (1957), and notes that she did much better in Jean-Luc Godard's *Breathless* (1959).

Collins, Tracy J. R. See Hadfield, below.

Conolly, Leonard. *Bernard Shaw and the BBC.* Toronto: University of Toronto Press, 2012. An Amazon: Kindle, release.

———. See Hadfield, below.

———. See *Misalliance,* below.

Cory-Wright, Susana. *Lady Tree: A Theatrical Life in Letters.* Raleigh, North Carolina: Lulu.com, 2012. Numerous references to Shaw. A paperback edition. Not seen.

Costello, Virginia. See Hadfield, above.

Doikas, Spiros. *No Sex Please: We're British! The Exploits of a Greek Student in Britain.* Luxembourg: CreateSpace, 2013. A paperback edition. Eleven references to Shaw. Not seen.

Dolmetsch, Arnold. An excerpt of a letter to Bernard Shaw in March 1928. *Bulletin of the Dolmetsch Foundation* 22 (Autumn 2012): 11–12. The letter contained Dolmetsch's trenchant view of "virtuosi." Not seen.

Dugan, Sally. *Baroness Orczy's The Scarlet Pimpernel: A Publishing History.* Burlington, Vermont: Ashgate, 2012. Seven references to Shaw. Not seen.

Dukore, Bernard F. *Bernard Shaw: Slaves of Duty and Tricks of the Governing Class.* Greensboro, North Carolina: ELT Press, 2012. The book's ten chapters include (1) "Duty Bound and Duty Free," (2) "Unpleasant and Pleasant Plays," (3) "Puritans and a Prizefighter," (4) "The Big Three," (5) "Late Edwardian Plays," (6) "Plays of the War Years," 7) "An Allegory, An Adaptation, and a Different War," (8) "Plays During Hard Times," (9) "Parables and Playfulness," and (10) "Slaves of Duty, Moral Duty, and Other Tricks of the Governing Class." The text is available on *Project Muse.*

Dunn, Anthony J. *The Worlds of Wolf Mankowitz: Between Elite and Popular Cultures in Post-War Britain.* Edgware, Middlesex: Vallentine Mitchell, 2013. His father gave him a complete set of Shaw works when he was twelve. He joined the screenwriting for *Millionairess* (1960), and included is a discussion of the differences between Shaw's script and the film script. Not seen.

Edwardian Opulence: British Art at the Dawn of the Twentieth Century. A catalogue. 28 February 2013 to 2 June 2013. An exhibition at Yale University. The exhibition is accompanied by a major publication, edited by the curators and published by the Center in association with Yale University Press. It contains twelve references to Shaw. <britishart.yale.edu/exhibitions/Edwardian-opulence-british-art-dawn-twentieth-century>.

Eltis, Sos. *Acts of Desire: Women and Sex on Stage, 1800–1930.* New York: Oxford University Press, 2013. Nineteen references to Shaw, including to *Candida, Superman, Widowers' Houses, Mrs Warren,* and *Philanderer.* Not seen.

Evans, T. F. *George Bernard Shaw*. New York: Routledge, 2013. A paperback complement of *Shaw: The Critical Heritage* (1995).

Farooqui, Shahnawaz. *Clash of Civilizations in Traditional Islamic Discourse*. Luxembourg: CreateSpace, 2012. Reviews the case of Shaw, as taken in by Rabindranath Tagore. However, after visiting him after Tagore won the Nobel Prize, Shaw reported he was a "fool."

Field-Lewis, Jane, and Tina Hiller. *My Cool Shed: An Inspirational Guide to Stylish Hideaways and Workspaces*. London: Pavilion, 2012. Includes "George Bernard Shaw's Writing Hut."

Fort, Adrian. *Nancy: The Story of Lady Astor*. London: Cape, 2012. Includes six references to Shaw—considered by Astor to be one of her closest friends. She last visited him a week before he died. Reviewed in *TLS*, 14 December 2012, 26.

Gahan, Peter. "Bernard Shaw: Dégringolade and Derision in Dublin City." *SHAW: The Annual of Bernard Shaw Studies* 32 (2012): 39–58.

——. "Bernard Shaw's Role in the Irish National Revival (*Shaw, Synge, Connolly, and Socialist Provocation* by Nelson O'Ceallaigh Ritschel)." *SHAW: The Annual of Bernard Shaw Studies* 32 (2012): 170–74.

Gibson, Andrew. *The Strong Spirit: History, Politics, and Aesthetics in the Writings of James Joyce, 1898–1915*. New York: Oxford University Press, 2013. Seven references to Shaw, including ones to *Blanco Posnet*, *John Bull*, and Michael Holroyd's biography of Shaw. Not seen.

Goldsworthy, Vesna. *Inventing Ruritania*. London: C. Hurst & Co. Publishers, 2013. Contains a section, "Bernard Shaw's Bulgaria." Not seen.

Gordan, John Dozier. *Bernard Shaw, 1856–1950: An Exhibition from the Berg Collection Manuscripts, Autograph Letters, First Editions*. Whitefish, Montana: Literary Licensing, LLC, 2013. Not seen.

Hadfield, D. A., and Jean Reynolds, eds. *Shaw and Feminisms: On Stage and Off*. Gainesville: University Press of Florida, 2012. Includes "Foreword" by Rodelle Weintraub, "Shaw's Athletic-Minded Women" by Tracy J. R. Collins, "Shaw and Cruelty" by Lawrence Switzky, "Shutting Out Mother: Vivie Warren as the New Woman" by Ann Wilson, "The Politics of Shaw's Irish Women in *John Bull's Other Island*" by Brad Kent, "Bernard Shaw and the Archbishop's Daughter" by Leonard Conolly, "Writing Women and Feminism behind the Scenes" by D. A. Hadfield, "Feminist Politics and the Two Irish "Georges": Egerton versus Shaw" by Margaret D. Stetz, "The Passionate Anarchist and Her Idea Man" by Virginia Costello, "*Mrs Warren's Profession* and the Development of Transnational Chinese Feminism" by Kay Li, "Shaw's Women in the World" by John M. McInerney, "The Energy behind the Anomaly: In Conversation with Jackie Maxwell" interview and editing by D. A. Hadfield, and "Bibliography" by Michel Pharand.

Harding, Desmond. "Staging the City: Bernard Shaw and the Production of Urban Space." *SHAW: The Annual of Bernard Shaw Studies* 32 (2012): 1–15.

Hauser, Thomas. *And the New . . . : An Inside Look at Another Year in Boxing.* Fayetteville: University of Arkansas Press, 2012. Two references to Shaw and Gene Tunney (171–72).

Hilder, Monika B. *The Gender Dance: Ironic Subversion in C. S. Lewis's Cosmic Trilogy.* New York: Peter Lang Publisher, 2013. Hilder argues there was evidence of the history of the assumed superiority of the classical hero, long before the *Übermensch*, named by Nietzsche's and borrowed by Shaw, who described the Christian ethos as a slave morality. Mentions *Major Barbara, Methuselah*, and *Man and Superman*.

Hiller, Tina. See Field-Lewis, Jane, above.

Hirsch, Laura. *The Other Side of Autism: Famous Spirits Unveil Regressive Autism's Causes and Remedies.* Highland City, Florida: Rainbow Books, 2012. Includes Chapter 19: "Featured Spirits: Poe, Shaw, Edgar Cayce, Einstein" (346–52). Not seen.

Holder, Heidi J. "Shaw, Class, and the Melodramas of London Life." *SHAW: The Annual of Bernard Shaw Studies* 32 (2012): 59–85.

Holroyd, Michael. "*Mrs. Warren's Profession.*" Gate Theatre, Dublin, production program. April 2012. The essay locates the play among Shaw's early "unpleasant" plays, credits its "well-made-play" technique, noting its scenes between Mrs. Warren and her daughter Vivie are among the strongest he wrote for the stage—and ahead of their time. The struggle between mother and daughter must be in part based on Shaw's distancing experience from both of his parents.

———. "The Shaw Beneath the Skin: Bernard Shaw." In *The Importance of Staying Earnest.* By Todd London. Raleigh, North Carolina, 2013: 283–88. Not seen.

Huckvale, David. *Ancient Egypt in the Popular Imagination: Building a Fantasy in Film, Literature, Music and Art.* Jefferson, North Carolina, 2012. Provides a discussion of Shaw's *Caesar and Cleopatra* and the popular representation of ancient Egypt—to which Shaw's representation adds very little.

Huckvale, David. "*Visconti and the German Dream: Romanticism, Wagner and the Nazi Catastrophe in Film.* Jefferson, North Carolina: McFarland, 2012. Eleven references to GBS.

Jackson, Holbrook. *Bernard Shaw.* Tyger Valley, South Africa: Ulan Press, 2012. A reproduction of the original 1923 edition. Paperback. Not seen.

Jamieson, Alasdair. *The Music of Hamish MacCunn*. Bloomington, Indiana: AuthorHouse, 2013. Paperback. Eight references to Shaw. Not seen.

Jenkes, Norma. Review of Sidney Albert's *Plato and Euripides: Currents in Major Barbara*; Stanley Weintraub's *Who's Afraid of Bernard Shaw*; Nelson O'Ceallaigh Ritschel's *Shaw, Synge, Conolly, and Socialist Provocation*; and Leonard Conolly's *The Shaw Festival: The First Fifty Years*. In *Text & Presentation*, Volume 9, 2012.

Judge, Tony. *Tory Socialist: Robert Blatchford and Merrie England*. Luxembourg: CreateSpace, 2013. Paperback. Five references to Shaw, who was one of Blatchford's opponents. Not seen.

Katz, Leon. *Cleaning Augean Stables: Examining Drama's Strategies*. Luxembourg: CreateSpace, 2012. Paperback. Western drama has become bland with its clichés. Many references to Shaw, including a ten-script list of "discussion" plays: *Don Juan, Dilemma, Buoyant Billions, Getting Married, Caesar, Joan, Apple Cart, On the Rocks, Superman* (act I), and *Major Barbara*. Not seen.

Kent, Brad. See Hadfield, above.

Kobatchnik, Amnon. *Blood on the Stage, 1975–2000: Milestone Plays of Crime, Mystery, and Detection*. Lanham, Maryland: Scarecrow Press, 2012. Shaw titles on a list of notable one-act plays of mayhem, mischief, and murder are *Augustus, Cymbeline Refinished, Passion, Poison, and Petrifaction, Blanco Posnet*, and *Six of Calais*. Other references to GBS include one of him as a cordially-met friend of Bram Stoker.

Kurin, Richard. *Madcap May: Mistress of Myth, Men, and Hope*. Washington, D.C.: Smithsonian Books, 2012. A life of May Yohe, who married the English Lord who owned the Hope diamond, remarried at least twice (maybe twelve!) more. She drew both praise and rebuke from Shaw.

Landry, Travis. *Subversive Seduction: Darwin, Sexual Selection, and the Spanish Novel*. Seattle: University of Washington Press, 2012. Paperback. Five references to Shaw, one of which refers to the change of Shaw's Don Juan sex to become Doña Juana.

Leask, Margaret. *Lena Ashwell: Actress, Patriot, Pioneer*. Hertfordshire: University of Hertfordshire Press, 2012. Ashwell played Lina in the 23 February 1910 production of *Misalliance*. Seven other references to Shaw.

Leonard, Maurice. *Hope and Glory: A Life of Dame Clara Butt*. Brighton, UK: Victorian Secrets, 2012. Paperback. Butt was one of the most celebrated singers of the Victorian and Edwardian eras. Appendix A is "Dame Clara and George Bernard Shaw" (212–14). A number of other references to Shaw. Not seen.

Li, Kay. See Hadfield, above.

Lodge, David. *A Man of Parts*. New York: Penguin Books, 2012. A biographical novel of H. G. Wells in which Shaw is a significant character.

Long, Cui. *1856 to 1950: George Bernard Shaw—Biographies* [sic] *Series of Nobel Prize Winners (Chinese edition)*. Beijing: Time Literature and Art Press, 2012. Not seen.

Malamud-Smith, Janna. *My Father is a Book: A Memoir of Bernard Malamud*. Berkeley, California: Counterpoint Press, 2013. Paperback. One reference to GBS: Malamud read and quoted Shaw. Not seen.

Malone, Aubrey. *The Mammoth Book of Irish Humor*. Philadelphia: Running Press, 2013. Paperback. A number of Shaw references. Not seen.

Martinson, Harry. *Chickweed Wintergreen: Selected Poems*. Tarset, Northumberland: Bloodaxe Books, 2011. Martinson was a Swedish co-winner of the Nobel Prize in Literature for 1974. This translation by Robin Fulton is the 2012 Winner of the Bernard Shaw Prize for translation from Swedish.

McGee, Gary. See Coates-Smith, Michael, above.

McHugh, Dominic. *Loverly: The Life and Times of My Fair Lady*. New York: Oxford University Press, 2012. Not seen. Reviewed by Gina Dalfonzo in Section III. Periodicals, below.

McInerney, John M. See Hadfield, above.

McKay, James. *The Films of Victor Mature*. Jefferson, North Carolina: McFarland, 2013. One major reference is to the 1952 RKO production of Shaw's *Androcles*, starring Mature.

McNamara, Audrey. "*John Bull's Other Island:* Taking the Bull to Ireland." SHAW: *The Annual of Bernard Shaw Studies* 32 (2012): 133–42.

Meilaender, Gilbert. *Should We Live Forever? The Ethical Ambiguities of Aging*. Grand Rapids, Michigan: William B. Eerdmans, 2013. Paperback. Three references to Shaw, one to *Methuselah*. Shaw proposed that "immortality is natural." Not seen.

Mencken, H. L. *George Bernard Shaw: His Plays*. Forgotten Books, 2012. No postal address. Offers print-on-demand titles of a number of Shaw works. Not seen.

Miller, Elizabeth. *Slow Print: Literary Radicalism and Late Victorian Print Culture*. Stanford: Stanford University Press, 2013. Includes many references to Shaw and his very substantial role in the progression named in this title. Includes a chapter, "The Black and White Veil: Shaw, Mass Print Culture, and the Antinovel Turn" (82–124). Not seen.

The Millionairess. Shaw Festival 2012. (Shaw Festival production program). Includes "Director's Notes" by Blair Williams and "You Must Learn to

Take Chances in the World" by Ann Saddlemyer: "A comedy" wherein "one by one a group of hapless eccentric individuals find themselves dancing through a tangle of money and power, sex and marriage, led by a glittering, irresistible and willfully domineering plutocrat of the plutocrats"—Epifania, a "daughter of centuries of financiers." She will search for a husband with her father's "Portia-like test, that no suitor should win her hand until he has proved his own genius for money-making." This enterprise fails. But the Life Force will join her to the Doctor, who has "no talent for making money," and who "rejects all who leave the world no better than they found it." The play ends with the possibility that the two might find a way together.

Misalliance. Shaw Festival 2012 (Shaw Festival production program). Includes "Director's Notes by Eda Holmes, and "Happy Families" by Leonard Conolly: *Misalliance* is one of his many plays that refracts Shaw's unsettled deliberation of "family," signaled by its long preface, "Parents and Children." The play's barely functional Tarleton family is another specimen case. A solution, "especially for women," is represented in the "wonderful visitor [Ms Szczepanowska] . . . who appears literally, from the sky with, literally, such smashing effect" to represent "what Shaw seems to be suggesting in the play . . . that any kind of alliance is a threat to independence and creativity." To Ms S, this would include the family.

Murray, Christopher. "Shaw's Ibsen and the Idea of an Irish Theatre." In *Ibsen and Chekhov on the Irish Stage.* Edited by Irina Ruppo Malone. Dublin: Carysfort Press, 2012. An Amazon: Kindle offering. Not seen.

Mutch, Deborah, ed. *British Socialist Fiction, 1884–1914.* Five volumes. London: Pickering & Chatto, forthcoming, September 2013. Offers at least 100 titles (example authors: William Morris, Maxim Gordy, Robert Blatchford, and "Teddy Ashton"). Shaw's titles are not included. Price: £450/$795.

Nassar, Sylvia. *Grand Pursuit: The Story of Economic Genius.* Roseburg, Oregon: Simon & Schuster, 2012. Paperback. Thirteen references to Shaw. Not seen.

Oulton, Carolyn W. de la L. *Below the Fairy City: A Life of Jerome K. Jerome.* Brighton, UK: Victorian Secrets, 2012. Paperback. Seven references to Shaw, with whom Jerome had disagreements over the years. Not seen.

Pembarton, Marilyn. *Out of the Shadows: The Life and Works of Mary de Morgan.* Newcastle upon Tyne, Cambridge Scholars Press, 2012. The book begins with Shaw's recollection of the unhappy reputation of de Morgan before he ever met her. Nine more references to GBS. Not seen.

Pharand, Michel W. "Shaw's Mexican Disciple (*You Have Nothing to Learn from Me: A Literary Relationship Between George Bernard Shaw and Rodolfo Usigli* by Ramón Layera and Katie Gibson)." SHAW: *The Annual of Bernard Shaw Studies* 32 (2012): 190–93.

———. See Hadfield, above.

P.H.U. [Pedro Henrique Urena]. *Obras completas*. Luxembourg: CreateSpace, 2013. Paperback. Ureña (1884–1946) was a Dominican intellectual, essayist, philosopher, humanist, philologist, and literary critic. His very famous article was "The Utopia of America." Eighteen references to Shaw. Not seen.

Preece, Rod. *Animal Sensibility and Inclusive Justice in the Age of Bernard Shaw*. Vancouver: University of British Columbia Press, 2012. A paperback edition of the 2011 issue.

Ramakrishnan, Niranjan. *Reading Gandhi in the Twenty-First Century*. New York: Palgrave Pivot, 2013. Seven references to Shaw. Gandhi and money were not the same as Shaw and money.

Reynolds, Jean. See Hadfield, above.

Ritschel, Nelson O'Ceallaigh. "Shaw, Murder, and the Modern Metropolis." SHAW: *The Annual of Bernard Shaw Studies* 32 (2012): 102–16.

———. *Shaw, Synge, Conolly, and Socialist Provocation*. Gainesville: University Press of Florida, 2012. A paperback issue of the 2011 edition.

Rodriguez, Gustavo A. "Shaw's Subversions of Biblical Language." In *Godly Heretics: Essays on Alternative Christianity in Literature and Popular Culture*. Edited by Marc Dipaolo. Jefferson, North Carolina: McFarland Books, 2013: 114–32. Not seen.

Rong, Tang. *George Bernard Shaw (Humor and Irony Wordsmith) World Celebrities (Chinese edition)*. Beijing: China Social Press, 2012. A paperback edition. Not seen.

Russell, Sandra Joy. "The Devil Inside: London's Slums and the Crises of Gender in Shaw's *Widowers' Houses*." SHAW: *The Annual of Bernard Shaw Studies* 32 (2012): 86–101.

Saddlemyer, Ann. See *The Millionairess*, above.

Saslav, Isidor. "Celebrating Shaw's Chicago Century and Beyond." SHAW: *The Annual of Bernard Shaw Studies* 32 (2012): 151–69.

Sharland, Elizabeth. *Classical Destinations*. iUniverse.com, 2013. A reissue of Sharland's *Passionate Pilgrimages* (New York: Welcome Rain Publishers, 2008), with its chapter on Shaw's Ayot.

Slater, Michael. *The Great Charles Dickens Scandal*. New Haven: Yale University Press, 2012. Shaw came to think that Dickens's daughter Kate Perugini might have letters between Dickens and his mistress Ellen Ternan, but they were never found. Three more references to Shaw. Not seen.

Soboleva, Olga, and Angus Wrenn. *The Only Hope of the World: George Bernard Shaw and Russia*. Pieterlen, Switzerland: Peter Lang AG, 2012. "Traces the Russian sources that contributed to the formation of Shaw's literary style. By reflecting on these parallels, as well as by drawing on archive reports in the Russian and Western media, . . . attempt(s) to establish the extent to which Shaw's obsession with the socialist cause affected the evolving character of his dramatic output. The book also explores the enduring positive reception of Shaw's plays on the Russian stage." A paperback edition. Not seen.

Stafford, Tony J. "St. Dominic's Parsonage: The Best View of Victoria Park." SHAW: *The Annual of Bernard Shaw Studies* 32 (2012): 143–50.

———. *Shaw's Settings: Gardens and Libraries*. Gainesville: University Press of Florida, forthcoming in October 2013.

Steinmeyer, Jim. *Who Was Dracula? Bram Stoker's Trail of Blood*. Los Angeles: Tarcher, 2013. Many references to Shaw and his plays. Not seen.

Stetz, Margaret. See Hadfield, above.

Switzky, Lawrence. See Hadfield, above.

Tabachnick, Stephen E. "Lawrence of Arabia and the Shaws (T. E. Lawrence, *Correspondence with Bernard Shaw and Charlotte Shaw*, Volume 4, 1929–35, edited by Jeremy and Nicole Wilson)." SHAW: *The Annual of Bernard Shaw Studies* 32 (2012): 182–86.

Updike, John. *Odd Jobs: Essays and Criticism*. New York: Random House, 2012. Paperback. Updike's attention to GBS was substantial. This includes references to *Caesar*, *Saint Joan*, and his review of Michael Holroyd's biography of Shaw and Dan Laurence's edition of the Shaw letters. Not seen.

Villis, Tom. *British Catholics and Fascism: Religious Identity and Political Extremism Between the Wars*. New York: Palgrave Macmillan, 2013. Chapter 4, "The Chesterbelloc," reviews the origin and impact of Shaw's conceit joining the proto-liberal G. K. Chesterton and Hilaire Belloc, the proto-fascist.

Walters, Margaret. See *Manual de socialismo y capitalismo . . .* in Section I. Works by Shaw, above.

Warwick, Sarah. *Upstairs & Downstairs: The Illustrated Guide to the Real World of Downton Abbey*. London: Carlton Books, 2012. Includes a "feature spread" on Bernard Shaw. Not seen.

Wearing, J. P. "Shaw and Some Contemporaries (*Whos's Afraid of Bernard Shaw? Some Personalities in Shaw's Plays* by Stanley Weintraub)." *SHAW: The Annual of Bernard Shaw Studies* 32 (2012): 175–76.

Weintraub, Rodelle. See Hadfield, above.

Weintraub, Rodelle, and Stanley Weintraub. "Shaw's London Then and Now." *SHAW: The Annual of Bernard Shaw Studies* 32 (2012): 31–38.

Weintraub, Stanley. *Who's Afraid of Bernard Shaw? Some Personalities in Shaw's Plays*. Gainesville: University Press of Florida, 2013. A paperback edition on the 2011 issue.

———. See Weintraub, Rodelle, above.

Welsh, Olie Mae Trost. *Fault Zone: Over the Edge*. Stanford, California: Sand Hill Review Press, 2012. Includes a four-page story by Welsh: "Shaw: A One-Act Story." In it, "George Bernard Shaw, a life-long atheist, dies and finds himself in heaven. God soon comes in and the four-page dialogue intelligently and with gentle cleverness reveals a Shavian personality that used his wits" to help people, and who in the end comes to believe that there is a god and a heaven and an eternity of happiness to enjoy after all.

West, Anna Nagar. *George Bernard Shaw: A Biography*. Tamil Nadu, India: Spider Books, 2012. Paperback. Not seen.

West, John G. *The Magician's Twin: C. S. Lewis on Science, Scientism, and Society*. Seattle: Discovery Institute Press, 2012. Paperback. Two references note differences between Lewis and GBS. Not seen.

Williams, Jim. *Tango in Madeira: A Dance of Life, Love, and Death*. Marble City Publishing, 2013. No postal address. Fiction. In this work "Bernard Shaw learns to tango." Not seen.

Wilson, Ann. See Hadfield, above.

Wilson, Colin. *The Decline and Fall of Leftism*. Amazon: Kindle, 2012. Uses the Nottingham: Paupers' Press, 1989, edition. Wilson was a longtime admirer of Shaw before his political view changed.

Wrenn, Angus. See Soboleve, Olga, above.

Wynn, Anthony, and Robert Wood. *Valiant for Truth: Barry Morse and His Lifelong Association with Bernard Shaw*. Portland, Oregon: Lulu.com, 2012. A paperback edition. Not seen.

Yde, Matthew. *Bernard Shaw and Totalitarianism: Longing for Utopia*. London: Palgrave, forthcoming in 2013.

———. "Building the New City of God: Shaw's Provisional Supermen." *SHAW: The Annual of Bernard Shaw Studies* 32 (2012): 117–32.

III. Periodicals[3]

"Books Received." *European Legacy* 17.3 (June 2012): 435–37. Includes Charles A. Carpenter's *Bernard Shaw as-Artist Fabian.*

Breon, Robin. "A Tale of 2 Festivals." *American Theater* 29.5 (May/June 2012): 32–37. "For a large cadre of theatre critics and arts journalists, covering the Stratford Shakespeare Festival and the Shaw Festival has become a rite of spring. Just as surely as the rude Canadian winter surrenders to the coming warmth of summer, the miracle of these two sancta sanctorum renews itself annually—and for many who labor in the theatre, these institutions represent two great tabernacles of the art form."

[*Candida*]. "Pittsburgh Public Theater" production announcement. *Back Stage, National ed.* 54.13 (28 March 2013): 31.

Constenla, Tereixa. "La ley de la renta de Bernard Shaw." *El pais: Cultura.* 17 January 2013. 18 January 2013 <cultura.elpais.com/cultura2013/01/17/ actualidid. A review of Dolors Udina's translation into Spanish of Shaw's *The Intelligent Woman's Guide.* . . . See *Manual de socialismo y capitalismo* in Section I. Works by Shaw, above.

Dalfonzo, Gina. "Their Fair Lady: The Making of a Postwar/Broadway/ Hollywood Musical Blockbuster." *The Weekly Standard* 18.9 (12 November 2012). Review of Dominic McHugh's *Loverly: The Life and Times of My Fair Lady.* New York: Oxford University Press, 2012.

Danvers-Walker, Michael. "A Compulsion to Act: Famous Actor Michael Danvers-Walker Outlined his Career to the Shaw Society." *The Shavian* 12.2 and 3 (Autumn 2012/Spring 2013): 28–34. "I have been fortunate," Michael continued, "to have travelled far and wide playing parts in plays

---

3. In his article in SHAW 25, "Tracking Down Shaw Studies: The Proper Use of Printed and Online Bibliographical Sources," Charles A. Carpenter names an array of online reference tools, the use of which in the period covered by this 2012 Checklist discovers hundreds of serial reviews of performances of Shaw works, and many other pieces on Shaw topics of every kind—often not formally "scholarly." The principle of selection of those pieces included in this "Periodicals" listing is intended to be selective and illustrative. In some cases, articles found published in hard copy are listed here as "Web," as available in electronic archives from which they were retrieved for this checklist. Articles published only in online serials or on websites are listed in Section "VI. Bernard Shaw on the World Wide Web," below. Reviews of performances and publications about Shaw are not annotated in the Checklist.

by Bernard Shaw." This article, condensed from a talk, retails numerous experiences playing Shaw roles.

Dunford, Lizzie. "Shaw's Other Island: Prints of Dublin in the Dining Room at Shaw's Corner." *The Shavian* 12.2 and 3 (Autumn 2012/Spring 2013): 41–49. "It is clear to see many of the buildings whose portraits now hang in Shaw's Dining Room would have been near-daily sights of Sonny." Shaw's favorite room in the house was the "Dining Room, where he would spend two hours over his lunch, reading through his post and papers. It is also the room that he died in, the place where he chose to spend his last weeks." He "waved goodbye to Ireland thirty years before he moved to Ayot St Lawrence, and he lived in this tiny village for twice as long as his youth in Dublin. But even a brief walk around his home shows us that he never truly left it behind."

Einsohn, H. I. Review of Sidney Albert's *Shaw, Plato, and Euripides*. *Choice* 49.12 (August 2012): 2275.

———. Review of Rod Peece's *Animal Sensibility and Inclusive Justice in the Age of Bernard Shaw*. *Choice* 49.11 (July 2012): 2058.

———. Review of Stanley Weintraub's *Who's Afraid of Bernard Shaw? Choice* 49.9 (May 2012): 1650.

Emerson, Caryl. "Krzhizhanovsky as a Reader of Shakespeare and Bernard Shaw." *Slavic and East European Journal* 56.4 (2012): 577–611. "In the first footnote to his published essay on Shaw's 'images and thought' (1935), Krzhizhanovsky alerts his reader that he is 'preparing a book on Shaw.' That book never materialized, although the typescript of a talk prepared in the 1940s suggests that the topic remained active for him. Like Shakespeare and Lord Kelvin (who in the typescript replaces Francis Bacon of the earlier essays), Shaw is an 'experimenter.' His style is that of a natural scientist, 'the steel sound of a scalpel against its plank,' and also that of a person whose words 'recall the ring of a fool's bell-infested cap.' He creates his plays with three tools: the writer's pen, the conductor's baton, and the boxer's glove. This final item combined with militant optimism with the appeal of the knockout—appropriately, for boxing tournaments and the pugilistic images were popular metaphors in the 1930s for the struggle between political systems. Success in the ring was all in the 'lightness, simplicity, and accurate targeting of the blow.' However serious the war, winners were obliged to be of a comic, not a tragic, disposition. Krzhizhanovsky quotes an *Encyclopaedia Britannica* definition of this martial sport: 'the noble art of dealing out and receiving blows with a smile on one's face.' [paragraph] Krzhizhanovsky had his favorites among the forty-odd 'smiling plays' that Shaw had written by the outbreak of

World War II. It is quite a different list from the *Pygmalion [My Fair Lady]* / *Man and Superman*/*Major Barbara* staples of the Anglophone canon. In pride of place are *The Devil's Disciple* (in which Tairov, as a young actor in Gaideburov's Traveling Theater, had played Richard Dudgeon), the early Chekhovian *Heartbreak House, The Doctor's Dilemma, Candida, Androcles and the Lion,* some lesser-known texts such as *You Never Can Tell, Fanny's First Play, Too True to Be Good, Augustus Does His Bit*—and the obligatory 'political extravaganza' *The Apple Cart [1929],* Shaw's spoof on dysfunctional monarchy and parliamentary democracy in the grip of plutocrats, which was widely taken as sympathetic to Stalinism. What intrigues Krzhizhanovsky, however, is never the politics and always the 'concentrated idea' as a formal kinetic problem. How does Shaw generate dramatic excitement out of the movement of idea alone? In Shaw 'everything—like thread through a needle—is drawn through consciousness. All his dramatic devices are X-rayed by reason. These are devices in the full sense of the word."

Eom, Tae-yong. "*Mrs Warren's Profession*: Shaw and Marx's Criticism of Capitalism." *Journal of Modern British and American Drama* 25.2 (August 2012): 121–60. In Korean; with English summary. Not seen.

Gibbs, A. M. "Weintraub on Shaw" [review of Stanley Weintraub's *Who's Afraid of Bernard Shaw? English Literature in Transition: 1880–1920*] 55.4 (Fall 2012): 519.

Gribben, Alice. "Webb of Influence." *New Statesman* (20 February 2012): 51. Announcement: 9,000 pages of Beatrice Webb's diaries have been published digitally and in full for the first time by the London School of Economics. Access is at <digital.library.lse.ac.uk/collections/webb>.

Grode, Eric. "Shaw's View of a Woman Headed to a Burning Stake" [review of the Bedlam Troupe production at Access Theater, New York]. *New York Times* (5 May 2012): C2.

Hadfield, D. A. Review of Leonard Conolly's *Bernard Shaw and the BBC. University of Toronto Quarterly* 81.3 (Summer 2012): 750–52.

Hevesi, Dennis. "Jerome Kilty, 90, Who Made a Career of Interpreting Shaw." *New York Times* (16 September 2012): A24. Obituary. Kilty's most notable creation was *Dear Liar*, his adaptation of forty years of amorous correspondence between Mrs. Patrick Campbell and GBS.

Hunt, Joanne. "President Pays Tribute to GB Shaw." *Irish Times* (30 May 2012): 3. Ten inches of print accompanied by a bio-box on Shaw, reporting President of Ireland Michael Higgins's appearance at the National Gallery of Ireland to give the plenary address for the

"G.B. Shaw: Back in Town" conference that convened for sessions at University College Dublin, co-sponsored by the International Shaw Society. It was the first international conference in Ireland for Shaw. The text of Higgins's speech and photographs of him are at www.president .ie/media-gallery/photo-gallery/?album=6&gallery=63

Juan, Du. Review of Peter Gahan's *Shaw Shadows: Rereading the Texts of Bernard Shaw. Foreign Literature Studies* 34.6 (December 2012): 170–73.

Kent, Brad. "Eighteenth-Century Literary Precursors of *Mrs Warren's Profession.*" *University of Toronto Quarterly* 81.2 (Spring 2012): 187–207. "*Mrs Warren's Profession* is almost solely discussed in terms of its portrayal of prostitution in relation to the theatre of its day. In this light, the work is defined as a decisive break with what came before it. But Shaw warned against this tendency to label literature that challenges contemporary norms as necessarily original. Instead, he called on his audience to recognize the cyclical nature of literature, noting that what is new to one generation is most often merely that which was discarded by the previous one. By adopting the longer view, this essay examines *Mrs Warren's Profession* alongside some well-known prostitute narratives of the Eighteenth-Century to argue that while Shaw might have overturned one tradition, there is much to suggest that he concurrently tapped into another."

Kornhaber, David. "Nietzsche, Shaw, Stoppard: Theater and Philosophy in the British Tradition." *Philosophy and Literature* 36.1 (April 2012): 79–95. "Stoppard is not the sort of playwright one might call anti-intellectual, yet he has persistently singled out the field of academic philosophy for special assault in his plays. Stoppard's antipathy emerges from a history of contention between the theater and philosophy in England, one that originates in Friedrich Nietzsche's *Birth of Tragedy* and particular reception at the hands of George Bernard Shaw. Stoppard offers an apotheosis of this disputation in his 1972 farce *Jumpers*, which imagines a marriage between a philosopher and an actress meant to demonstrate the superiority of the theater as a mode of speculative discourse."

———. "The Philosopher, the Playwright, and the Actor: Friedrich Nietzsche and the Modern Drama's Concept of Performance." *Theatre Journal* 64.1 (March 2012): 25+. "This essay explores the impact of Friedrich Nietzsche's *The Birth of Tragedy* and *The Case of Wagner* on conceptualizations of the theatrical event during the emergence of modern drama, focusing specifically on the writings of August Strindberg, George Bernard Shaw, and Eugene O'Neill—all avowed devotees of Nietzsche's work. To these playwrights, Nietzsche offered a particular vision of theatrical creation as a coequal marriage of the representational and embodied artistries of author and actor, each manifested only through its engagement with the other in the moment of performance. Nietzsche's schematization would help to inform much of the rethinking of the actor–author relationship that would mark these dramatists approach to the stage, variously interpreted in Strindberg's call for a semi-improvisatory actor . . . Shaw's celebration of the virtuosic actor as the author's essential partner . . . and O'Neill's insistence on masked actors as an antidote to time-worn stage traditions."

———. Review of Sidney Albert's *Shaw, Plato, and Euripides. Comparative Drama* 46.4 (Winter 2012): 569–71.

———. Leonard, Robert Sean. An interview with Leonard. *American Theatre* 30.1 (January 2013): 160. On his interpretation of Henry Higgins in *Pygmalion*, Leonard says he is different from that portrayed by Rex Harrison or Leslie Howard. Not seen.

Lou, Harry. "By George in Canada, a Top-Notch Theater Festival has been Celebrating Shaw and Company for 50 Years: Perfect for a Vacation Visit." *Indianapolis Business Journal* 33.23 (6 August 2012): 33A. The Shaw Festival PR people get the message out.

McEwan, Alice. "George Bernard Shaw and His Writing Hut: Privacy and Publicity as Performance at Shaw's Corner." *Interiors: Design, Architecture, Culture* 2.3 (November 2011): 333–56. "In 1906 George Bernard Shaw and his wife Charlotte moved to an Arts and Crafts house set on two acres of beautiful gardens in the countryside in Hertfordshire. Despite its potential as a refuge from city living, a place of comfort and quiet domesticity away from their London flat, Shaw denied the possibility of habitation in any conventional sense, preferring to exist on the margins. Indeed he acted as if no boundaries existed between the interiors and landscapes that surrounded the house, typically occupying the luminal zones of windowsills and verandas. This article will argue that the locus of this fluidity and theatrical imagination was a writing hut in the form of a revolving shelter, built in a secluded part of the garden, hidden from view. Equipped with a bed and a writing table, Shaw fashioned an outside study as an intermediate space. A site for the performance of the self and an advertisement for his socialist ideas, it was particularly constructive in the promotion of health reform. He ensured that his hut gained notoriety worldwide through the mass media in the form of journal articles and photographs, against the backdrop of his own burgeoning interest in photography and the media. Through the Habermasian theory of 'audience-oriented subjectivity' and the ideas of architectural historian Beatriz Colomina, Shaw is considered in ways that have not previously been recognized: anticipating the concerns of modern architecture and Modernism, dematerializing boundaries between inside and outside, between privacy and publicity."

Miller, Derek. "Performative Performances: A History and Theory of the 'Copyright Performance.'" *Theatre Journal* 64.2 (May 2012): 161–77. "Copyright performances reveal the complex interaction between economics and aesthetics in the late Nineteenth Century. Although contemporary markets and styles shaped copyright law's development, the legal forms that emerged—by accident and design—shaped, in turn, the evolution of theatrical commerce and art. Although this performance genre no longer exists, the story of its emergence and rapid expansion uncovers the deeply rooted tensions between performance and commodity capitalism. Peggy Phelan's claim that performance develops 'an economy of cultural capital independent of object commodification' is too absolute; nineteenth-century copyright law inscribed performance as a commodity. The process of that inscription, however, created disturbances both in the legal system and in the theatrical community, in the wake of which the copyright performance fleetingly thrived." The article is prologued with a summary of the copyright performance and subsequent career of *Mrs Warren's Profession*, which, "although notable for the author's active mutilation of his text, was an otherwise unremarkable example of the remarkable practice known as the 'copyright performance.'"

"A Noise Within [Pasadena], Acting Interns" [production announcement for *Doctor's Dilemma*]. *Back Stage, National ed.* 53.30 (26 July 2012): 28.

"The Old Globe Theatre Season, San Diego, California" [production announcement for *Pygmalion*]. *Back Stage, National ed.* 53.34 (14 June 2012): 24.

Pellisa, Teresa Lopez. "Automatas y robots; fantoches tecnologicos en R.U.R. de Karel Capek y El Senor de Pigmalion de Jacinto Grau." *Anales de la Literatura Española contemporánea* 38.3 (2013): 137–59. R.U.R. (1920) by Karel Capek and *The Lord of Pygmalion* (1921) by Jacinto Grau are dystopian science-fiction plays, contemporaries, and with similar themes, in spite of the fact that the robot/android protagonists do not have the same function in the texts. Both authors employed the genre in their dramas and, in the case of the Capek, also in a novel. They were written and presented during the period of avant-garde, near to the time of Bernard Shaw's return to (in the manner of science fiction) the myth of Pygmalion in [*Back to Methuselah*, Act 5] "As Far as Thought Can Reach" (in 1921), and the maturation of the modern dystopian genre with the appearance of *We* (in 1921) by Zamiatin, *Brave New World* (in 1932) by Huxley and, later, *1984* (in 1949) by Orwell. Translation by Tracy J. R. Collins.

Pharand, Michel. "Shaw and Militant Irish Socialism" [review of Nelson O'Ceallaigh Ritschel's *Shaw, Synge, and Conolly, and Socialist Provocation. English Literature in Transition: 1880–1920*]. 55.4 (Fall 2013): 522.

Ramert, Lynn. "Lessons from the Land: Shaw's *John Bull's Other Island*. *New Hibernia Review/Iris Éireannach Nua: A Quarterly of Irish Studies* 16.3 (Autumn 2012): 44–59. "Shaw's beliefs on the relationship between humans and nature fit better within the emerging ethical and environmental ideologies and movements of today than in his own time. His treatment of modern social and environmental concerns in *John Bull's Other Island* gives the play a sense of presence and urgency today, though these ideas may have baffled or completely eluded audiences in the early Twentieth Century. In England, the audiences apparently appreciated the humor of the play, but lost the deeper meaning. Irish audiences would not get a chance to see the play until 1916, and it was widely interpreted as a play about Home Rule above all else. It is likely, then, that Shaw's message about the environment was generally overlooked."

Riley, Phillip. "Why we Need a Shaw National Theatre." *The Shavian* 12. 2 and 3 (Autumn 2012/Spring 2013): 1–15. Historians of Shakespeare might wish to refer to this account which uses a considerably detailed history of the progress to a Shakespeare National Theatre to imagine the possibility of a Shaw National Theatre. Riley appeals for a scheduling of 2020 as "the year to give Shaw a theatre where it is recognized that the company will concentrate on his works."

Rivers, Bryan. "'Miss Vavasour' in Bernard Shaw's *Mrs Warren's Profession*." *The Explicator* 70.3 (2012): 175–78. "Mrs. Warren's former professional pseudonym, 'Miss Vavasour,' is alluded to only once in the play; however, its strategic placement, at the climactic conclusion to act I, operates on three levels simultaneously. The allusion injects a note of social realism by reflecting the actual use of nicknames by Victorian prostitutes; provides an important thematic key to understanding the play's central sociopolitical preoccupation with the unhealthy entrenched power of the essentially feudal Victorian Establishment; and deconstructively ironic, denotes the potentially ambivalent self image of Mrs. Warren concerning her relationship with Sir George Crofts."

Rodriguez-Martín, Gustavo A. "Comparison and Other 'Modes of Order' in the Plays of Bernard Shaw." *International Journal of English Studies* 12.2 (July 2012): 151. "Shaw is widely regarded as one of the most important playwrights in the English language, ranking often second only to Shakespeare. This literary prominence, however, is not matched by a significant number of stylistic analyses, much more so in the case of linguistically-oriented ones. One of the few studies in Shaviana with a clear stylistic approach is R. M. Ohmann's (1962) monograph. However, it focuses on Shaw's non-dramatic writings and due to its publication date, it does not utilize *software* tools for corpus stylistics. The purpose of this paper is to analyze Bernard Shaw's use of certain comparative structures in his dramatic writings (what Ohmann calls 'Modes of Order' in his book) with the aid of the technical and methodological advances of computer-based stylistics, thus utilizing an innovative outlook because of the combination of stylistics and corpora research."

Sharma, Susheel Kumar. "Antifeminism in Bernard Shaw's *Candida. Points of View* 17.1 (Summer 2010): 54–62. Not seen.

"Shaw, George Bernard." IASIL Bibliography Bulletin for 2011. *Irish University Studies: A Journal of Irish Studies* 42.2 (Autumn–Winter 2012): 398ff. Twenty-four entries. Three have not been listed in this *SHAW* Checklist.

Smoker, Barbara. "Smoker at 90." *The Shavian* 12.2 and 3 (Autumn 2012/ Winter 2013): 19–23. This autobiographical piece is full of information about Smoker, reporting that she intended a writer's life and that she has had one. She refers to much recognition of her successes, a main one in the 1972 Ward Lock Educational Ltd publication of her *Humanism*, 5th edition, South Place Ethical Society, 2008. Another notice that her contribution and patronage to the ongoing global industry in Shavian revivals have been formidable and will be indelible.

———. "Transcribing Shaw's Shorthand." *The Shavian* 12.1 (Summer 2012): 21–27. Smoker learned and used Pitman phonetic shorthand, which Shaw used for seventy years. Her account of his use of it is therefore expert. Among the neat facts here, she corrects the record that Shaw first used Pitman for a creative draft of *Widowers' Houses* in 1884 (not 1885). She reminds us that the first draft of *Saint Joan* was in Pitman. But much more important is the indispensible role she played in establishing texts for Shaw's editor, Dan Laurence, critiquing Blanche Patch's sometimes loose Pitman representation of Shaw's dictation, and the work of Michael Holroyd for Shaw's biography. "All in all, however, Shaw's use of the Pitman system of shorthand proved a nice little earner for me— being employed, so to speak, as his part-time posthumous secretary."

Switzky, Lawrence. Review of Stanley Weintraub's *Who's Afraid of Bernard Shaw. The Modern Language Review* 108.2 (April 2013): 637–38.

Webster, Andy. "Shaw's Battle of the Sexes, Waged Slyly if Vigorously." Review of Irish Repertory Theater, New York, production of *Man and Superman. New York Times* (17 May 2012): C7.

Weintraub, Stanley. "Bernard Shaw Besieged: Early Progresses to Oxbridge, 1888–1892." *English Literature in Transition: 1880–1920* 56.1 (2013): 51–61. From a nearly unmatched command of the fugitive details of Shaw's life comes this fascinating narrative of the nonacademic Shaw in his early thirties, in his visits and impertinent receptions at first Cambridge and then Oxford.

Williams, Nicholas R. *"How He Lied to Her Husband*: Shaw's Experiment with a One-act Comedy." *GBS* 34 (June 2012): 3. Is this play best considered as a satire or a parody of a typical comedy of the period? "The play works in both ways to satirize a segment of privileged London society represented by a bored married woman and her wealthy husband, with the plot complication created by the wife's young lover who wants to elope with her. At the same time the play parodies the use made by the commercial theatre of a mildly erotic situation. Shaw is taking the old Victorian melodrama plot of the unfaithful wife being confronted by an aggrieved husband and turning it into a light comedy bordering on farce."

Wixson, Christopher. "'These Noxious Microbes': Pathological Dramaturgy in George Bernard Shaw's *Too True to Be Good*." *Modern Drama* 56.1 (Spring 2013): 1–18. "This essay charts the interdependency of form and content in Bernard Shaw's *Too True to Be Good* (1931). In this late play, the playwright, building upon his well-known attacks against medical theory and practice, views class privilege, colonial relations, and dramatic structure itself through the lens of disease. Angrily taking the stage in act one, the unusually acerbic Microbe inaugurates Shaw's dissection of imperialist discourse and attempts to purge the theatrical textual body of its pathogenic conventions."

Woods, Michelle. "Framing Translation: Adolf Hoffmeister's Comic Strips, Travelogues, and Interviews as Introductions to Modernist Translations." *Translation and Interpreting Studies* 7.1 (2012): 1–18. Hoffmeister . . . was one of the translators of James Joyce's *Anna Livia Plurabelle* and the illustrator of Czech translations of George Bernard Shaw's plays. His paratextual work for translated modernist literature—prefaces, caricatures, comic strips, travelogues and interviews—engaged with modernist practice in producing an abusive mimesis is his re-presentation of authors and their writing. This included a verbal and visual insertion of the translator and re-presenter that makes him visible and also fallible, unreliable and humorous. Hoffmeister's use of humor and demystification made the complex modernist translations more accessible to a wider readership while also bringing into question the practices and mechanics of translations and cultural domestication."

Yde, Matthew. "Bernard Shaw's Stalinist Allegory: *The Simpleton of the Unexpected Isles*." *Modern Drama* 56.1 (Spring 2013): 19–37. "For over fifty years, playwright George Bernard Shaw called for the state extermination of the incorrigibly criminal or anti-social. Yet these statements have usually been dismissed as expressions of Shaw's well-known propensity for comic exaggeration and hyperbole, his pugnacious rhetoric, his love of paradox, and especially, his addiction to antagonizing the British political establishment. Nonetheless, as this article shows, Shaw was not joking, and in fact, gave full support to the liquidation policies that arose in the totalitarian countries in the thirties, especially those in the Soviet Union. His 1934 play *The Simpleton of the Unexpected Isles*, although rarely recognized as such, is actually an allegory of the Soviet Union that gives especial attention to the totalitarian state's uncompromising policy of disposing of recalcitrant citizens. The article analyses the play in light of Shaw's 1931 visit to the Soviet Union and his vociferous support of its political agenda under Stalin."

Yoon, So Young. "Habitus Represented by Body in Pygmalion." *Journal of Modern British and American Drama* 25.2 (August 2012): 189–213. In Korean, with English summary. Not seen.

GBS 35 (June 2012). The Bernard Shaw Society of Japan. Includes "Forty Years of the Bernard Shaw Society of Japan" by M. Ogiso; "The International Shaw Conference and Shaw Festival" by H. Morikawa; *"How He Lied to Her Husband*: Shaw's Experiment with a One-act Comedy" by Nicholas R. Williams; "The Martyrdom Hidden from the Sight: An Analysis of Cognition in *Saint Joan*" by Y. Isobe; "Joan's Art of Encouragement in *Saint Joan*" by T. Iida; *"Heartbreak House* Translated by Shohei Iijima" by R. Suzuki; *"O'Flaherty V.C.*: Irish Business Side of Colonialism" by S. Matsumoto; "From *Pygmalion* to *My Fair Lady*" by M. Oe; "Friendship and Love between Bernard Shaw and Mrs Patrick Campbell in *Dear Liar*" by M. Morioka; "Eliza's Self-Formation in Society and Sociability" by M. Ochiai; "Bernard Shaw and Tsukiji Little Theatre" by R. Oura; and "Activities of the Society in 2011." A performance announcement: *Major Barbara*, translated by Professor Kurokawa, was presented by the Aristophanes Company at Studio AR, Tokyo between 16 and 25 November, 2012. See also Williams, Nicholas R., above.

The Shavian 12.1 (Summer 2012). The Journal of the Shaw Society. Includes "An Evening with Sylvia Syms, "They Could Write Like Bernard Shaw," "Malvern Plaque," "National Theatre" a review of *Doctor's Dilemma* by Francis Evans, "Alan [Knight] on Shaw on Acting," "Transcribing Shaw's Shorthand" by Barbara Smoker, "Looking Back at Bernard Shaw" by Tony Kanal and Richard Digby Day, and "Reviews" of *Saint Joan* and *You Never Can Tell*. See also Smoker, Barbara, above.

The Shavian 12.2 and 3 (Autumn 2012 and Spring 2013). The Journal of the Shaw Society. Includes "Why We Need a Shaw National Theatre" by Phillip Riley, "Shaw 'At Home,'" "Smoker at 90" by Barbara Smoker, "Shaw Films at the Cinema Museum," "A Compulsion to Act" by Michael Danvers-Walker, "In the Name of GBS," "Shaw at the Proms," "Shaw's Other Island" by Lizzie Dunford, "TF Evans Award," "Shaw on War,"

"Obituary: Lord Archer of Sandwell," "Slaves of Duty and Tricks of the Governing Class" by Bernard Dukore, "Shaw Portrait Goes to Labor," and "Reviews" of *The Doctor's Dilemma, Heartbreak House, and Overruled*. See also Dunford, Lizzie; Riley, Phillip; Smoker, Barbara; and Danvers-Walker, Michael, above.

IV. Dissertations and Selected Theses

Ajtony, Zsuzsanna. *Britain and Britishness in G. B. Shaw's Plays: A Linguistic Perspective*. Ph.D. Dissertation, University of Bucharest, 2011. *WorldCat Dissertations and Theses*. See also, Ajtony, in Section II. Books and Pamphlets.

Cabaj, Stacey. "The Eliza-Higgins Model: The Ideology, Rapport, and Methods of Dialect Acquisition." M.A. Thesis, Virginia Commonwealth University, 2012. Digarchive.library.vcu.edu. 23 April 2013. "The centenary of *Pygmalion* is also a prime juncture to document, in contrast or complement to Higgins's model, contemporary theories and techniques of dialect acquisition. Chapter one of this thesis explores the ideology of dialect acquisition, addressing the issues of dialect prestige and standard speech. Chapter two examines the rapport between teacher/coach and learner/actor, including a comparison of teacher-centered and learner-centered pedagogies and the influence of expectancy theories on learner growth. Chapter three details the methods of dialect acquisition, addresses language learning theories as applied to dialect learning, and offers practical exercises and techniques. The conclusion outlines areas of future consideration to enhance the dialect acquisition process in the classroom and rehearsal hall."

Martin, Benjamin H. "You again? Character Rerepresentation in George Bernard Shaw's *Back to Methuselah* and *Man and Superman*. M.A. Thesis, Southern Connecticut State University, 2012. *Proquest Dissertations and Theses*, 41. "Explores Shaw's use of a literary/stage device called rerepresentation (defined briefly as the means by which a transformed character reappears physically or characterologically) and this device's utility in Shaw's depiction of social change throughout history."

Rhodes, Evan Wright. "Kin Aesthetics: Boxing and the Public Arenas of Modernism." Ph.D. Dissertation, University of Virginia, 2012. *Proquest Dissertations and Theses*, 281. "Across four chapters covering authors such as George Bernard Shaw, Ernest Hemingway, Djuna Barnes, Ezra Pound, Mina Loy, James Joyce, and others, I aim to show how modernism's trials in pugilistic writing were less the collapse of a high/low divide or cultural transgression and more a set of novel claims about the ways that modernist writing could signify in the public sphere."

Snodgrass, Lindsay. "To Be Natural . . . is such a Difficult Pose to Keep Up": Elocution's Extended Denouement, a Case for the Revival of Thomas Sheridan's Sincere Performer in Contemporary English Studies." M.A. Thesis, Texas A & M University, 2012. Repository.tamu.edu. 23 April 2013. "Focusing on the dramatic works of Oscar Wilde, George Bernard Shaw and Brian Friel, this thesis contends that Irish drama, in addition to presenting a forceful illustration of the way in which Sheridan's elocutionary theories have been adapted and challenged on the national and civic level, provides current scholars access to recent dramatic representations of authenticity and voice as well as the virtue/pitfalls of performativity. Wilde, Shaw and Friel specifically present linguistic performance as a process of negotiation and exchange, using the stage to reflect and construct Irish national and civic identity. Each playwright offers a lens through which to reevaluate ongoing debates over language acquisition, particularly as such debates arise within the context of composition studies. . . . This study encourages contemporary composition scholars and pedagogues to reconsider the role of authenticity and performance within the writing classroom, prompting students and teachers to explore writing as an expression of both the public and private self."

Tien, Yuk. "Literary Humor and Chinese Modernity: The Adaptation and Translation of Shakespeare, Wilde, and Shaw." Ph.D. Dissertation, Pennsylvania State University, 2012. Etda.libraries.psu.edu. 23 April 2013. Looking at the adaptations and translations of Shakespeare, Wilde, and Shaw: "Issuing from contemporary time and space, adaptation demonstrates an emerging new sense of self in the negotiation of identity in the translational process. There are plays that fuse comedy and tragedy, or laughter and tears, but adaptation allows us to see how comedy can be transformed from tragedy, through changing perspectives and the distance or detachment created by time and culture. The adaptation and translation of bawdy humor represents a site of implicit censorship. New constraints, however, also bring new comic creativity and encourage different ways of thinking and speaking about what is supposed to be 'forbidden.' The employment of specific local and provincial dialects has also become an important marker of the comic imaginary. Different dialectal strands that make up literary texts and film or stage productions offer a new perspective from which to look into the formation of identity at various levels. Further, when the translation of a comedy is adapted to be performed, what is involved is the intersection and collaboration of verbal and visual humor, as well as the dynamic between the character in a text and the role actualized by an actor on stage."

V. Recordings

Back to Methuselah (2012). Durham, North Carolina: Duke Classics, 2012. Available as a computer file or eBook. Also available: *Caesar* and *Pygmalion*.

Caesar (2012). See *Back to Methuselah*, above.

Candida (2013). Audible Audio Edition, 139 min. Washington, D.C.: Audio Book Contractors, LLC, 2013. $12.24, at Amazon.

Heartbreak House (2013). LibriVox Free Audiobook Collection. Approx. 198 min. Montreal: LibriVox, 2013. Contact: LibriVox.org. for more free audio books, or to become a reader.

Pygmalion (2013). Audible Audio Edition, 89 min., "unabridged." Moscow: IDDK [Multimedia Products in Russian], 2013. $4.95, at Amazon. A Russian-language sound recording.

Pygmalion (2012). 2 CDs, 90 min., "unabridged." North Kingston, Rhode Island: BBC Radio 4, 2012. Baker and Taylor vendor price: $29.95.

Pygmalion (2012). See *Back to Methuselah*, above.

Saint Joan (2012). $19.19 at Amazon. See *Candida*, above.

Widowers' Houses (n.d.). 119 min. See *Heartbreak House*, above.

Fanny's First Play (2011). 2 DVDs, 132 min. Washington, D.C.: Washington Stage Guild, 2006, 2011. Videotaped 1 April 2006 for the Washington Area Performing Arts Video Archive. Director: John MacDonald. Restricted to individual viewing only at the Michelle Smith Performing Arts Library, University of Maryland.

The George Bernard Shaw Collection (2010, 2011). Sound recording, 13 hours, 3 min. Solon, Ohio: Playaway Digital Audio, 2011. $94.99. Contains eight plays adapted for radio: *Mrs Warren, Major Barbara, Arms, Doctor's Dilemma, Candida, Misalliance, Disciple, and Pygmalion*. Previously released by Los Angeles: L.A. Theatre Works.

Hossick, Malcolm. *George Bernard Shaw: A Concise Biography*. Projected-image computer file. 36 min. New York: Films Media Group, 2011. Access through Films on Demand, Films Media Group, Cambridge Educational, Meridian Education, and Shopware.

An Ideal Husband (2011). 2 DVDs, 154 min. Washington, D.C.: Shakespeare Theatre, 2011. Live performance recorded 7 April 2011 for the Washington Area Performing Arts Video Archive. Director: Daniel Rehbehn. Restricted to individual viewing only at the Michelle Smith Performing Arts Library, University of Maryland.

Major Barbara (29 April 2012). Audio, 47.04 min. LibriVox Free Audiobook Collection. Sample of cast: Undershaft: Chuck Williamson; Lady Britomart Undershaft: Amy L. Gramour; Barbara: Elizabeth Klett.

A Minister's Wife (26 June 2011). CD. New York: Avatar Studios, 2011. Based on the play *Candida*. An original off-Broadway cast recording. Recorded and mixed by Bart Migal.

A Minister's Wife (8 June 2011). DVD, 93 min. New York: The New York Public Library's Theatre on Film and Tape Archive at Lincoln Center Theater, 8 June 2011. Directors: André Bishop and Bernard Gersten. "Restricted to qualified researchers."

Misalliance. See *Candida*, above.

Mrs. Warren's Profession (2010). 2 DVDs, 131 min. Director: Keith Baxter. Videotaped 19 June 2010 for the Washington Area Performing Arts Video Archive. See *Fanny's First Play*, above.

VI. Shaw on the World Wide Web[4]

Albert, Sidney P. 11 April 1914–9 January 2013. Obituary. legacy.com/ obituaries/latimes/obituary. 12 January 2013.

---

4. The search terms "George Bernard Shaw" and "Bernard Shaw" on a search engine such as *Google* in 2013 produce nearly 17 million hits. Research of Shaw on the web is especially productive through the agency of websites devoted to Shaw. In addition, persons with access to *J-Stor, Muse, MLA International Bibliography Online*, and *WorldCat*, for example, perhaps through a university library subscription, may complete as much as 90 percent of primary and secondary research online. Available at commercial websites such as Amazon.com are generous pdf sample pages of many new books for sale, in addition to downloadable out-of-copyright, republished "etexts" or "ebooks" of primary and secondary Shaw publications on *Google*. In this list, URLs are furnished when other retrieval information is insufficient. Most of these listings are of production announcements or reviews of Shaw plays, representing an effort to count the number of them between April 2012 and May 2013. This Checklist again identifies nearly 100 productions and broadcasts of Shaw works or excerpts from his works around the world. Daniel Janes in "The Shavian Moment: Why Are There So Many George Bernard Shaw Revivals?" Newstatesman.com. 20 July 2012, speaks a question based on four Shaw revivals in the London metropolitan area for a single season. The numerous Internet sightings logged in this section of the Checklist support the same question. There is what appears to be a subscription to Shaw readings, performances, societies, and festivals greater than ever. Although there is more than one notice for a very few productions, entries in this section of the Checklist are representative and selected to try include nonduplicate notices of hem.

"Arthur Miller, George Bernard Shaw in Reader's Theater Presentations this Summer." Announcement of reading of *Devil's Disciple* at University of North Carolina at Ashville Center for Creative Retirement. Unca.edu. 7 June 2012.

Bard, Frank. "Quintessence of Shaw on Mr. Airy Stage." Review of Sedgewick Theatre, Philadelphia, production of *Arms and the Man*. Montgomerynews.com. 30 April 2013.

Barnidge, Mary Shen. *"You Never Can Tell."* Review of the Remy Bumppo Theatre, Chicago, production. Windycitymediagroup.com. 6 December 2012.

Begel, Dave. "Boulevard's [Milwaukee] *Don Juan In Hell* Finds Richness in Minimalism." Onmilwaukee.com. 18 November 2012.

Bement, Colleen. "Conversation with Authors Robert E. Wood and Anthony Wynn." About their book on Barry Morse, *Valiant For Truth: Barry Morse and his Lifelong Association with Bernard Shaw*, in Section II. Books and Periodicals, above. Examiner.com. 23 August, 2012.

Beckerman, Jim. *"Pygmalion* Comes to Bergen Community College [Paramus, New Jersey]." Northjersey.com. 11 April 2013.

Bhattacharyya, Rica. "Literature Goes to B[usiness]School: IIM [Indian Institute of Management](s), Top Institutes Using Old Classics to Teach Leadership." Economictimes.indiatimes.com. 21 March 2013. Mumbai has schools that have students reading Arthur Miller, Ibsen, Gandhi, and Shaw to learn how to lead in "the challenging business environment of modern times."

Billington, Michael. "Blue/Orange." Review of the Cottesloe Theatre, London, production of *Doctor's Dilemma*. Guardian.co.uk. 21 July 2012.

———.*"Heartbreak House—Review."* Of the Chichester Festival Theatre production. Guardian.co.uk. 14 July 2012.

Blouke, Kate. Penfold Theatre, Austin, Texas, production review of *Minister's Wife*. Statesman.com. 4 April 2013.

Bogart, Mat, and Jessica Burrows. "A Noise Within Theater [Los Angeles] Announces 2012–2013 Season." *Doctor's Dilemma* will be produced. Theatrermania.com. 15 June 2012.

"Boho Theatre [Chicago] and Stage Left Theatre Present *Pygmalion*, 1/5–2/10." Chicago.broadwayworld.com. 21 November 2012.

Boorman, Emma. "UC Davis [California] Professor Elizabeth Miller Talks Socialism in Print with Santa Barbara [California]." Thebottomline. as.ucsb.edu. 14 November 2012. Miller's talk on "the work and influence of William Morris and George Bernard Shaw offered, to an intimate group of people in the Interdisciplinary Humanities Center at UC

Santa Barbara, a brief but fulfilling look at socialist print media in the late 1800s."

Borges-Accardi, Millicent. "At *Heartbreak House*, Things Are Not as They Seem." Review of the Will Geer Theatricum Botanicum, Topanga, California, production. Topangamessenger.com. 20 March 2013.

Braccini, Sophie. "Bernard Shaw's *Pygmalion* at Town Hall Theatre [Lafayette, California]." Lamorindaweekly.com. 6 June 2012.

Breeding, Lucinda. "The Rain in Spain." Denton, Texas, Community Theatre production announcement of *Pygmalion*. Dentorrc.com. 13 September 2012.

Bretz, Mark. "[John Morogiello's] *Engaging Shaw*: Theater Review." The West End Players Guild, St. Louis, Missouri. Laduenews.com. 31 February 2013.

Broaddus, Will. "To Hell and Back with George Bernard Shaw." Review of the Mainstage Theatre production, Salem, Massachusetts, of an abridged script of the "whole" *Man and Superman. Salemnewws.com.* 4 April 2013.

"*Candida.*" Review of the Sarah Thorne Theatre Club production, at Hilderstone College, Broadstairs, Kent. Thisiskent.co.uk. 10 August 2012.

Carpenter, Charles A. *A Selective, Classified International Bibliography of Publications about Bernard Shaw: Works from 1940 to Date, with Appendix of Earlier Works.* Last updated on 27 July 2013, http://chuma. cas.usf.edu/~dietrich/Carpenter-Shaw-Bibliography-TOC. This update of Carpenter's bibliography includes items not listed in this Checklist. International Shaw Society (ISS) members may also reach this link by clicking on "Bibliographies" under "Menu B." This online bibliography is a segmented version. E-mail Professor Carpenter for a one-piece version if you wish to search the entire database as a single page. Carpenter has made the bibliography available on the ISS website as a gift to Shaw Society members. For a very nominal cost, bibliographies of similar design and scope by Carpenter are on Barker, Beckett, O'Casey, O'Neill, Pinter, Stoppard, Synge, Yeats, and Miller. He may be reached at "Al Carpenter" (ccarpen@binghamton.edu).

Chamberlain, Adrian. "The Joy of Speaking Parts: The Stars of *Arms and the Man* are Fresh from Mostly Silent Roles—at Stratford and in a Tribeca-screened Film." Review of the McPherson Playhouse production, Victoria, British Columbia. Timescolonist.com. 3 June 2012.

Citron, Cynthia. "A Girl and Her Mother Are Soon Parted." Review of the Antaeus Company production of *Mrs. Warren*, North Hollywood. Examiner.com. 5 April 2013.

"Clackamas Community College [Oregon City, Oregon]: *Arms and the Man* Opens Feb. 28." Clackamas.edu. 27 February 2013.

"Classic Play [*Pygmalion*] Will Be Performed in Kirkintilloch." In East Dunbartonshire, Scotland. Kirkintilloch-herald.co.uk. 6 November 2012.

Cochran, Allison. "Shaw Festival Announces Appointment of New Executive Director [Elaine Calder]." Tracking.wordfly.com. 14 June 2012.

Coleman, Marc. "Labour Must Quit to Save Itself and Us." Independent.ie. 3 June 2012. Attacks Michael Higgins with suggestion that he might not have known that Shaw defended Hitler.

"Community Theatre Group Celebrating Play's [Pygmalion's] Centenary." In Axbridge, Somerset, England. Thisissomerset.co.uk. 21 June 2012.

Craig, Pat. "*Pygmalion* Opens at Town Hall Theatre in Lafayette [California]." Mercurynews.com. 21 May 2012.

Credit, Cali. "Conservatory Students Explore Love Shaw Style in *Candida*." Announcement of the Cook Theatre, Florida State University, Sarasota, production. Jeraldtribune.com. 4 April 2013.

Crist, Cindy. "The Play's the Thing: [excerpts from] *Arms and the Man*." Film viewed at North Shore Senior Center, Northfield, Illinois. Lifelonglearning@nssc.org. 11 July 2012.

Crosby, Johanna. "*Dear Liar*—Long distance Love in Cotuit." Review of the Wits End, Cape Cod, production. Wickedlocal.com. 8 November 2012.

Crowder, Marcus. "Sacramento Live: *Widowers' Houses* a Play to Think About." Announcement of the California Stage Theater production. Sacbee.com. 12 April 2013.

Daglish, Darren. "*The Doctor's Dilemma*: Tower Theatre at Bridewell [London]." A production announcement. Londontheatre.co.uk. 13 May 2013.

——. "*The Man of Destiny* & *Fascinating Foundling*." Pentameter Theatre, London, production announcement. Londontheatre.co.uk. 27 March 2013.

Dear Liar. Review of the Regent Park Arts and Cultural Center, Toronto, production. Mooneyontheatre.com. 29 September 2012.

Despain, Karen. "Readers' Theatre Production Shows Shaw's [*Black Girl in Search of God*] Stands Test of Time." In Prescott, Arizona. Dcourier.com. 29 March 2013.

"*Devil's Disciple*." Announcement of Pantagleize Theatre Company, Forth Worth, Texas, production. Listings.dfw.com. 10 January 2013.

Dietrich, Richard. Dietrich's websites, *Shaw Bizness: Links to the Life, Times, and Work of Irish Playwright George Bernard Shaw*, 16http://chuma.cas.usf. edu/~dietrich/shawbizness.html, and the *International Shaw Society Home Page* www.shawsociety.org, are, in combination, by far, the most important websites for matters about Shaw. Accessed 16 May 2013.

"Don Juan in Hell by George Bernard Shaw." Announcement of the Paper Wing Theatre Company, Monterey, California, production. Zvents.com. 10 September 2012.

Englehardt, Joanne. "Pear Avenue Theatre [Mountain View, California] Offers Polished Production of Shaw's [*Mrs Warren's*] *Profession.*" Mercurynews.com. 26 June 2012.

Everett-Green, Robert. "Meet Five in the Shaw's [Festival] Spotlight: They are more than Ingenues." Theglobeandmail.com. 11 May 2013. Provided are substantial introductions to actresses Harveen Sandhu, Julia Course, Kate Besworth, Jacqueline Thair, and Ijeoma Emesowum.

"Flagler Theater Group [Daytona Beach, Florida] Tackles Staged Reading of *Pygmalion.*" News-journalismonline.com. 10 November 2012.

"Florida State University/Asolo Conservatory for Actor Training [Saratoga], Presents *Candida* by George Bernard Shaw." Tampabaynewswire.com. 25 March 2013.

"Fundit, Performance: George Bernard Shaw—*Heartbreak House.*" Production announcement and appeal for production funding by Spoonlight Theatre Company, Dublin. Fundit.ie. 5 June 2012.

Gans, Andrew. "*Book of Mormon* Tony Winner Nikki M. James Will Play Title Role in [New York's Project Shaw] Reading of *Saint Joan.*" Playbill. com. 28 November 2012.

———, and Kenneth Jones. "[New York's Project Shaw] *Man and Superman* with Brian Murray, Will Be Preserved for Lincoln Center [New York] Archives." Playbill.com. 20 March 2013.

Gardner, Lyn. "*Meine Faire Dame* [*My Fair Lady*]—ein Sprachlabor." Review of the Edinburgh International Festival Theater Basel production. Guardian.co.uk. 15 August 2012.

"George Bernard Shaw." *Wikiquote*. Wikiquote.org. 18 March 2013. Twenty-three electronic pages. "A goldmine for Shaw quotations."—Richard Dietrich.

"George Bernard Shaw Aficionado Directs Comedy that Features 'Variety of Emotions. John McInerney Delivers *Arms and the Man* as the Final Show of Actors Circle's [Scranton, Pennsylvania] 32nd Season." Timesleader. com. 30 April 2013.

"George Bernard Shaw's *Candida.*" Announcement of Actors Studio, Newburyport, Massachusetts, staged reading. Escapesnorth.com. 12 September 2012.

"George Bernard Shaw's *Pygmalion* Hits Iranian Bookshelves." Ibna.ir. 15 December 2012. The translation is by Arezo Shojaei, published by Qatreh Publications, Iran.

"George Bernard Shaw's *Pygmalion*—First-Rate! Go See." Review of Old Globe Theatre production, San Diego, California, production. Tripadvisor.ca. 25 February 2012.

"Girls Dominate [Bruton School, Somerset, UK] Production of Shaw Classic [*Pygmalion*]. Thisissomerset.co.uk. 20 March 2013.

Heffley, Lynne. "Stage Preview: A Pared-Down *Pygmalion*." Review of Parson's Nose Theatre, Pasadena, California, production. Passadenasun. com. 14 January 2013.

Higgins, Michael D. "Remarks at the First Irish International Shaw Conference." www.president.ie/speeches/remarks-at-the-first-international-shaw-conference-to-be-held-in-ireland. This Internet destination provides both a link to an electronic recording of the speech and a photo gallery featuring Higgins. 3 June 2012.

Holroyd, Michael. "Bernard Shaw and His Lethally Absurd *Doctor's Dilemma*." Guardian.co.uk. 13 July 2012. A feature piece to announce the National Theatre, London, production. "Shaw subtitled his Play 'A Tragedy,' but, in fact, writes Holroyd, it's a brilliant satire on the pre-National Health Service medical profession."

Hughes, Andrew S. "*Smash* Weds Love and Politics." Review of the Indiana University, South Bend, production. Southbentribune.com. 11 October 2012.

Hunt, Joanne. "President Pays Tribute to GB Shaw." Irishtimes.com. 2 June 2012. An online address for the *Irish Times* report of Ireland's President Michael Higgins's plenary address to the members, guests of the International Shaw Society, and the public at the National Gallery of Ireland.

Isidor Saslav. See Saslav, Isidor, below.

Janes, Daniel. "The Shavian Moment: Why Are There So Many George Bernard Shaw Revivals?" *New Statesman*. Newstatesman.com. 20 July 2012. "In January 1993, when the UK was in recession and unemployment exceeded 10 per cent, theatre critic Irving Wardle observed a number of George Bernard Shaw revivals: 'His stock always goes up when we are in trouble.' Fast forward almost 20 years and little has changed. The past month alone has seen the opening of *Heartbreak House* at the Chichester Festival Theatre, *The Doctor's Dilemma* at the National and *The Man of Destiny* at the Bridewell. Combine this with the recent production of *Saint Joan* at The Rose, Bankside, and we are in the throes of the most serious spate of Shaviana since Britain's last economic slump."

Jesensek, Antonius J. "A Glance at the Reception of Bernard Shaw in Italy." *Upstage: A Journal of Turn-of-the-Century Theatre* 5 (Winter 2012–13).

Oscholars.com. 22 January 2013. "Research into Bernard Shaw's reception in Italy has until recently been minimal. I will begin by locating Shaw in the Italian cultural context in which his plays first appeared and trace the early response to his plays by Italian audiences and critics. . . . Shaw was a novelty and a controversial playwright for at least four decades since his introduction to Italian theatre in 1909. First, because his polemical plays, his controversial ideas and unusual playwriting techniques came as a shock to the audience; secondly, because Shaw brought social reality to the theatre—which was exactly what audiences wanted to escape from. He even suggested that the social conventions and institutions, which were the very fabric of their lives, should be demolished. It was little wonder that in Italy, like in many other countries, some audiences failed to understand his plays, rejected his ideas and considered him a threat to the status quo they wanted to preserve."

"John Murrell Revisions Shaw in Festival's 2013 Season: *Peace in Our Time* an Adaptation of *Geneva* for Shaw Festival." CBC.ca. 24 September 2012.

"Kokomo Civic Theatre [Indiana University] Kicks off Season 2012–3 with *My Fair Lady*." Kokomoperspecive.com. 9 August 2012.

Kruger, Charles. "*My Fair Lady* is as Charming as can be at San Francisco Playhouse." Examiner.com. 17 August 2012.

LeRoy, Bridget. "*Pygmalion* by George Bernard Shaw." Announcement of East Hampton, New York, High School, production. Easthamton.patch.com. 12 November 2012.

Letts, Quentin. "*Doctor's Dilemma*: Putting Medics Under the Microscope." Review of the Royal National Theatre, London, production. Dailymail. co.uk. 25 July 2012.

Li, Kay. *The SAGITTARIUS-ORION SHAW Digitizing Project* at http:// libra.appsoi.yorku.ca/. A Virtual Tour of Shaviana has moved to http:// libra.appsoi.yorku.ca/virtual-tour-of-shaviana/. The SAGITTARIUS-ORION Shaw Digitizing Project continues to undergo substantial expansion, in research projects funded by the Social Sciences and Humanities Research Council of Canada. There are two main sections: (1) an open access platform and (2) a restricted access platform accessible only on the Ontario Research and Innovation Optical Network (ORION), which will ensure copyright restrictions. The open access platform is much enhanced. The highlights include: (1) an introduction to Shaw with an article on "Who is Bernard Shaw" written by Stanley and Rodelle Weintraub specially for SAGITTARIUS; (2) a calendar of productions of Shaw's plays around the world; (3) theatre productions with links to reviews and videos of performances around the world;

(4) footsteps of Bernard Shaw with videos showing Shaw world tour; (5) links to Charles Carpenter's Shaw bibliography; (6) the virtual tours of Isidor Saslav's Shaw collections; (7) links to Shaw holiday shopping; (8) a page with links to a large number of electronic Shaw texts; (9) links to Shaw Festival Study Guides; and (10) other classroom resources on specific plays. The restricted access platform continues to feature classroom resources such as annotated full texts, study guides, reference materials written by world-renowned Shaw scholars, annotated bibliography, complete with concordances and a search engine. It has also become a portal for pilot studies on Shaw.

There is a new feature: Sagittarius has developed an interactive collaborative platform on ORION O3 at https://shaw.othree.ca/ complete with a "Fantasia for Shaw Scholars". Among the many features are Individual blogs for Shaw Scholars, Shaw Wiki, and Shaw Forum. People can have their individual blogs, and post topics for the Shaw Wiki and Shaw Forum. Strongly interested visitors are encouraged to apply for access to this platform. The site is fully interactive with new social media features.

Long, Benjamin. "*Mrs Warren's Profession* as Relevant as Ever." Review of the Illawarra Performing Arts Center, Wollongong, New South Wales, production. Illawarramercury.com. 8 April 2013.

"*Major Barbara*: George Bernard Shaw's Comedy of Conflict." Announcement of the Southern Methodist University, Dallas, production. Goldstar.com. 31 October 2012.

"*Major Barbara* at Radford University [Radford, Virginia]." Review. Nrvnews. com. 18 April 2013.

Man and Superman. Announcement of Eastern New Mexico University, Portales, production. Pntonline.com. 28 October 2012.

McInerney, John. *Doing Shaw Now*, at http://gbshawnow.wordpress.com. Or from a link on the ISS homepage at www.shawsociety.org. A new website for those particularly interested in the staging aspects of Shaw's plays. John says, "If you would like to comment on a stage production of a Shaw play you have seen, this site can be your forum. If you are working on a Shaw production, this site can be a resource to consult. Either way, we are interested in what you have to say." From a September 2012 announcement.

McKeown, John. "Theatre." Review of Shaw's *Comedieta for Two Voices* [*Village Wooing*], at Bewley's Café Theatre, Dublin. Independent.ie. 23 August 2012.

"Michigan Shakespeare Festival [Jackson, Michigan] to Run [*Pygmalion*]." Detroit.broadwayworld.com. 12 June 2012.

Morris, Stacey. "TV Anchors Make News in *Dear Liar* Staged Readings." Announcement of performances in Saratoga Springs and Albany. Saratogian.com. 29 March 2013.

"Neoteny Theatre Presents: *Overruled* by GB Shaw." Announcement of Red Sandcastle Theatre, Toronto, production. 29 March 2013.

"Newton's Verne Vance Wins Evans Award for Essay on G. B. Shaw." Wickedlocal.com. 3 November 2012. The essay was written as a new Preface to Shaw's play *The Apple Cart*. The prize is £500.

"90 Years of *Time* Cover Stars: The Celebrities Who Defined a Century of Entertainment." Entertainment.time.com. 27 February 2013. A reproduction of the 24 December 1925 *Time* cover that features GBS is included in the article.

North, Natalie. "Wartime Farce Retains Message 100 Years Later." Review of the McPherson Playhouse, Victoria, British Columbia, *Arms and the Man* production. 5 June 2012.

O'Connor, Jack Courtney. "George Bernard Shaw's English Bores in Comedies at the Old Red Lion [London]." Review of *How He Lied to Her Husband, Overruled,* and *Village Wooing.* Camdennewjournal.com. 10 January 2013.

O'Connor, Terry. "[Boxing] Champion's Son [Jay Tunney] Sets Epic [Gene] Tunney-Shaw Tale in Boca Grande, Florida." Gasparillagazette.com. 29 March 2013.

Palm, Matthew. "Mad Cow Theatre [Orlando] Announces [production of *Mrs Warren's Profession*]." Orlandosentinel.com. 19 June 2012.

Parkin, Simon. "Rare and Funny Play [*You Never Can Tell*] Gets Norwich [England] Performance." 22 June 2012.

"Perth's Studio, Ontario, Wins Praise" for production of *Overruled.* Emcperth.ca. 15 November 2012.

Putnam, Caurie. "Theatre Review [Black Sheep Theatre, Rochester, New York]: *Widowers' Houses . . .*" Democratandchronicle.com. 13 September 2012.

"Red Mask Players [Danville, Illinois] Announce Shows." *Arms and the Man* is one of the offerings. Commercial-news.com. 7 September 2012.

Reeves, Lisa. "Youth Theatre Group [Cheshire, England] to Present George Bernard Shaw Comedy," *Annajanska.* Wilmslow.co.uk. 18 October 2012.

Retzel, Rebecca J. "*Pygmalion.*" Review of Washington Stage, D.C., production. Washingtoncitypaper.com. 31 October 2012.

Rogovoy, Seth. "George Bernard Shaw, Marx Bros Comedy, Musical 'Bridges' Top WTF [Williamstown, Massachusetts, Theatre Festival] 2013 Season." Announcement of *Pygmalion* production. Rogovoyreport.com. 27 February 2013.

Rothstein, Edward. "Jacques Barzun Dies at 104: Cultural Critic Saw the Sun Setting on the West." New YorkTimes.com. 25 October 2012.

"Saslav, Isidor. Obituary." By Kelly Gooch. Tylerpaper.com/article/20130131/News01/130139979/-1/news. 29 January 2013. See also a Saslav obituary in *Longview News-Journal*. 29 January 2013.

"Shakespeare . . . Shaw [Abbey Theatre production announcement of *Major Barbara*]." Tracking.wordfly.com. 13 November 2012.

"The Shaw and Shah Show." Announcement of Mumbai production of *Arms and the Man*. Indianespress.com. 11 August 2012.

Shaw vs. Chesterton. Provision Theatre, Chicago, performance announcement. Gazettechicago.com. 7 September 2012.

ShawChicago Theater Company. 2012. 16 May 2013. www.shawchicago.org/about.html. ShawChicago presents the plays of Bernard Shaw and his contemporaries. Promotion and production information for the 2012–2013 season. Shaw productions associated with ShawChicago this season: *Village Wooing, Shaw vs Shakespeare*, A Shaw Lecture, *Widowers' Houses, Millionairess*, and *Saint Joan*.

Sidney P. Albert. See Albert, Sidney P., above.

Sjostrom, Jan. "*Palm Beach Hillbillies* on Tap? Four Arts to Offer Sitcom-writing Class in Summer Lineup." Palmbeachdailynews.com. 14 June 2012. The summer's program offers a play-reading series that will feature *Pygmalion, My Fair Lady*, and *Major Barbara*.

"Stage Tube: First Look at Manna Nichols and More in Rehearsal for [Washington, D.C's] Arena Stage's *My Fair Lady*." Broadwayworld.com. 10 October 2012.

Sullivan, Mark. "Now I Know How Joan of Arc Felt: Stripped Down, A Production of Shaw's *Saint Joan* Crackles with Energy." The New York, Bedlam Theater production. Capitalnewyork.com. 29 March 2013.

Toynbee, Polly. "Bernard Shaw's Guide to the Post-Crash World." Guardian.co.uk. 13 October 2012. A review of a 2013 edition of Shaw's *Intelligent Woman's Guide*. The playwright's passionate and indignant guide for women, which tells how social injustice destroys lives, suddenly looks remarkably fresh.

"University of Alabama [Tuscaloosa] Theater Department Presents George Bernard Shaw Play [*Misalliance*]." Cw.ua.edu. 12 November 2012.

Urbani de la Paz, Diane. "*Heartbreak House* to Open Its Doors at Key City Public Theatre [Port Townsend, Washington]." Peninsuladailynews.com. 25 April 2013.

"*Village Wooing* in Roundwood House, [Leinster, Ireland]." Leinsterexpress, ie. 12 October 2012.

"Vintage High Students [Little Theater, Napa, California] Bring Shaw's *Pygmalion* to Life." Napavalleyregister.com. 18 April 2013.

"WCSU [Western Connecticut State University, Danbury, Connecticut] to Stage Shaw's *Major Barbara*." Norwalkplus.com. 7 October 2012.

"Westfield [New Jersey] Community Band Begins Centennial Summer Concert Series." Will feature songs from *My Fair Lady*. Nj.com. 11 June 2012.

"*Widowers' Houses* by Bernard Shaw." California Stage Production, Sacramento. Sacbee.com. 27 April 2013.

Wilke, Hannah. "Turnaround Is Fair Play—*My Fair Lady* Coming to Muscatine [Iowa]. Muscatinejournal.com. 27 September 2012.

Wilson, Simon. "People's Theatre Brings Bernard Shaw Classic to the Stage." A Nottingham Arts Theatre, Nottingham, UK, production of *Pygmalion*. Thisisnottingham.co.uk. 10 April 2013.

"*You Never Can Tell*." Announcement of Remy Bumppo Theatre, Chicago, production. Remybumppo.org. 20 June 2012.

VII. Other Media

"Calico Dragon Teaching a Child Not to Step on a Caterpillar George Bernard Shaw Vegan Handbag." $46.95 + $7.96 shipping. At Amazon. 11 October 2012.

Epstein, Jacob. "Second Portrait of George Bernard Shaw," 1934. Sold at Sotheby's for £27,500. 11 May 2012.

"Mens Pocket Watch Pewter George Bernard Shaw Design 4973." Currently unavailable. Advertised at Amazon.co.uk. 5 July 2012.

"Painting 'given back' to Labour." Oxfordmail.co.uk. 4 August 2012. Labour leader Ed Miliband took delivery at the party's new London headquarters of a "missing portrait" of Bernard Shaw, from John Ruskin principal, Professor Audrey Mullender. The painting, believed to have been lost in World War II, was found hanging for years at Ruskin College's Walton Street campus. The painting, by Bertha Newcomb, with whom Shaw was perhaps romantically involved, and titled "GBS—The Platform Spellbinder," is believed to be worth between £10,000 and £20,000.

VIII. Miscellany

Gray, John, director. *The Makeover*. ABC Hallmark Hall of Fame, 2013, forthcoming. "*Makeover* puts a modern twist on George Bernard Shaw's *Pygmalion*," including changing the genders of the main characters. Julia Stiles will play Hannah Higgins, a professor who completes an unsuccessful bid for Congress. For the next election, she and her biz partner

Colleen Pickering recruit sincere yet unpolished Elliott Doolittle, played
by David Walton, to enter the race." From AJ Marechal's announcement
in *Variety* (29 August 2012).

Gregory, Timothy, adaptation, arrangement, and director. *Shaw vs.
Chesterton: The Debate.* Performed at Chicago's Provision Theater,
September–October 2012.

Iscove, Robert, director. *She's All That.* Miramax, 1999. Based on Shaw's
Pygmalion.

Kemper, Theodore P. *Candida, Act IV.* 2011. This original script is the winner
of the first annual T. F. Evans Award, made by the Shaw Society. The
£500 prize is a T. F. Evans legacy to the society. The script may be downloaded at the Shaw Society website. Copyright remains with the author.

Lonergan, Kenneth, director. *Margaret.* Fox Searchlight Pictures, 2011 and 2012.
John Bertolini wrote to ISS members: "There's a complimentary reference to
Shaw in . . . *Margaret* . . . In a telephone conversation between the main character, the daughter, and her father (played by Lonergan), she says, 'Not that
I'm trying to make this woman's horrible death into my own personal moral
gymnasium,' and the father comments, 'Right. Well, that's that Shaw quote,
right?' . . . The Shaw quote? The great Shaw quote. 'The Englishman sees the
world as expressly designed to be his own personal moral gymnasium.' I think
it's in one of those wonderful prefaces.' The daughter then remarks, 'I don't
know where I read it.' Of course, the father is referring to Tanner's admonish-
ing Octavius in Act I of *Man and Superman.* It isn't quite accurate, but pretty
close. I suspect Lonergan may be a Shaw admirer, so I thought I'd pass this on....
Best, JB."

Senna, Lorraine, director. *Americanizing Shelley.* UniGlobe Entertainment,
2008. A woman from the Himalayas is "Americanized" by an American
man. Thanks to Julie Sparks.

Untermeyer, Louis. "The Heaven of Queer Stars." *Heavens.* Ann Arbor:
University of Michigan Library, 1922. Reissued by Evergreen Review, 2011.
Reviewed by David Langford, *Magazine of Fantasy and Science Fiction*
(November–December 2012): 258. G. K. Chesterton in this vignette engages
in his "favorite pastime of debate. His Father Brown-like mouthpiece brilliantly out-argues a Mephistophelian adversary resembling GKC's old spar-
ring partner Bernard Shaw, whose protests are swamped by the incoming
flood of paradoxical rhetoric. It's Chesterton at his most exhausting."

Weldon, Fay. *Habits of the House.* New York: St. Martins, 2013. The *TLS* (3
August 2012), 3, reviewer writes: "Bernard Shaw is mentioned in one
particularly bizarre scene during which the Earl of Dilberne manages to
quote from *Major Barbara* over dinner—impressive, given that Shaw's
play was written in 1905, six years after Weldon's novel is set."

CONTRIBUTORS

SIDNEY P. ALBERT (1914-2013) was professor emeritus of philosophy at California State University, Los Angeles, and author of *Shaw, Plato, and Euripides: Classical Currents in 'Major Barbara'* (2012). He was a founding member of the International Shaw Society, a former member of the *Shaw Review* editorial board, and a frequent contributor to SHAW.

CHARLES A. CARPENTER, a founding member of the International Shaw Society, is Emeritus Professor of English at Binghamton University. His publications on Shaw, stretching over forty-nine years, include *Bernard Shaw and the Art of Destroying Ideals: The Early Plays* (1969) and *Bernard Shaw as Artist-Fabian* (2009). He is completing an edition of the correspondence of Shaw and Gilbert Murray, and maintains a continuing bibliography of Shaw on his website. His most recent book is *The Dramatic Works of Samuel Beckett: A Selective, Classified International Bibliography of Publications About His Plays and Their Conceptual Foundations* (2011).

PETER CONOLLY-SMITH is an Associate Professor of American culture and history at CUNY–Queens College in New York City. He has published articles on war, immigration, ethnicity, film, and theater, including several articles on Shaw, and is the author of *Translating America: An Ethnic Press Visualizes Popular American Culture, 1895–1918* (2004).

R. F. DIETRICH ruined his retirement by founding the International Shaw Society, of which he is now Treasurer. Brought it on himself, is all.

A. M. GIBBS is Emeritus Professor of English at Macquarie University, Sydney. His *Bernard Shaw: A Life* (2005) was runner-up for the Robert Rhodes Prize for a book on Literature awarded by the American Conference for Irish Studies; shortlisted for the Nettie Palmer Prize for nonfiction in the Victorian Premier's Literary Awards, and for the General History Prize in the NSW Premier's History Awards; included in the U.S. Choice list of outstanding academic titles of 2006; and highly commended in the 2007 Australian National Biography Award Competition. His publications include *Shaw* (Writers and Critics Series, 1969); *The Art and Mind of Shaw: Essays in Criticism* (1983); *Shaw: Interviews and Recollections* (1990); *"Man and Superman" and "Saint Joan": A Casebook* (1992); *"Heartbreak House": Preludes of Apocalypse* (1994), and *A Bernard Shaw Chronology* (2001).

D. A. HADFIELD is lecturer in English at the University of Waterloo. She is author of *Re: Producing Women's Dramatic History* (Talon, 2007) and co-editor, with Jean Reynolds, of *Shaw and Feminisms: On Stage and Off* (2013), published in the University Press of Florida Bernard Shaw series.

BARRY KEANE holds a Ph.D. from Trinity College, Dublin, and is an Adjunct Professor in Translation and Comparative Studies at Warsaw University and an Associate Professor at the Warsaw School of Humanities and Social Sciences. He is the author of works on Jan Kochanowski and the Skamander Poets, and is completing postdoctoral research with Dublin City University in partnership with An Foras Feasa (the Institute for Research in Irish Historical and Cultural Traditions at National University of Ireland, Maynooth) on the staging of Irish drama in Poland.

LAGRETTA TALLENT LENKER recently retired from the University of South Florida University College. She taught modern, late Victorian, and American drama and has written or edited eight books and several articles, primarily on the works of Shaw. She was guest editor of SHAW 28: *Shaw and War.*

KAY LI, a founding member of the International Shaw Society, is Project Leader of the SAGITTARIUS—ORION Digitizing Project on Bernard Shaw and the author of *Bernard Shaw and China: Cross-Cultural Encounters* (2007). She is Adjunct Professor in the Faculty of Liberal Arts and Professional Studies, York University, and President of Asian Heritage Month—Canadian Foundation for Asian Culture (Central Ontario) Inc.

GUSTAVO A. RODRÍGUEZ MARTÍN holds a Ph.D. in English from the Universidad de Extremadura, Extremadura, Spain, where he is an Assistant Professor. He also lectures in English language and literature at the IES

Trassierra in Córdoba. His research interests include stylistics, phraseology, and corpus linguistics, and he is a member of the GIALIRE research group (devoted to stylistics).

DEREK MCGOVERN is an Assistant Professor in the English Language and Literature Department at Dong-A University in Busan, South Korea. His Ph.D. dissertation, "Eliza Undermined: The Romanticization of Shaw's *Pygmalion*," examines how successive adaptations of *Pygmalion* often radically depart from Shaw's feminist and antiromantic conceptions of his play. Future research will include the analysis of screen adaptations of other Shaw plays.

JOHN R. PFEIFFER is Professor of English at Central Michigan University and bibliographer of *SHAW*. He has written on Günter Grass, John Stuart Mill, Sir Richard Francis Burton, John Christopher, John Brunner, Etheridge Knight, Ray Bradbury, Aldous Huxley, Margaret Walker, George Eliot, Octavia Butler, and nineteenth-century science fiction. His recent publications include reviews of Avrom Fleishmann's *George Eliot's Intellectual Life*, Ian Morris's *Why the West Rules . . . For Now*, and Sven Wagner's *The Scientist as God: A Typological Study of a Literary Motif, 1818 to the Present*.

MICHEL W. PHARAND, general editor of *SHAW*, is the author of *Bernard Shaw and the French* (2000), editor of Robert Graves's *The Greek Myths* (2001), and of *Bernard Shaw and His Publishers* (2009), and general editor of *Benjamin Disraeli Letters, Volume IX: 1865–1867* (2013). He is director of the Disraeli Project at Queen's University, Kingston, Canada.

NELSON O'CEALLAIGH RITSCHEL holds a Ph.D. in Theatre History from Brown University and is a Professor of Humanities, and department chair, at Massachusetts Maritime Academy. He has published extensively on Synge and modern Irish theater, and his fourth book, Shaw, Synge, Connolly, and Socialist Provocation (2011), was reprinted in paperback in 2012.

ISIDOR SASLAV (1938–2013), a professional violinist, retired as Head of the String Department in the School of Music at Stephen F. Austin State University. He was an avid collector of Shaviana and, at the time of his death, was cataloguing the Archibald Henderson scrapbooks relating to Shaw housed at the University of North Carolina at Chapel Hill.

STANLEY WEINTRAUB has been researching Shaw since the 1950s and has edited and authored two dozen GBS-related books. His latest is *Who's Afraid of Bernard Shaw? Some Personalities in Shaw's Plays* (2011).

CHRISTOPHER WIXSON is Associate Professor of English at Eastern Illinois University and teaches courses in early modern, modern, and contemporary drama. He has staged plays by Albee, Beckett, Chekhov, Pinter, Shakespeare, John Webster, Christopher Durang, and Sarah Kane. His articles have appeared in *Studies in English Literature, Comparative Drama, Notes on Contemporary Literature, Pamphlet, The Harold Pinter Review, American Drama*, and the *Columbia Encyclopedia of Modern Drama*.

MATTHEW YDE is a Lecturer in the Department of Theatre at Ohio State University, where he graduated in 2011 with a Ph.D. in Theatre History, Literature, and Criticism. His research is on modern and contemporary drama, especially as it relates to politics, philosophy, and religion, and he is the author of *Bernard Shaw and Totalitarianism: Longing for Utopia* (2013). The provisional title of his current book project is *The Gospel According to Stephen Adly Guirgis*, an examination Guirgis's plays and film roles in relation to Christianity.

NOTICES

Request for Manuscripts: Future SHAW Volumes

The editorial board of SHAW: The Annual of Bernard Shaw Studies seeks article-length manuscripts for upcoming volumes.

SHAW 34 will be a theme issue devoted to "Shaw and Health," with Christopher Wixson as guest editor. SHAW 34 seeks to address Shaw's views on and personal experiences with any aspect of physical and mental health: vegetarianism and other diets, vivisection, vaccination, smallpox and other diseases, medication, illness, death and dying, mortality and longevity, euthanasia, doctors and the medical profession, hospitals, operations, health care, osteopathy, public sanitation, personal hygiene, pollution, exercise (walking, cycling, swimming, etc), alcohol and tobacco, drugs and addiction, venereal diseases, birth control, psychiatry and psychoanalysis, and related topics. Inquiries and manuscript submissions should be sent to cmwixson@eiu.edu or mailed to Dr. Christopher Wixson, Department of English, Eastern Illinois University, 600 Lincoln Avenue, Charleston, IL 61920, USA.

Beginning in 2015, SHAW will be published bi-annually. SHAW 35.1 (June 2015) will be a theme issue devoted to "Shaw and Modernity," with Lawrence Switzky as guest editor. SHAW 35.1 will consider Shaw's significance as an artist and critic during the emergence of artistic, social, political, and cultural modernity. Essays might address Shaw's responses to and representations of the rise of mass culture, the "culture industry," and modernism and the avant-gardes; the influence of new technology (cars, airplanes, telephones) and new media (film, radio, television) on social, political, and perceptual practices; the industrialization of manufacturing and warfare; new "modern" disciplines like psychoanalysis, sociology, and literary criticism; and bureaucratization, the welfare state, global governance, and the persistence of nationalism. Essays are also welcome on individual plays and prose writings that engage problems of modernity, as well as essays on Shaw in relation to other theorists of modernity (e.g., Marx, Nietzsche, Weber, Wells, Eliot, Adorno, Woolf, and Brecht). Inquiries and manuscript submissions should be sent to lawrence.switzky@utoronto.ca or mailed to Dr. Lawrence Switzky, Department of English, University of Toronto, 170 St. George Street, Toronto, Ontario M5R 2M8, Canada.

SHAW 35.2 (December 2015) will include articles on general topics, book reviews, the Checklist of Shaviana, Notices, and ISS information. For inquiries, contact Dr. Michel Pharand at michelpharand@yahoo.com.

SHAW submissions should preferably be sent as email attachments (in Microsoft Word). For matters of style, please refer to recent *SHAW* volumes.

The 52nd Annual Shaw Festival, Niagara-on-the-Lake, Ontario, Canada

The 2013 Shaw Festival (3 April–27 October 2013) featured *Major Barbara* (2 May–19 October), directed by Jackie Maxwell, and an adaptation of *Geneva* by John Murrell entitled *Peace in Our Time: A Comedy* (19 May–12 October), directed by Blair Williams. The playbill also included *Guys and Dolls*, directed by Tadeusz Bradecki, *Lady Windermere's Fan* by Oscar Wilde, *Enchanted April* by Matthew Barber, *The Light in the Piazza*, based on a novel by Elizabeth Spencer, *Trifles* by Susan Glaspell, *A Wife for a Life* by Eugene O'Neill, *Our Betters* by W. Somerset Maugham, *Faith Healer* by Brian Friel, and *Arcadia* by Tom Stoppard.

For further information, write to Shaw Festival, P.O. Box 774, Niagara-on-the-Lake, Ontario, Canada, L0S 1J0; or call 1-800-511-SHAW [7429] or 905-468-2153; or go to www.shawfest.com.

Shaw's Corner

For information about summer performances of Shaw plays by Michael Friend Productions, contact Sue Morgan at Sue.Morgan@nationaltrust.org.uk. The Shaw plays staged in 2013 were *The Man of Destiny*, *The Fascinating Foundling*, *Buoyant Billions*, *Geneva*, and *Misalliance*.

ShawChicago Theater Company

The Shaw plays performed at the Ruth Page Center for the Arts during ShawChicago's 2012–13 season were *The Millionairess* and *Widowers' Houses*.

Outreach performances included *A Shaw Lecture, Village Wooing, Saint Joan, Shaw vs. Shakespeare, Shaw's Women,* and *Saint Joan.* See www.shawchicago .org/.

Project Shaw

Since 2006, the Gingold Theatrical Group, headed by producer and director David Staller, has staged a concert reading of one Shaw play per month at The Players Club in New York City. The 2013 season included *Misalliance, Caesar and Cleopatra, The Admirable Bashville, Mrs Warren's Profession, Too True to Be Good, On the Rocks,* and Shaw-related events. See www.project-shaw.com.

Comparative Drama Conference, Baltimore, Maryland

The three Shaw sessions at the 37th annual Comparative Drama Conference (4–6 April 2013) at Stevenson University in Baltimore were chaired by Tony J. Stafford (University of Texas, El Paso) and included papers by Tony Stafford, Glen Clifton (West Virginia University), Amjad Ali (Pakistan), Ellen Dolgin (Dominican College), Sanjit Mishra (Indian Institute of Technology, Roorkee, India), Justin Tackett (Stanford), Manisha Patil (Yashwantrao Chavan Institute of Science, India), Al Turco (Wesleyan College), and Adewale Ajayi (Federal Polytechnic, Nigeria). Abstracts for next year's conference may be sent to Tony J. Stafford at tnyorzb@sbcglobal.net or tstaffor@utep.edu until 1 December 2013.

"Shaw at Home": The Ayot St. Lawrence / London, England, Shaw Conference

Co-sponsored by the National Trust, The Shaw Society, and the International Shaw Society, "Shaw at Home" (17–22 June 2013) featured numerous events—such as a visit to the London School of Economics (co-founded by Shaw) and, at "Shaw's Corner," performances of *Buoyant Billions* and *Geneva*—and many papers, including presentations by four distinguished speakers: Shaw biographer Sir Michael Holroyd, journalist Polly Toynbee, drama critic Michael Billington, and eminent Shaw scholar Stanley Weintraub. Special thanks go to Sue Morgan, Steward of "Shaw's Corner," for helping to organize this conference.

Summer Shaw Symposium, Niagara-on-the-Lake, Ontario, Canada

Brad Kent (Université Laval, Québec) organized the 10th annual Summer Shaw Symposium at Niagara-on-the-Lake (26–28 July 2013), sponsored by the Academy of the Shaw Festival and the International Shaw Society. See www.shawsociety.org/summersymposium-2013.htm.

Midwest Modern Language Association Convention

The theme of the 55th annual MMLA Convention in Milwaukee, Wisconsin (7–11 November 2013), will be "Art & Artifice" and will include a Shaw session organized by Christopher Wixson.

Modern Language Association Convention

The 129th annual MLA Convention in Chicago (9–12 January 2014) will include a Shaw session entitled "Shaw and Adaptation" organized by Lawrence Switzky. Presenting papers will be Brett Gamboa (Dartmouth College), Jennifer Buckley (University of Iowa), and Elizabeth Carolyn Miller (University of California, Davis).

International Shaw Society

The Shaw Symposium at Niagara-on-the-Lake and the Shaw sessions at the MLA and the MMLA conventions and at the Comparative Drama conferences are sponsored by the International Shaw Society. For information about the ISS, see www.shawsociety.org. For details about calls for papers, see www.shawsociety.org/Calls-for-Papers.htm.

INTERNATIONAL SHAW SOCIETY

Benefits of Membership – 2014

Membership in the ISS brings many benefits, but one of the chief benefits comes from providing to the ISS tax-deductible funds that can be used to support the scheduling of Shaw conferences, symposia, sessions, and seminars and the giving of travel grants to the young to attend such events. In this way your regard and enthusiasm for Shaw can best be passed on. Please be as generous as you can in choosing your level of membership (see form following). For all gifts, the Recording Shaw will write your name in the Book of Life.

LIST OF BENEFITS

- With paid membership, <u>the option</u> of a substantially discounted subscription to the journal SHAW: *The Annual of Bernard Shaw Studies.* Generally, it is published in the late fall. See http://www.psupress.org/journals/jnls_shaw.html.
- Eligibility for and opportunity to contribute to whatever travel and research grants and prizes the ISS offers to encourage the study of Shaw and his circle.
- A discount of at least $25 on the registration fee for ISS conferences and other ISS events.

- 40% discount on the University Press of Florida Shaw Series books. A purchase code is given to members. See http://www.upf.com/ seriesresult.asp?ser=gbshaw.
- Access to all levels of an ISS Homepage at www.shawsociety.org that will keep everyone informed of relevant activities and provide links to valuable research tools and to opportunities for discussion. The ISS Homepage links to the Members Page via a password available through membership.
- The latest news on Shaw doings via email, newsletters, Facebook, Twitter, WikiShaw, and a Shaw blog—such as upcoming conferences, symposia, and other meetings; theater and book notices; theater and book reviews; editorials; and much more. Serves as a listserv that invites participation. The blog is at http://gbs.shawsociety.org. The webmaster's email is dietrich@usf.edu.
- The right to vote in ISS elections and referendums and the right to hold elected and appointed office and to serve on committees.

ISS Scholarships, Grants, and Prizes

As one of the principal goals of the ISS is to encourage younger generations to experience the delights of reading and seeing Shaw's works and participating in the discussion of them, the ISS offers a generous program of support in the form of scholarships, grants, and prizes, most of which are allied with particular events, such as symposia and conferences. To that end, in ten years fifty-nine young scholars have been awarded seventy-seven ISS Travel Grants to attend the annual Symposia at the Shaw Festival in Niagara-on-the-Lake, Ontario, the first Chicago Symposium in 2010 co-sponsored by the ShawChicago Theater Company, and the Shaw Conferences in 2004, 2006, 2009, 2011, 2012, and 2013, respectively at the University of South Florida, Brown University, Catholic University of America, the University of Guelph (Canada), University College Dublin, and the National Trust's "Shaw's Corner" at Ayot St. Lawrence, UK. *If you give a minimum of $500, the grant the ISS gives with that can carry your name, if you wish.*

INTERNATIONAL SHAW SOCIETY

2014 Membership Form

The annual ISS membership fee is due on January 1 of each year, regardless of when you started during the year. As the ISS is a non-profit organization, the fee is tax-deductible in the U.S., as are gifts, and may be in other countries as well. Membership brings an **optional** discount subscription to the annual journal *SHAW* (300 pages or more) at $33 per year ($55 retail + up to $20 in mailing costs). To become a member or renew your membership or give a membership, please complete the form below and mail it with your check/cheque or Western Union money order *in U.S. dollars* made out to "**International Shaw Society**" and addressed to: **ISS, P.O. Box 728, Odessa, FL 33556-0728.** You can speed this process up by emailing via attachment the completed form to the ISS Treasurer at dietrich@shawsociety.org and by using PayPal for the fee. Credit cards can be used if registered on PayPal. **Questions? Email the ISS Treasurer at dietrich@shawsociety.org.**

Circle One of the Following: 1. Renewal   2. New   3. Gift
(if "Gift," who is the giver? _____)

Membership Fee (in U.S. dollars). Below, circle whichever applies & fill in Totals:

STEP 1 – (Required) Select Type of Membership Below:	Fee for 1 Year - 2014	Totals
1A. Standard Membership for One:	$25	Step 1:
1B. Standard Spousal Membership (both listed):	$35	$
1C. Standard Student Membership:	$10	

STEP 2 – Optional Donation - Select a gift amount for 2014 and enter in the column to the right:	Step 2: $
2A. Contributor: $25 to $175	
2B. Sponsor: $200 to $400	
2C. Partner: $500 or more (specify):_____. If your gift is $500 or more, your name may go on a specific ISS grant. Do you wish to be acknowledged in the giving of the grant: YES NO	
STEP 3 – Optional Subscription to SHAW 33 The journal *SHAW 33* (Penn State University Press) is available to members at a discount price. Enter $33 in the column to the right if you want the journal, or enter a zero if you *don't* want the journal.	Step 3: $
STEP 4 – Optional Subscription to *The Shavian* and Membership in the UK Shaw Society The UK Shaw Society offers a subscription to the paperback journal *The Shavian* (3 editions per year) at $25, and with that comes membership in the UK Shaw Society. Enter $25 to the right if you want this:	Step 4: $
STEP 5 – PayPal Fees (optional) If using PayPal, direct payment to the dietrich@shawsociety.org account and please add 4% of total to this point for PayPal fees and enter rounded up amount in column to the right under Step 5:	Step 5: $
STEP 6 – TOTAL of Totals (add up the totals in Steps 1, 2, 3, 4 & 5 in the column to the right:	Step 6: $

Please print or type:

Name(s) of Member(s): _____

Address (please indicate if different from last year for those renewing):

_____

_____

Phone Number(s):   _____

E-mail Address(es):   _____

ISS business is conducted more online than not. If you do not have access to email and need a hard copy, please initial here _____. Thank you for your membership and contribution.

www.shawsociety.org

Bernard Shaw's Book Reviews, Vol. 1
Originally Published in the *Pall Mall Gazette* from 1885 to 1888

Edited by Brian Tyson

These hitherto uncollected book reviews of Shaw—his first journalistic efforts—reveal much not only about the writer but also the culture of the time in which he lived. Between 1885 and 1888, Bernard Shaw published 111 book reviews in the *Pall Mall Gazette*. In spite of their importance as the first regular journalism Shaw wrote and the fact that the books (fiction, nonfiction, plays, and poetry) he read during these years must have formed the nucleus of his permanent library, the reviews have never before been analyzed in connection with Shaw's work. Brian Tyson has assembled the book reviews, complete with the books' titles, authors, and a brief biography of each author, including any comments Shaw made about the review, and has placed them in historical context, elucidating any interesting, difficult, or obscure references.

Tyson's critical introduction places the reviews in the context of Shaw's work and Victorian society. The reviews are often characterized by the wit and brilliance that we associate with the later Shaw, shedding light on his development as a writer at his most formative stage.

Regardless of the merits of the material Shaw was reviewing, it is amusing and enlightening to follow him down to the wandering tributaries of Late Victorian fiction and poetry, which reveal as much about Shaw as they do about the preoccupations and prejudices of the average reader of the day.

522 pages | $36.95 paper

penn state press

820 N. University Drive, USB 1, Suite C | University Park, PA 16802 | info@psupress.org
WWW.PSUPRESS.ORG | 1-800-326-9180